Little mama

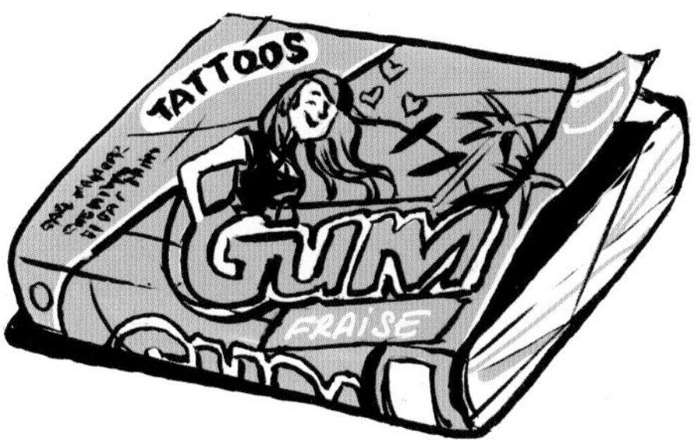
TATTOOS
GUM
FRAISE

BY

HALIM

Translation by Montana Kane

Localization, Layout, and Editing by Mike Kennedy

LION FORGE
MAGNETIC

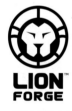

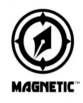

ISBN: 978-1-5493-0795-9
Library of Congress Control Number: 2019936688

Little Mama, Published 2019 by The Lion Forge, LLC.

10 9 8 7 6 5 4 3 2 1

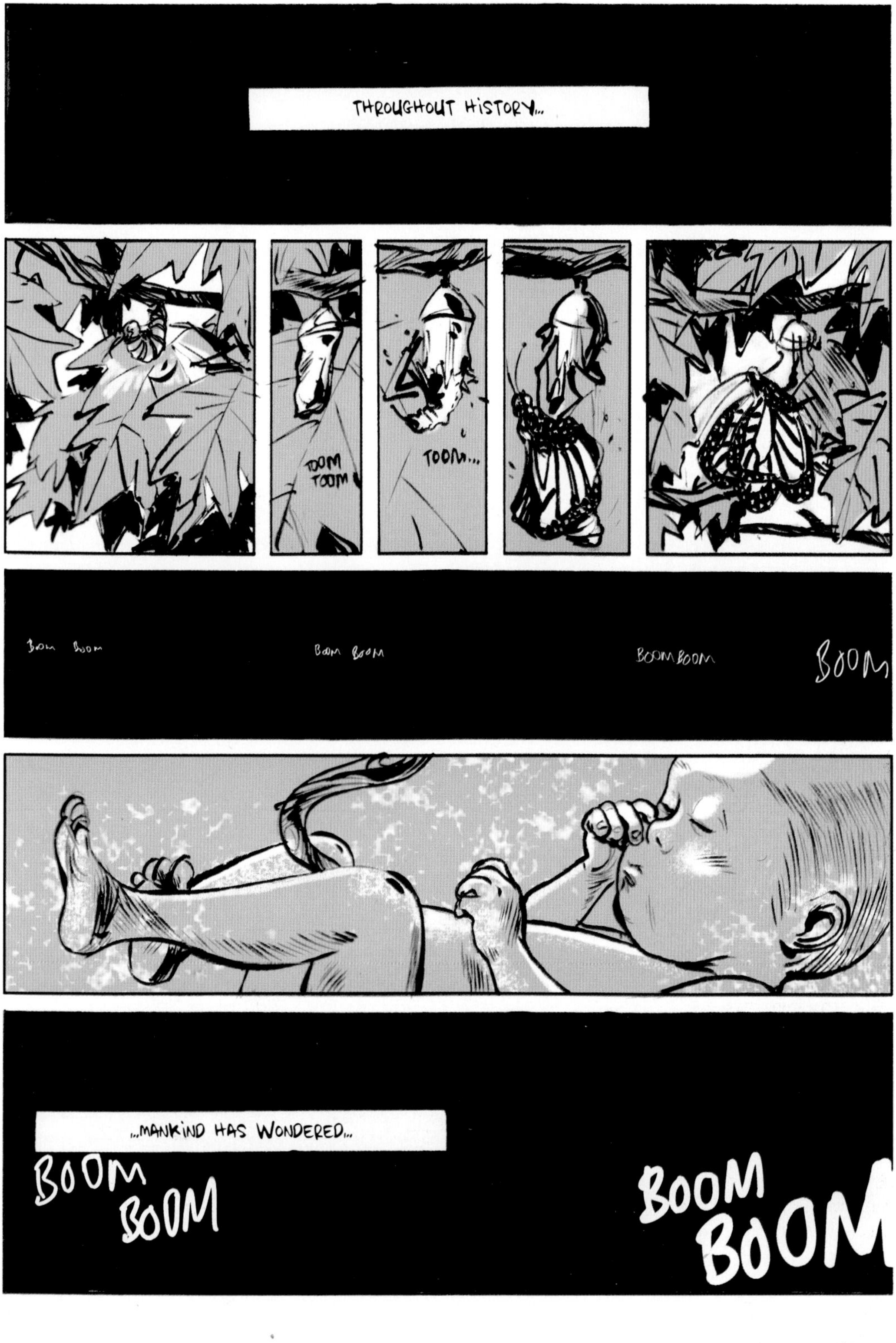
THROUGHOUT HISTORY...
TOOM TOOM
TOOM...
BOOM BOOM
BOOM BOOM
BOOMBOOM
BOOM
...MANKIND HAS WONDERED...
BOOM BOOM
BOOM BOOM

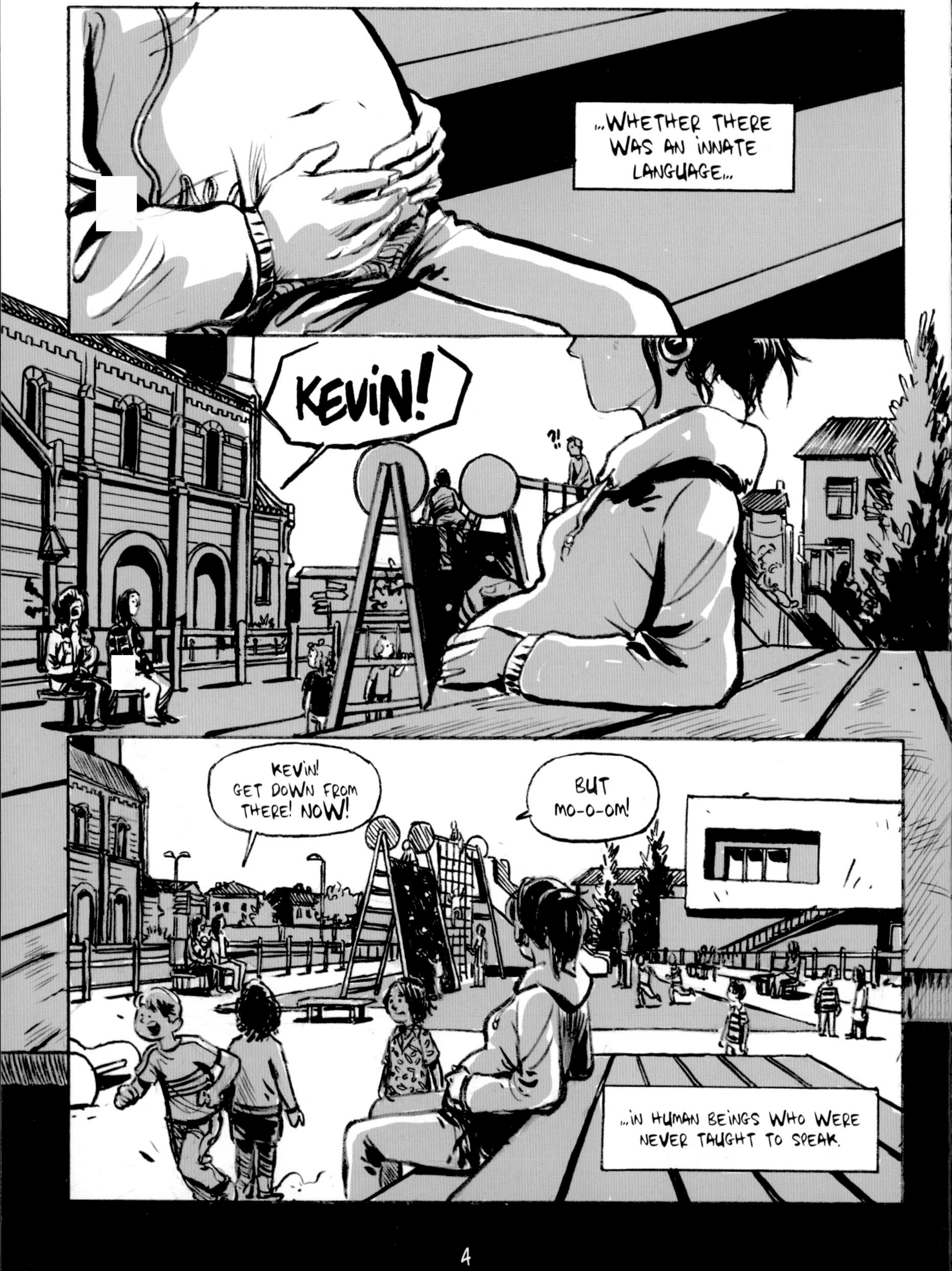
...WHETHER THERE WAS AN INNATE LANGUAGE...
KEVIN!
?!
KEVIN! GET DOWN FROM THERE! NOW!
BUT MO-O-OM!
...IN HUMAN BEINGS WHO WERE NEVER TAUGHT TO SPEAK.

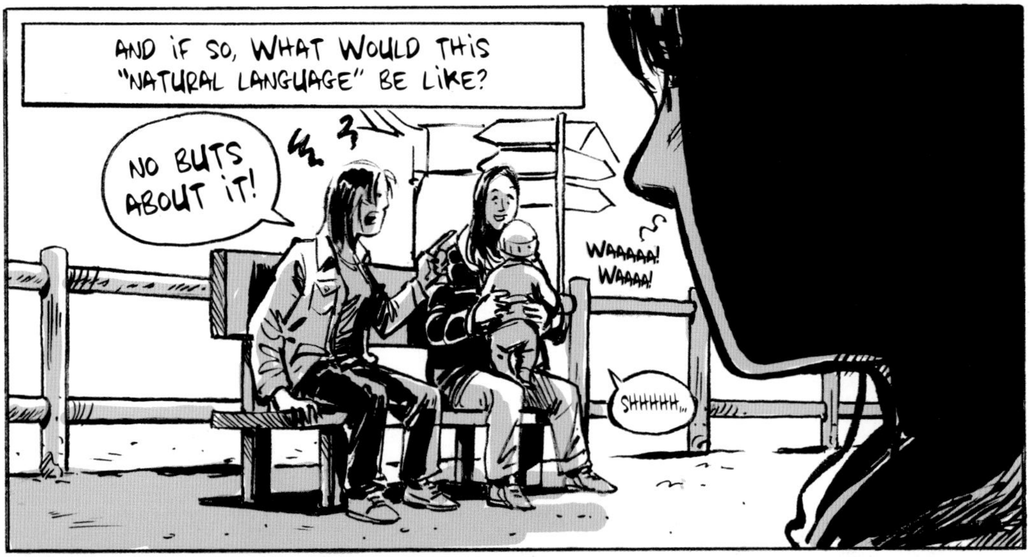
AND IF SO, WHAT WOULD THIS "NATURAL LANGUAGE" BE LIKE?
NO BUTS ABOUT IT!
WAAAAA! WAAAA!
SHHHHH...

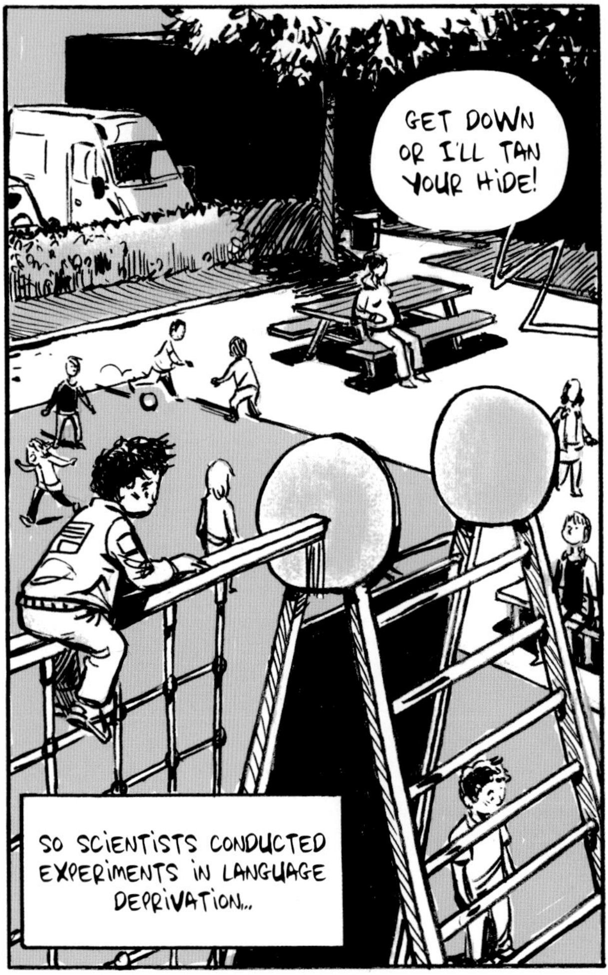
GET DOWN OR I'LL TAN YOUR HIDE!
SO SCIENTISTS CONDUCTED EXPERIMENTS IN LANGUAGE DEPRIVATION...

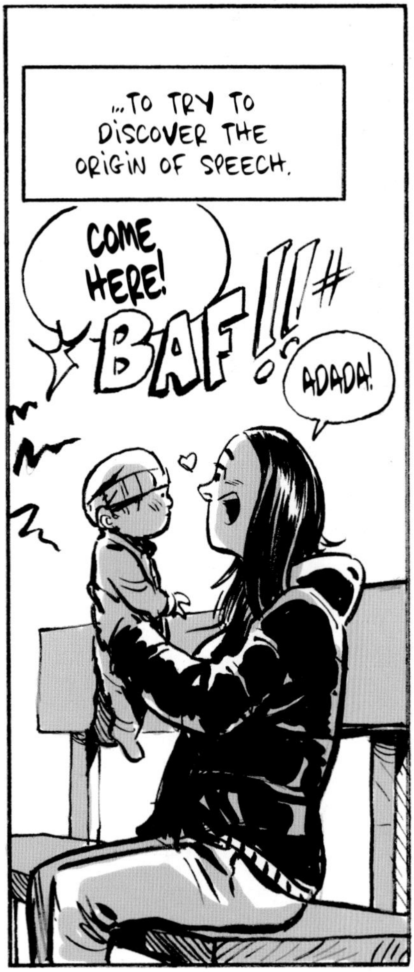
...TO TRY TO DISCOVER THE ORIGIN OF SPEECH.
COME HERE!
BAF!!!#
ADADA!

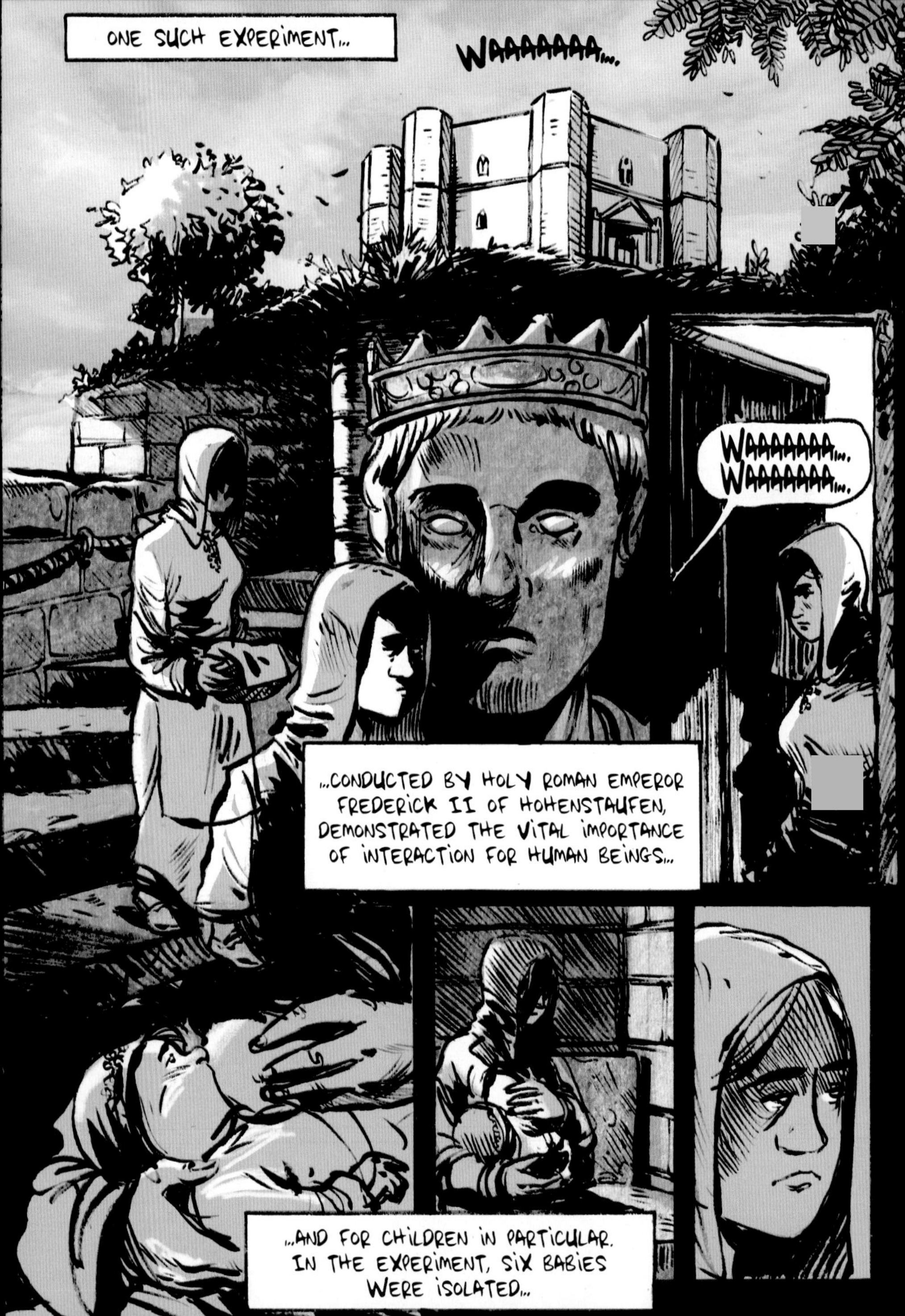
ONE SUCH EXPERIMENT...
WAAAAAAA...
WAAAAAAA... WAAAAAAA...
...CONDUCTED BY HOLY ROMAN EMPEROR FREDERICK II OF HOHENSTAUFEN, DEMONSTRATED THE VITAL IMPORTANCE OF INTERACTION FOR HUMAN BEINGS...
...AND FOR CHILDREN IN PARTICULAR. IN THE EXPERIMENT, SIX BABIES WERE ISOLATED...

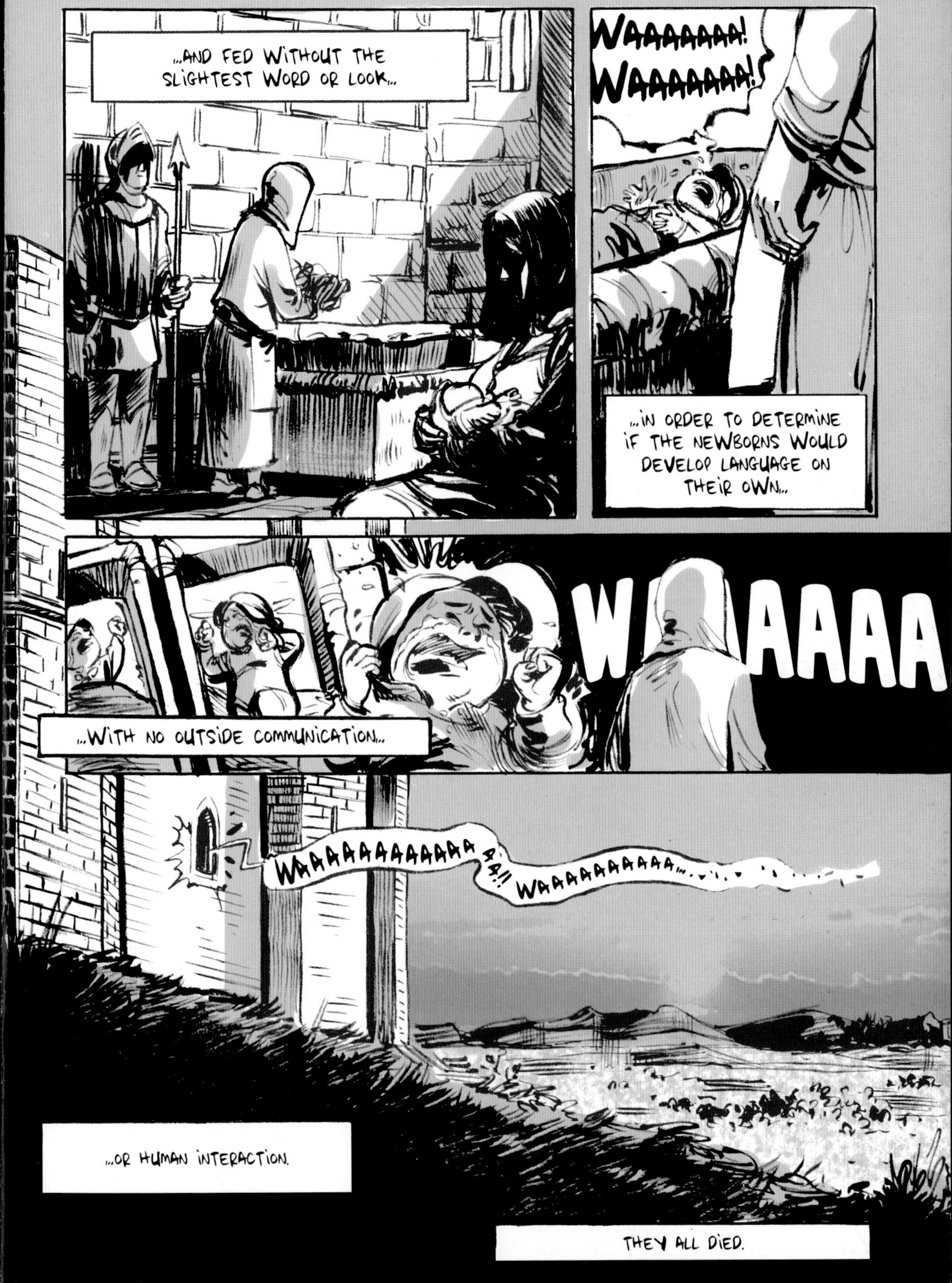
...AND FED WITHOUT THE SLIGHTEST WORD OR LOOK...
WAAAAAAA! WAAAAAAA!
...IN ORDER TO DETERMINE IF THE NEWBORNS WOULD DEVELOP LANGUAGE ON THEIR OWN...
WAAAAA
...WITH NO OUTSIDE COMMUNICATION...
WAAAAAAAAAAAAAA!!
WAAAAAAAAAA...
...OR HUMAN INTERACTION.
THEY ALL DIED.

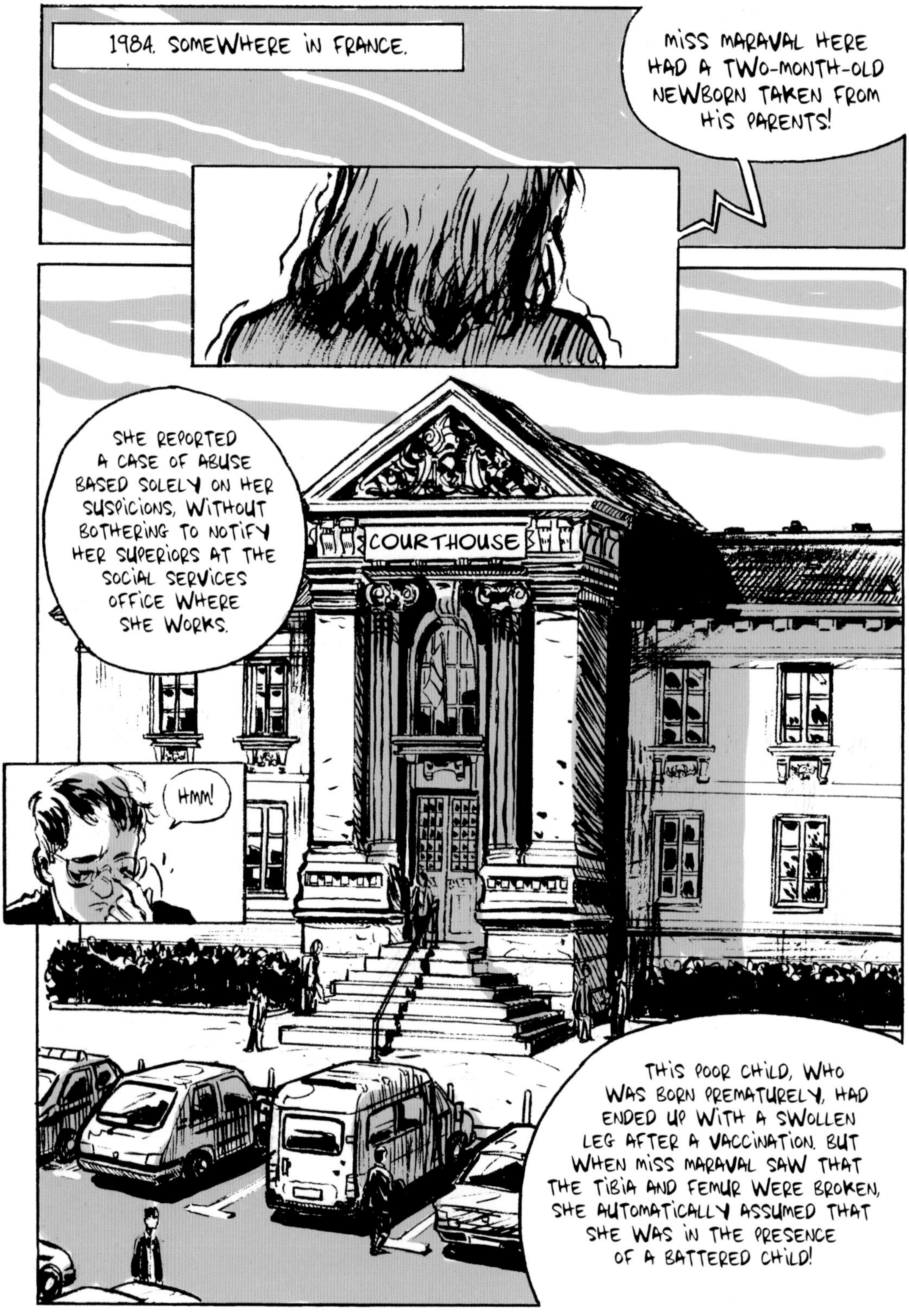
1984. SOMEWHERE IN FRANCE.
MISS MARAVAL HERE HAD A TWO-MONTH-OLD NEWBORN TAKEN FROM HIS PARENTS!
SHE REPORTED A CASE OF ABUSE BASED SOLELY ON HER SUSPICIONS, WITHOUT BOTHERING TO NOTIFY HER SUPERIORS AT THE SOCIAL SERVICES OFFICE WHERE SHE WORKS.
COURTHOUSE
HMM!
THIS POOR CHILD, WHO WAS BORN PREMATURELY, HAD ENDED UP WITH A SWOLLEN LEG AFTER A VACCINATION. BUT WHEN MISS MARAVAL SAW THAT THE TIBIA AND FEMUR WERE BROKEN, SHE AUTOMATICALLY ASSUMED THAT SHE WAS IN THE PRESENCE OF A BATTERED CHILD!

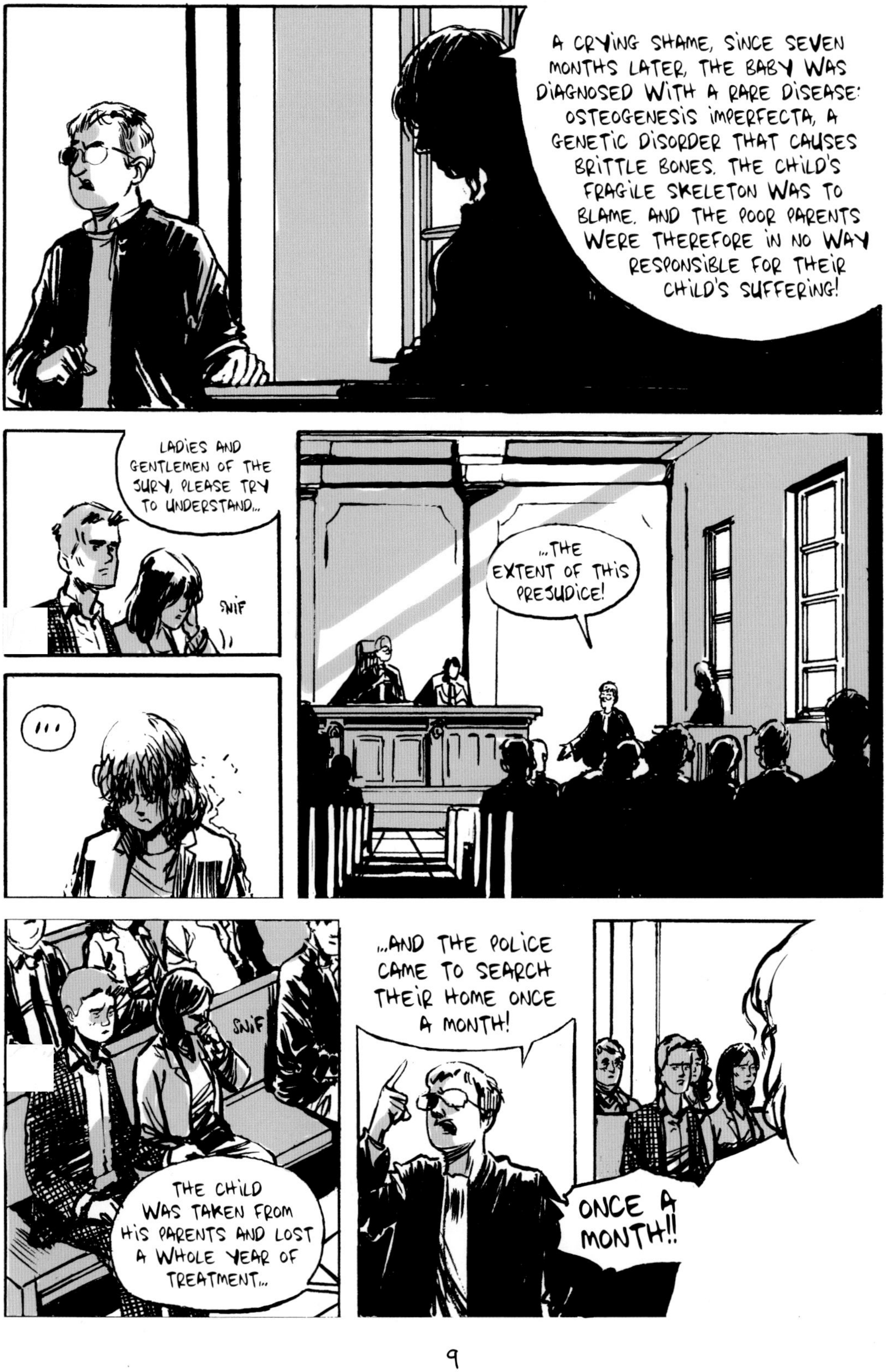

A CRYING SHAME, SINCE SEVEN MONTHS LATER, THE BABY WAS DIAGNOSED WITH A RARE DISEASE: OSTEOGENESIS IMPERFECTA, A GENETIC DISORDER THAT CAUSES BRITTLE BONES. THE CHILD'S FRAGILE SKELETON WAS TO BLAME. AND THE POOR PARENTS WERE THEREFORE IN NO WAY RESPONSIBLE FOR THEIR CHILD'S SUFFERING!
LADIES AND GENTLEMEN OF THE JURY, PLEASE TRY TO UNDERSTAND...
SNIF
...THE EXTENT OF THIS PREJUDICE!
...
SNIF
THE CHILD WAS TAKEN FROM HIS PARENTS AND LOST A WHOLE YEAR OF TREATMENT...
...AND THE POLICE CAME TO SEARCH THEIR HOME ONCE A MONTH!
ONCE A MONTH!!

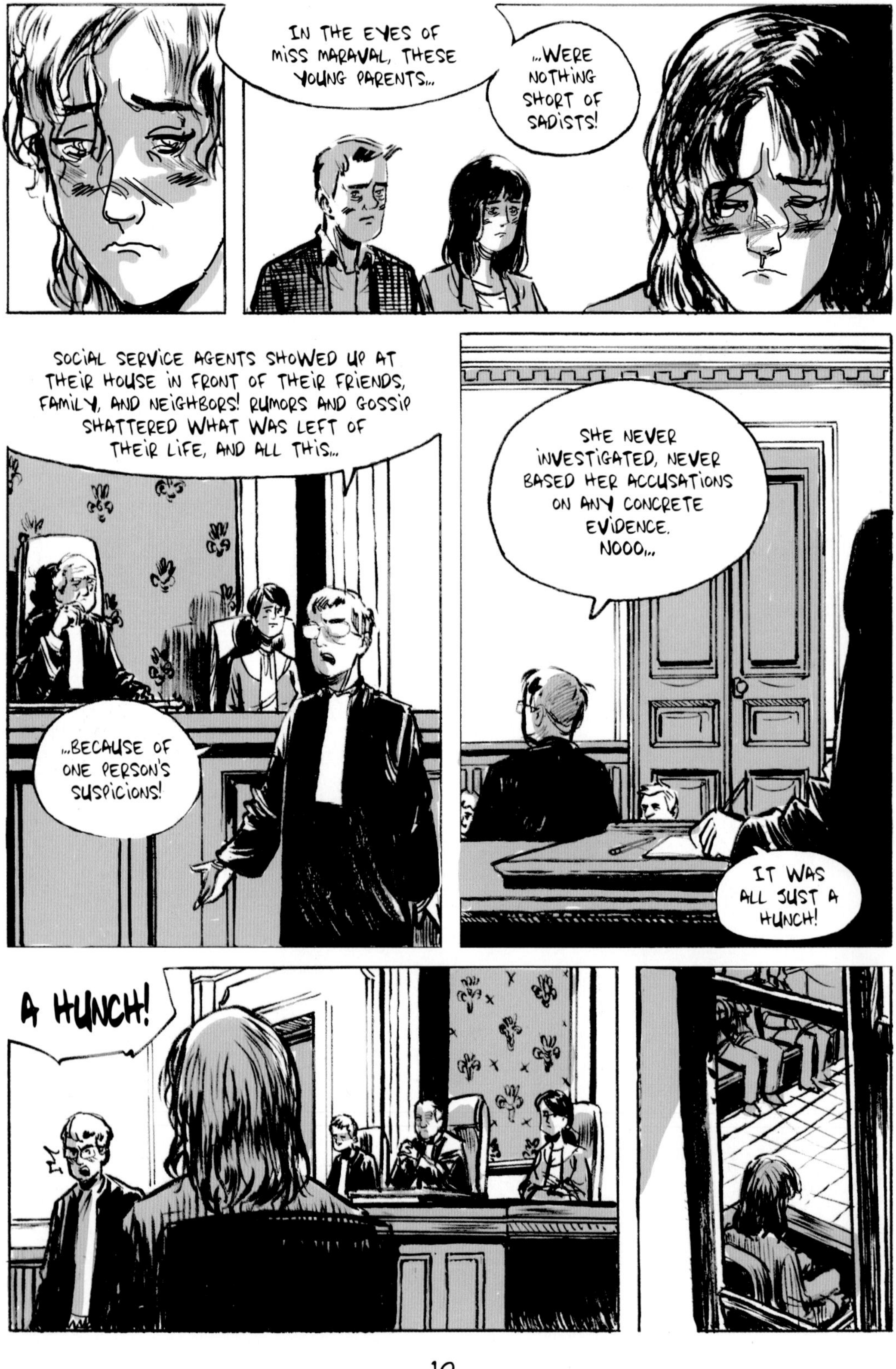
IN THE EYES OF MISS MARAVAL, THESE YOUNG PARENTS...
...WERE NOTHING SHORT OF SADISTS!
SOCIAL SERVICE AGENTS SHOWED UP AT THEIR HOUSE IN FRONT OF THEIR FRIENDS, FAMILY, AND NEIGHBORS! RUMORS AND GOSSIP SHATTERED WHAT WAS LEFT OF THEIR LIFE, AND ALL THIS...
...BECAUSE OF ONE PERSON'S SUSPICIONS!
SHE NEVER INVESTIGATED, NEVER BASED HER ACCUSATIONS ON ANY CONCRETE EVIDENCE. NOOO...
IT WAS ALL JUST A HUNCH!
A HUNCH!

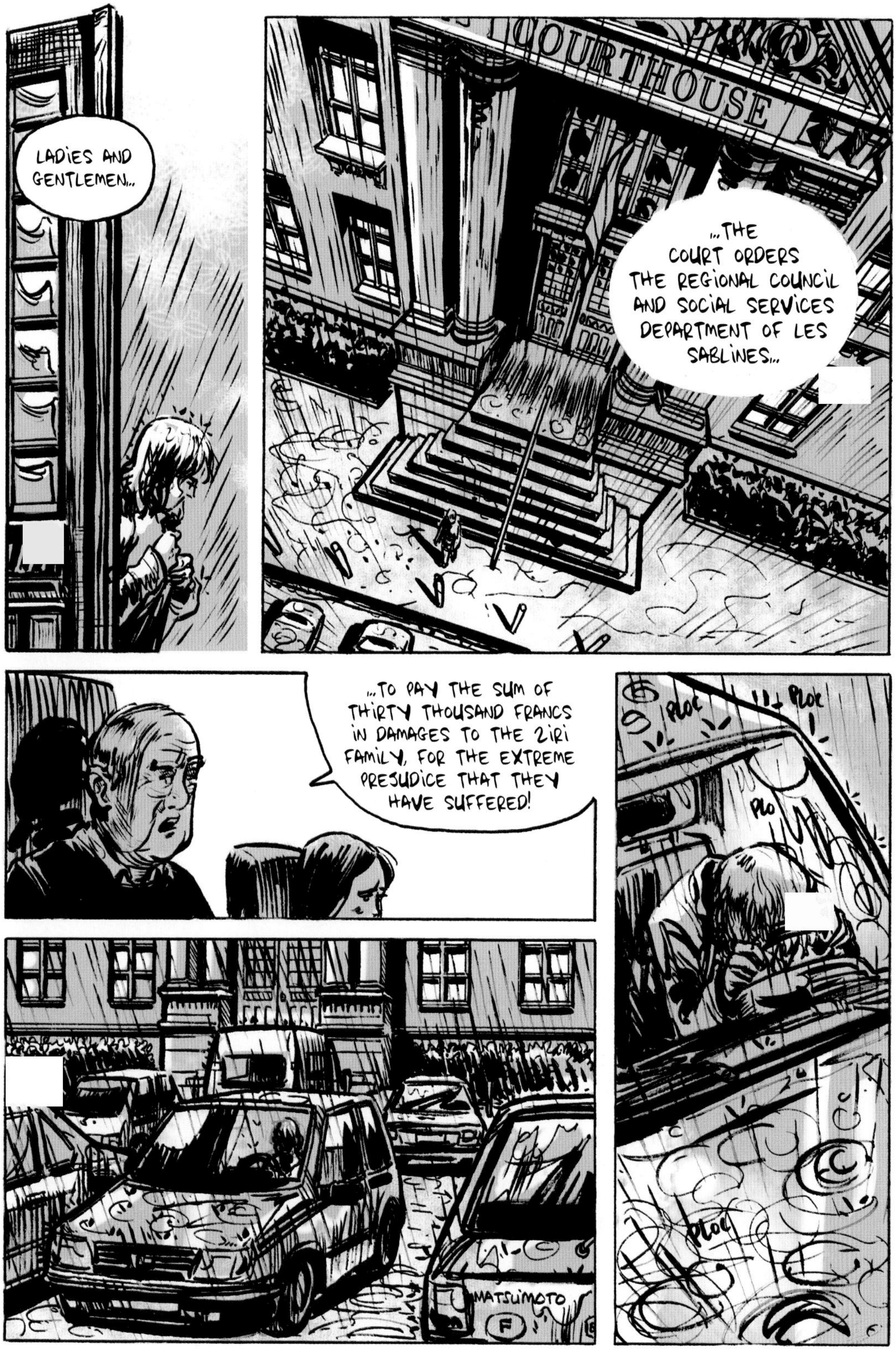
LADIES AND GENTLEMEN...
COURTHOUSE
...THE COURT ORDERS THE REGIONAL COUNCIL AND SOCIAL SERVICES DEPARTMENT OF LES SABLINES...
...TO PAY THE SUM OF THIRTY THOUSAND FRANCS IN DAMAGES TO THE ZIRI FAMILY, FOR THE EXTREME PREJUDICE THAT THEY HAVE SUFFERED!
PLOC
PLOC
PLO
PLOC
MATSUMOTO

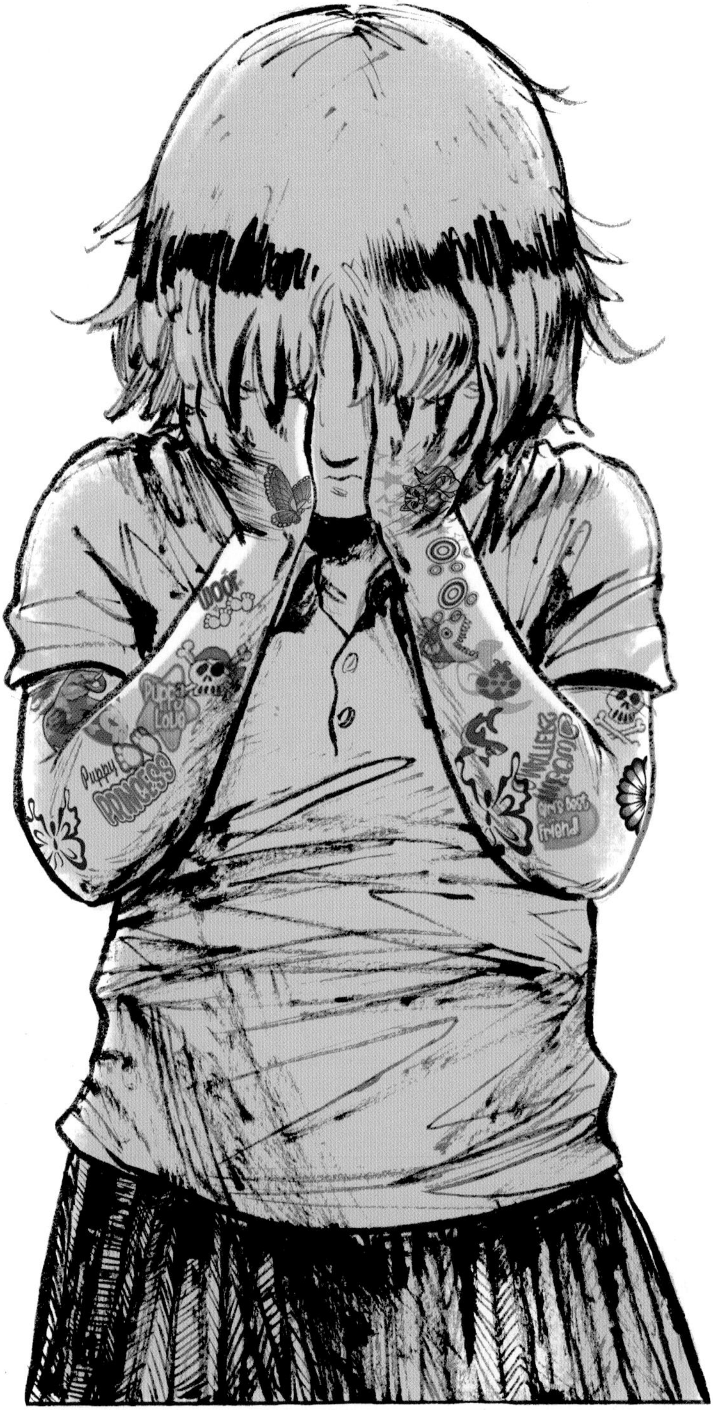
WOOF
Puppy
PRINCESS
friend

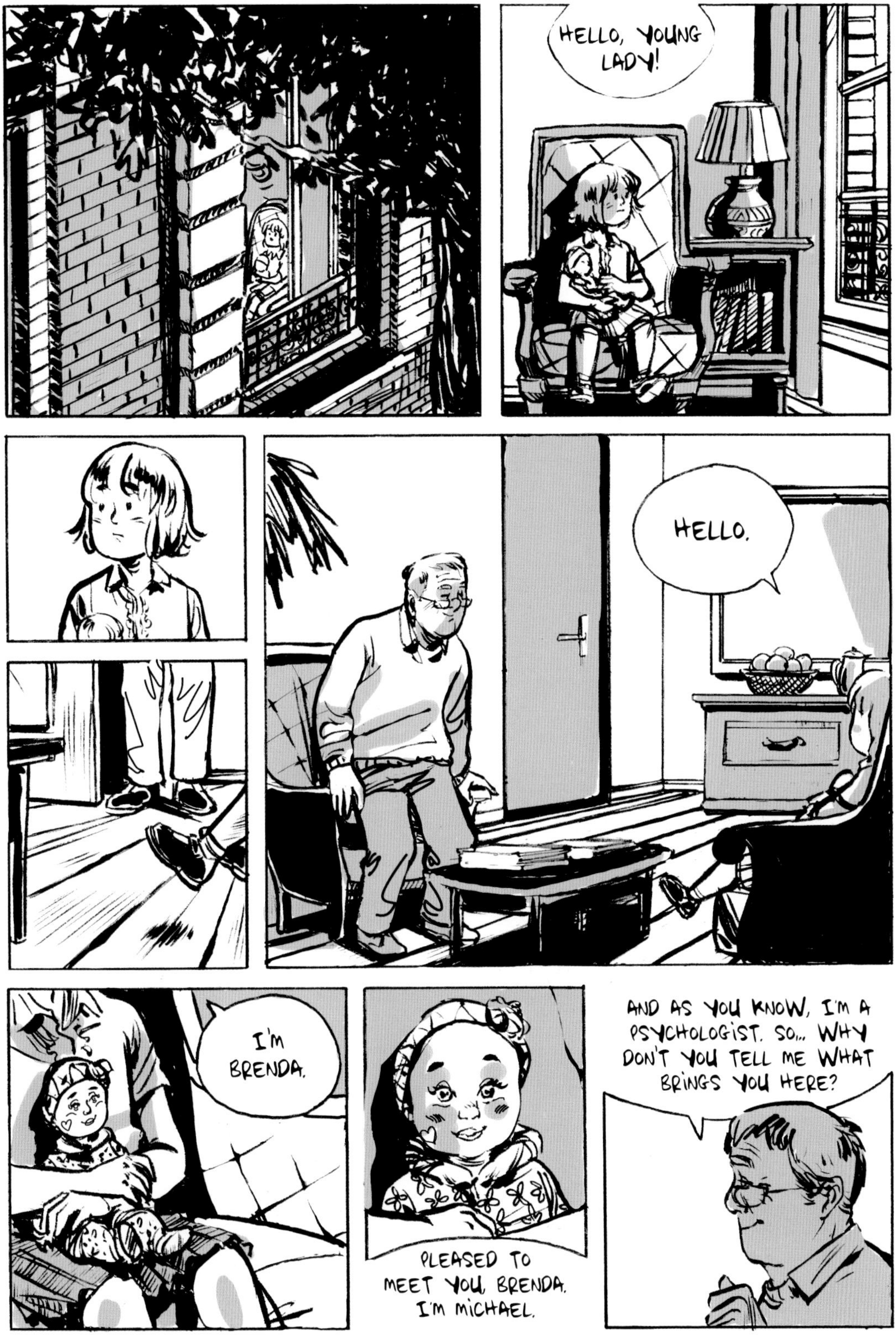
HELLO, YOUNG LADY!
HELLO.
I'M BRENDA.
PLEASED TO MEET YOU, BRENDA. I'M MICHAEL.
AND AS YOU KNOW, I'M A PSYCHOLOGIST. SO... WHY DON'T YOU TELL ME WHAT BRINGS YOU HERE?

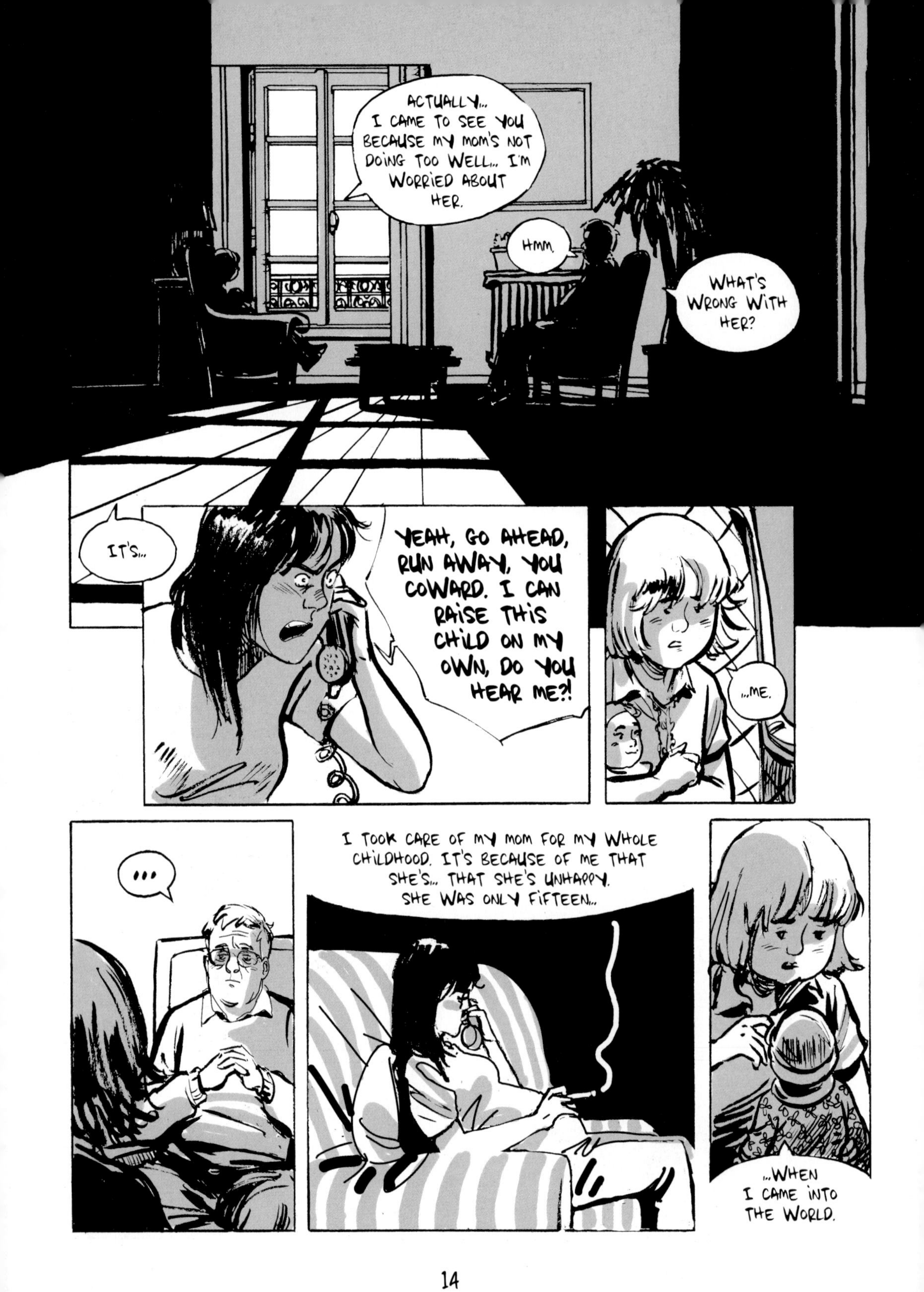

ACTUALLY... I CAME TO SEE YOU BECAUSE MY MOM'S NOT DOING TOO WELL... I'M WORRIED ABOUT HER.
HMM.
WHAT'S WRONG WITH HER?
IT'S...
YEAH, GO AHEAD, RUN AWAY, YOU COWARD. I CAN RAISE THIS CHILD ON MY OWN, DO YOU HEAR ME?!
...ME.
...
I TOOK CARE OF MY MOM FOR MY WHOLE CHILDHOOD. IT'S BECAUSE OF ME THAT SHE'S... THAT SHE'S UNHAPPY. SHE WAS ONLY FIFTEEN...
...WHEN I CAME INTO THE WORLD.

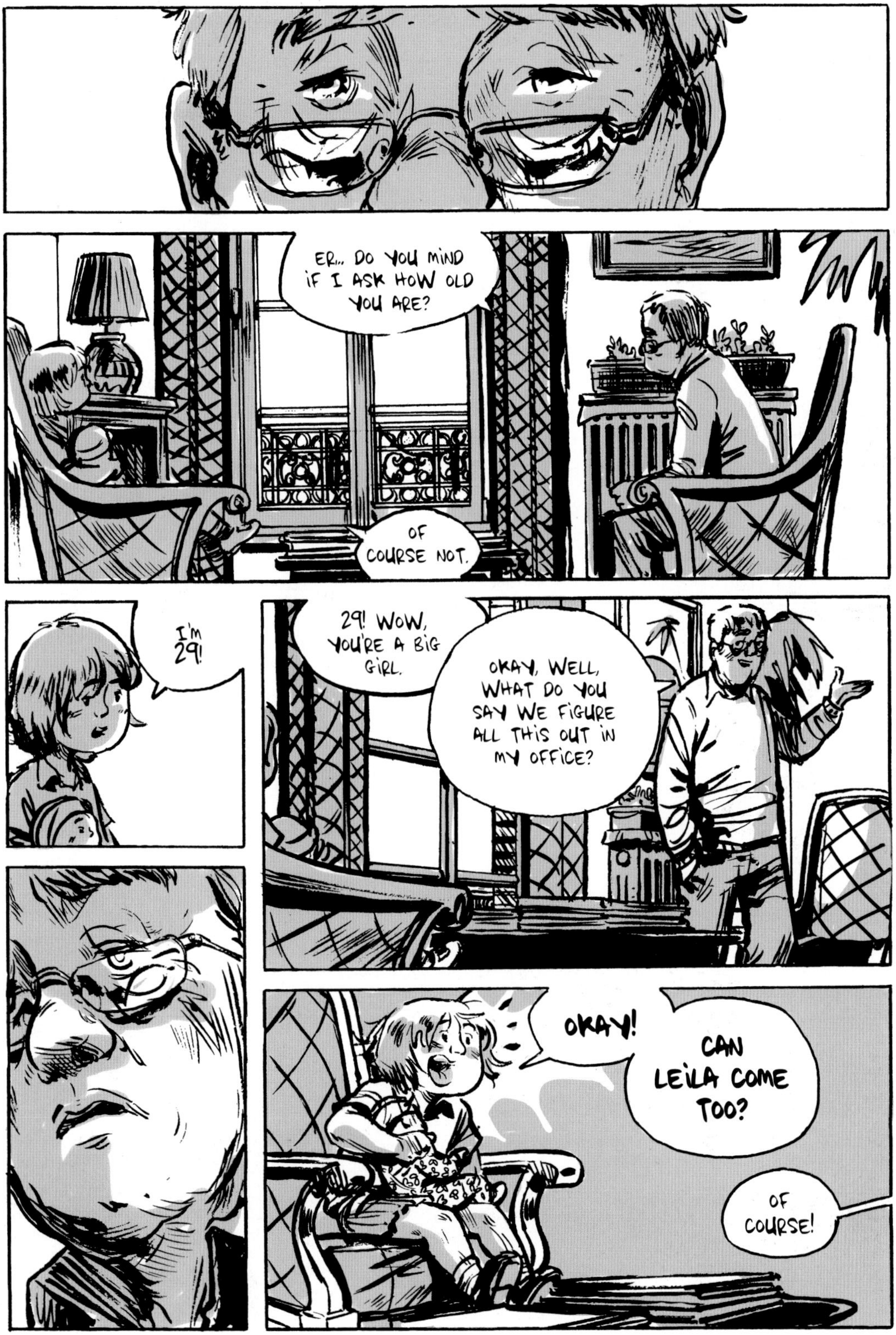
ER... DO YOU MIND IF I ASK HOW OLD YOU ARE?
OF COURSE NOT.
I'M 29!
29! WOW, YOU'RE A BIG GIRL.
OKAY, WELL, WHAT DO YOU SAY WE FIGURE ALL THIS OUT IN MY OFFICE?
OKAY!
CAN LEILA COME TOO?
OF COURSE!

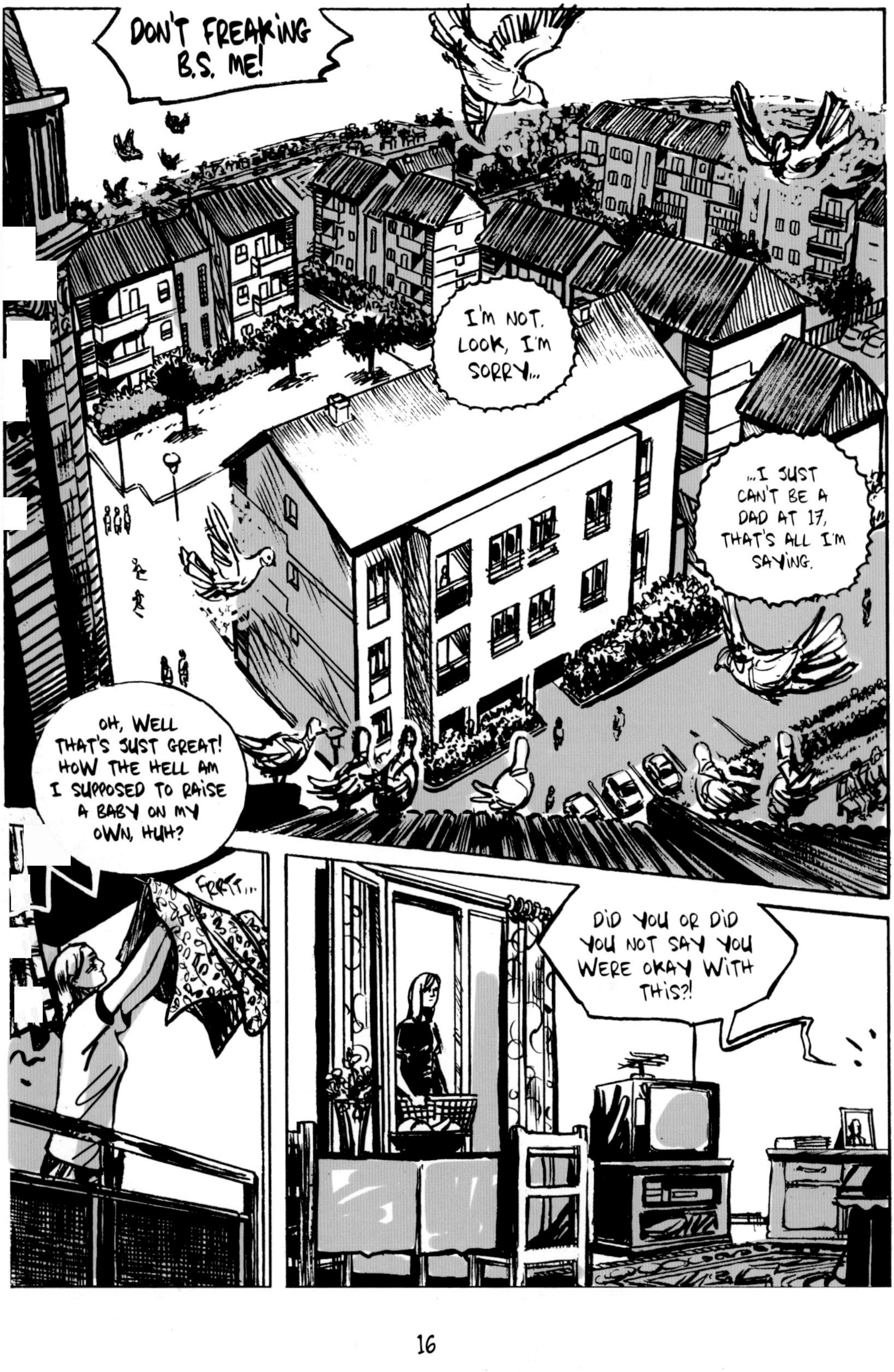
DON'T FREAKING B.S. ME!
I'M NOT. LOOK, I'M SORRY...
...I JUST CAN'T BE A DAD AT 17, THAT'S ALL I'M SAYING.
OH, WELL THAT'S JUST GREAT! HOW THE HELL AM I SUPPOSED TO RAISE A BABY ON MY OWN, HUH?
FRRT...
DID YOU OR DID YOU NOT SAY YOU WERE OKAY WITH THIS?!
!

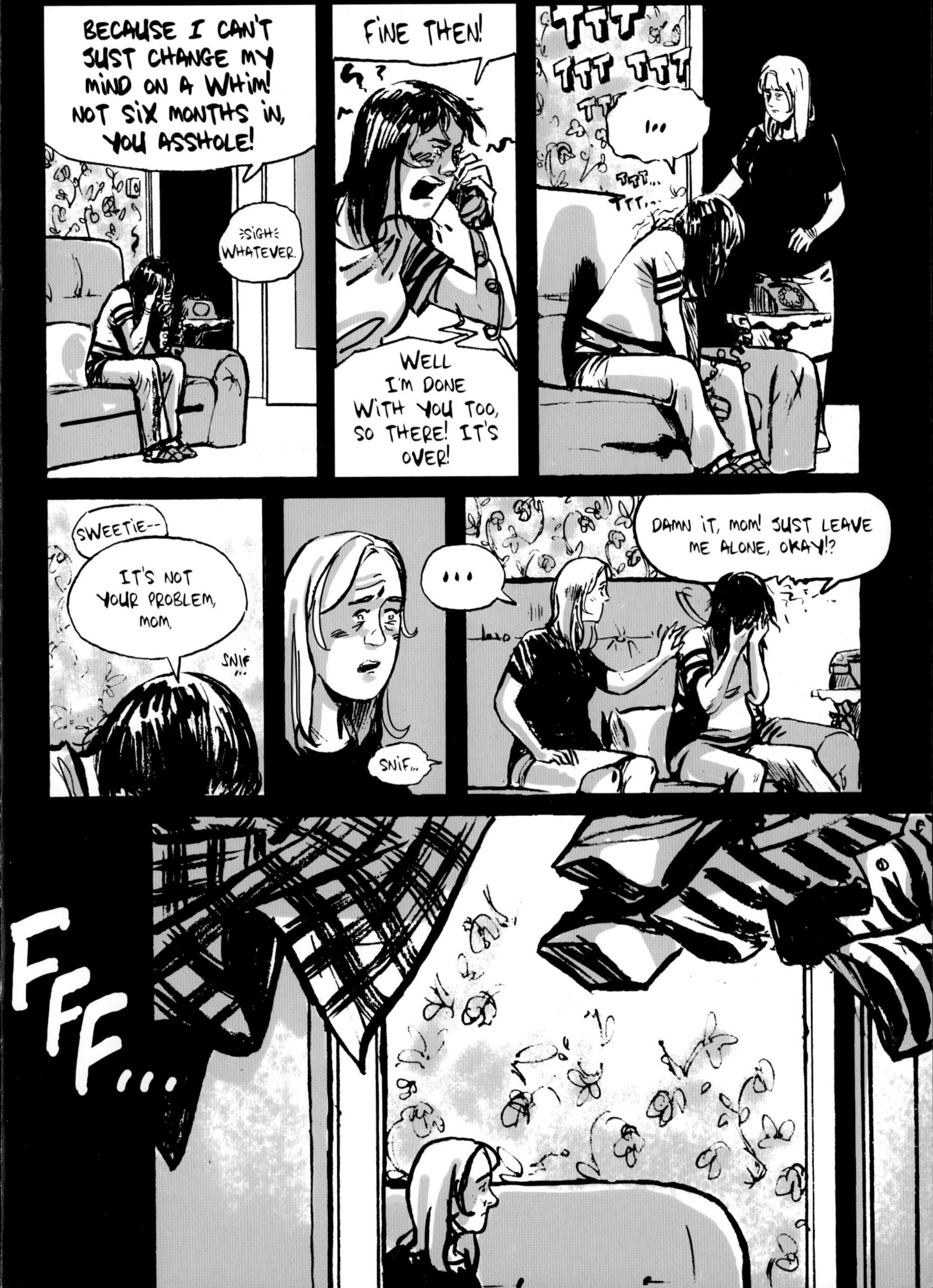
BECAUSE I CAN'T JUST CHANGE MY MIND ON A WHIM! NOT SIX MONTHS IN, YOU ASSHOLE!
SIGH WHATEVER.
FINE THEN!
WELL I'M DONE WITH YOU TOO, SO THERE! IT'S OVER!
TTT TTT TTT TT
...
TTT...
TTT...
SWEETIE--
IT'S NOT YOUR PROBLEM, MOM.
SNIF...
SNIF...
...
DAMN IT, MOM! JUST LEAVE ME ALONE, OKAY!?
FFF...

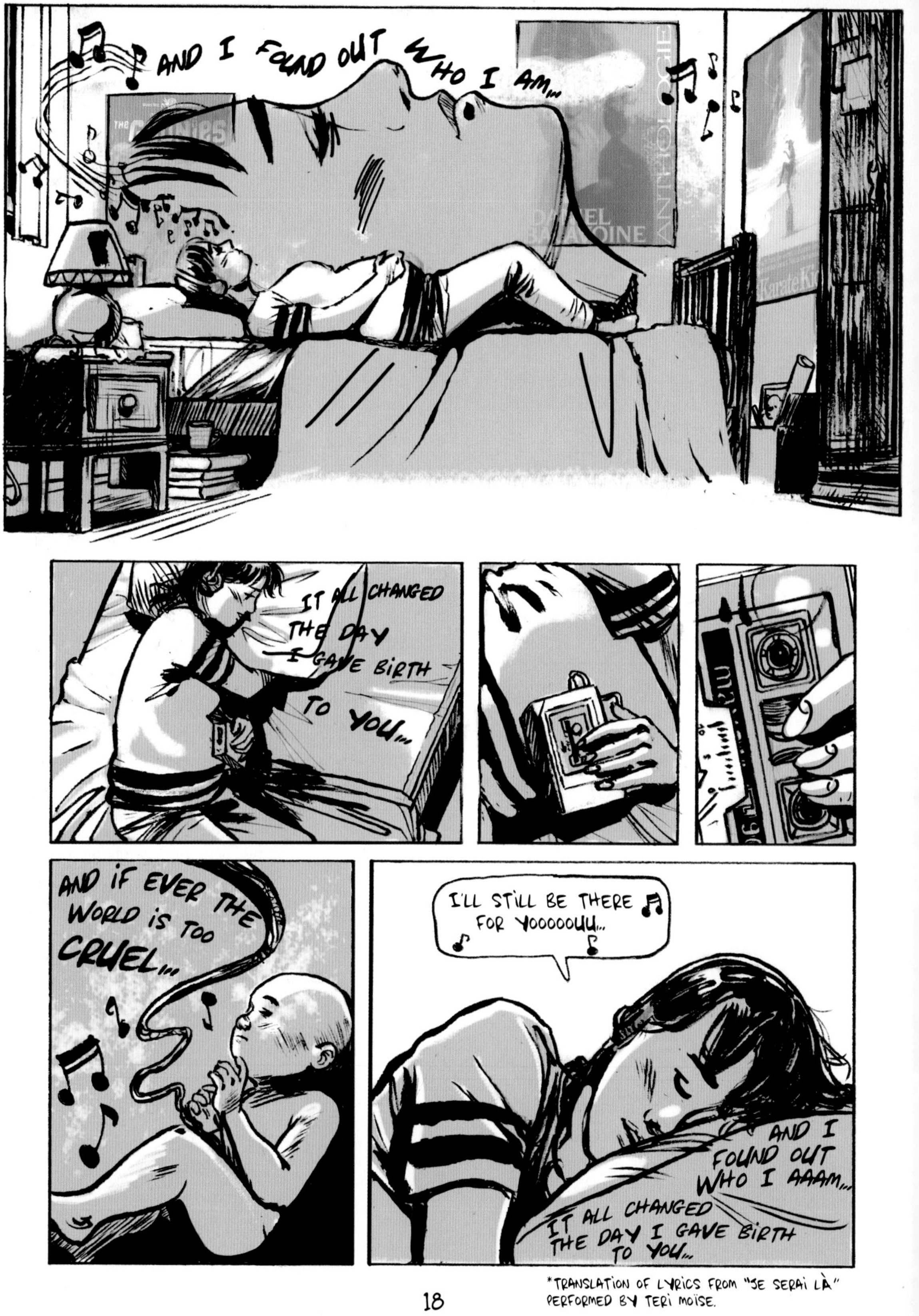
AND I FOUND OUT WHO I AM...
ANTHOLOGIE
IT ALL CHANGED THE DAY I GAVE BIRTH TO YOU...
AND IF EVER THE WORLD IS TOO CRUEL...
I'LL STILL BE THERE FOR YOOOOOUU...
AND I FOUND OUT WHO I AAAM...
IT ALL CHANGED THE DAY I GAVE BIRTH TO YOU...

*TRANSLATION OF LYRICS FROM "JE SERAI LÀ" PERFORMED BY TERI MOÏSE.

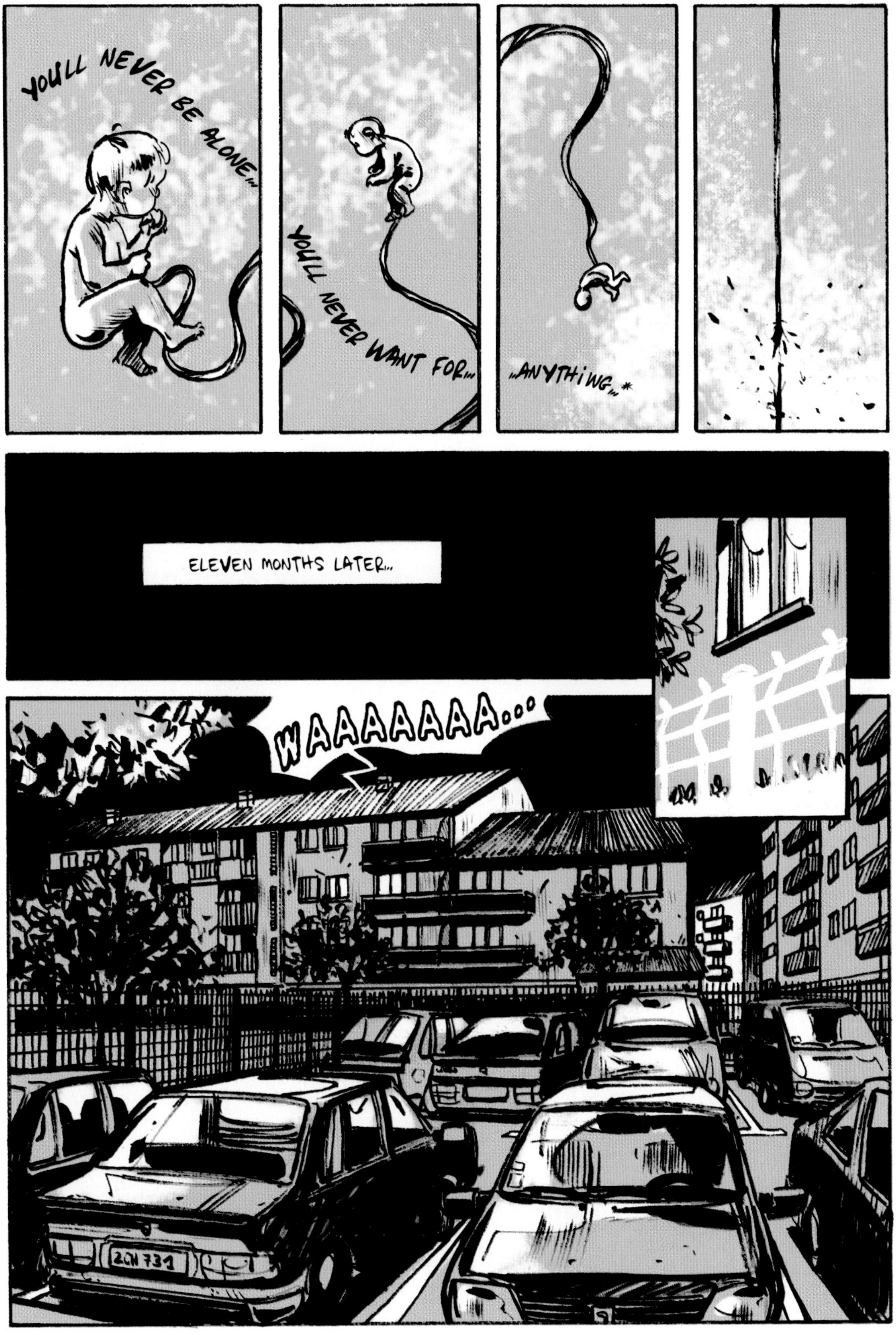
YOU'LL NEVER BE ALONE...
YOU'LL NEVER WANT FOR...
...ANYTHING...*
ELEVEN MONTHS LATER...
WAAAAAAA...
2CH 731

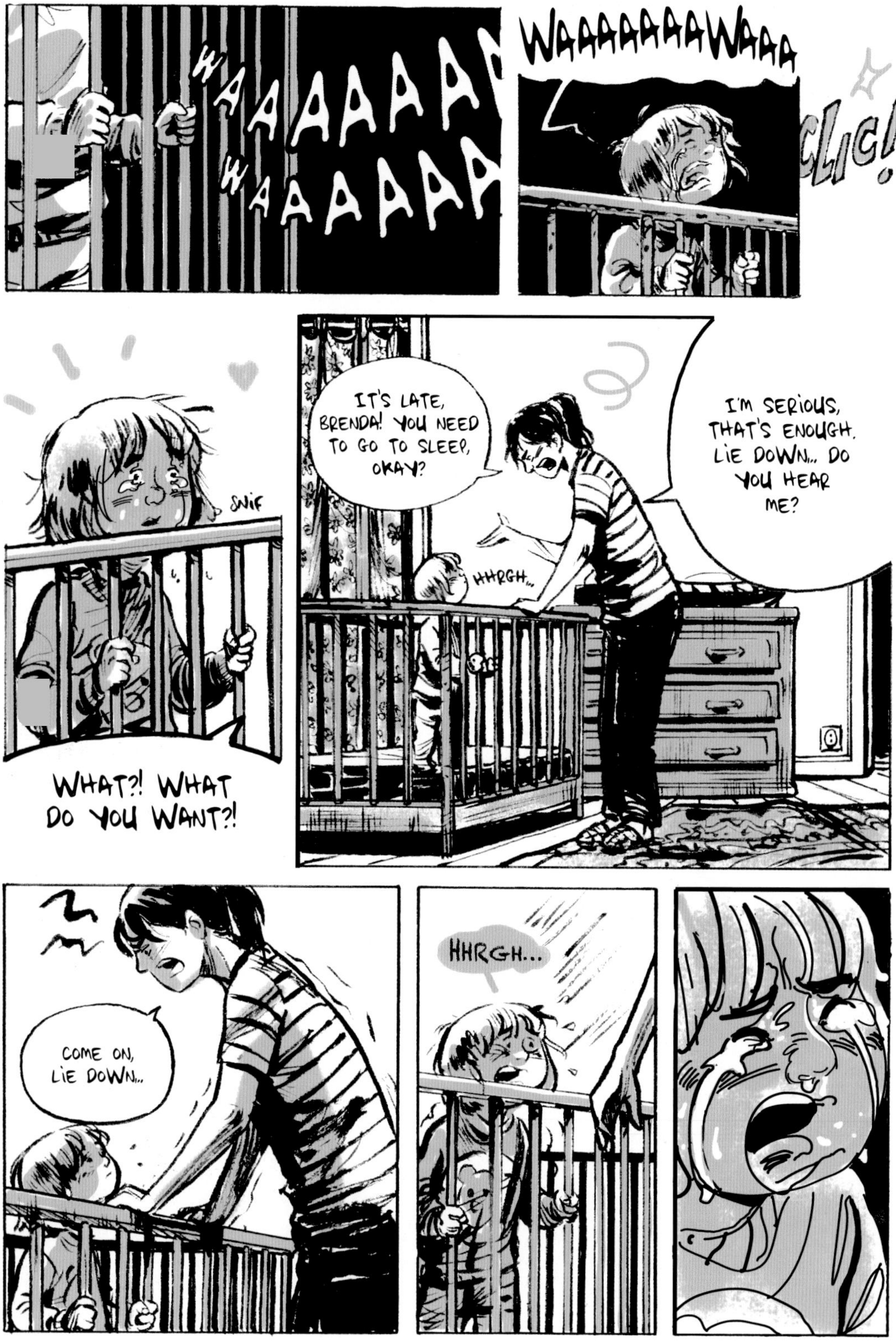
WAAAAAA
WAAAAAA
WAAAAAAAWAAA
CLIC!
SNIF
WHAT?! WHAT DO YOU WANT?!
IT'S LATE, BRENDA! YOU NEED TO GO TO SLEEP, OKAY?
HHRGH...
I'M SERIOUS, THAT'S ENOUGH. LIE DOWN... DO YOU HEAR ME?
COME ON, LIE DOWN...
HHRGH...

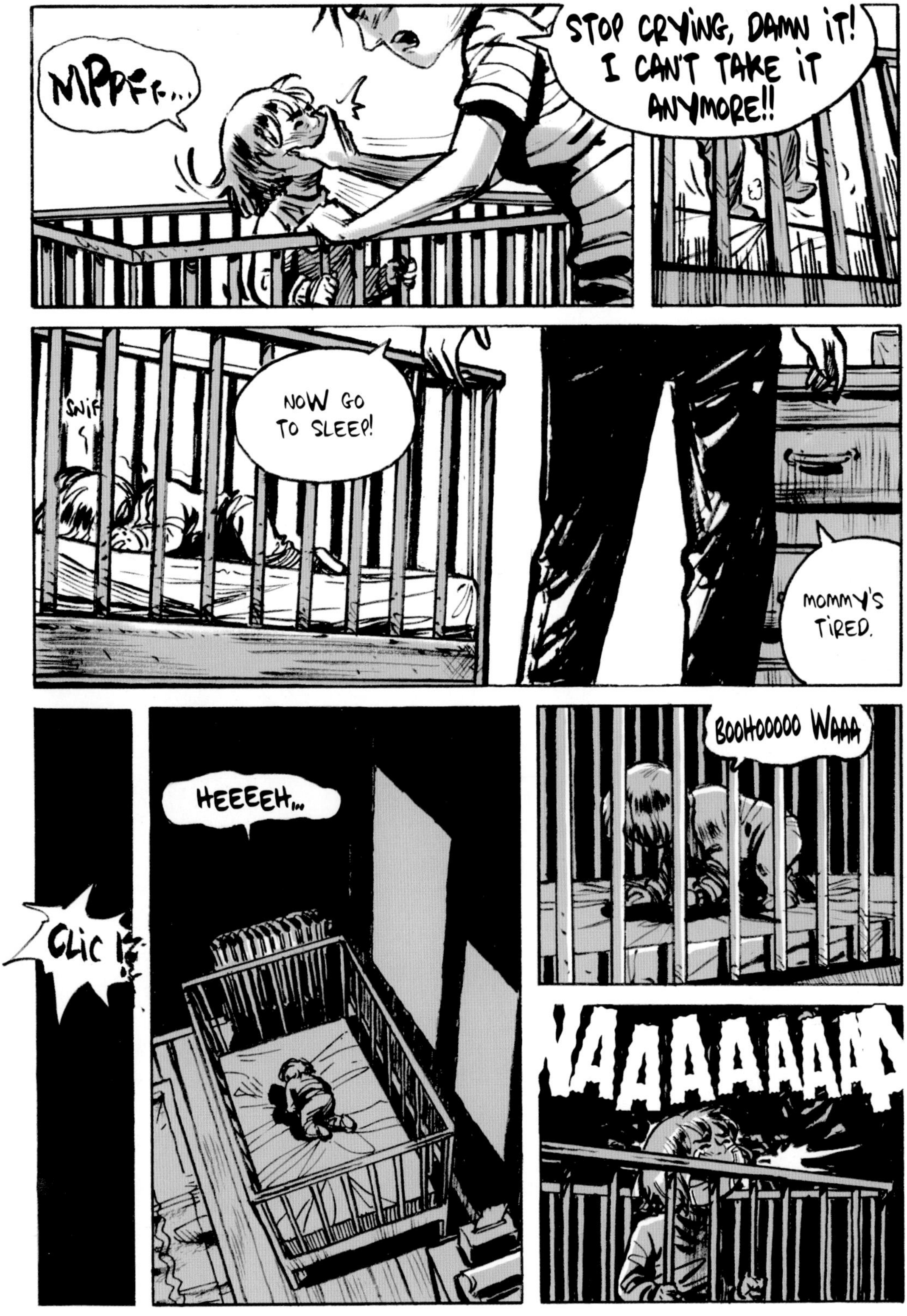
MPPFF...
STOP CRYING, DAMN IT! I CAN'T TAKE IT ANYMORE!!
SNIF
NOW GO TO SLEEP!
MOMMY'S TIRED.
HEEEEH...
CLIC
BOOHOOOOO WAAA
WAAAAAAA

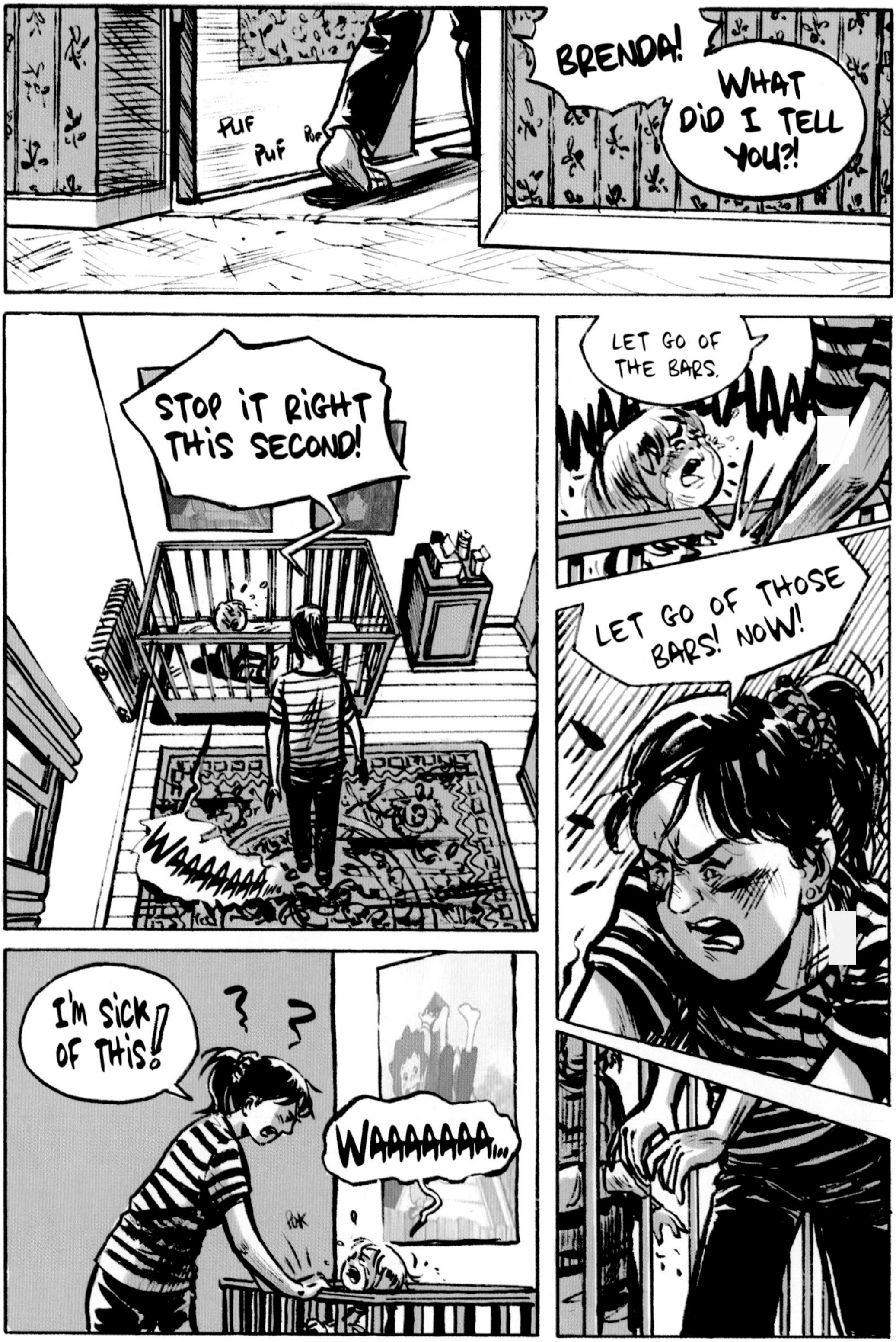
PUF
PUF
PUF
BRENDA!
WHAT DID I TELL YOU?!
STOP IT RIGHT THIS SECOND!
WAAAAAAA
LET GO OF THE BARS.
LET GO OF THOSE BARS! NOW!
I'M SICK OF THIS!
? ?
WAAAAAAA...
PUK

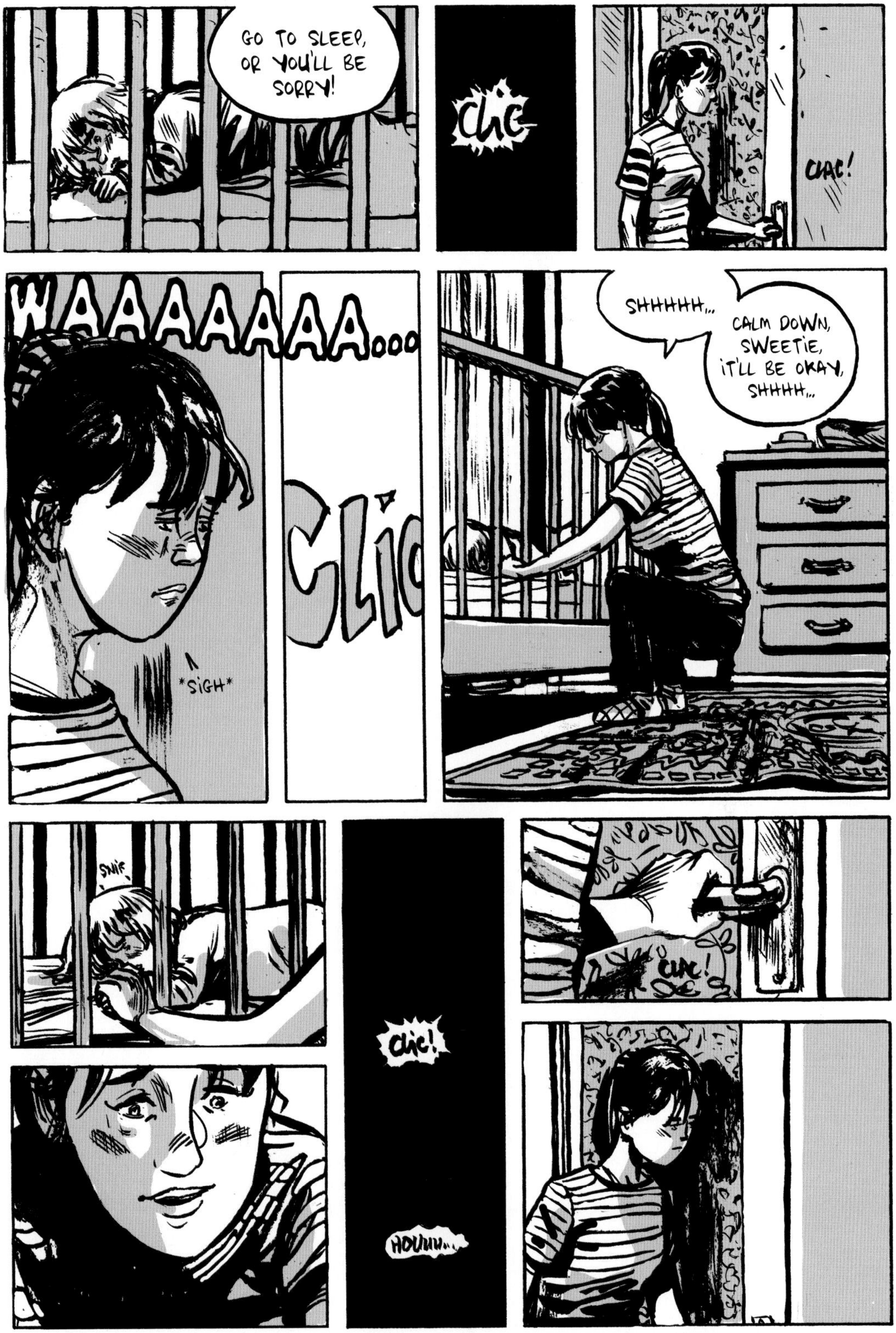
GO TO SLEEP, OR YOU'LL BE SORRY!
CLIC
CLAC!
WAAAAAAAA...
CLIC
SIGH
SHHHHH...
CALM DOWN, SWEETIE, IT'LL BE OKAY, SHHHH...
SNIF
CLAC!
CLIC!
HOUUU...

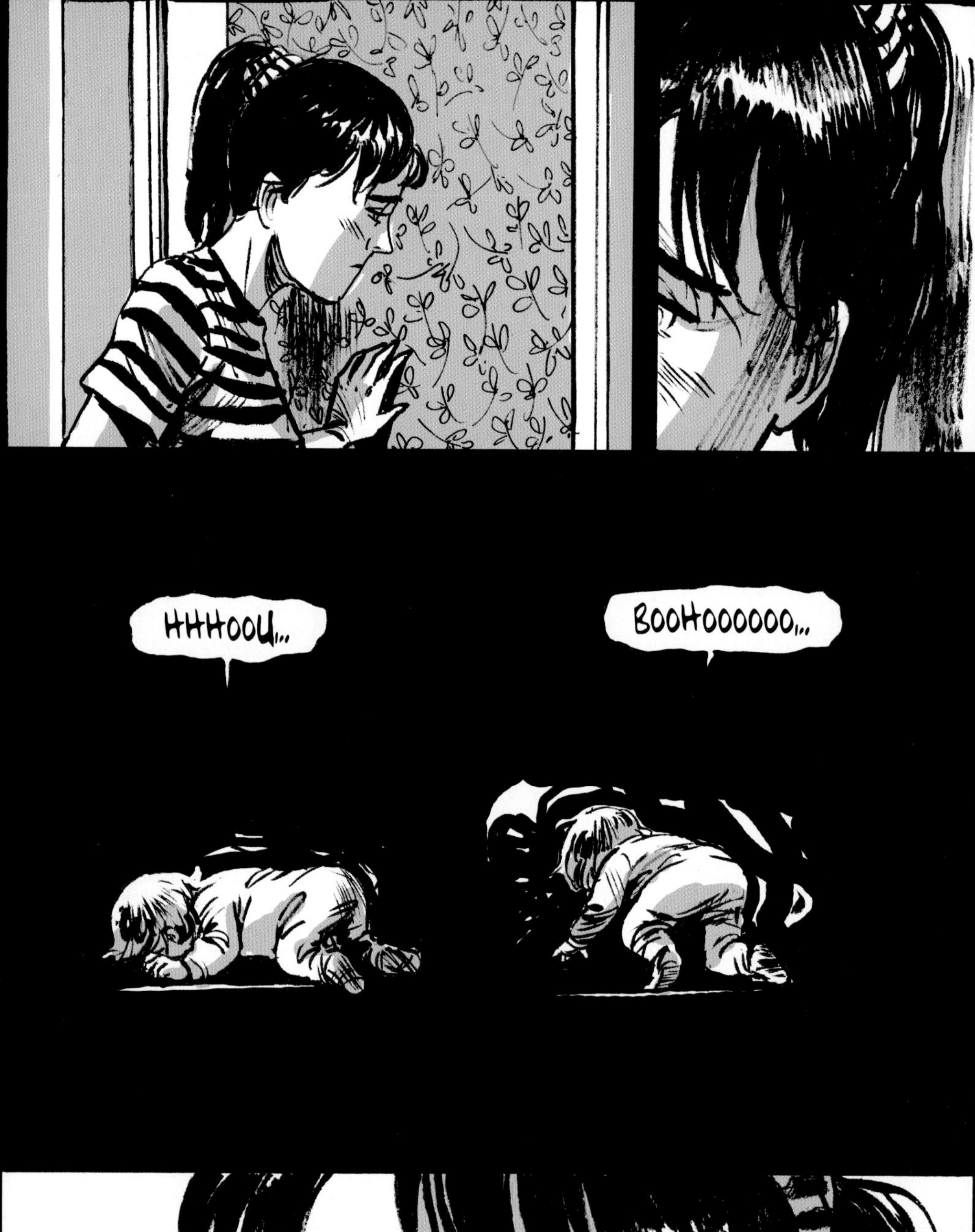
HHHOOU...
BOOHOOOOOO...

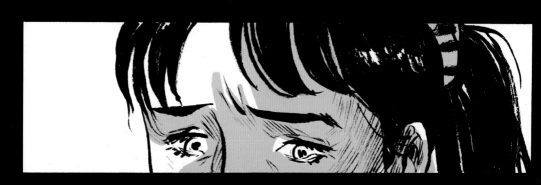

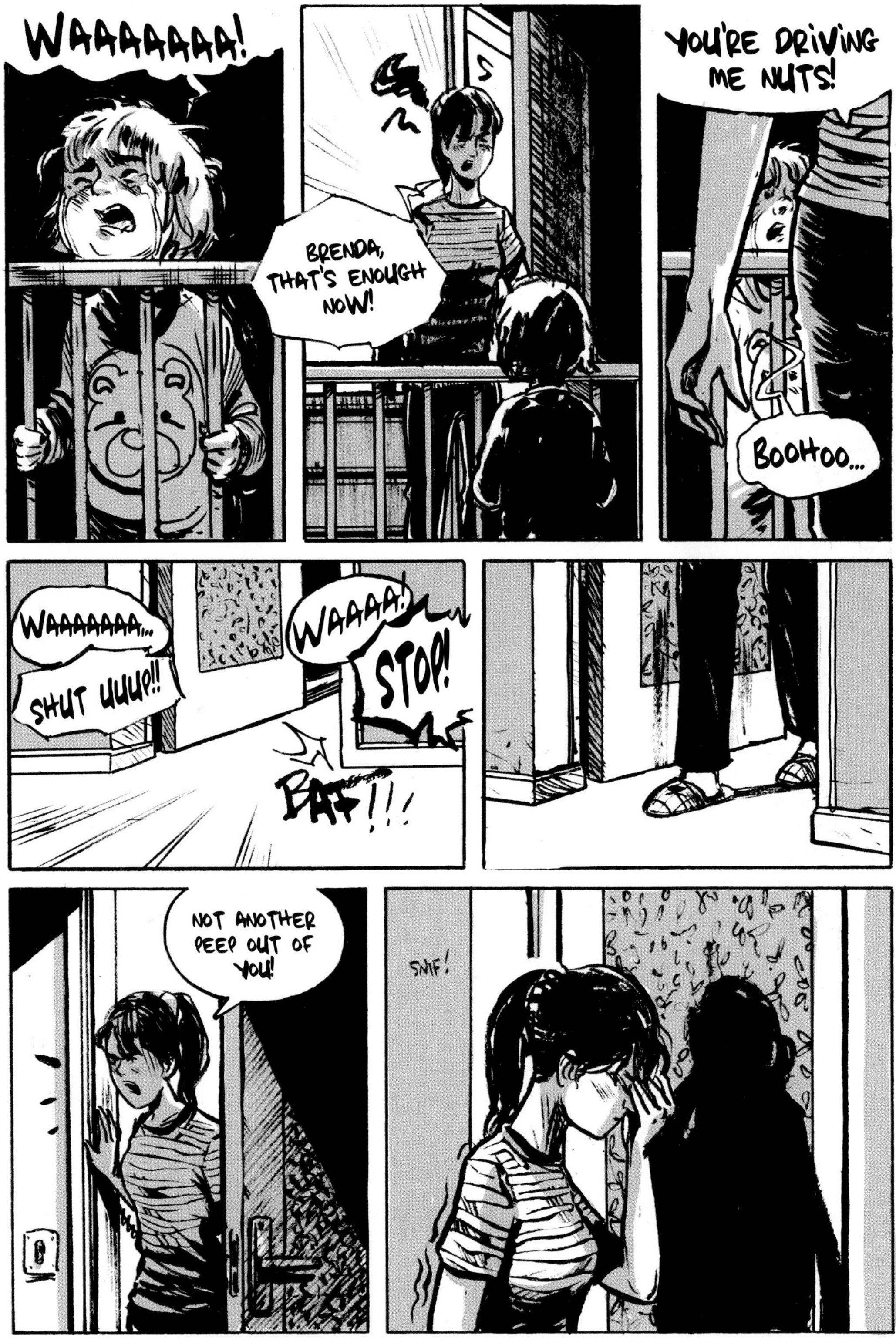
WAAAAAAA!
BRENDA, THAT'S ENOUGH NOW!
YOU'RE DRIVING ME NUTS!
BOOHOO...
WAAAAAAA...
SHUT UUUP!!
WAAAA!
STOP!
BAF!!!
NOT ANOTHER PEEP OUT OF YOU!
SNIF!

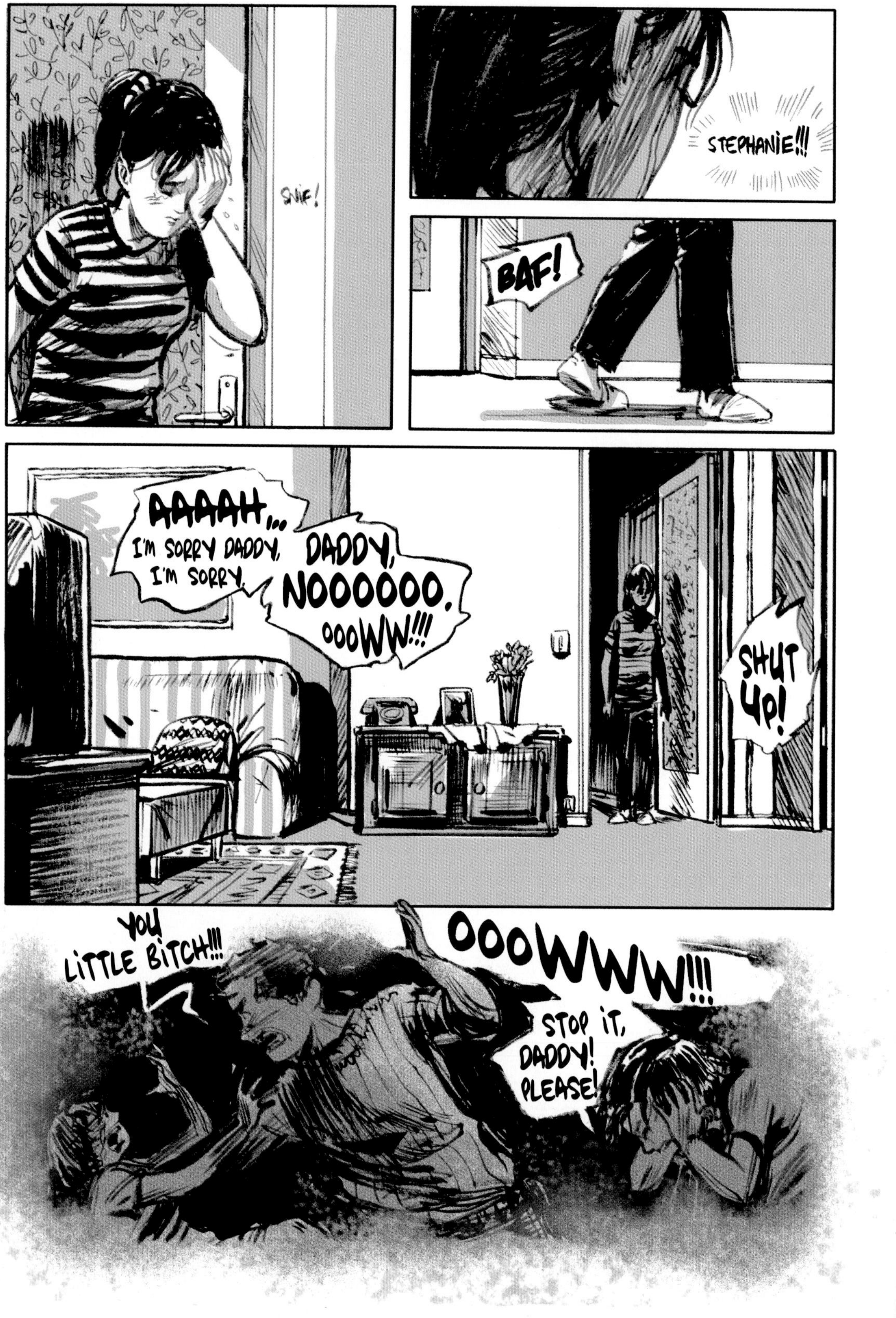
SNIF!
STEPHANIE!!!
BAF!
AAAAH... I'M SORRY DADDY, I'M SORRY.
DADDY, NOOOOOO. OOOWW!!!
SHUT UP!
YOU LITTLE BITCH!!!
OOOWWW!!!
STOP IT, DADDY! PLEASE!

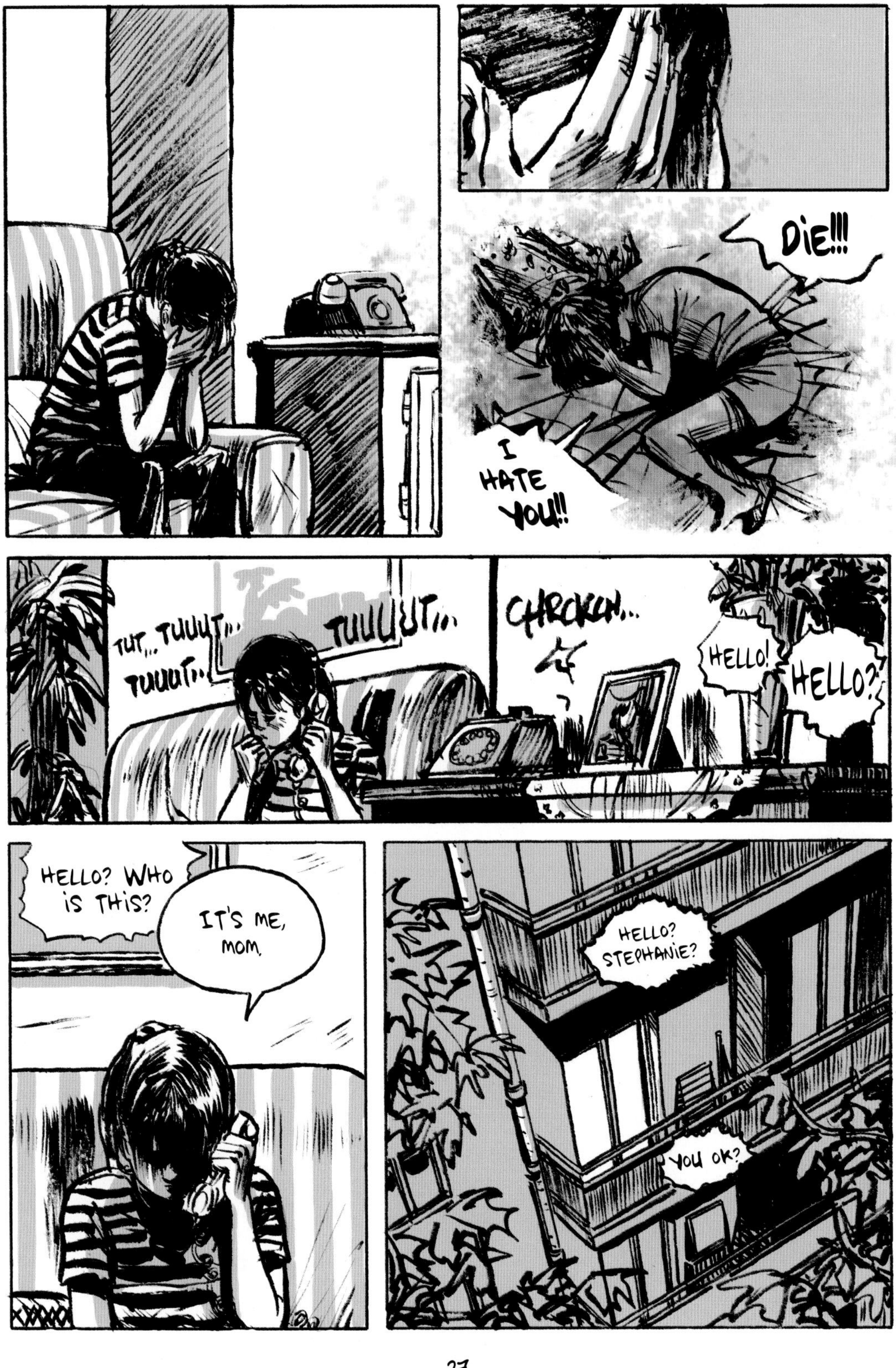
DIE!!!
I HATE YOU!!
TUT... TUUUT...
TUUUUT...
TUUUUT...
CHRCKCH...
HELLO!
HELLO?
HELLO? WHO IS THIS?
IT'S ME, MOM.
HELLO? STEPHANIE?
YOU OK?

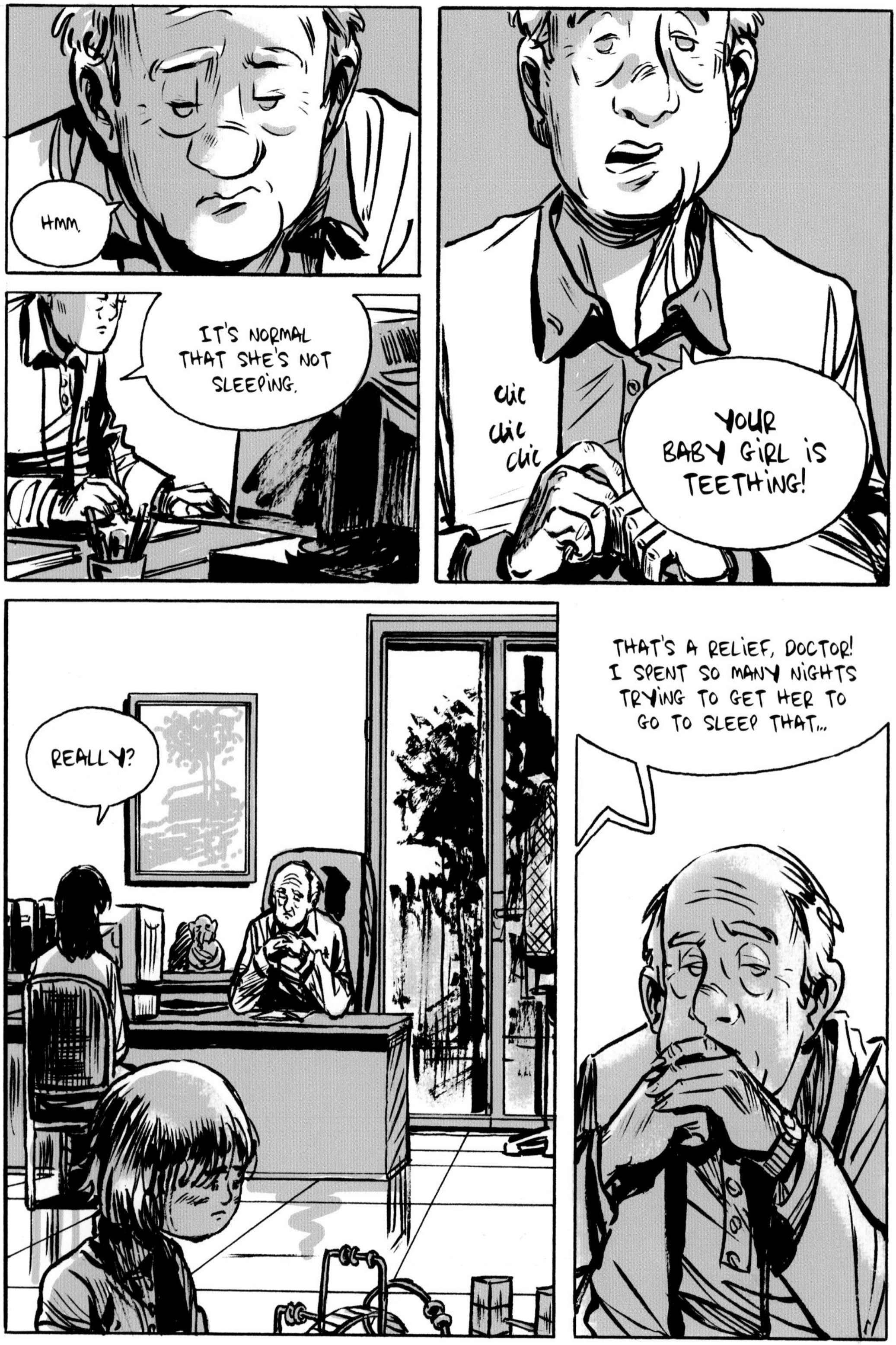
HMM.
IT'S NORMAL THAT SHE'S NOT SLEEPING.
CLIC CLIC CLIC
YOUR BABY GIRL IS TEETHING!
REALLY?
THAT'S A RELIEF, DOCTOR! I SPENT SO MANY NIGHTS TRYING TO GET HER TO GO TO SLEEP THAT...

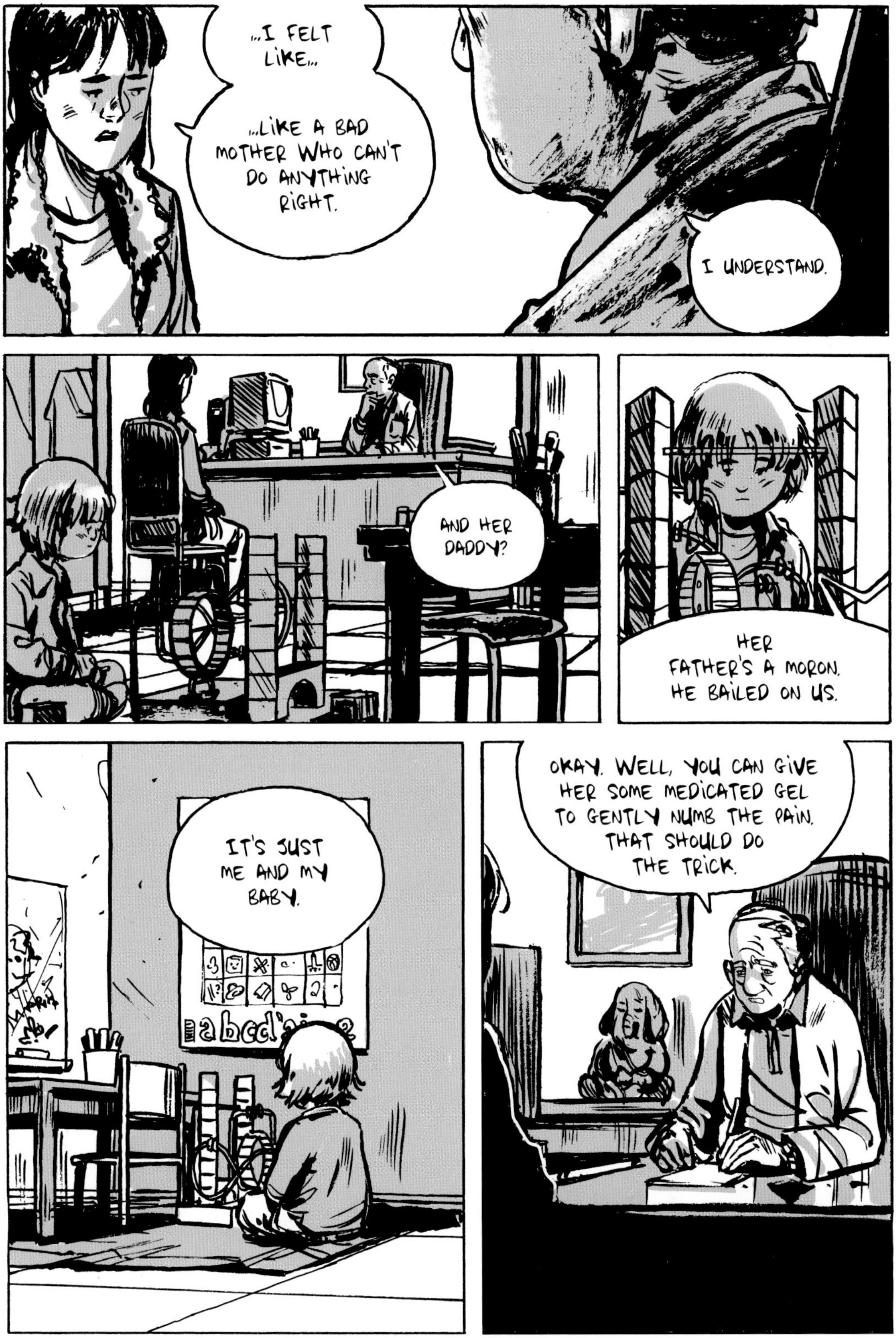
...I FELT LIKE...
...LIKE A BAD MOTHER WHO CAN'T DO ANYTHING RIGHT.
I UNDERSTAND.
AND HER DADDY?
HER FATHER'S A MORON. HE BAILED ON US.
IT'S JUST ME AND MY BABY.
OKAY. WELL, YOU CAN GIVE HER SOME MEDICATED GEL TO GENTLY NUMB THE PAIN. THAT SHOULD DO THE TRICK.

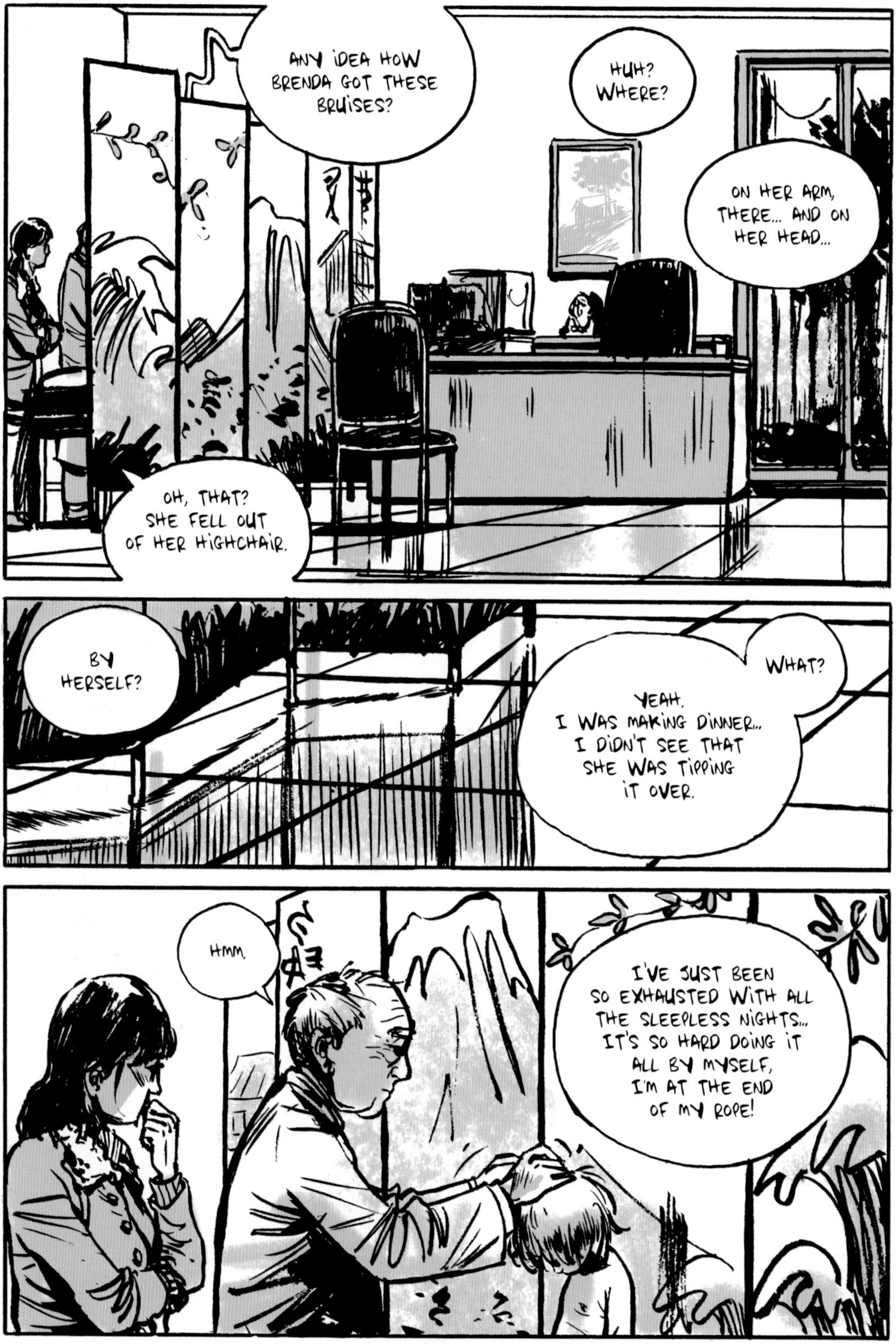
ANY IDEA HOW BRENDA GOT THESE BRUISES?
HUH? WHERE?
ON HER ARM, THERE... AND ON HER HEAD...
OH, THAT? SHE FELL OUT OF HER HIGHCHAIR.
BY HERSELF?
WHAT?
YEAH. I WAS MAKING DINNER... I DIDN'T SEE THAT SHE WAS TIPPING IT OVER.
HMM.
I'VE JUST BEEN SO EXHAUSTED WITH ALL THE SLEEPLESS NIGHTS... IT'S SO HARD DOING IT ALL BY MYSELF, I'M AT THE END OF MY ROPE!

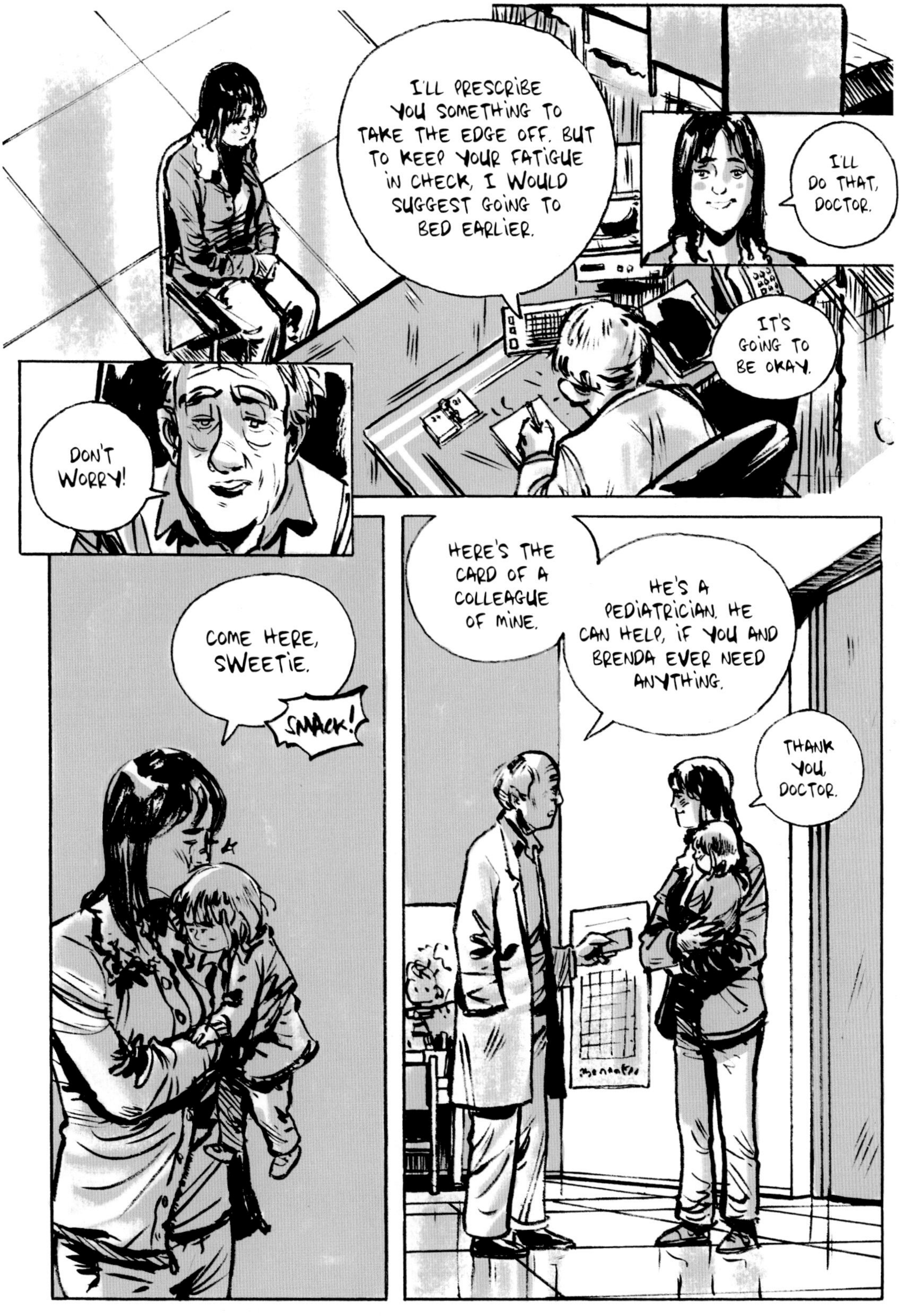
I'LL PRESCRIBE YOU SOMETHING TO TAKE THE EDGE OFF. BUT TO KEEP YOUR FATIGUE IN CHECK, I WOULD SUGGEST GOING TO BED EARLIER.
I'LL DO THAT, DOCTOR.
DON'T WORRY!
IT'S GOING TO BE OKAY.
COME HERE, SWEETIE.
SMACK!
HERE'S THE CARD OF A COLLEAGUE OF MINE.
HE'S A PEDIATRICIAN. HE CAN HELP, IF YOU AND BRENDA EVER NEED ANYTHING.
THANK YOU, DOCTOR.

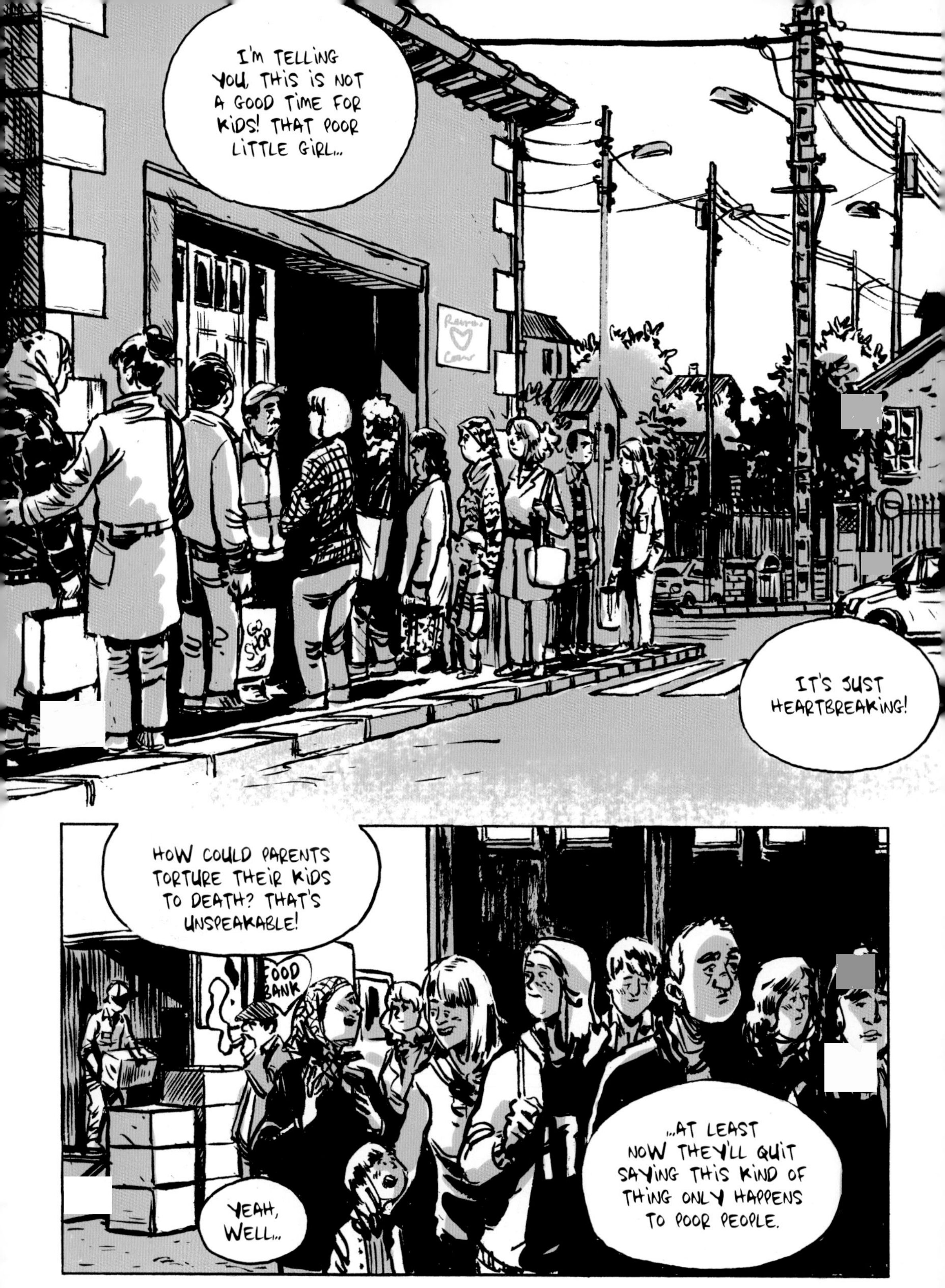
I'M TELLING YOU, THIS IS NOT A GOOD TIME FOR KIDS! THAT POOR LITTLE GIRL...
GO SHOP
IT'S JUST HEARTBREAKING!
HOW COULD PARENTS TORTURE THEIR KIDS TO DEATH? THAT'S UNSPEAKABLE!
FOOD BANK
YEAH, WELL...
...AT LEAST NOW THEY'LL QUIT SAYING THIS KIND OF THING ONLY HAPPENS TO POOR PEOPLE.

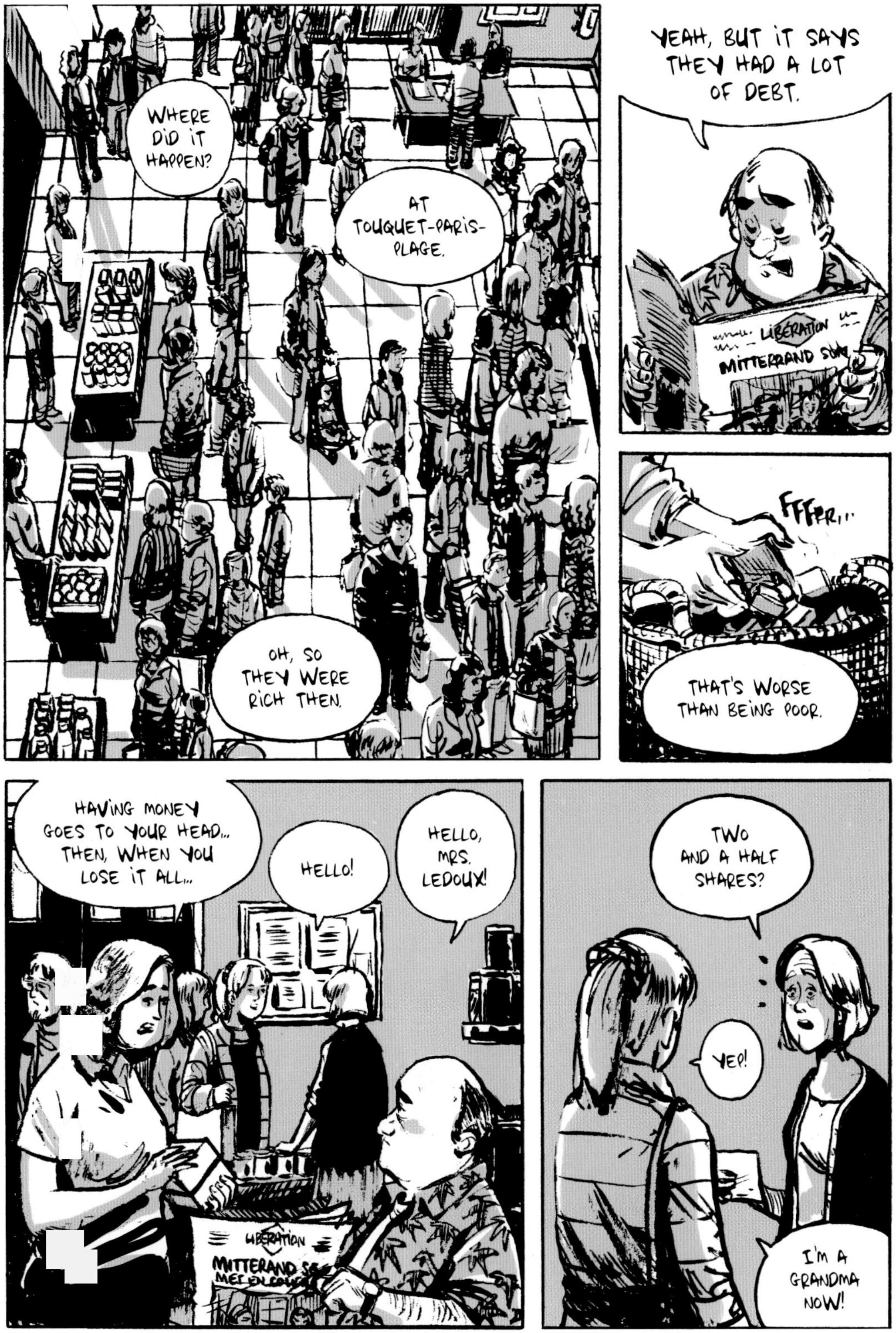
WHERE DID IT HAPPEN?
AT TOUQUET-PARIS-PLAGE.
OH, SO THEY WERE RICH THEN.
YEAH, BUT IT SAYS THEY HAD A LOT OF DEBT.
LIBÉRATION
FFFFR...
THAT'S WORSE THAN BEING POOR.
HAVING MONEY GOES TO YOUR HEAD... THEN, WHEN YOU LOSE IT ALL...
HELLO!
HELLO, MRS. LEDOUX!
TWO AND A HALF SHARES?
YEP!
I'M A GRANDMA NOW!

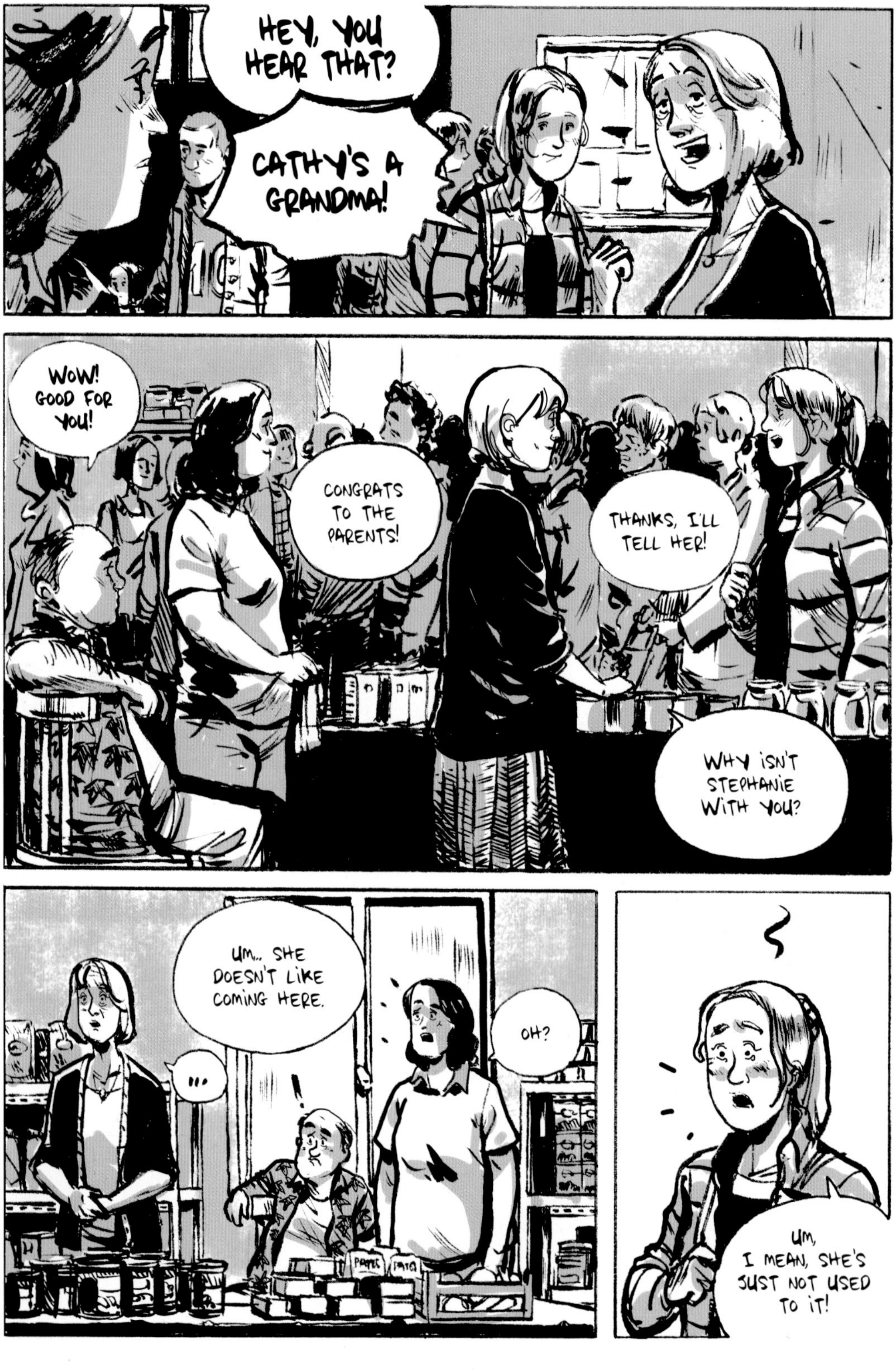
HEY, YOU HEAR THAT?
CATHY'S A GRANDMA!
WOW! GOOD FOR YOU!
CONGRATS TO THE PARENTS!
THANKS, I'LL TELL HER!
WHY ISN'T STEPHANIE WITH YOU?
UM.. SHE DOESN'T LIKE COMING HERE.
...
OH?
UM, I MEAN, SHE'S JUST NOT USED TO IT!

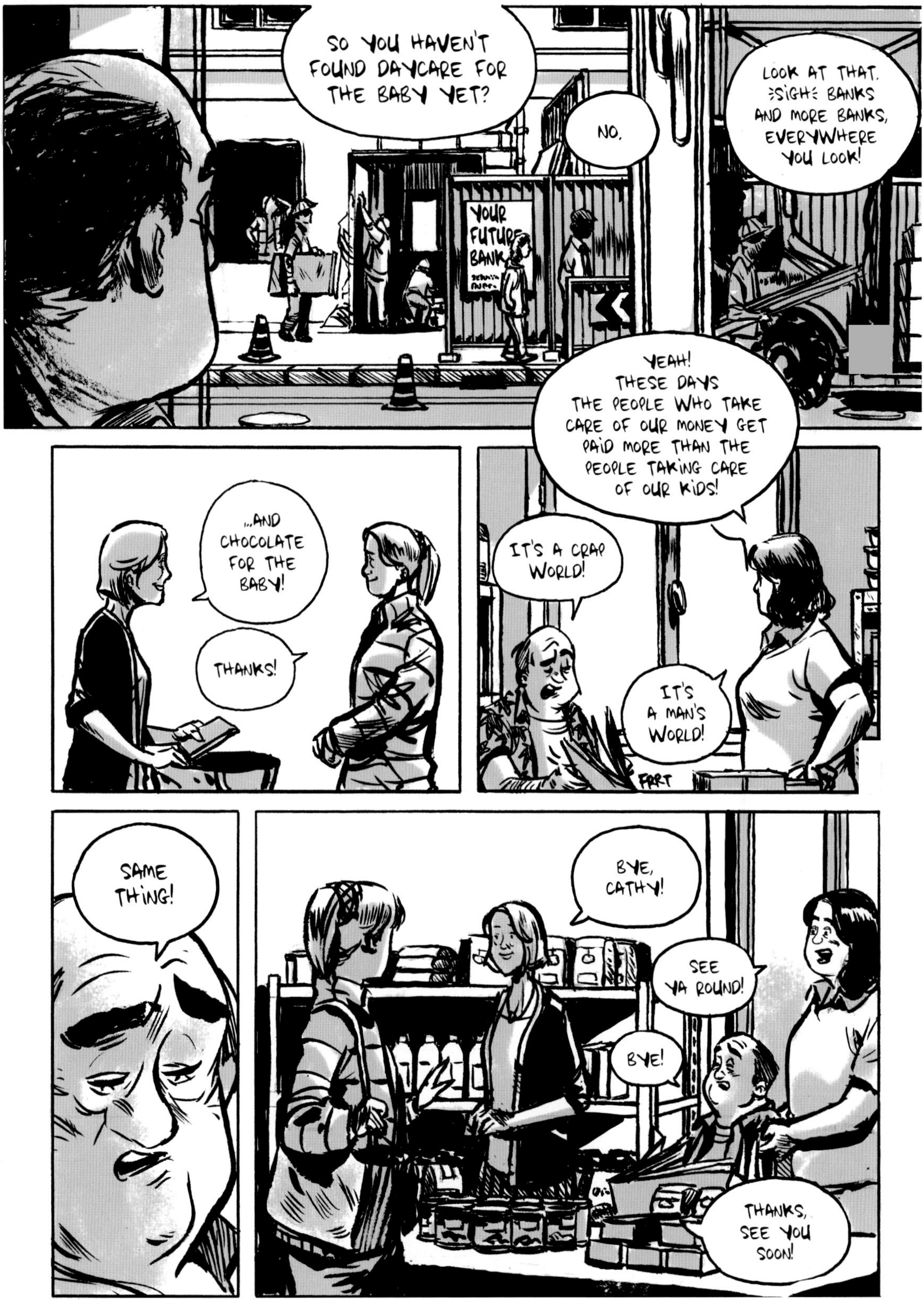
SO YOU HAVEN'T FOUND DAYCARE FOR THE BABY YET?
NO.
LOOK AT THAT. ≈SIGH≈ BANKS AND MORE BANKS, EVERYWHERE YOU LOOK!
YOUR FUTURE BANK
YEAH! THESE DAYS THE PEOPLE WHO TAKE CARE OF OUR MONEY GET PAID MORE THAN THE PEOPLE TAKING CARE OF OUR KIDS!
...AND CHOCOLATE FOR THE BABY!
THANKS!
IT'S A CRAP WORLD!
IT'S A MAN'S WORLD!
FRRT
SAME THING!
BYE, CATHY!
SEE YA ROUND!
BYE!
THANKS, SEE YOU SOON!

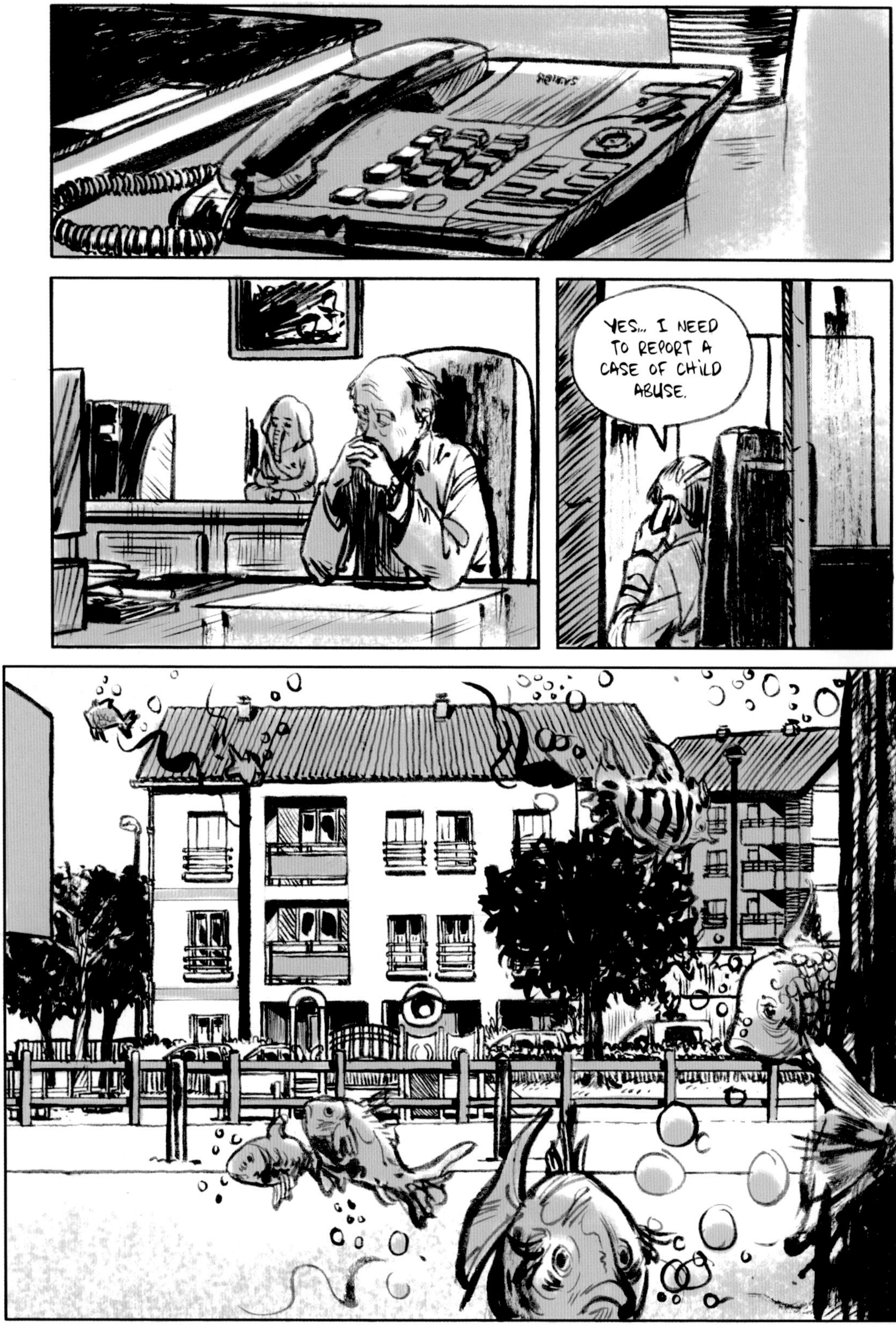
YES... I NEED TO REPORT A CASE OF CHILD ABUSE.

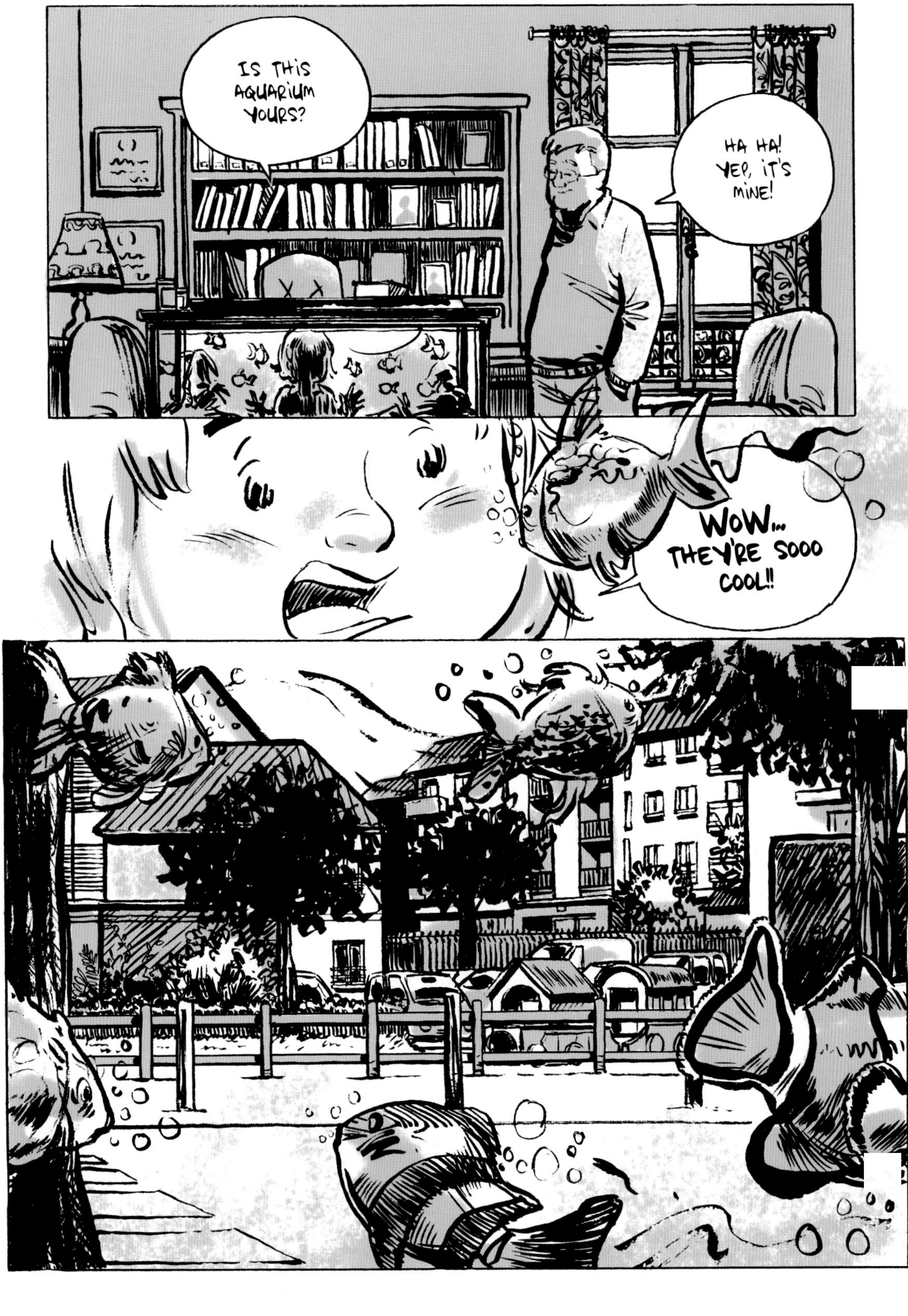
IS THIS AQUARIUM YOURS?
HA HA! YEP, IT'S MINE!
WOW... THEY'RE SOOO COOL!!

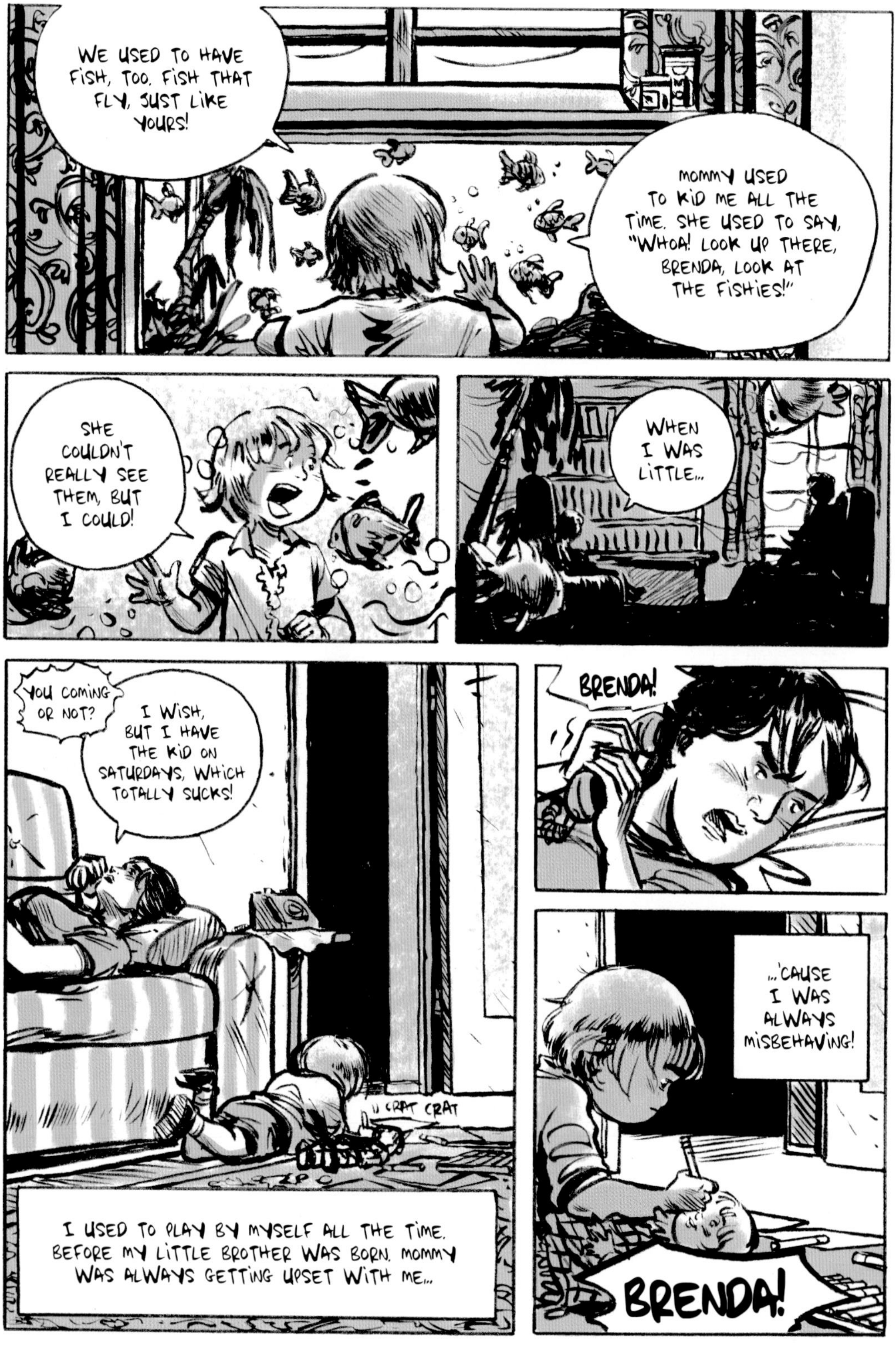
WE USED TO HAVE FISH, TOO. FISH THAT FLY, JUST LIKE YOURS!
MOMMY USED TO KID ME ALL THE TIME. SHE USED TO SAY, "WHOA! LOOK UP THERE, BRENDA, LOOK AT THE FISHIES!"
SHE COULDN'T REALLY SEE THEM, BUT I COULD!
WHEN I WAS LITTLE...
YOU COMING OR NOT?
I WISH, BUT I HAVE THE KID ON SATURDAYS, WHICH TOTALLY SUCKS!
CRAT CRAT
I USED TO PLAY BY MYSELF ALL THE TIME. BEFORE MY LITTLE BROTHER WAS BORN, MOMMY WAS ALWAYS GETTING UPSET WITH ME...
BRENDA!
...'CAUSE I WAS ALWAYS MISBEHAVING!
BRENDA!

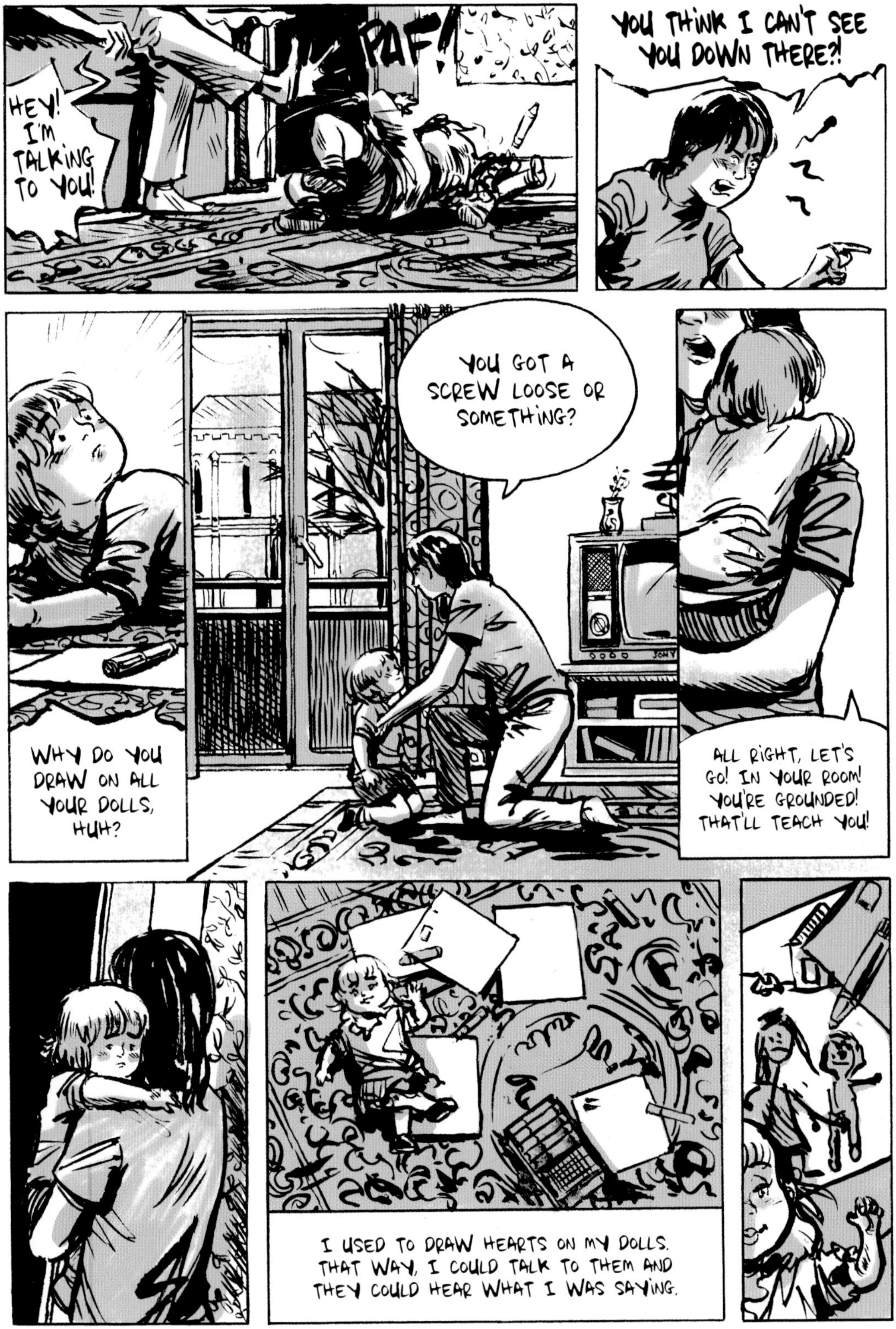

PAF!
HEY! I'M TALKING TO YOU!
YOU THINK I CAN'T SEE YOU DOWN THERE?!
YOU GOT A SCREW LOOSE OR SOMETHING?
WHY DO YOU DRAW ON ALL YOUR DOLLS, HUH?
ALL RIGHT, LET'S GO! IN YOUR ROOM! YOU'RE GROUNDED! THAT'LL TEACH YOU!
I USED TO DRAW HEARTS ON MY DOLLS. THAT WAY, I COULD TALK TO THEM AND THEY COULD HEAR WHAT I WAS SAYING.

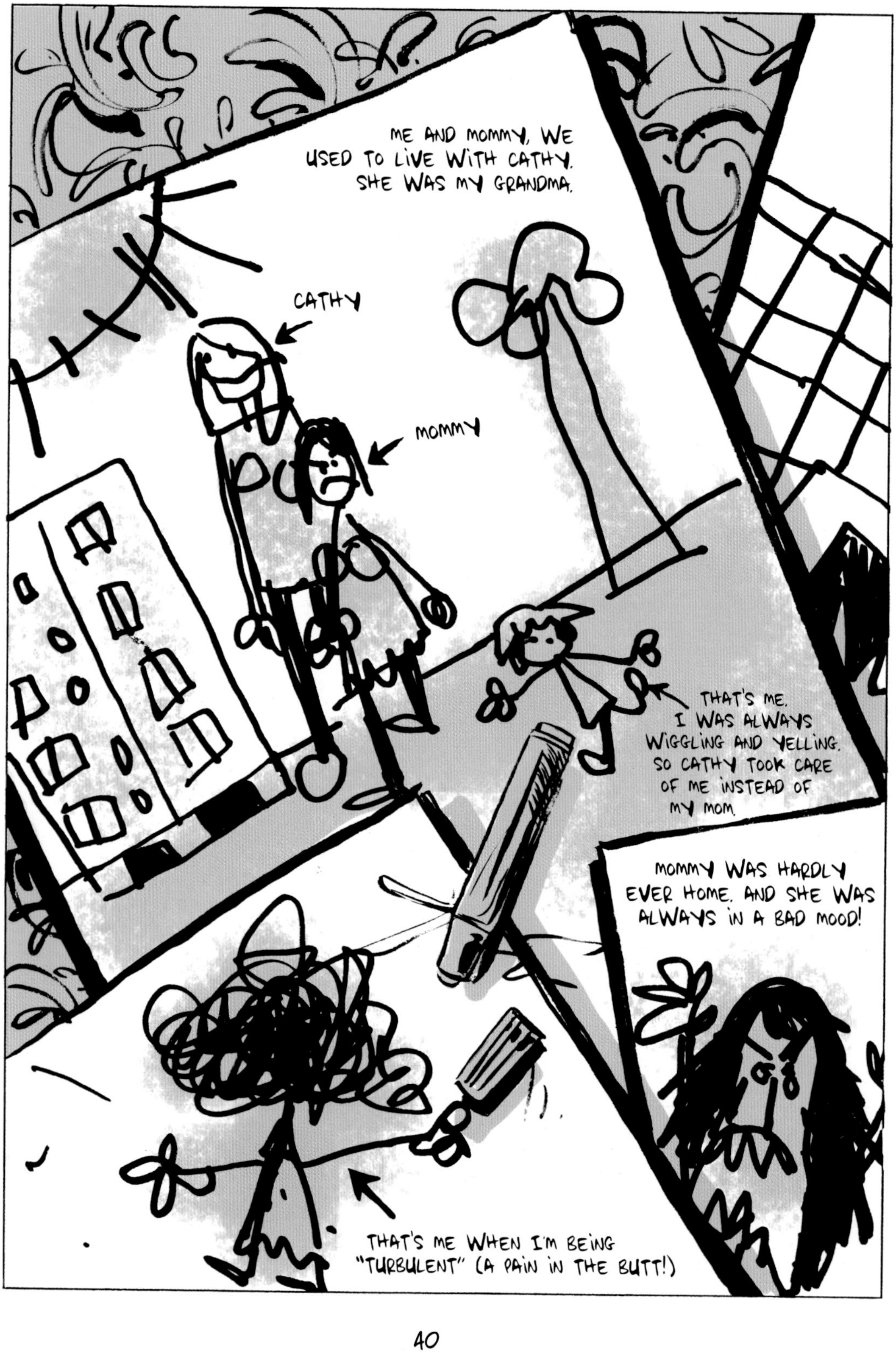

ME AND MOMMY, WE USED TO LIVE WITH CATHY. SHE WAS MY GRANDMA.
CATHY
MOMMY
THAT'S ME. I WAS ALWAYS WIGGLING AND YELLING, SO CATHY TOOK CARE OF ME INSTEAD OF MY MOM.
MOMMY WAS HARDLY EVER HOME, AND SHE WAS ALWAYS IN A BAD MOOD!
THAT'S ME WHEN I'M BEING "TURBULENT" (A PAIN IN THE BUTT!)

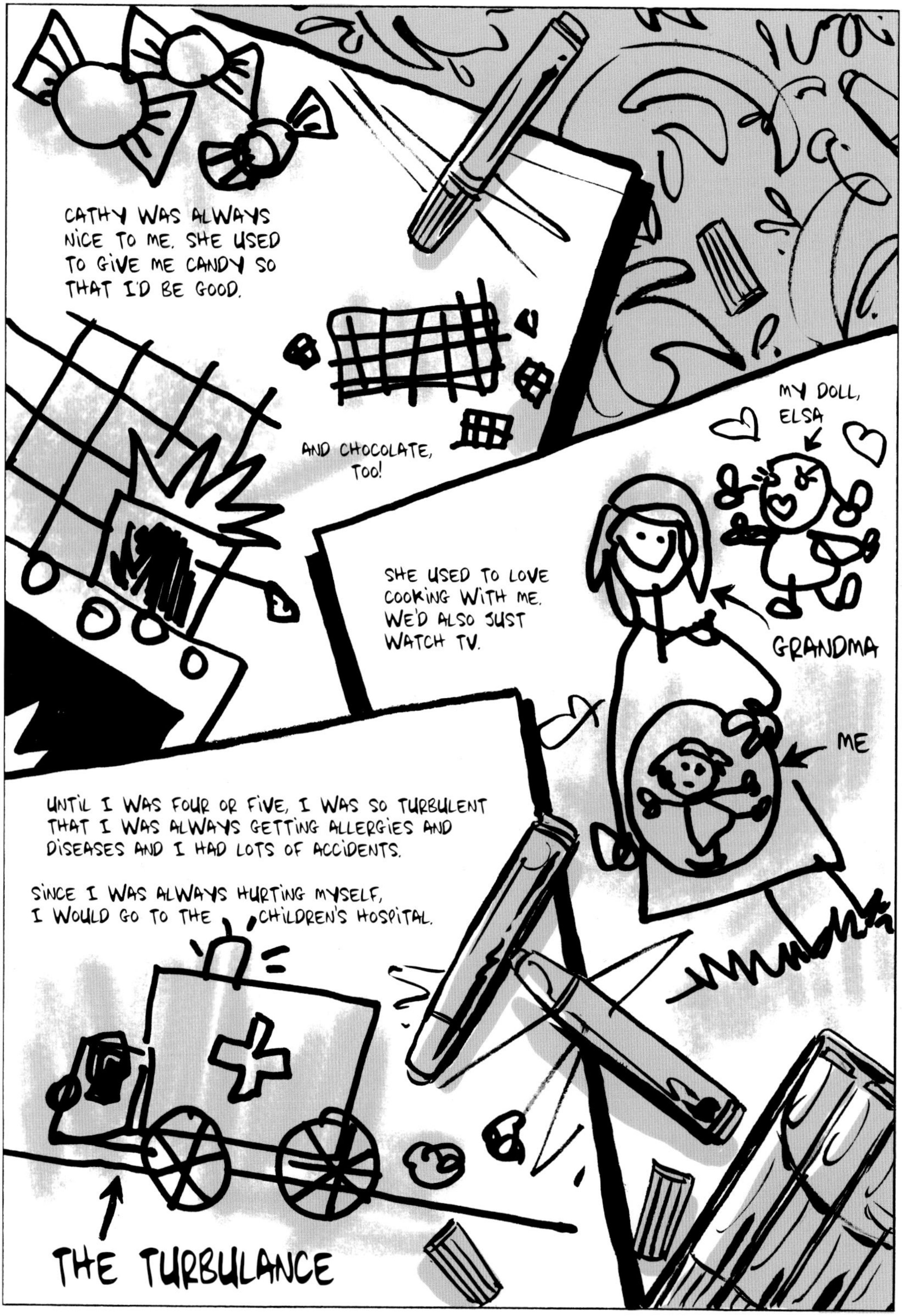
CATHY WAS ALWAYS NICE TO ME. SHE USED TO GIVE ME CANDY SO THAT I'D BE GOOD.
AND CHOCOLATE, TOO!
MY DOLL, ELSA
SHE USED TO LOVE COOKING WITH ME. WE'D ALSO JUST WATCH TV.
GRANDMA
ME
UNTIL I WAS FOUR OR FIVE, I WAS SO TURBULENT THAT I WAS ALWAYS GETTING ALLERGIES AND DISEASES AND I HAD LOTS OF ACCIDENTS.
SINCE I WAS ALWAYS HURTING MYSELF, I WOULD GO TO THE CHILDREN'S HOSPITAL.
THE TURBULANCE

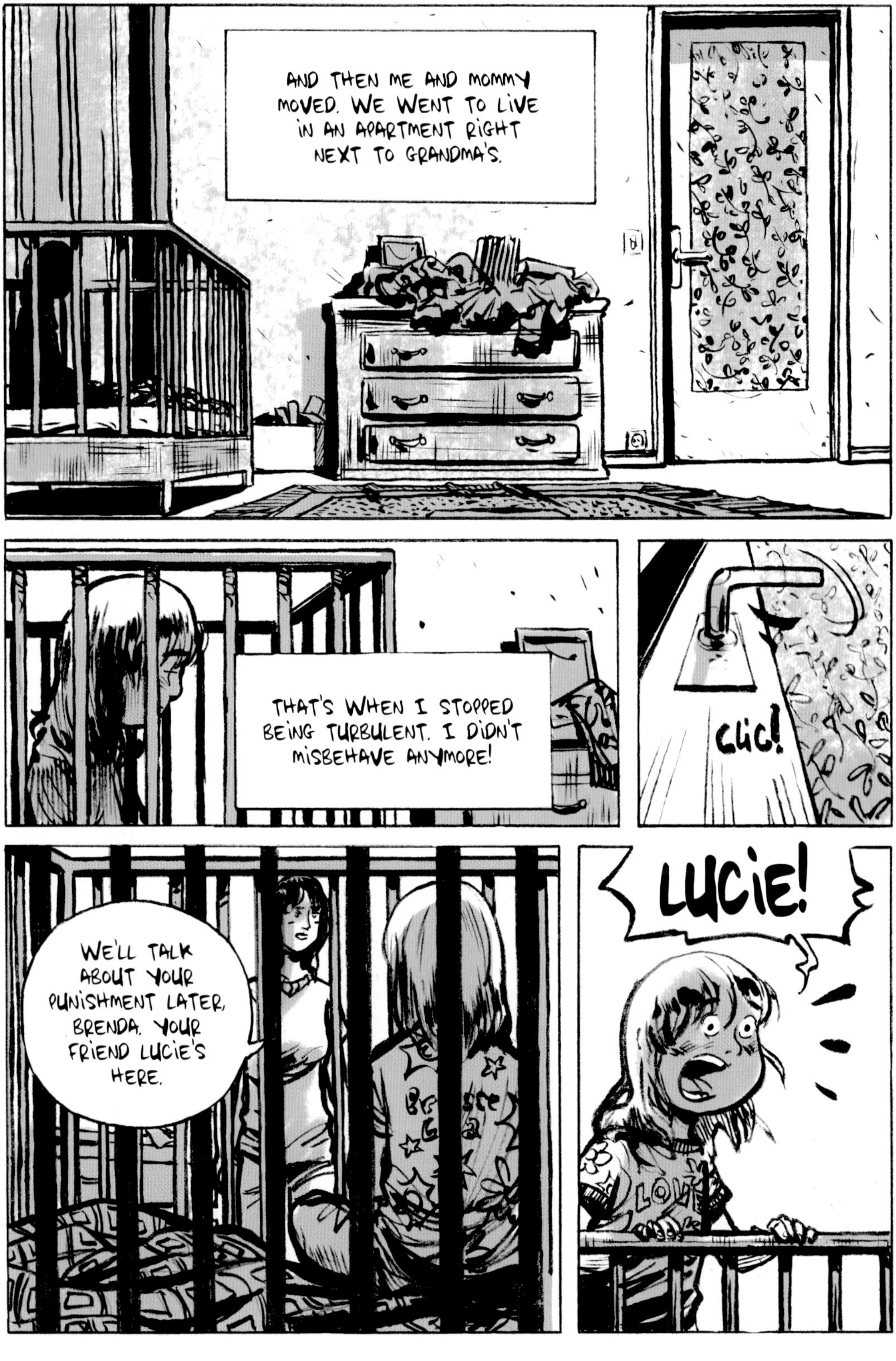
AND THEN ME AND MOMMY MOVED. WE WENT TO LIVE IN AN APARTMENT RIGHT NEXT TO GRANDMA'S.
THAT'S WHEN I STOPPED BEING TURBULENT. I DIDN'T MISBEHAVE ANYMORE!
CLIC!
WE'LL TALK ABOUT YOUR PUNISHMENT LATER, BRENDA. YOUR FRIEND LUCIE'S HERE.
LUCIE!

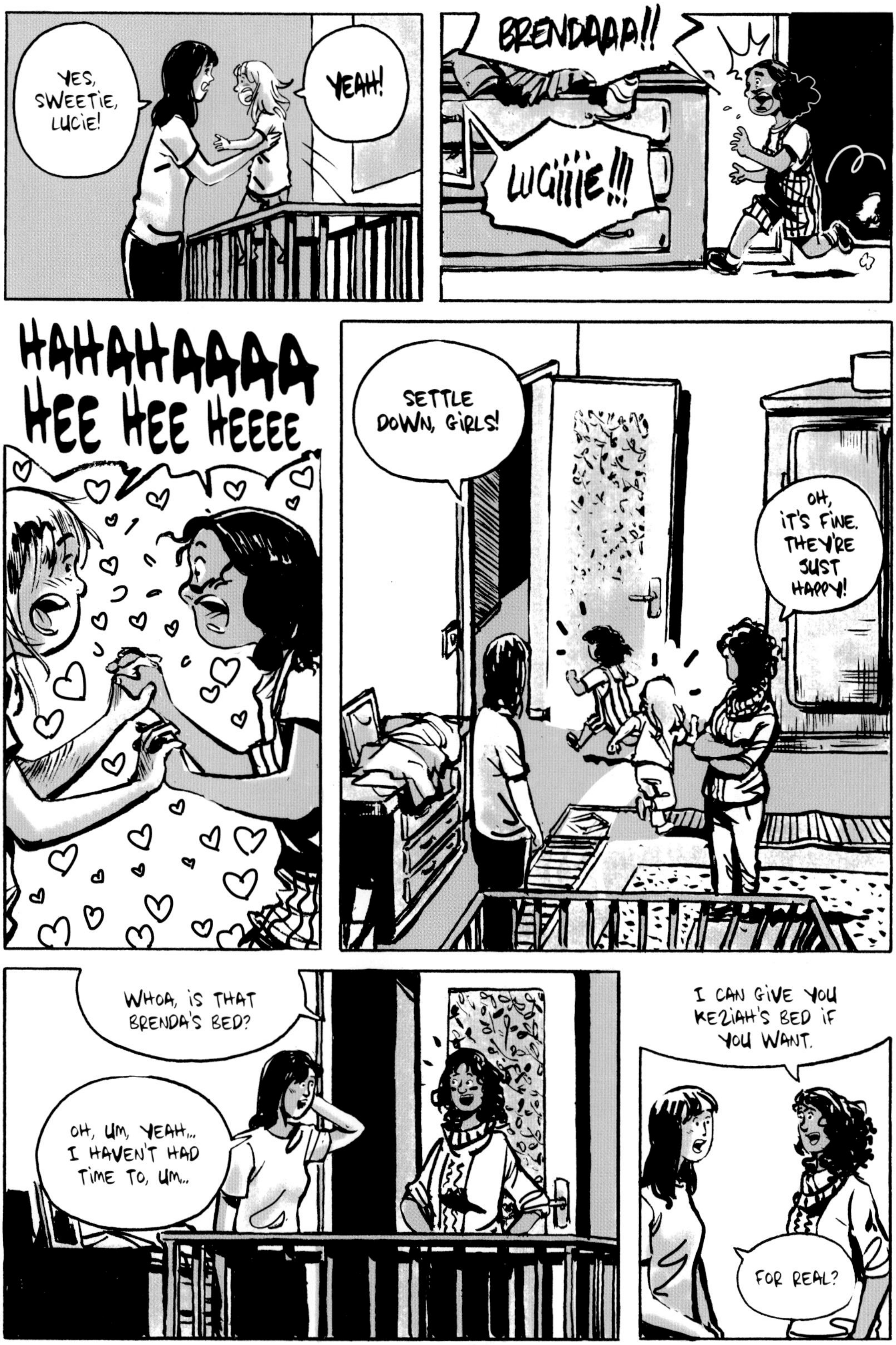
YES, SWEETIE, LUCIE!
YEAH!
BRENDAAA!!
LUCIIIIE!!!
HAHAHAAAA HEE HEE HEEEE
SETTLE DOWN, GIRLS!
OH, IT'S FINE. THEY'RE JUST HAPPY!
WHOA, IS THAT BRENDA'S BED?
OH, UM, YEAH... I HAVEN'T HAD TIME TO, UM...
I CAN GIVE YOU KEZIAH'S BED IF YOU WANT.
FOR REAL?

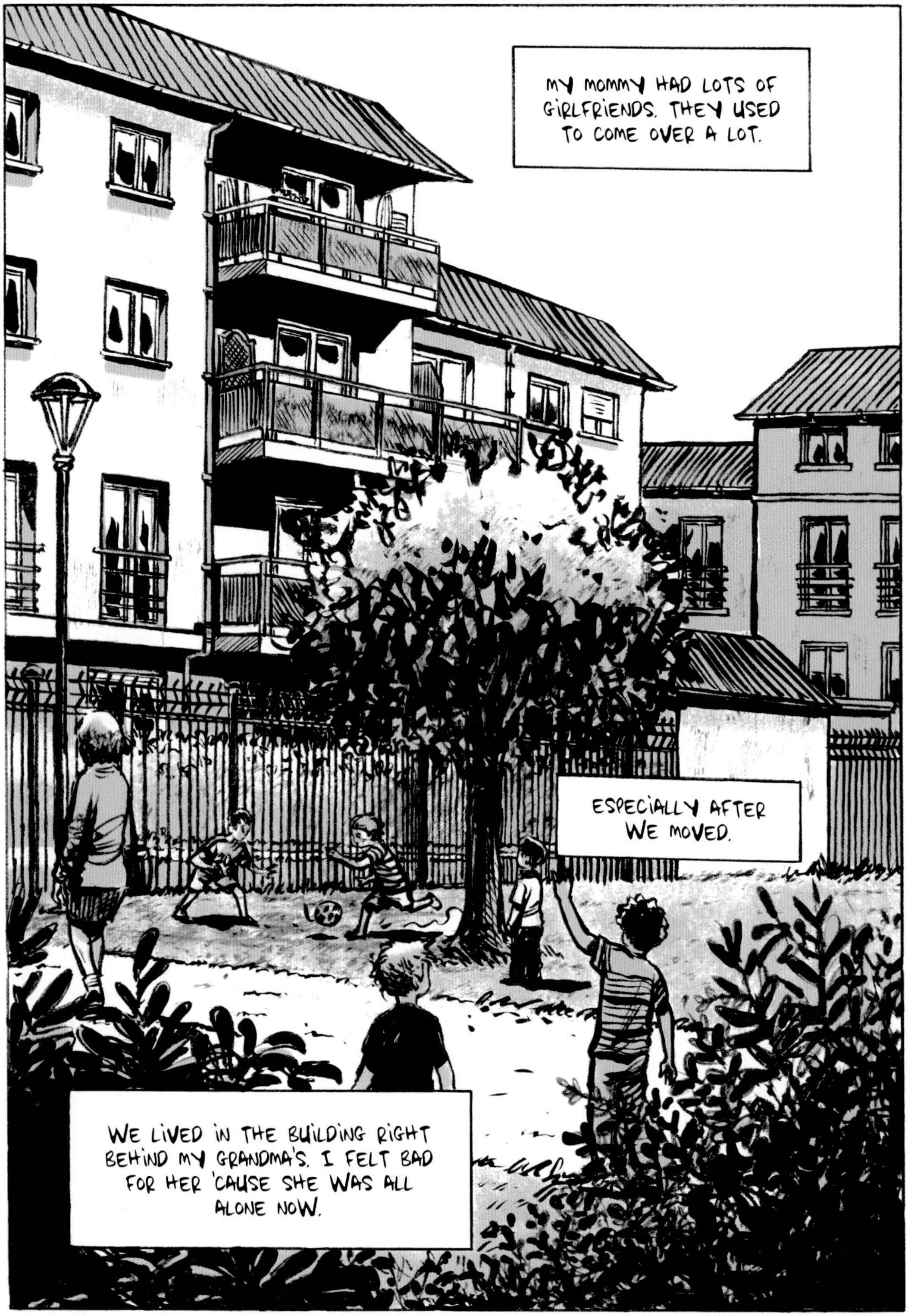
MY MOMMY HAD LOTS OF GIRLFRIENDS. THEY USED TO COME OVER A LOT.
ESPECIALLY AFTER WE MOVED.
WE LIVED IN THE BUILDING RIGHT BEHIND MY GRANDMA'S. I FELT BAD FOR HER 'CAUSE SHE WAS ALL ALONE NOW.

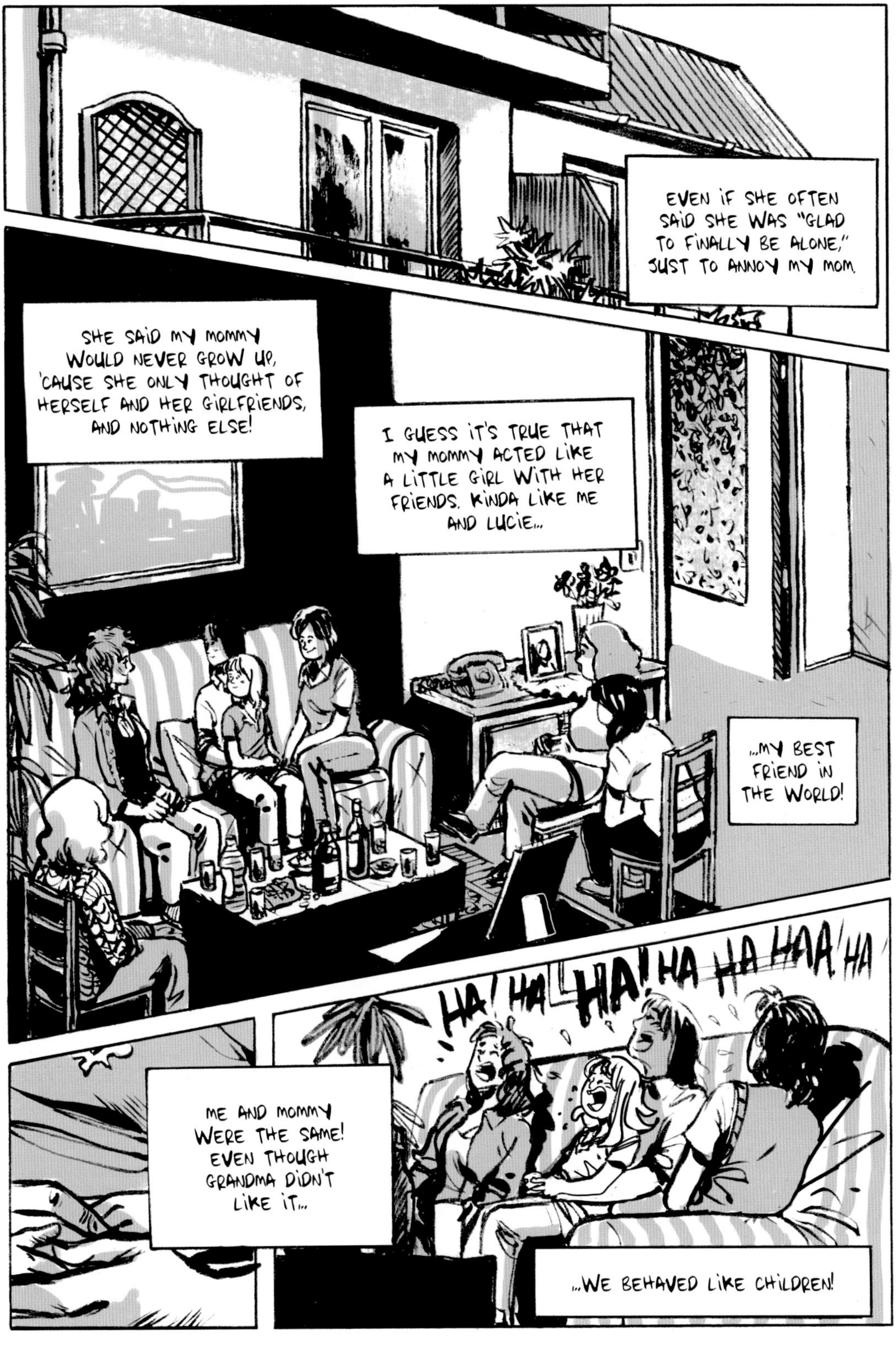

EVEN IF SHE OFTEN SAID SHE WAS "GLAD TO FINALLY BE ALONE," JUST TO ANNOY MY MOM.
SHE SAID MY MOMMY WOULD NEVER GROW UP, 'CAUSE SHE ONLY THOUGHT OF HERSELF AND HER GIRLFRIENDS, AND NOTHING ELSE!
I GUESS IT'S TRUE THAT MY MOMMY ACTED LIKE A LITTLE GIRL WITH HER FRIENDS. KINDA LIKE ME AND LUCIE...
...MY BEST FRIEND IN THE WORLD!
HA! HA HA! HA HA HAA! HA
ME AND MOMMY WERE THE SAME! EVEN THOUGH GRANDMA DIDN'T LIKE IT...
...WE BEHAVED LIKE CHILDREN!

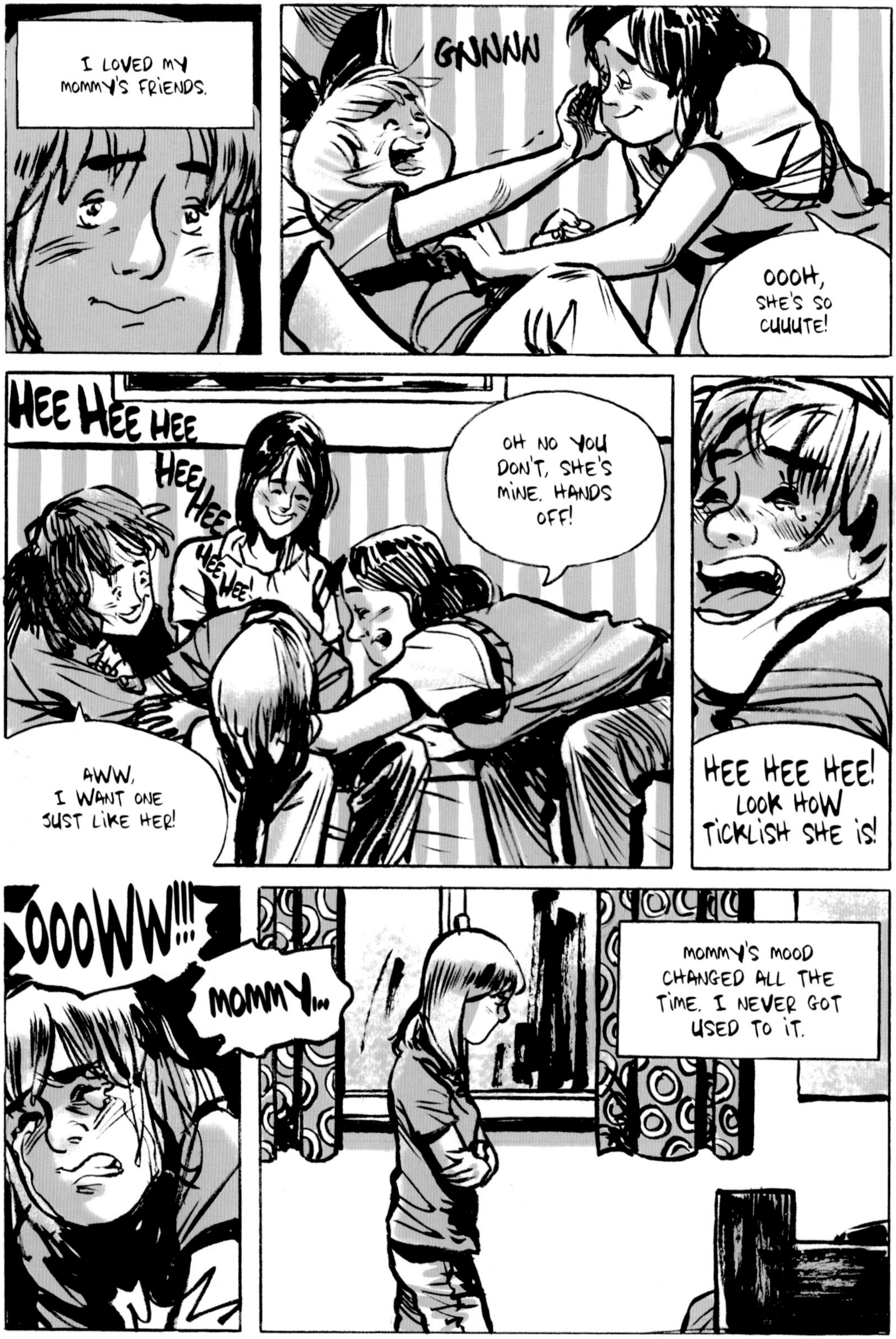
I LOVED MY MOMMY'S FRIENDS.
GNNNN
OOOH, SHE'S SO CUUUTE!
HEE HEE HEE HEE HEE HEE HEE!
OH NO YOU DON'T, SHE'S MINE. HANDS OFF!
AWW, I WANT ONE JUST LIKE HER!
HEE HEE HEE! LOOK HOW TICKLISH SHE IS!
OOOWW!!!
MOMMY...
MOMMY'S MOOD CHANGED ALL THE TIME. I NEVER GOT USED TO IT.

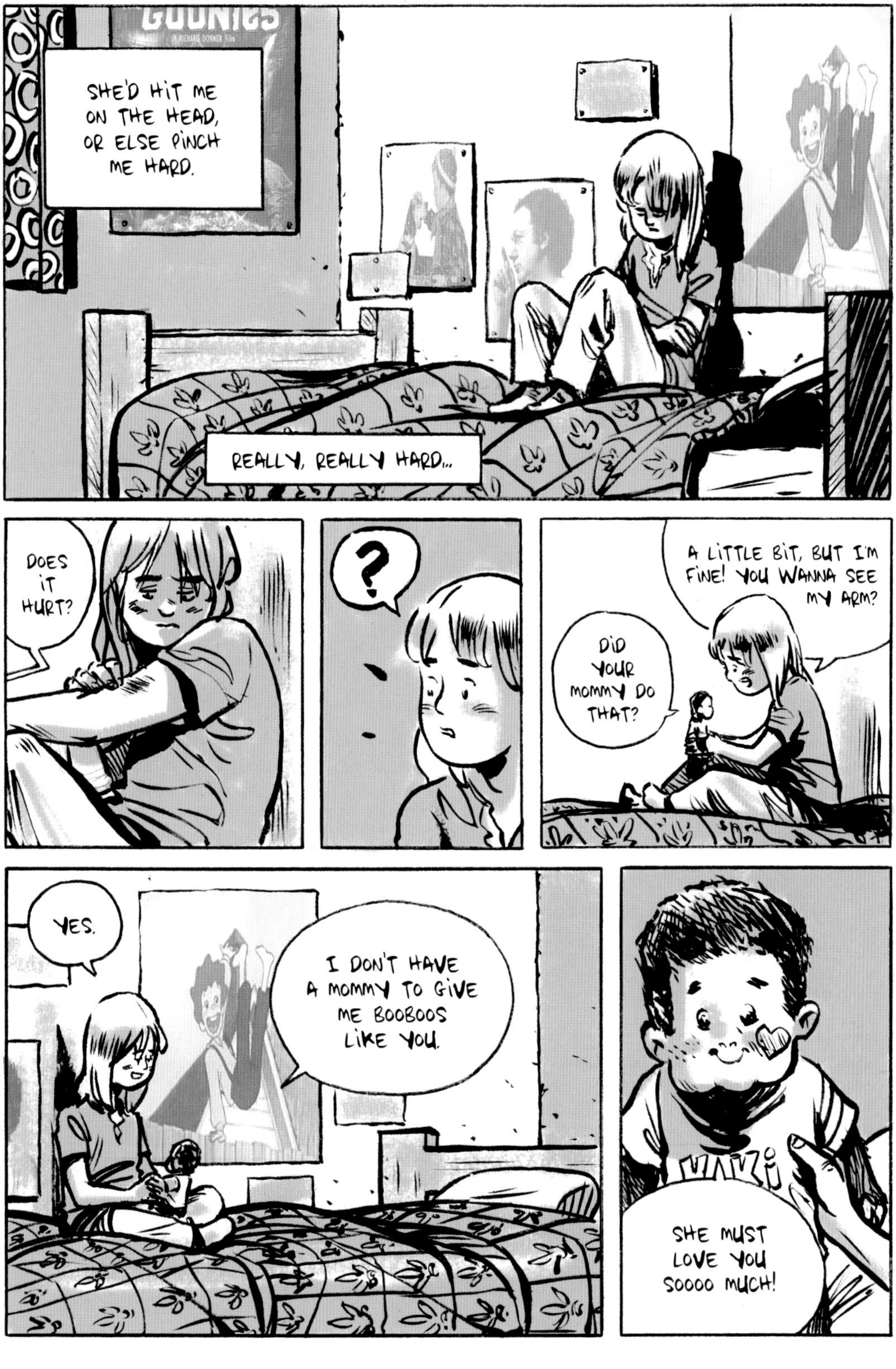
GOONIES
A RICHARD DONNER Film
SHE'D HIT ME ON THE HEAD, OR ELSE PINCH ME HARD.
REALLY, REALLY HARD...
DOES IT HURT?
?
A LITTLE BIT, BUT I'M FINE! YOU WANNA SEE MY ARM?
DID YOUR MOMMY DO THAT?
YES.
I DON'T HAVE A MOMMY TO GIVE ME BOOBOOS LIKE YOU.
SHE MUST LOVE YOU SOOOO MUCH!

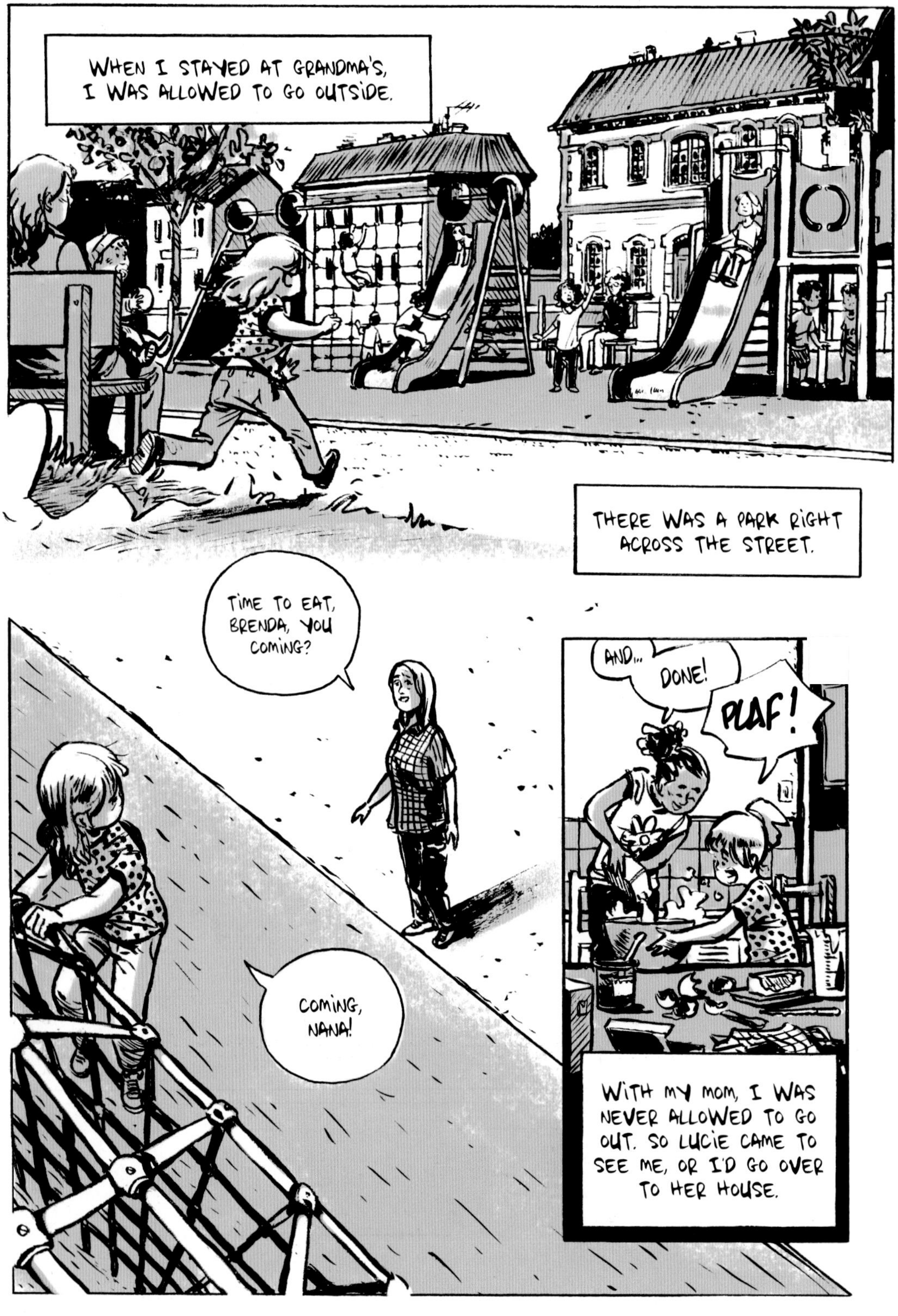
WHEN I STAYED AT GRANDMA'S, I WAS ALLOWED TO GO OUTSIDE.
THERE WAS A PARK RIGHT ACROSS THE STREET.
TIME TO EAT, BRENDA, YOU COMING?
COMING, NANA!
AND...
DONE!
PLAF!
WITH MY MOM, I WAS NEVER ALLOWED TO GO OUT. SO LUCIE CAME TO SEE ME, OR I'D GO OVER TO HER HOUSE.

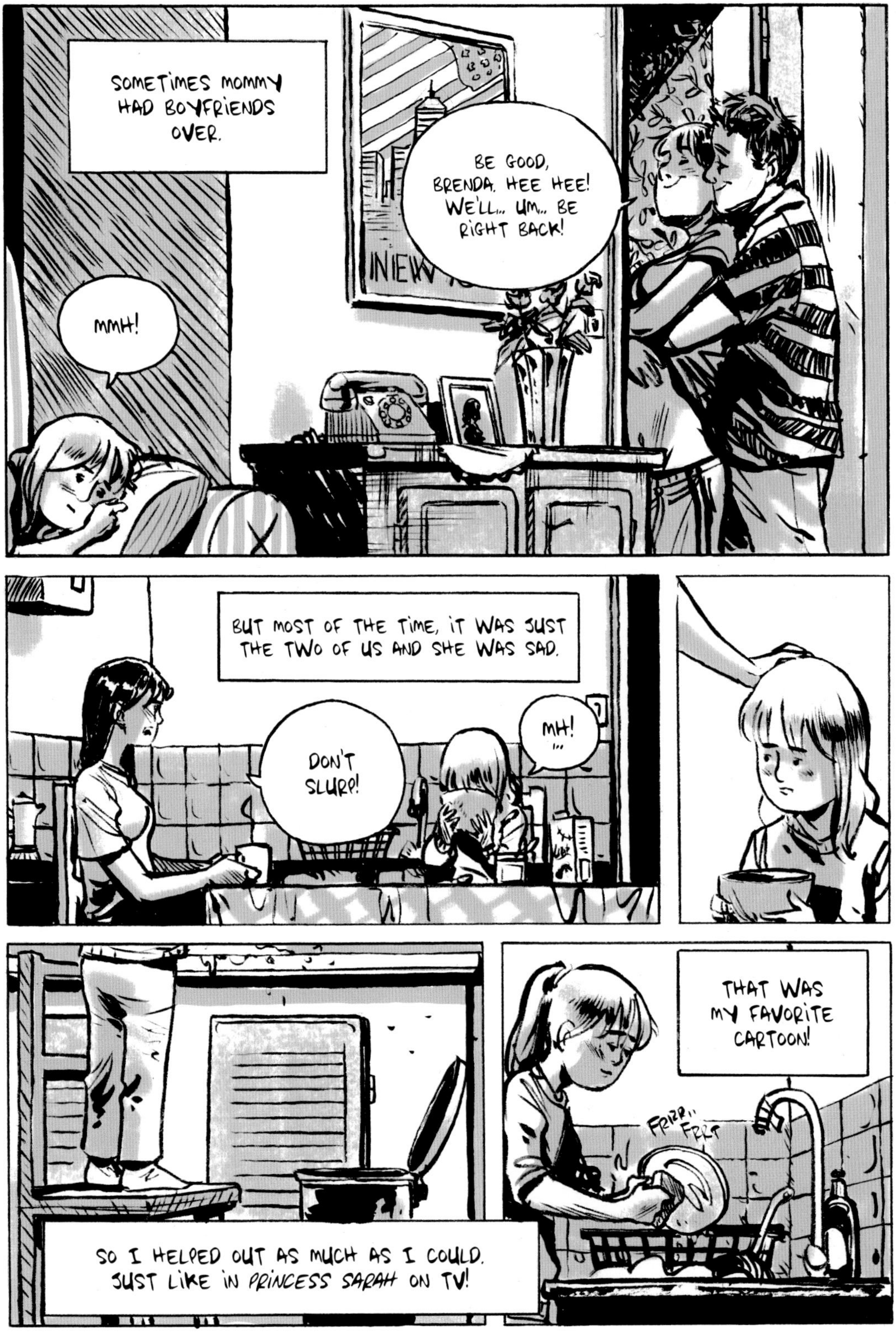
SOMETIMES MOMMY HAD BOYFRIENDS OVER.
BE GOOD, BRENDA. HEE HEE! WE'LL... UM... BE RIGHT BACK!
MMH!
NEW
BUT MOST OF THE TIME, IT WAS JUST THE TWO OF US AND SHE WAS SAD.
DON'T SLURP!
MH! ...
THAT WAS MY FAVORITE CARTOON!
FRIZR... FRRT
SO I HELPED OUT AS MUCH AS I COULD. JUST LIKE IN *PRINCESS SARAH* ON TV!

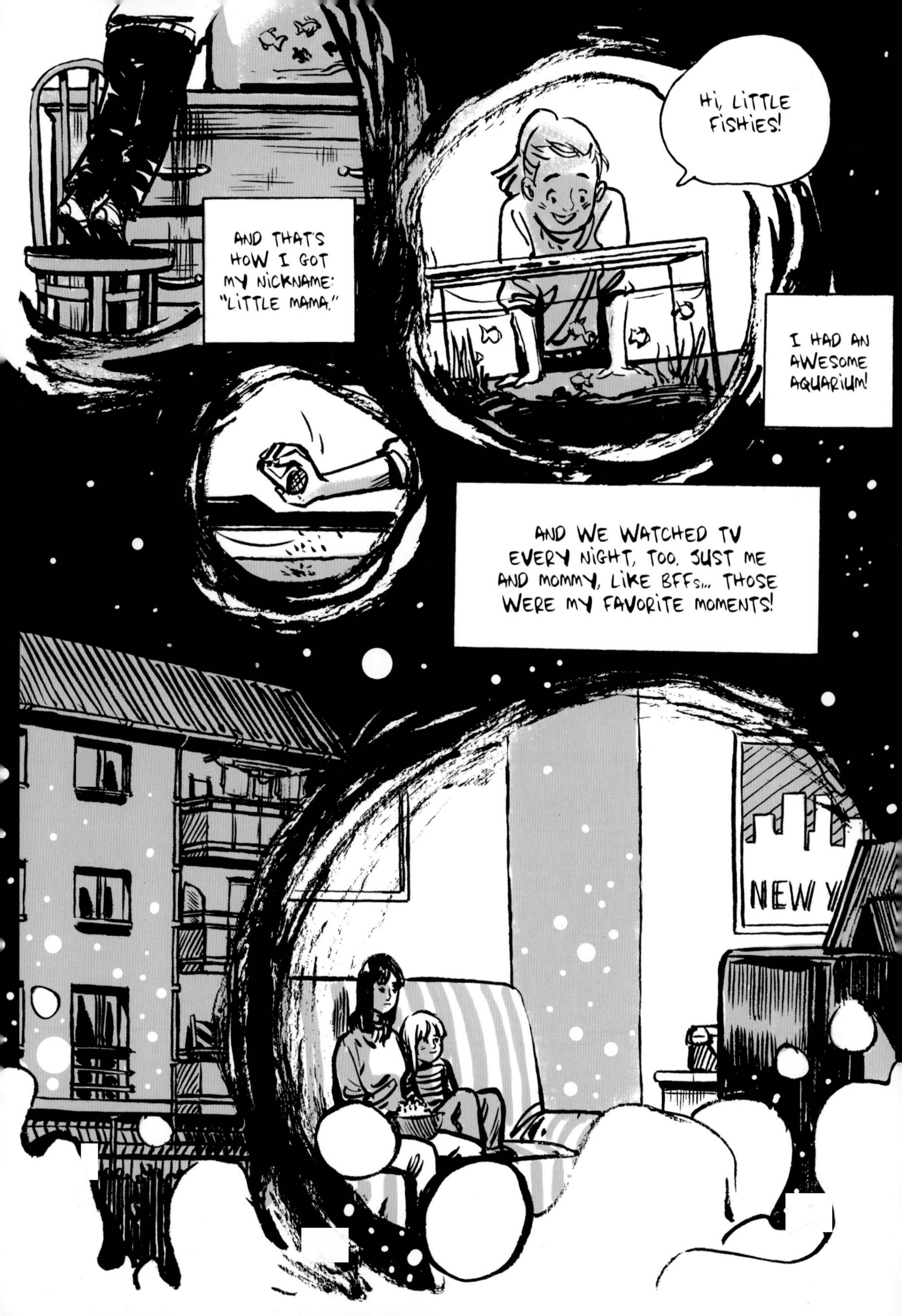
AND THAT'S HOW I GOT MY NICKNAME: "LITTLE MAMA."
Hi, LITTLE FISHiES!
I HAD AN AWESOME AQUARiUM!
AND WE WATCHED TV EVERY NiGHT, TOO. JUST ME AND MOMMY, LiKE BFFs... THOSE WERE MY FAVORiTE MOMENTS!
NEW Y

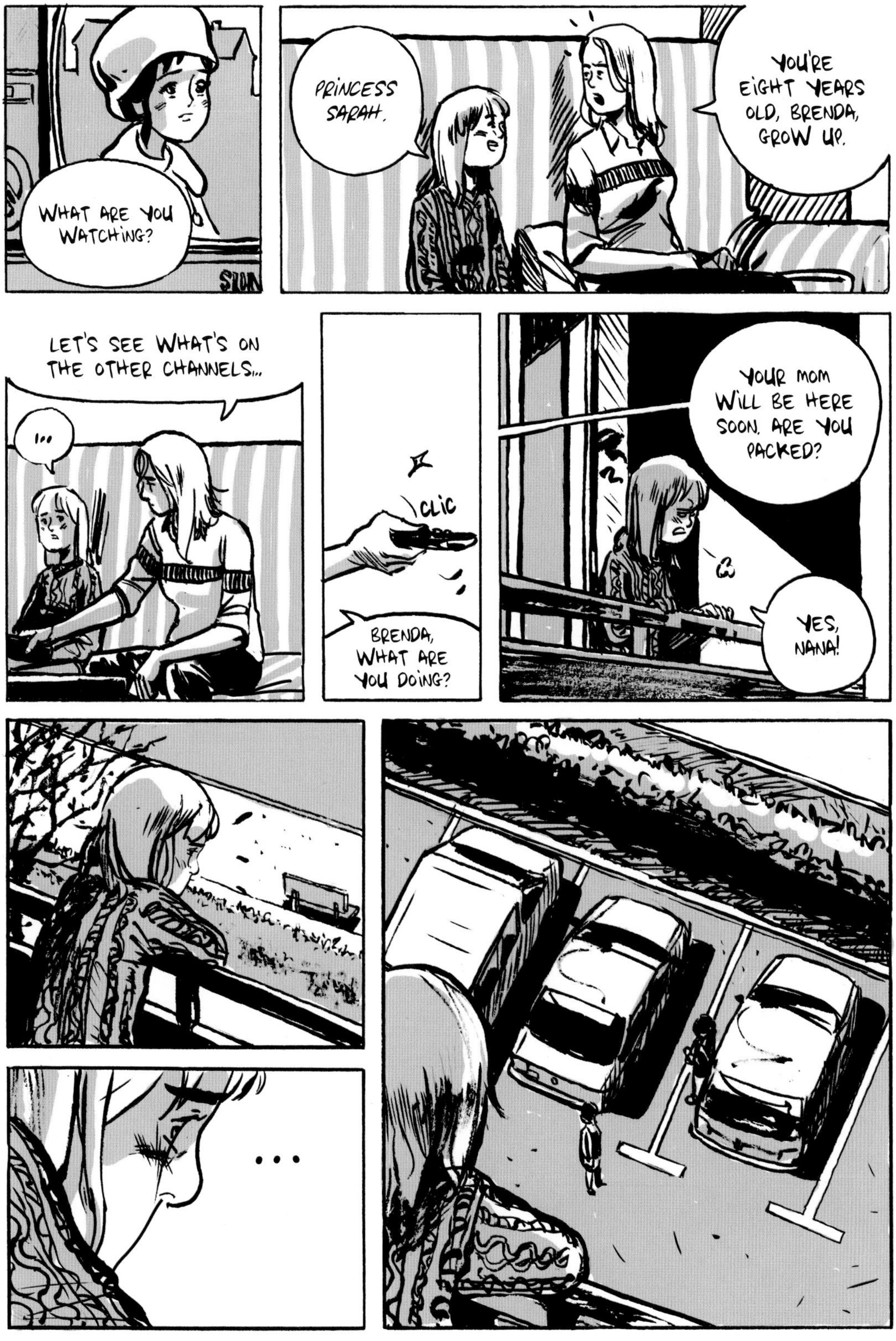
What are you watching?
Princess Sarah.
You're eight years old, Brenda, grow up.
Let's see what's on the other channels...
...
Clic
Brenda, what are you doing?
Your mom will be here soon. Are you packed?
Yes, Nana!
...

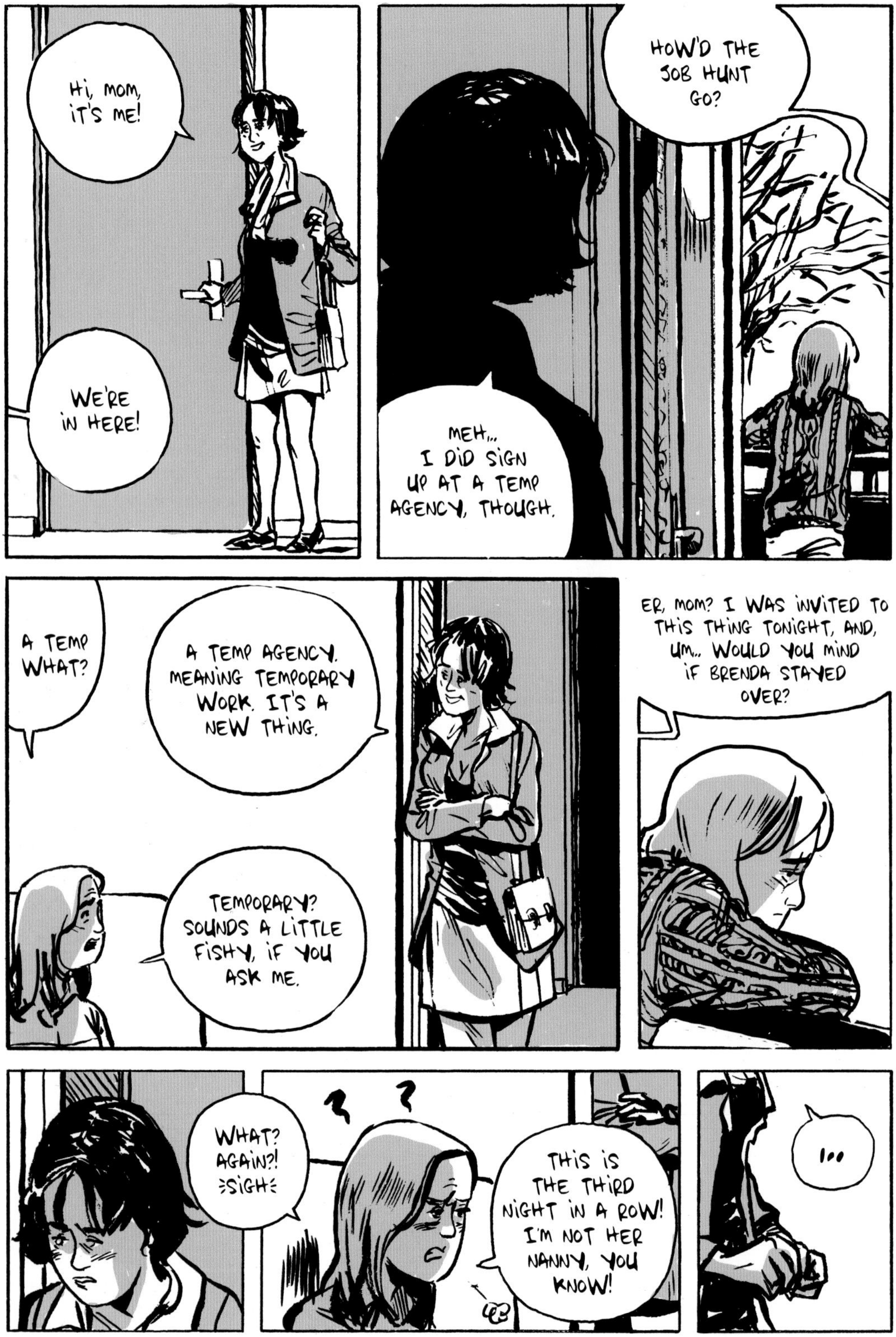
Hi, mom, it's me!
We're in here!
How'd the job hunt go?
Meh... I did sign up at a temp agency, though.
A temp what?
A temp agency. Meaning temporary work. It's a new thing.
Temporary? Sounds a little fishy, if you ask me.
Er, mom? I was invited to this thing tonight, and, um... would you mind if Brenda stayed over?
What? Again?! ≶sigh≷
This is the third night in a row! I'm not her nanny, you know!
...

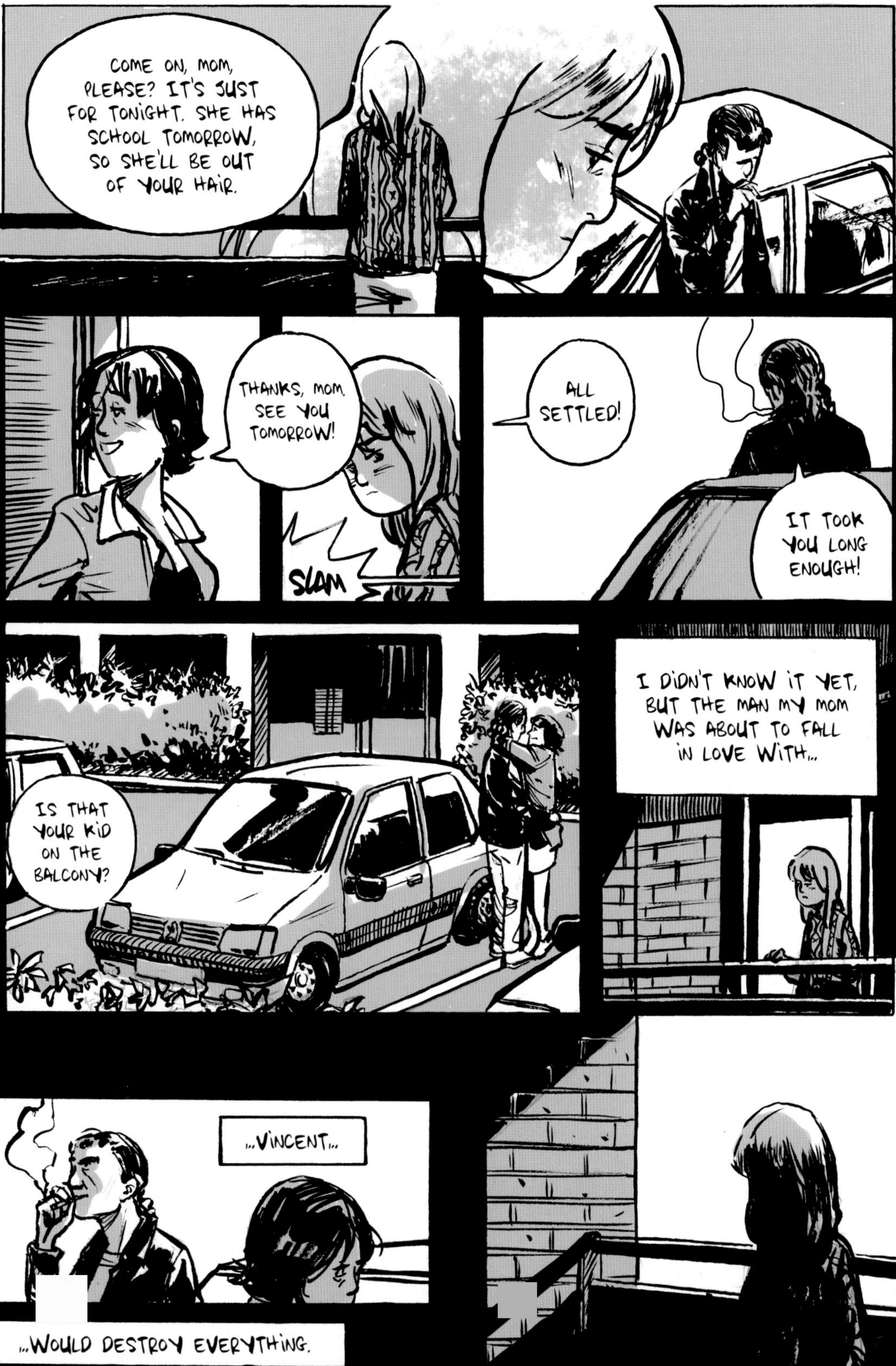
COME ON, MOM, PLEASE? IT'S JUST FOR TONIGHT. SHE HAS SCHOOL TOMORROW, SO SHE'LL BE OUT OF YOUR HAIR.
THANKS, MOM. SEE YOU TOMORROW!
SLAM
ALL SETTLED!
IT TOOK YOU LONG ENOUGH!
IS THAT YOUR KID ON THE BALCONY?
I DIDN'T KNOW IT YET, BUT THE MAN MY MOM WAS ABOUT TO FALL IN LOVE WITH...
...VINCENT...
...WOULD DESTROY EVERYTHING.

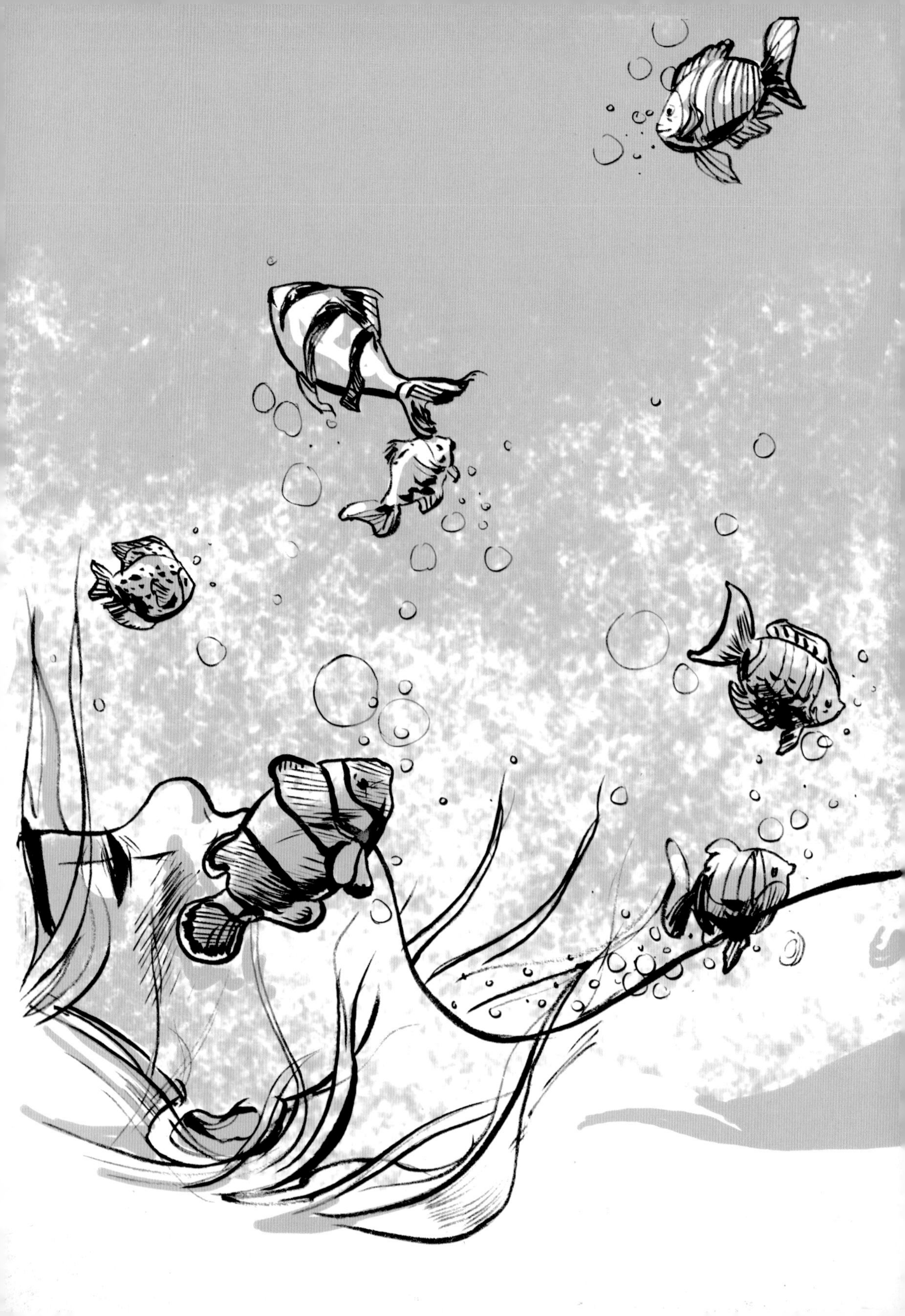

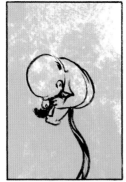

mommy?!

snif...

MY MOM DATED A LOT. SOMETIMES, SHE'D COME HOME ALONE...

...AND IN TEARS.

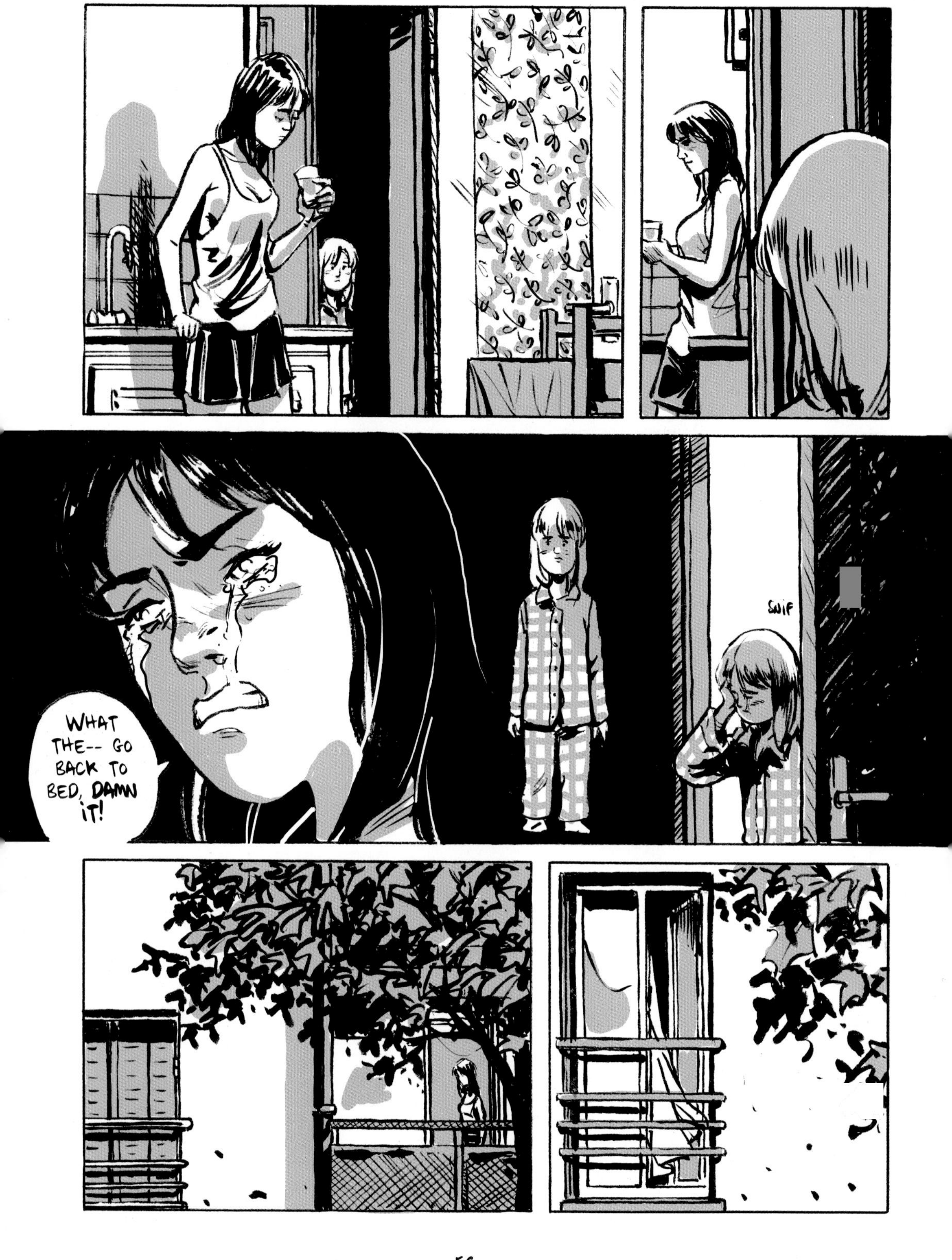
SNIF
WHAT THE-- GO BACK TO BED, DAMN IT!

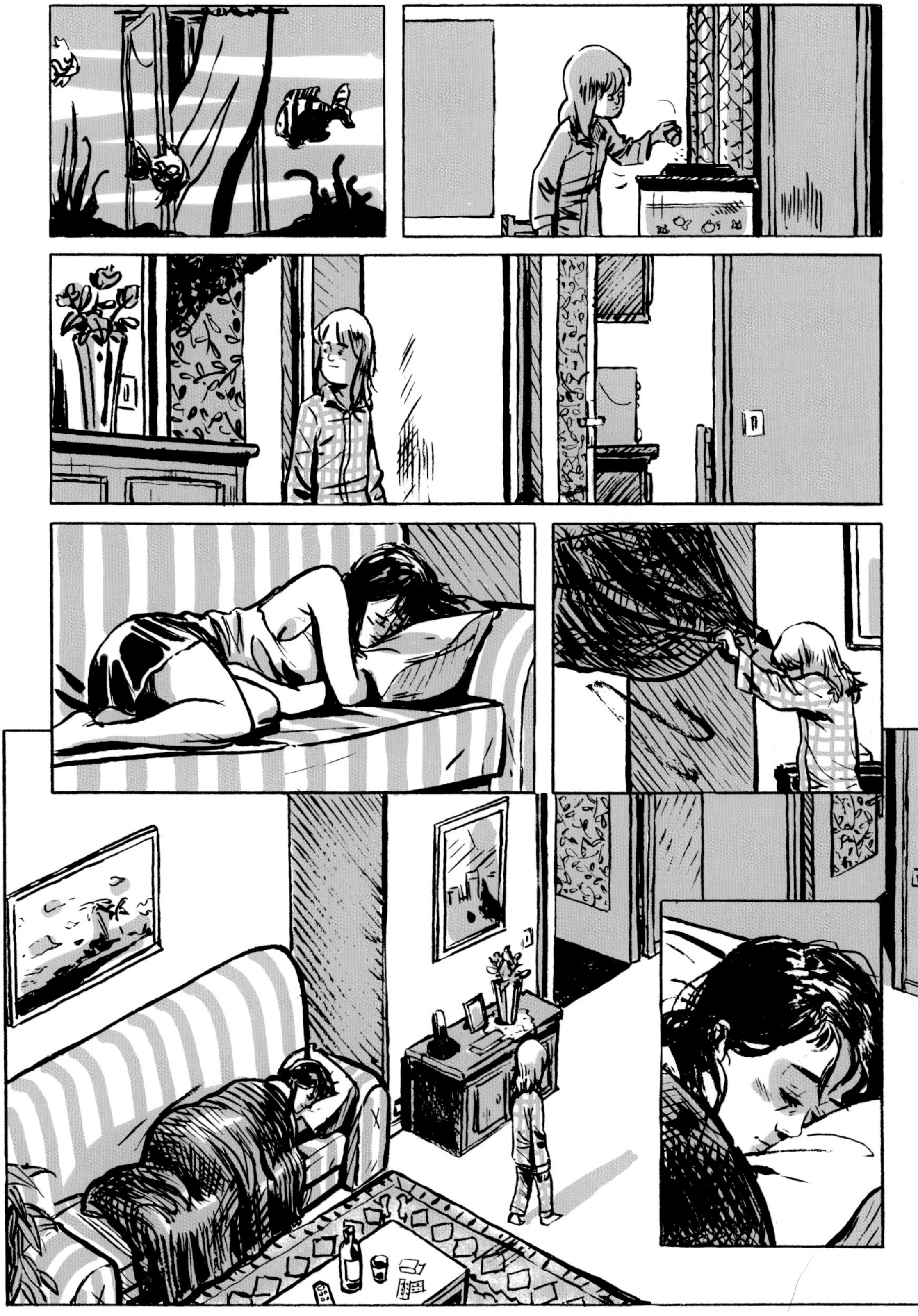

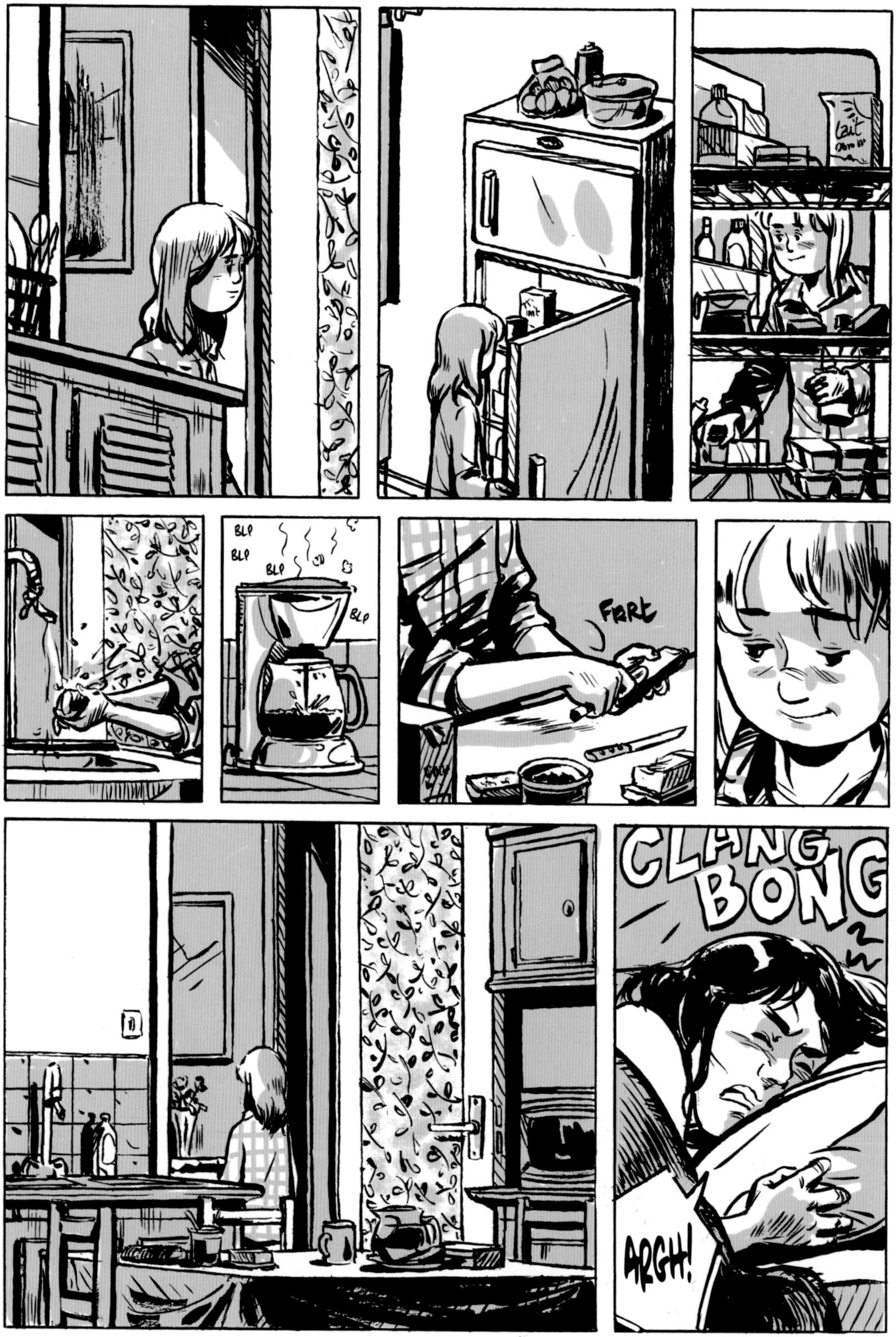
lait
BLP
BLP
BLP
BLP
FRRT
CLANG
BONG
ARGH!

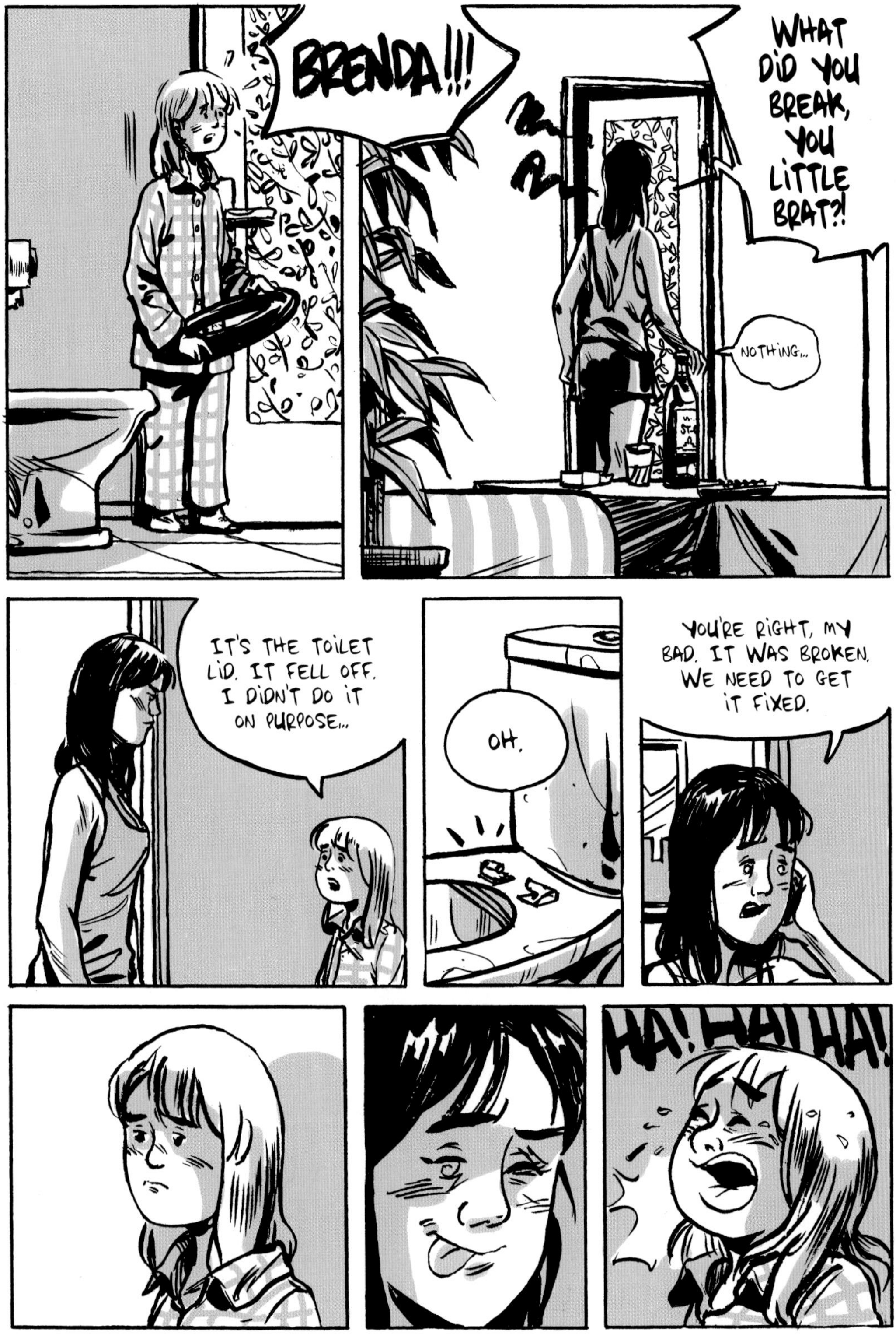
BRENDA!!!
WHAT DID YOU BREAK, YOU LITTLE BRAT?!
NOTHING...
IT'S THE TOILET LID. IT FELL OFF. I DIDN'T DO IT ON PURPOSE...
OH.
YOU'RE RIGHT, MY BAD. IT WAS BROKEN. WE NEED TO GET IT FIXED.
HA! HA! HA!

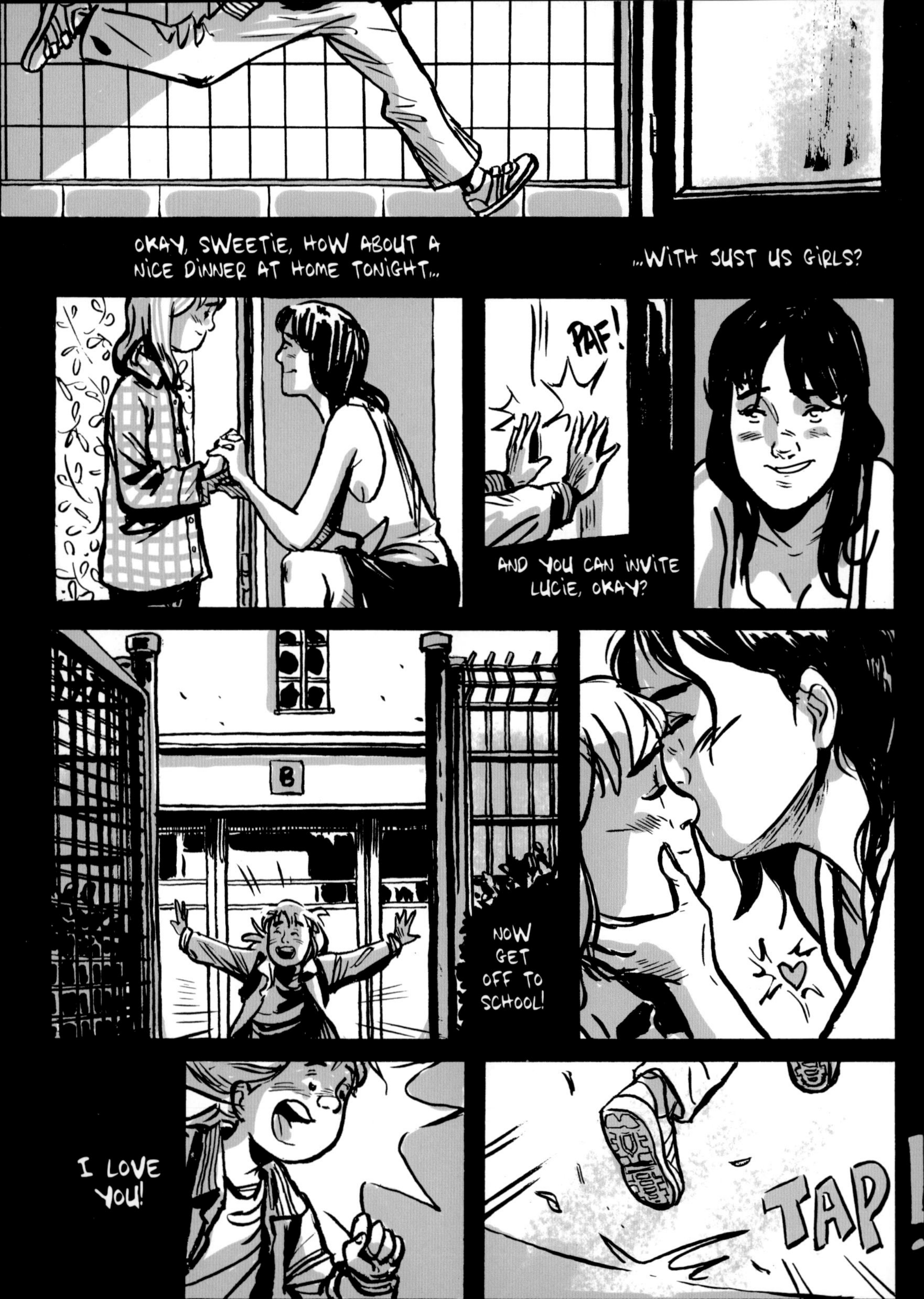
OKAY, SWEETIE, HOW ABOUT A NICE DINNER AT HOME TONIGHT...
...WITH JUST US GIRLS?
PAF!
AND YOU CAN INVITE LUCIE, OKAY?
NOW GET OFF TO SCHOOL!
I LOVE YOU!
TAP!

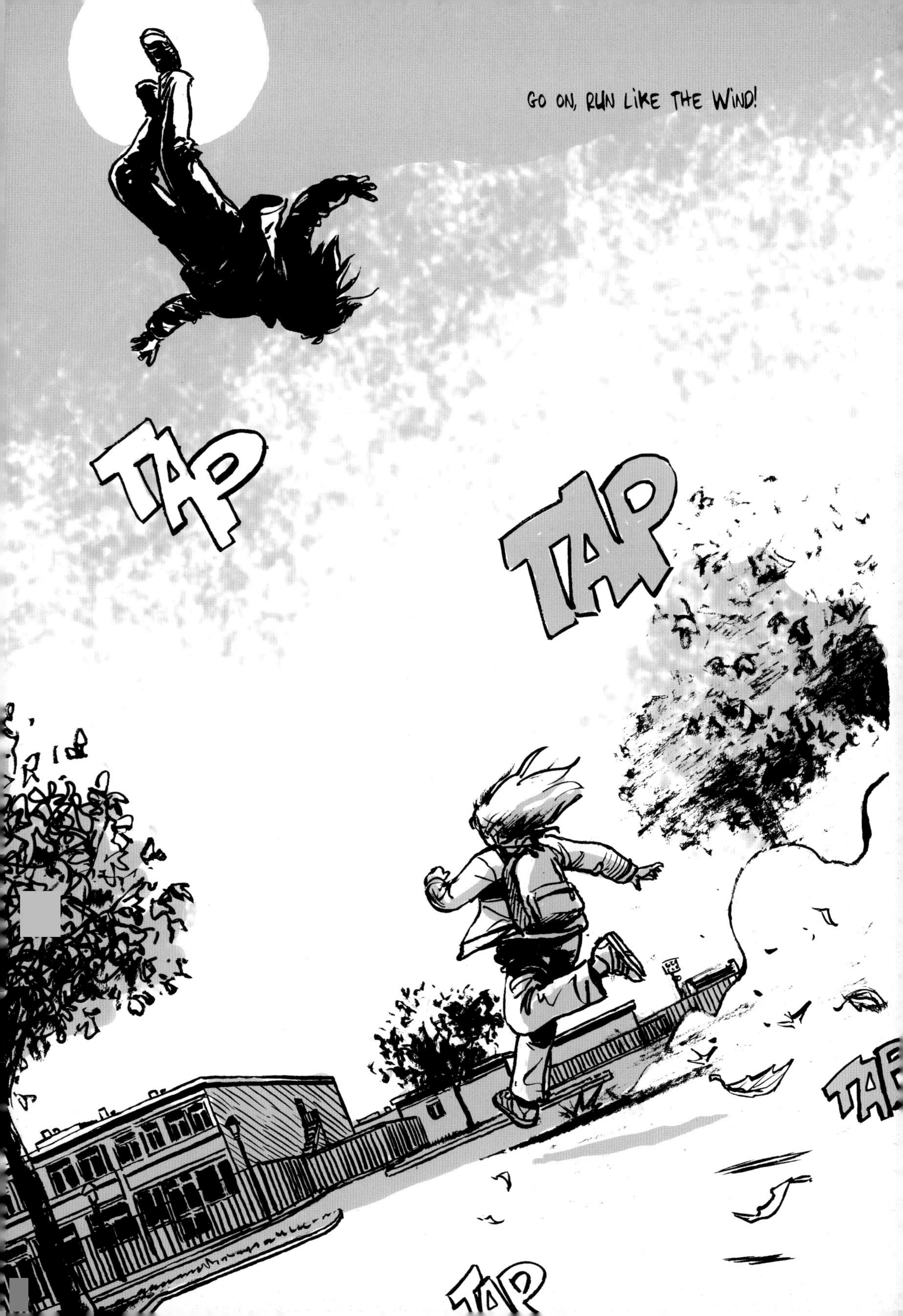
GO ON, RUN LIKE THE WIND!
TAP
TAP
TAP
TAP

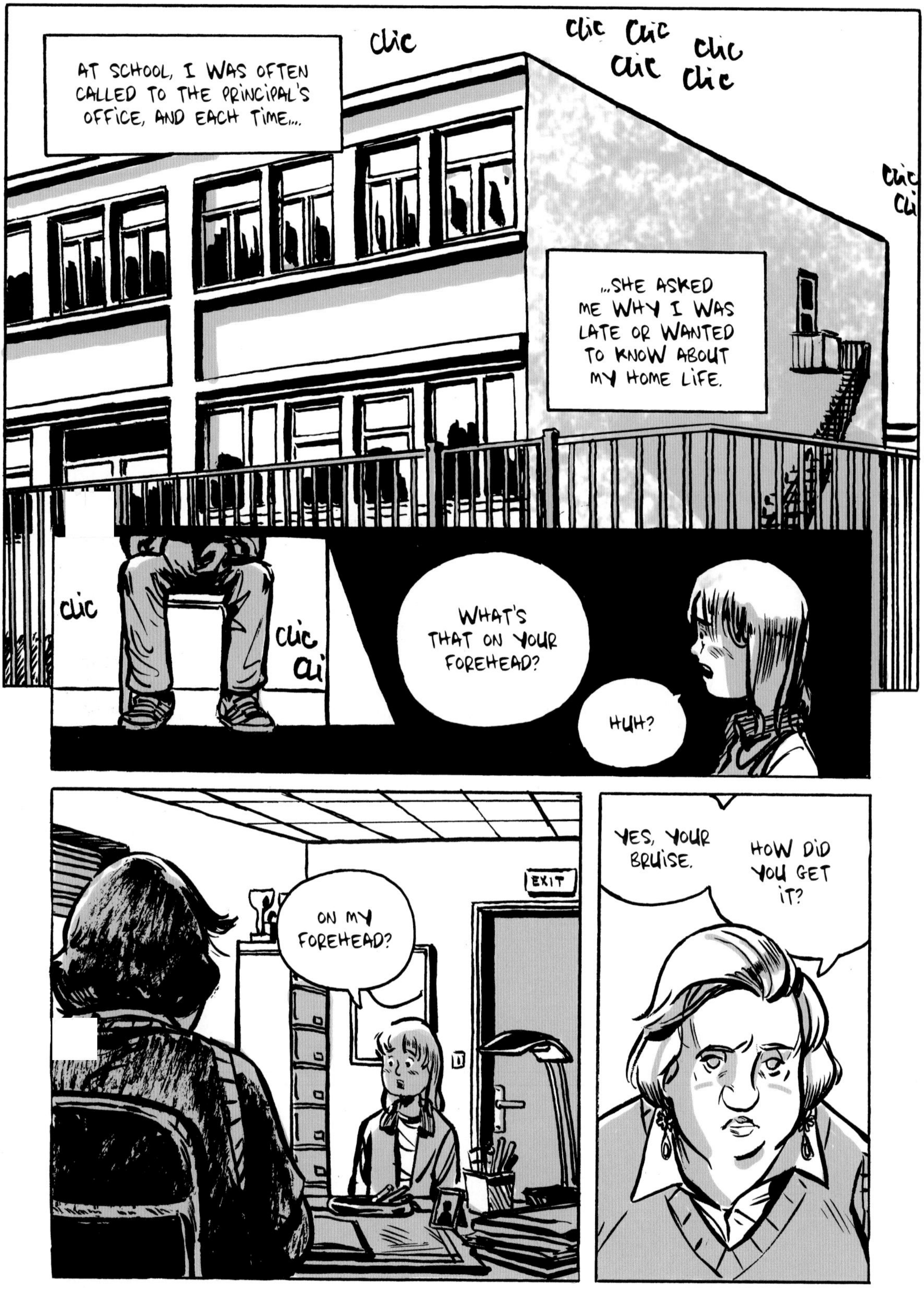

AT SCHOOL, I WAS OFTEN CALLED TO THE PRINCIPAL'S OFFICE, AND EACH TIME...
clic
clic clic
clic
clic clic
clic
...SHE ASKED ME WHY I WAS LATE OR WANTED TO KNOW ABOUT MY HOME LIFE.
clic
clic
WHAT'S THAT ON YOUR FOREHEAD?
HUH?
EXIT
ON MY FOREHEAD?
YES, YOUR BRUISE.
HOW DID YOU GET IT?

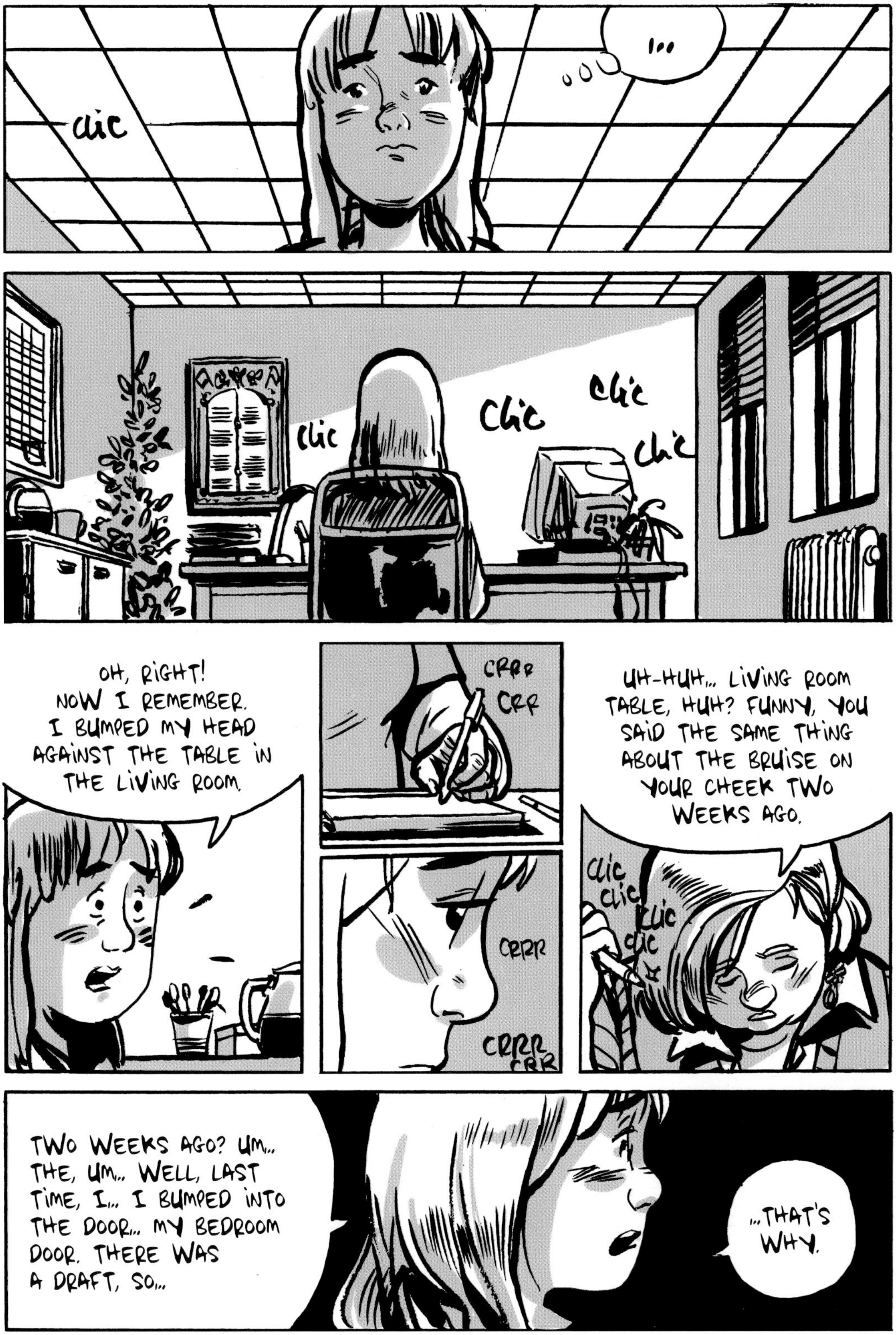
...
CLIC
CLIC
CLIC
CLIC
CLIC
OH, RIGHT! NOW I REMEMBER. I BUMPED MY HEAD AGAINST THE TABLE IN THE LIVING ROOM.
CRRR
CRR
CRRR
CRRR
CRR
UH-HUH... LIVING ROOM TABLE, HUH? FUNNY, YOU SAID THE SAME THING ABOUT THE BRUISE ON YOUR CHEEK TWO WEEKS AGO.
CLIC
CLIC
CLIC
CLIC
TWO WEEKS AGO? UM... THE, UM... WELL, LAST TIME, I... I BUMPED INTO THE DOOR... MY BEDROOM DOOR. THERE WAS A DRAFT, SO...
...THAT'S WHY.

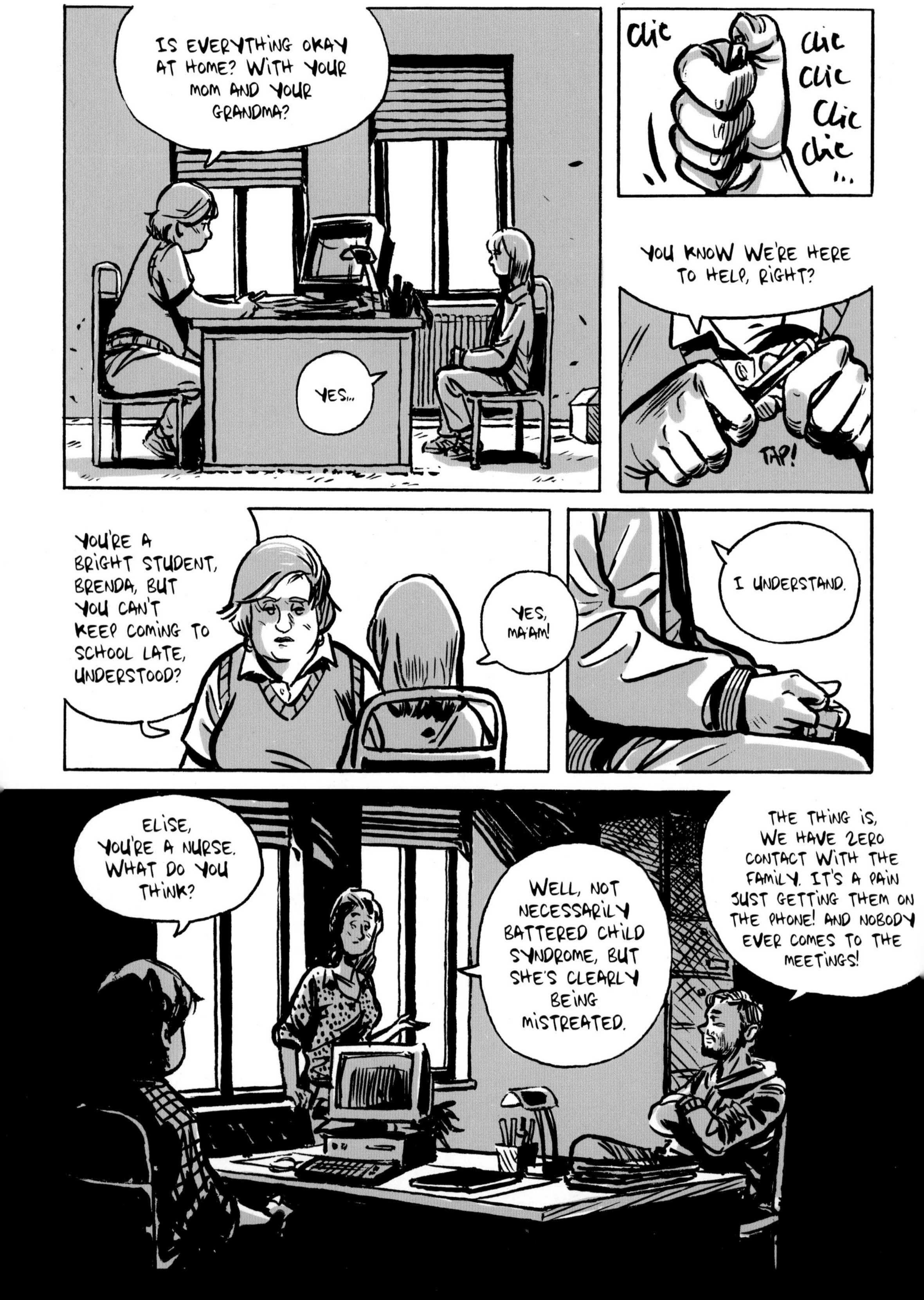
IS EVERYTHING OKAY AT HOME? WITH YOUR MOM AND YOUR GRANDMA?
YES...
Clic
Clic
Clic
Clic
Clic
...
YOU KNOW WE'RE HERE TO HELP, RIGHT?
TAP!
YOU'RE A BRIGHT STUDENT, BRENDA, BUT YOU CAN'T KEEP COMING TO SCHOOL LATE, UNDERSTOOD?
YES, MA'AM!
I UNDERSTAND.
ELISE, YOU'RE A NURSE. WHAT DO YOU THINK?
WELL, NOT NECESSARILY BATTERED CHILD SYNDROME, BUT SHE'S CLEARLY BEING MISTREATED.
THE THING IS, WE HAVE ZERO CONTACT WITH THE FAMILY. IT'S A PAIN JUST GETTING THEM ON THE PHONE! AND NOBODY EVER COMES TO THE MEETINGS!

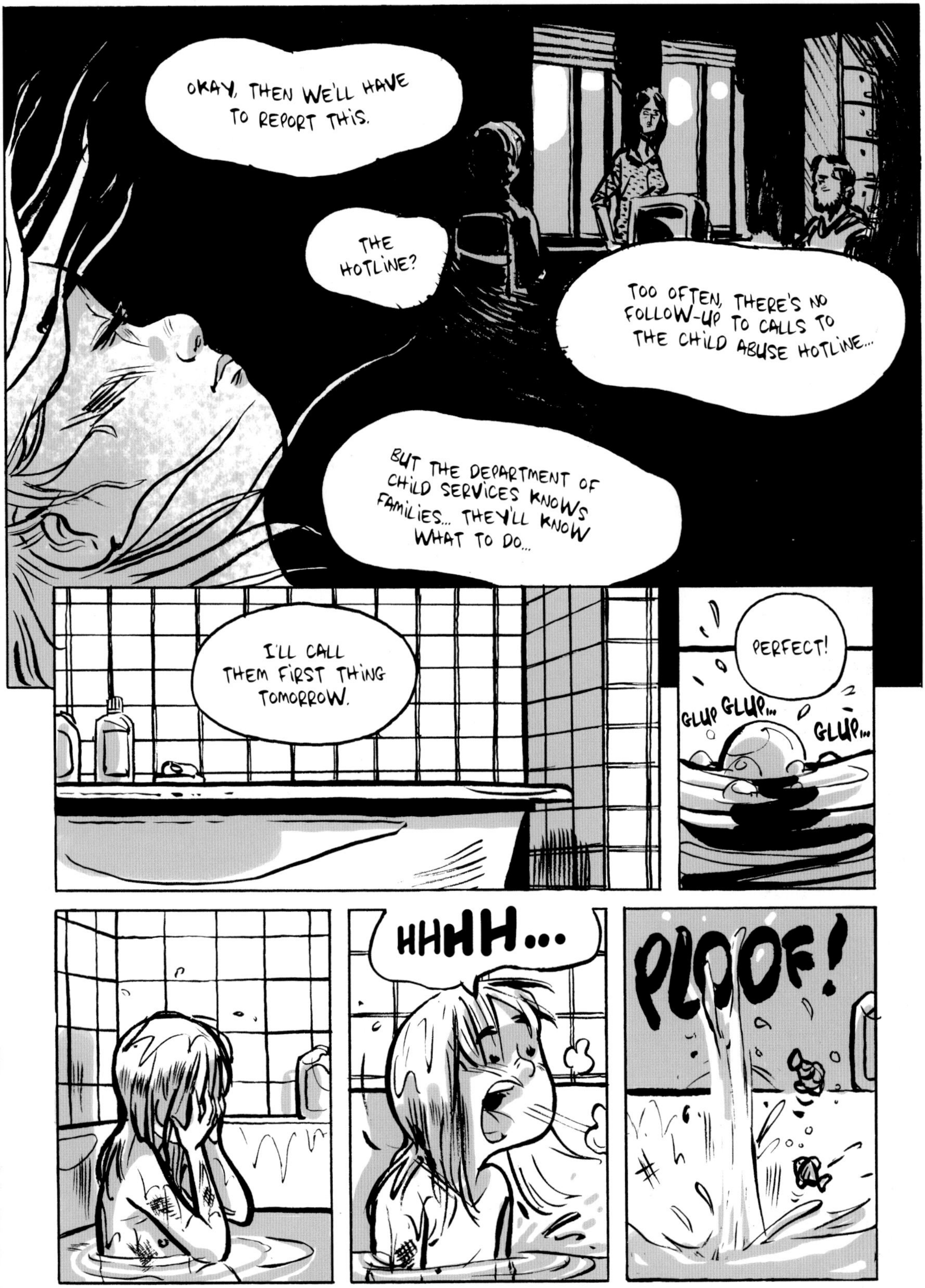
OKAY, THEN WE'LL HAVE TO REPORT THIS.
THE HOTLINE?
TOO OFTEN, THERE'S NO FOLLOW-UP TO CALLS TO THE CHILD ABUSE HOTLINE...
BUT THE DEPARTMENT OF CHILD SERVICES KNOWS FAMILIES... THEY'LL KNOW WHAT TO DO...
I'LL CALL THEM FIRST THING TOMORROW.
PERFECT!
GLUP GLUP... GLUP...
HHHH...
PLOOF!

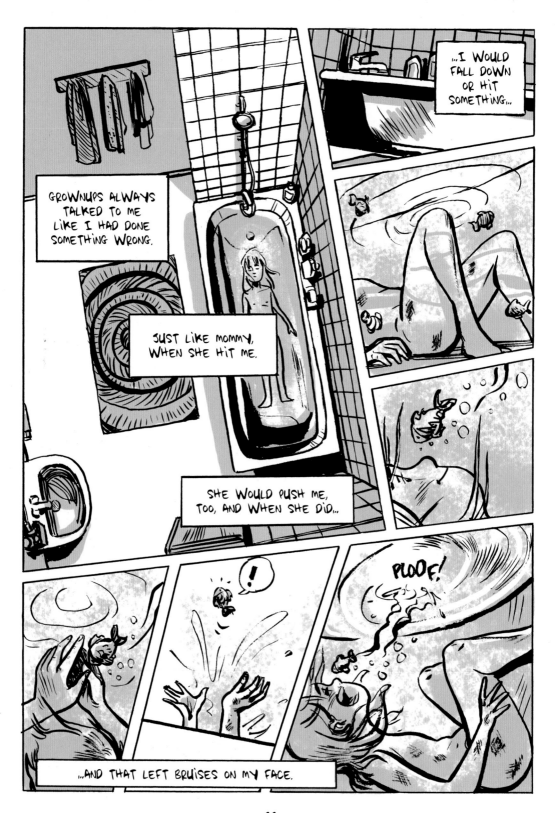

...I WOULD FALL DOWN OR HIT SOMETHING...

GROWNUPS ALWAYS TALKED TO ME LIKE I HAD DONE SOMETHING WRONG.

JUST LIKE MOMMY, WHEN SHE HIT ME.

SHE WOULD PUSH ME, TOO, AND WHEN SHE DID...

!

PLOOF!

...AND THAT LEFT BRUISES ON MY FACE.

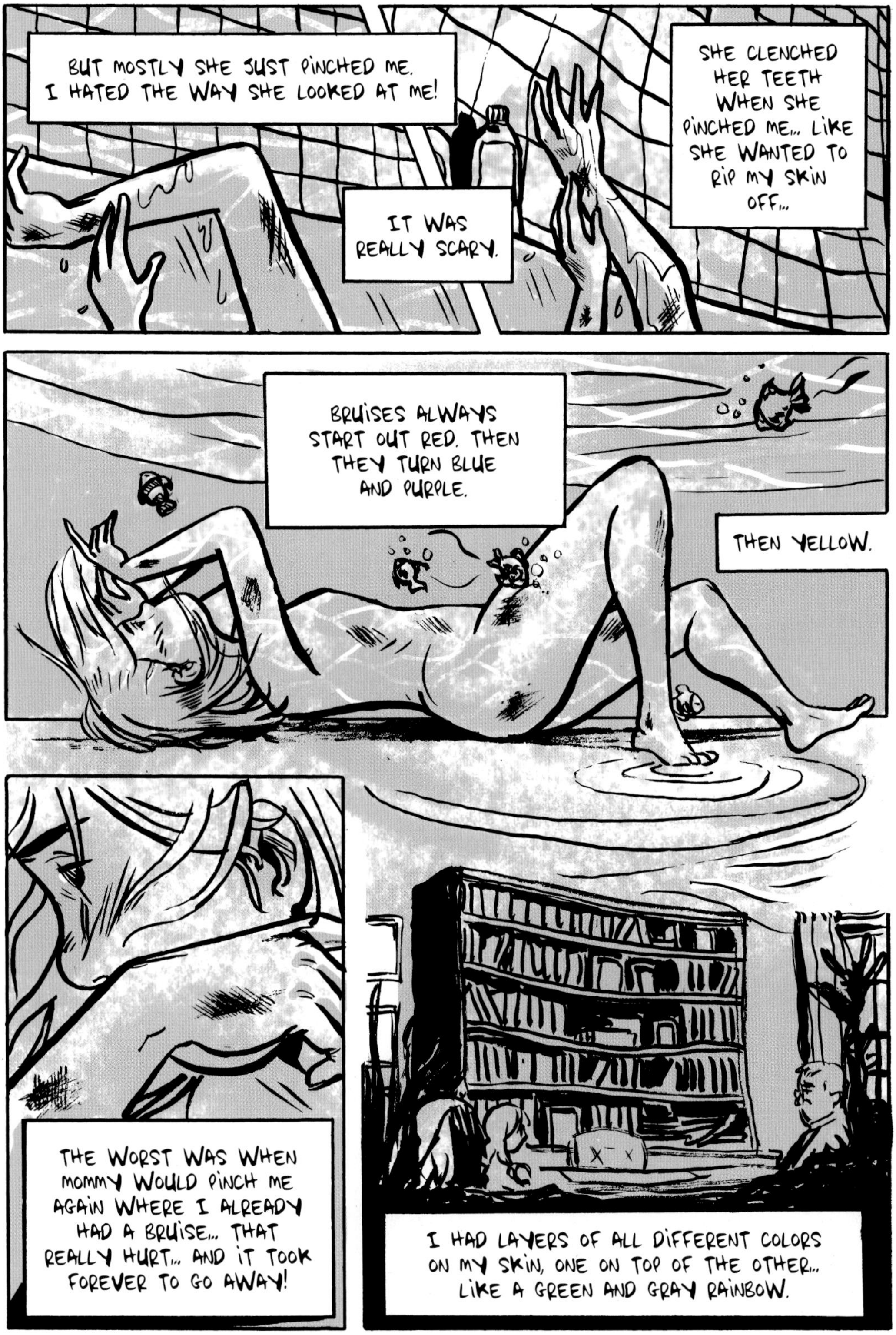

BUT MOSTLY SHE JUST PINCHED ME. I HATED THE WAY SHE LOOKED AT ME!
IT WAS REALLY SCARY.
SHE CLENCHED HER TEETH WHEN SHE PINCHED ME... LIKE SHE WANTED TO RIP MY SKIN OFF...
BRUISES ALWAYS START OUT RED. THEN THEY TURN BLUE AND PURPLE.
THEN YELLOW.
THE WORST WAS WHEN MOMMY WOULD PINCH ME AGAIN WHERE I ALREADY HAD A BRUISE... THAT REALLY HURT... AND IT TOOK FOREVER TO GO AWAY!
I HAD LAYERS OF ALL DIFFERENT COLORS ON MY SKIN, ONE ON TOP OF THE OTHER... LIKE A GREEN AND GRAY RAINBOW.

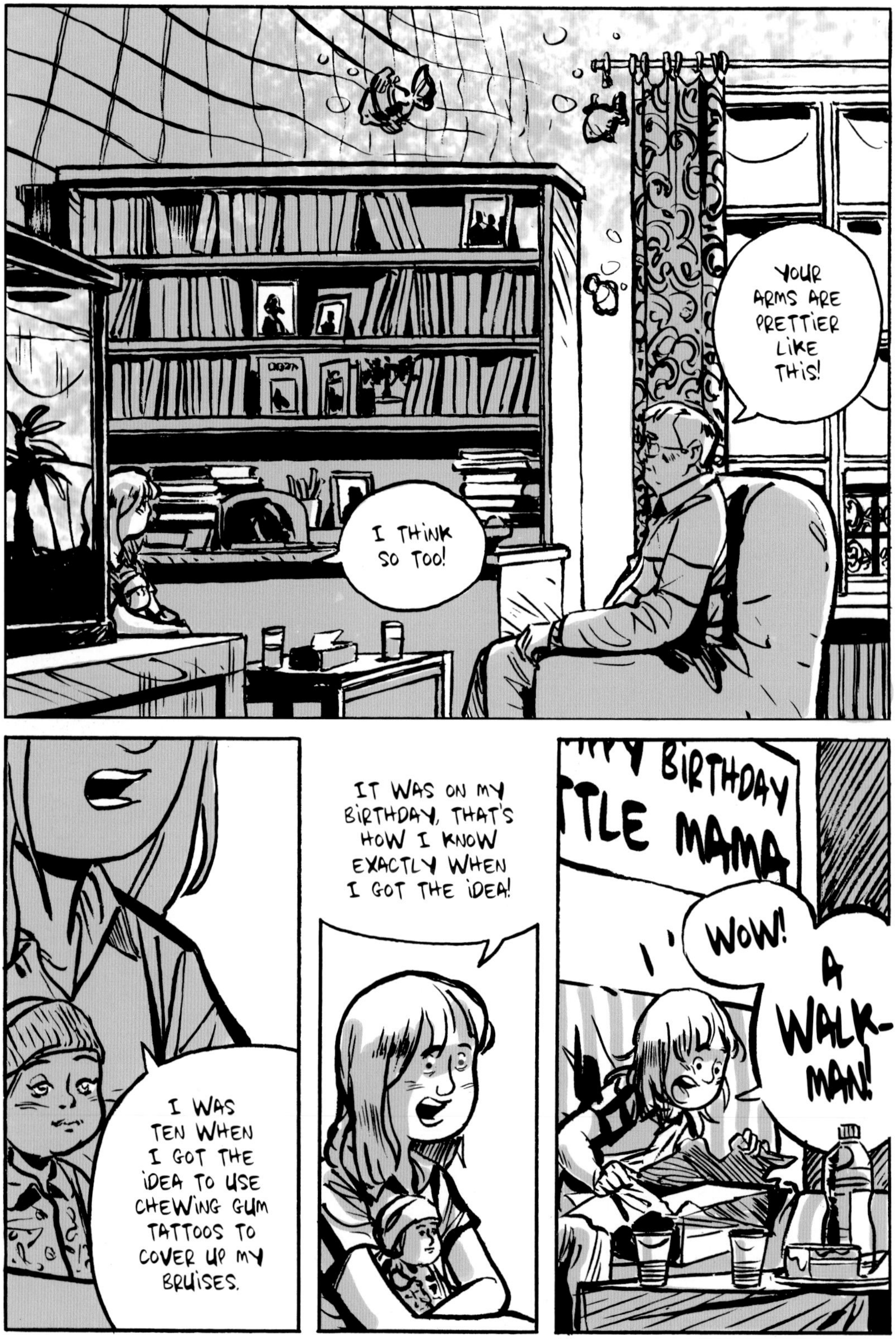
YOUR ARMS ARE PRETTIER LIKE THIS!
I THINK SO TOO!
I WAS TEN WHEN I GOT THE IDEA TO USE CHEWING GUM TATTOOS TO COVER UP MY BRUISES.
IT WAS ON MY BIRTHDAY, THAT'S HOW I KNOW EXACTLY WHEN I GOT THE IDEA!
BIRTHDAY
TTLE MAMA
WOW!
A WALK-MAN!

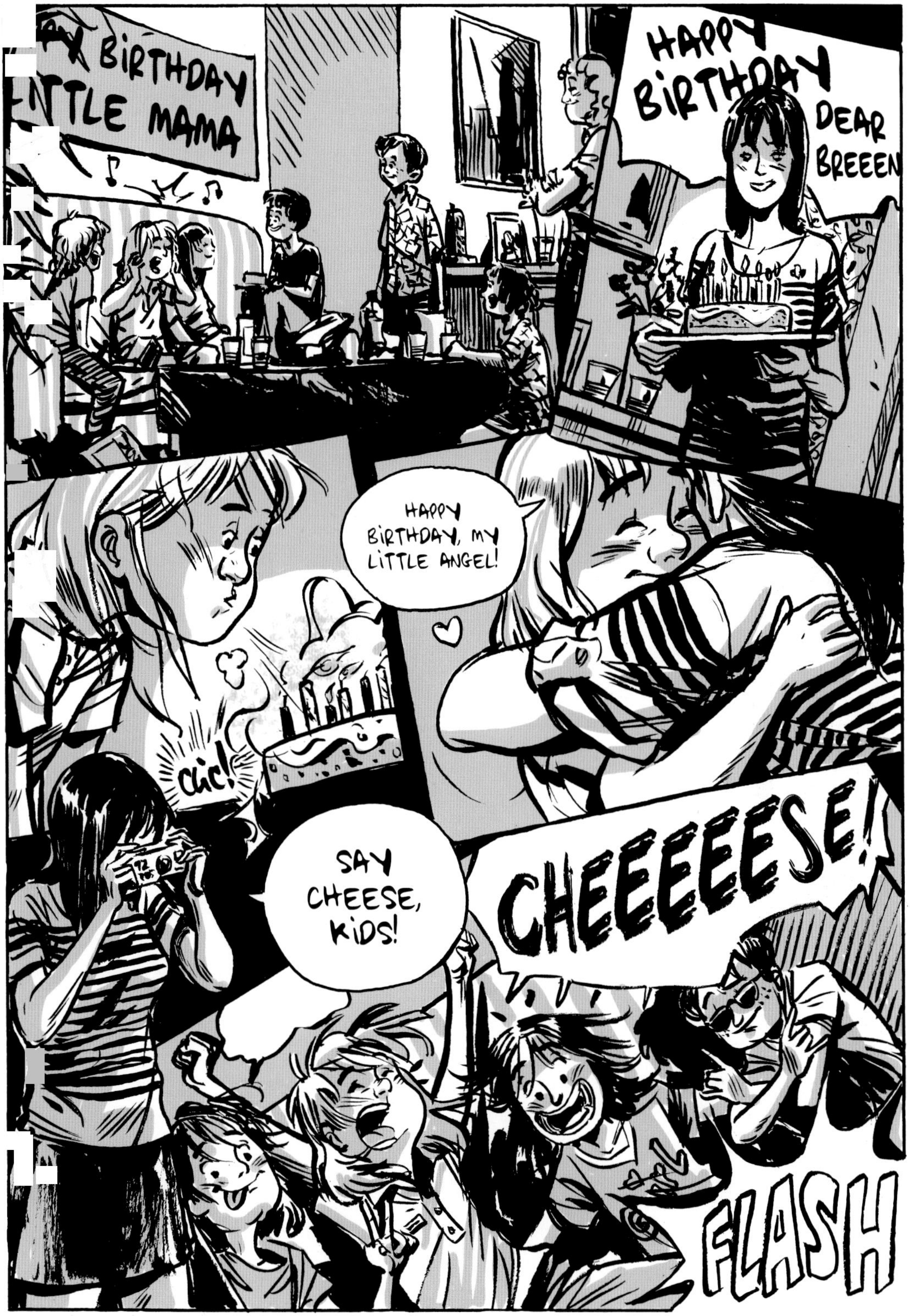
BIRTHDAY
ITTLE MAMA
HAPPY BIRTHDAY DEAR BREEEN
HAPPY BIRTHDAY, MY LITTLE ANGEL!
CLIC!
SAY CHEESE, KIDS!
CHEEEEEESE!
FLASH

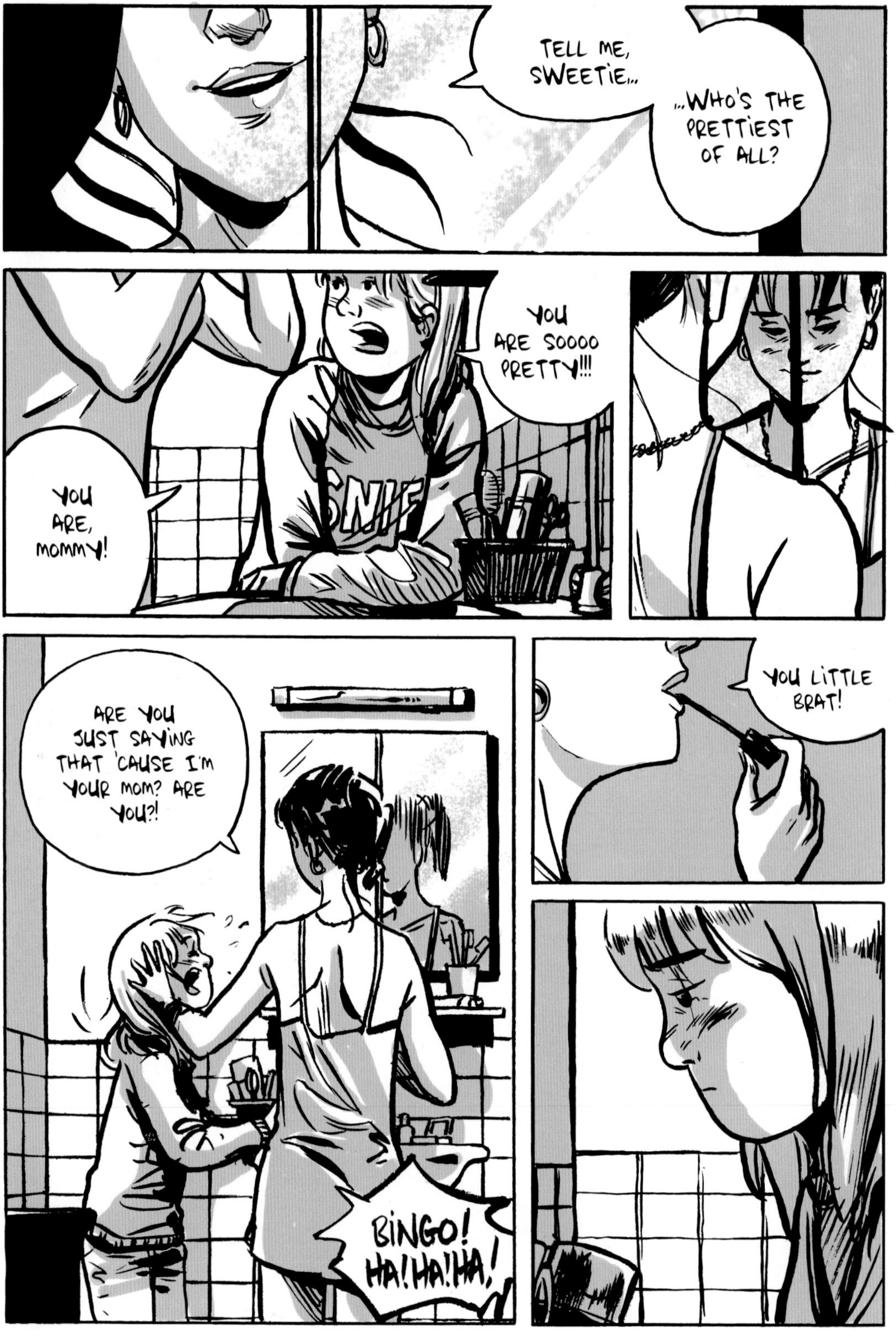
TELL ME, SWEETIE...
...WHO'S THE PRETTIEST OF ALL?
YOU ARE, MOMMY!
YOU ARE SOOOO PRETTY!!!
ARE YOU JUST SAYING THAT 'CAUSE I'M YOUR MOM? ARE YOU?!
BINGO! HA! HA! HA!
YOU LITTLE BRAT!

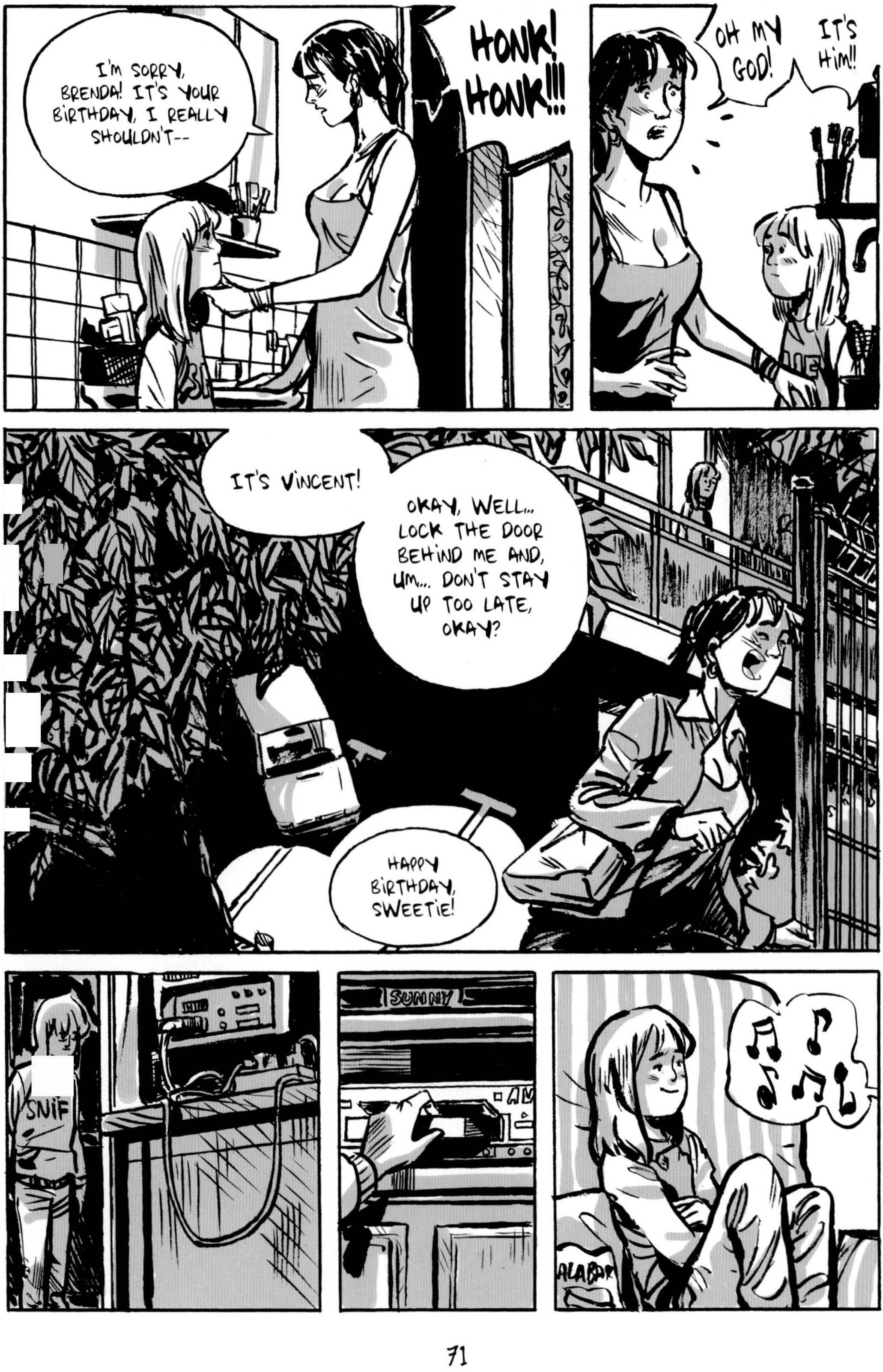
I'M SORRY, BRENDA! IT'S YOUR BIRTHDAY, I REALLY SHOULDN'T--
HONK! HONK!!!
OH MY GOD!
IT'S HIM!!
IT'S VINCENT!
OKAY, WELL... LOCK THE DOOR BEHIND ME AND, UM... DON'T STAY UP TOO LATE, OKAY?
HAPPY BIRTHDAY, SWEETIE!
SNIF
SUNNY

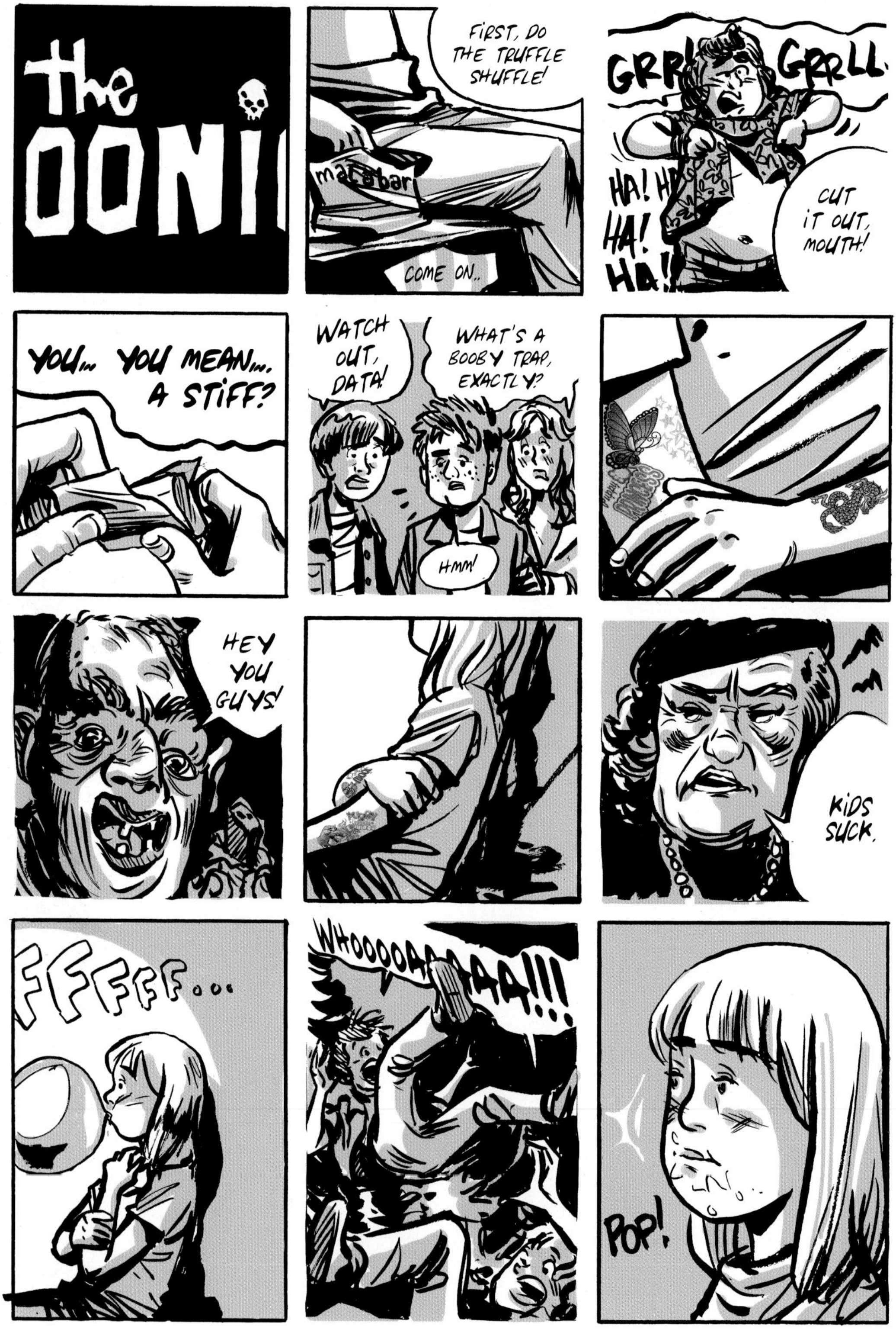
the
OONI
FIRST, DO THE TRUFFLE SHUFFLE!
mataba
COME ON..
GRR!
GRRLL
HA! HA! HA! HA!
CUT IT OUT, MOUTH!
YOU... YOU MEAN... A STIFF?
WATCH OUT, DATA!
WHAT'S A BOOBY TRAP, EXACTLY?
HMM!
HEY YOU GUYS!
KIDS SUCK.
FFFFF...
WHOOOOAAAAAA!!!
POP!

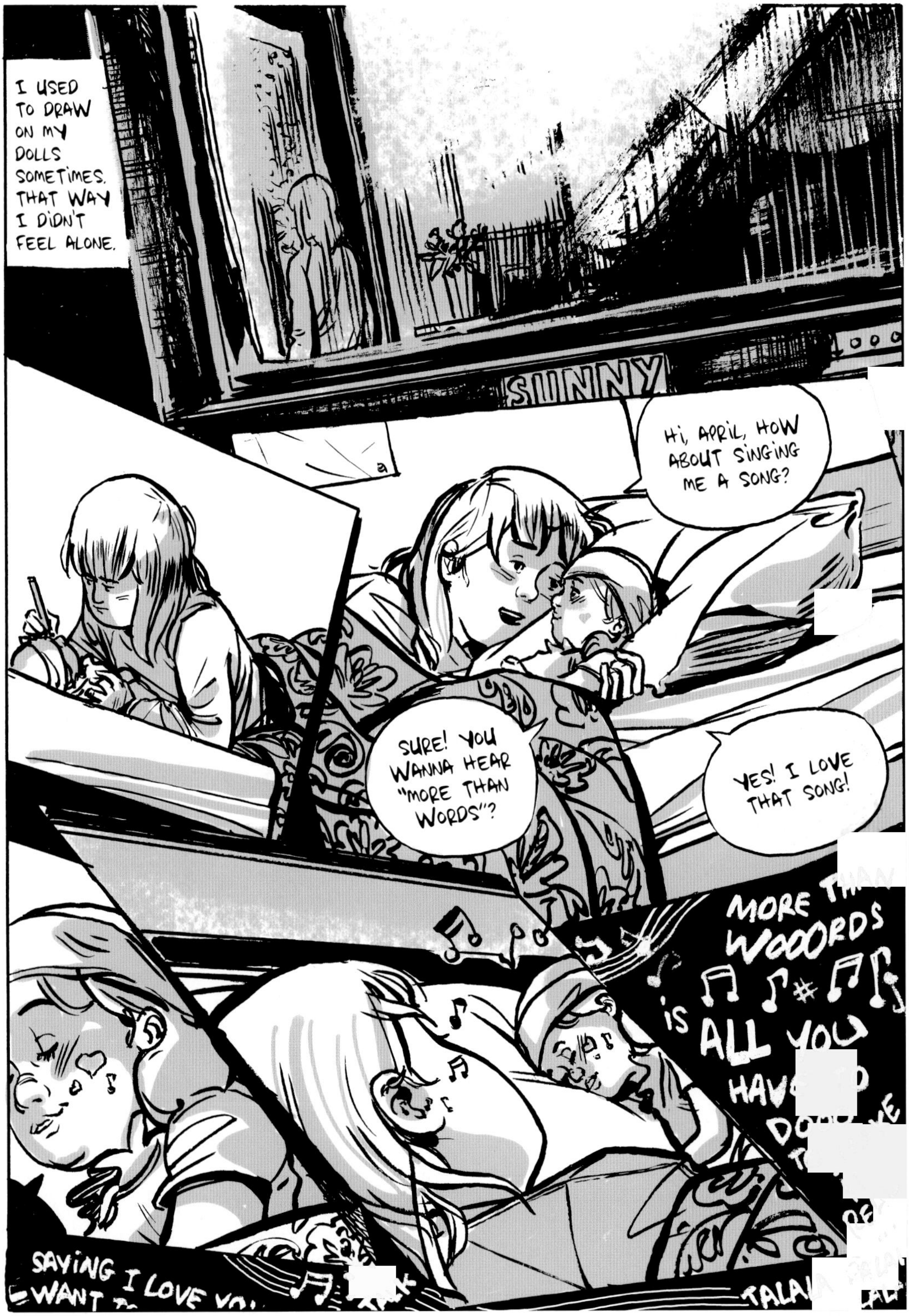
I USED TO DRAW ON MY DOLLS SOMETIMES. THAT WAY I DIDN'T FEEL ALONE.
SUNNY
Hi, APRIL, HOW ABOUT SINGING ME A SONG?
SURE! YOU WANNA HEAR "MORE THAN WORDS"?
YES! I LOVE THAT SONG!
MORE TH
WOOORDS
IS ALL YOU
SAYING I LOVE

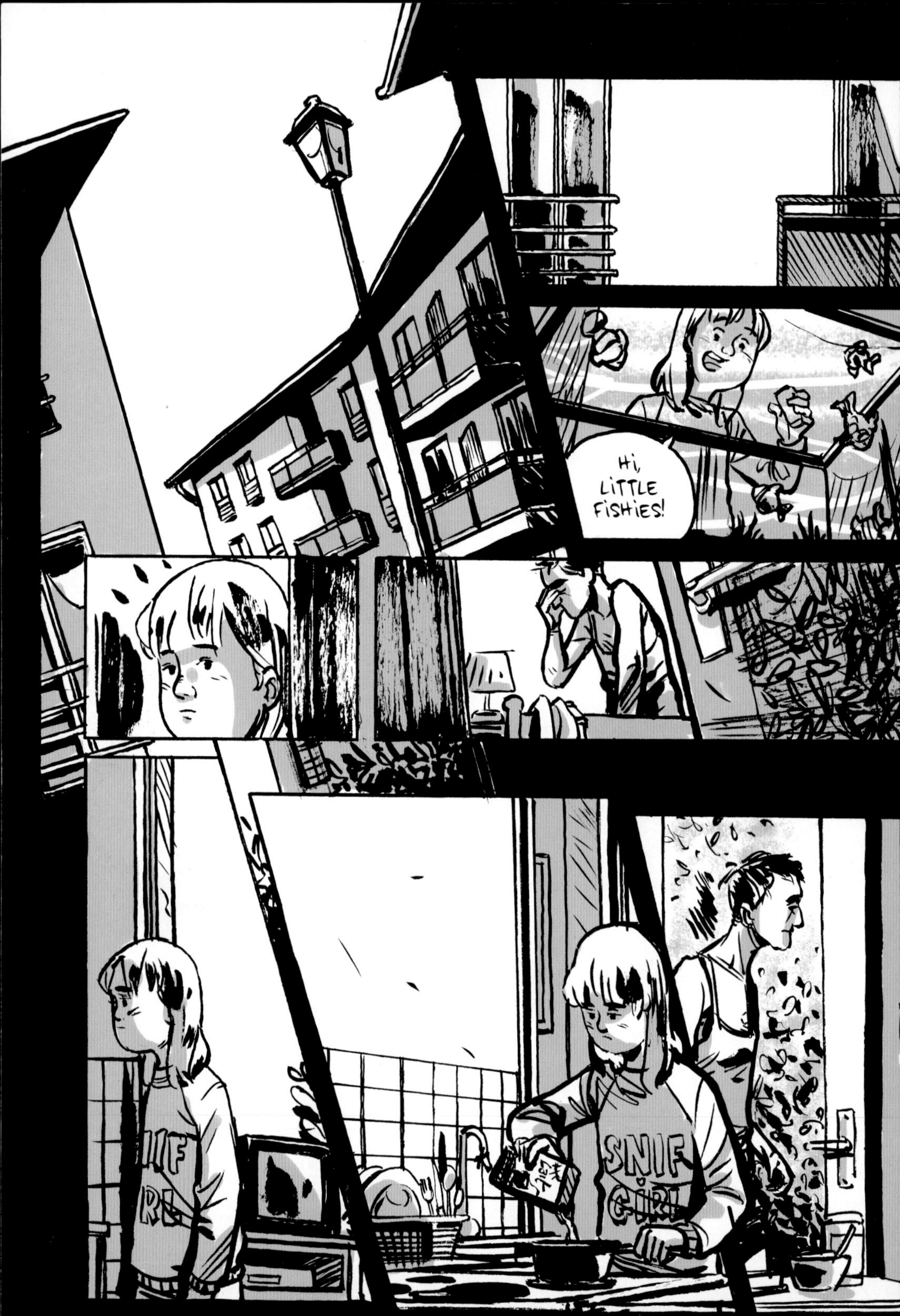
Hi, LITTLE FISHIES!
SNIF GIRL

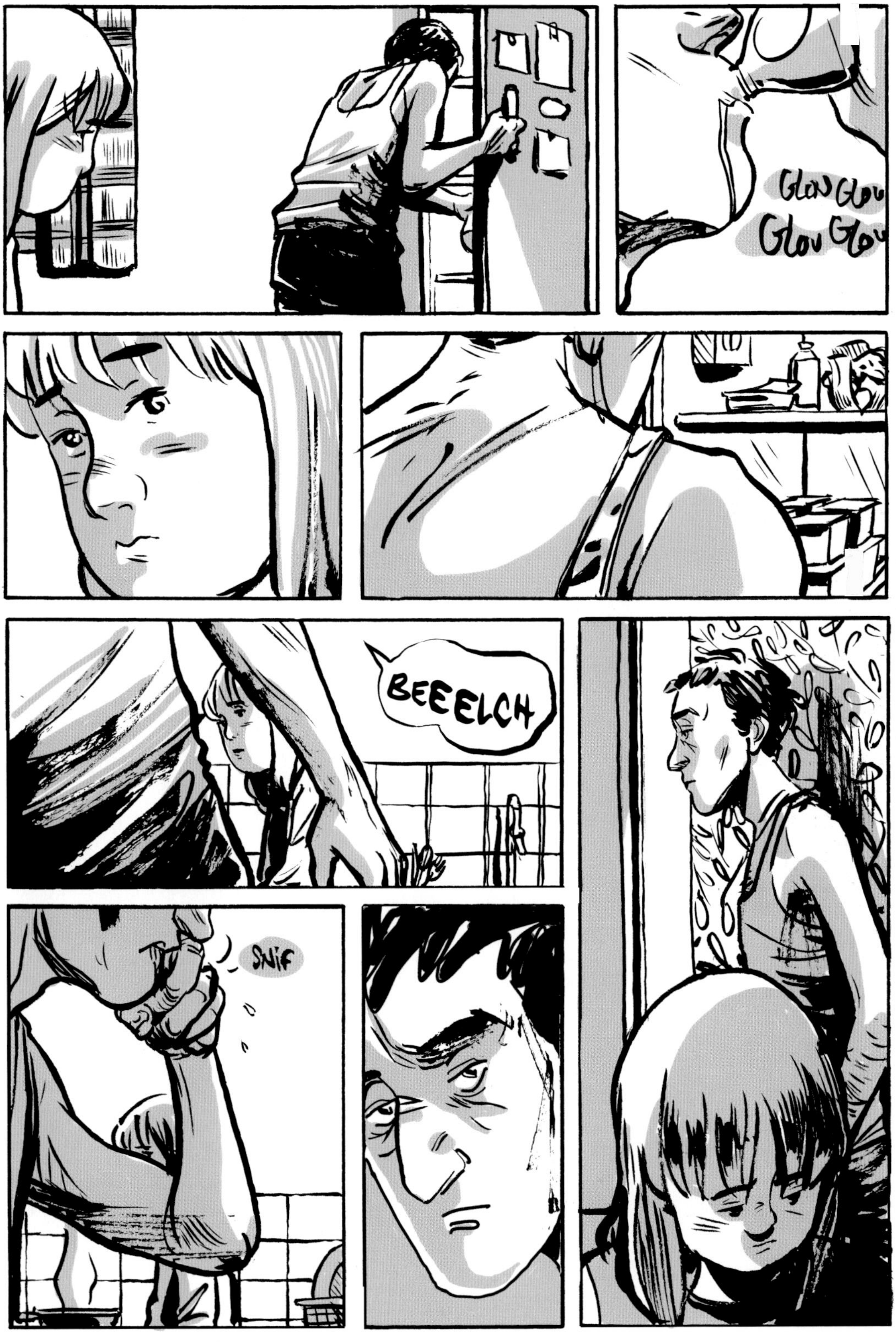
Glou Glou
Glou Glou
BEEELCH
SNIF

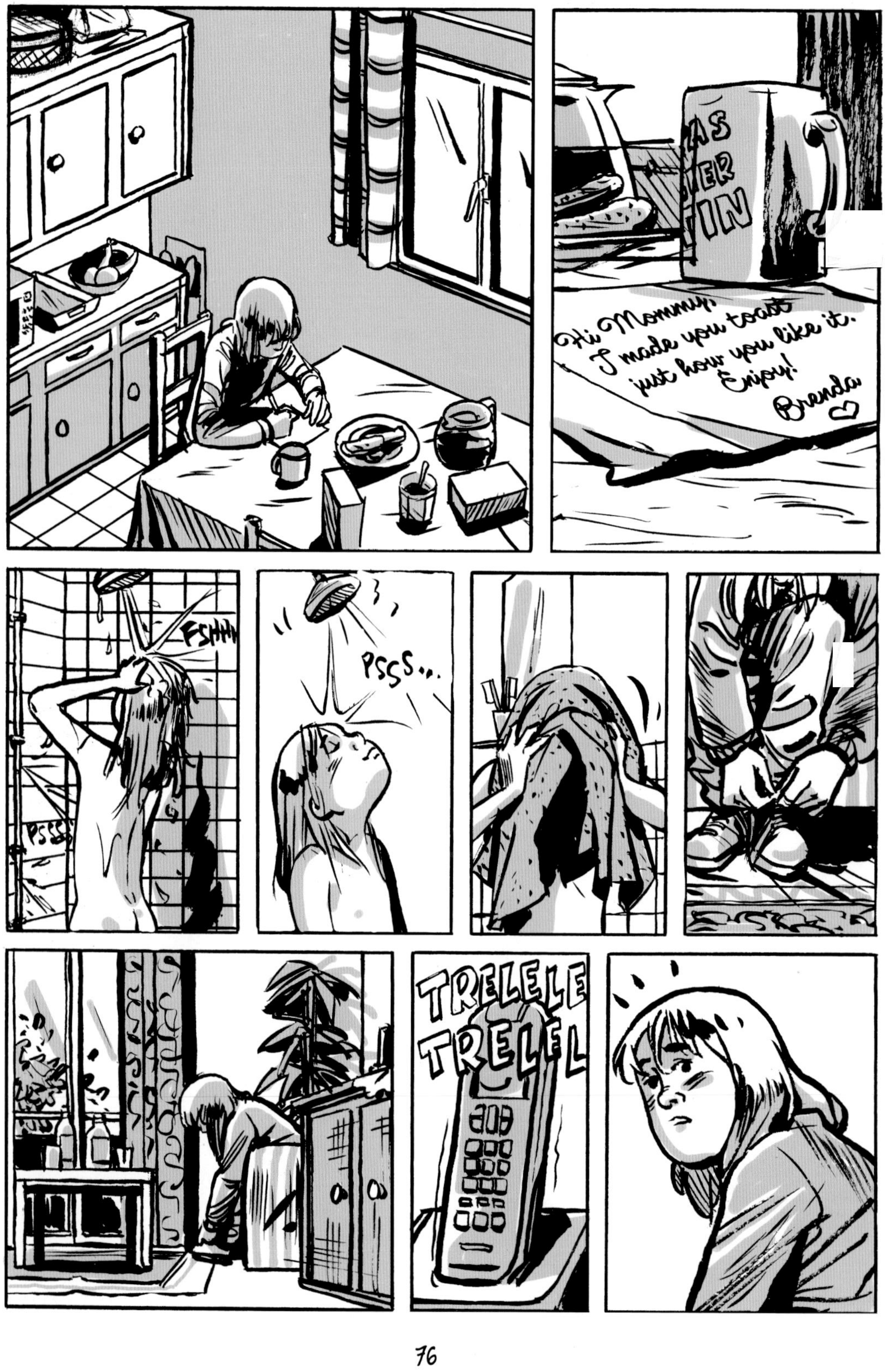
Hi Mommy,
I made you toast
just how you like it.
Enjoy!
Brenda
FSHH
PSSS
PSSS...
TRELELE
TRELEL

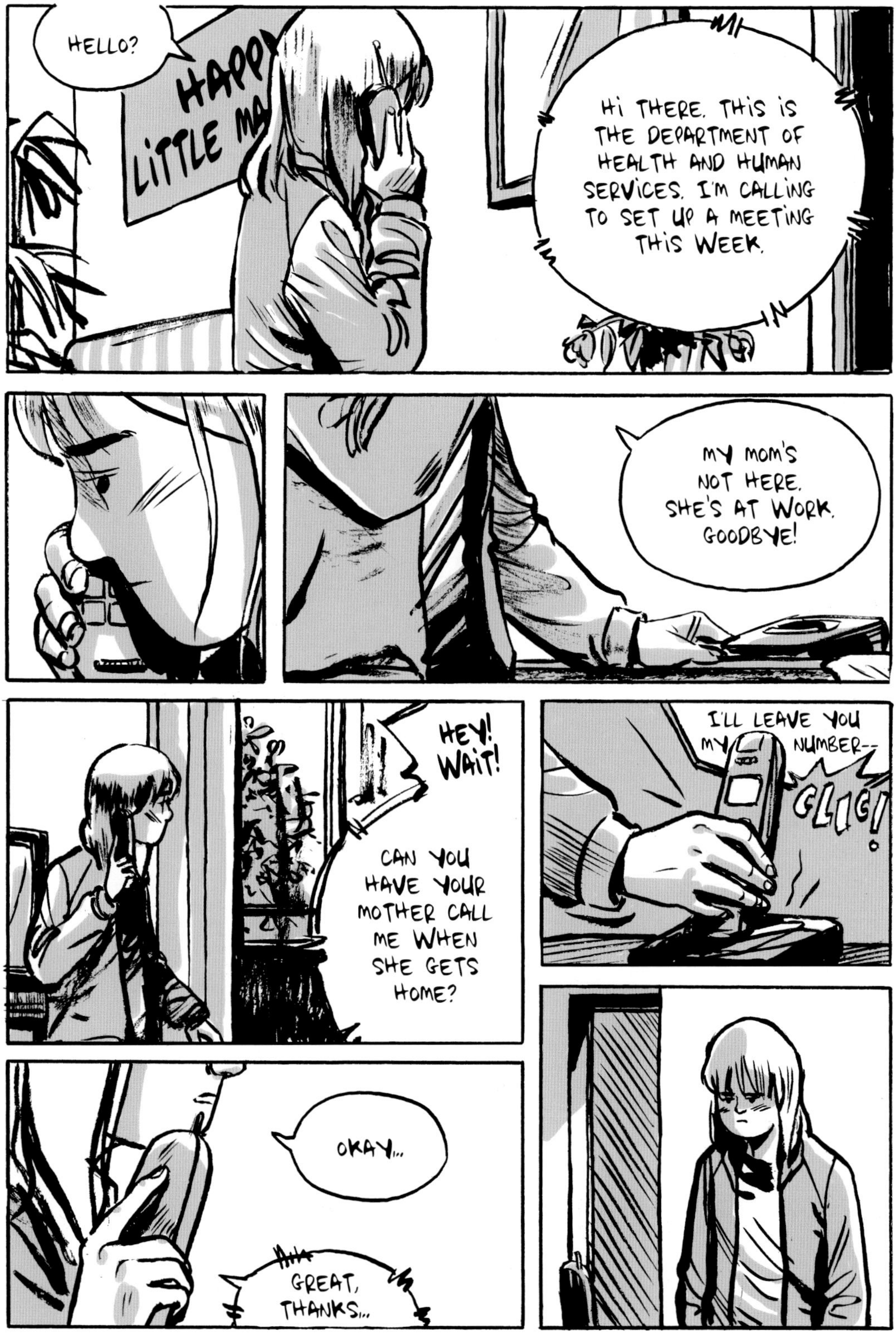
HELLO?
HAPPY
LITTLE MA
HI THERE. THIS IS THE DEPARTMENT OF HEALTH AND HUMAN SERVICES. I'M CALLING TO SET UP A MEETING THIS WEEK.
MY MOM'S NOT HERE. SHE'S AT WORK. GOODBYE!
HEY! WAIT!
CAN YOU HAVE YOUR MOTHER CALL ME WHEN SHE GETS HOME?
I'LL LEAVE YOU MY NUMBER--
CLIC!
OKAY...
GREAT, THANKS...

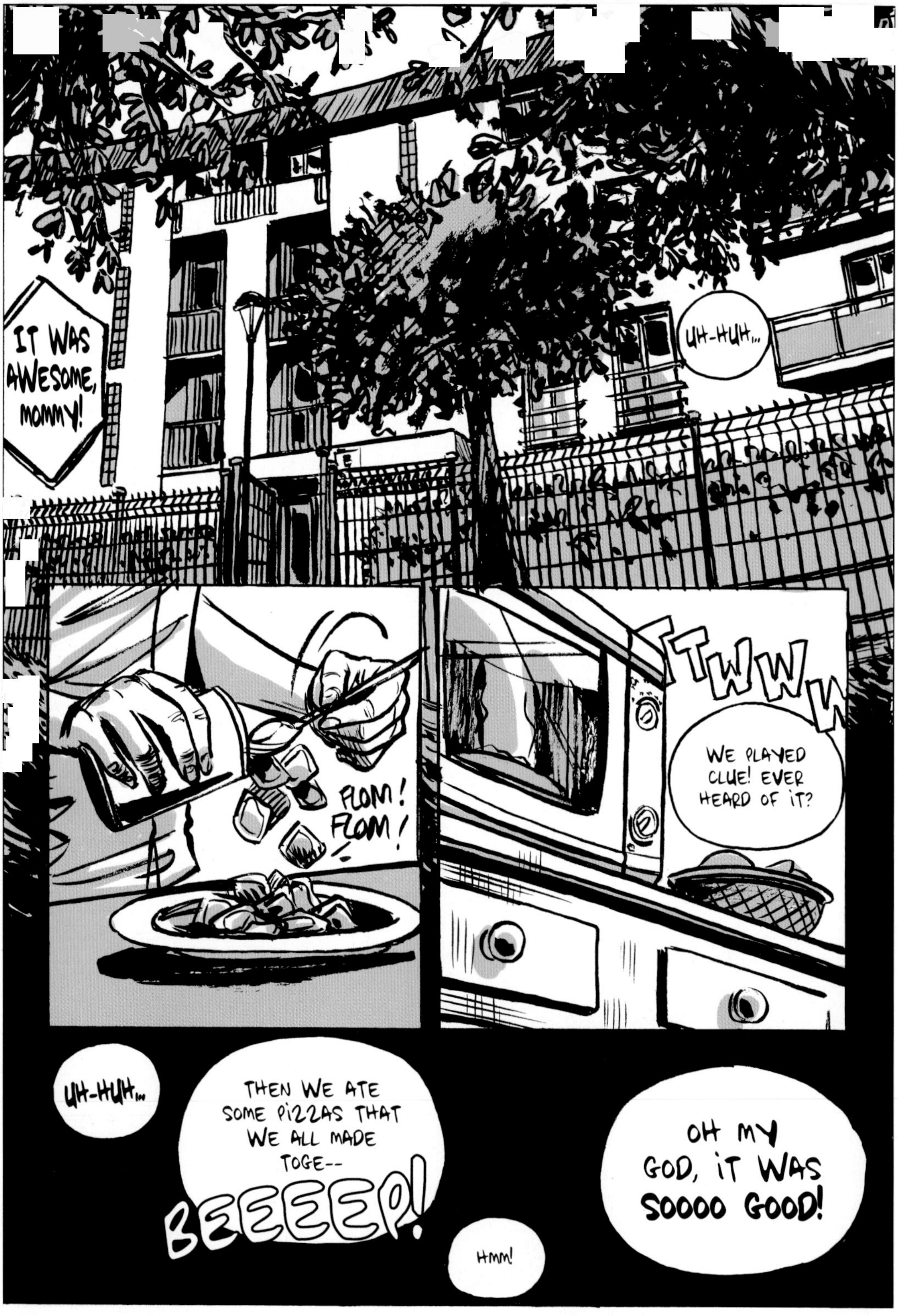
IT WAS AWESOME, MOMMY!
UH-HUH...
FLOM! FLOM!
TTWWWW
WE PLAYED CLUE! EVER HEARD OF IT?
UH-HUH...
THEN WE ATE SOME PIZZAS THAT WE ALL MADE TOGE--
BEEEEP!
HMM!
OH MY GOD, IT WAS SOOOO GOOD!

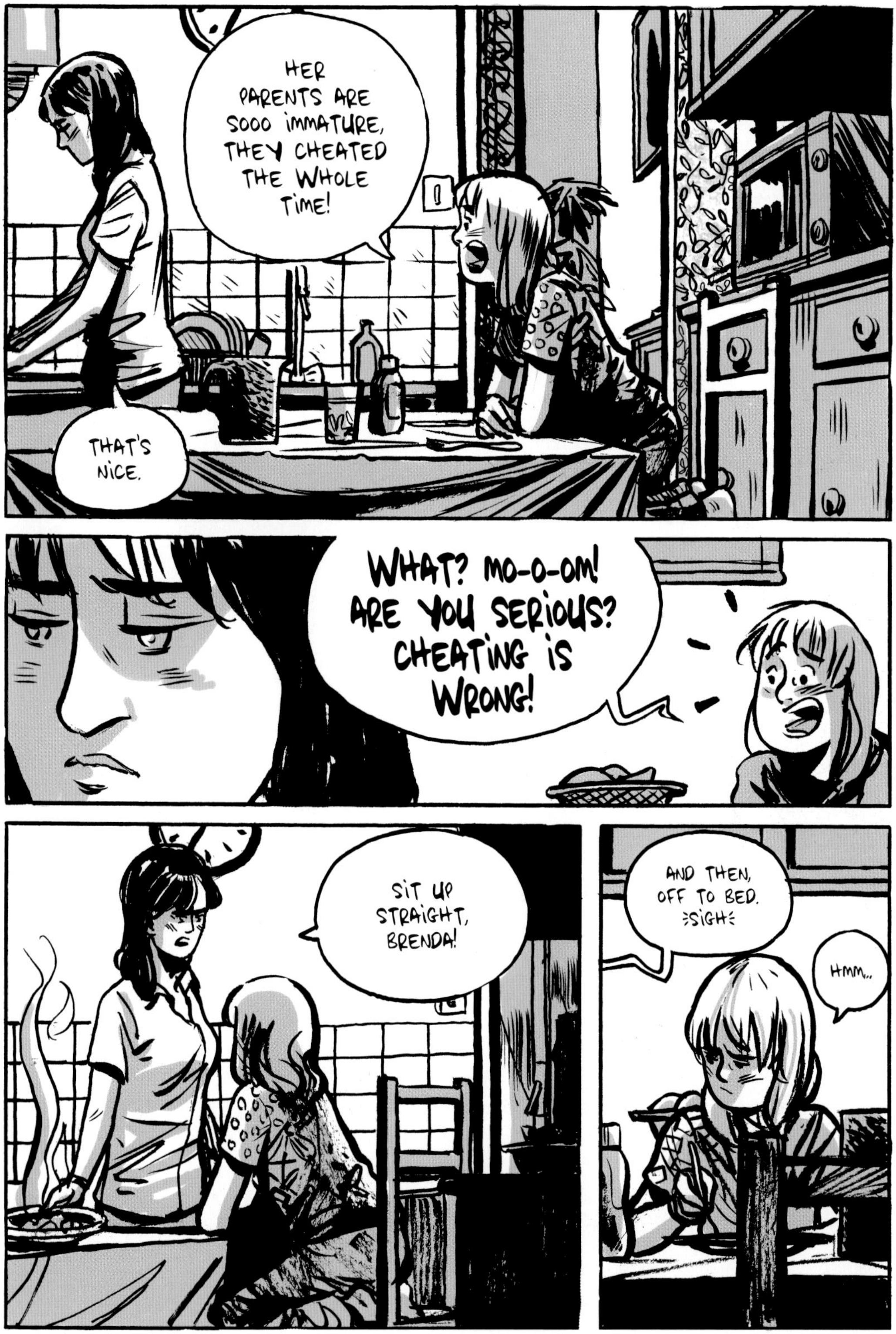
HER PARENTS ARE SOOO IMMATURE, THEY CHEATED THE WHOLE TIME!
THAT'S NICE.
WHAT? MO-O-OM! ARE YOU SERIOUS? CHEATING IS WRONG!
SIT UP STRAIGHT, BRENDA!
AND THEN, OFF TO BED. SIGH
HMM..

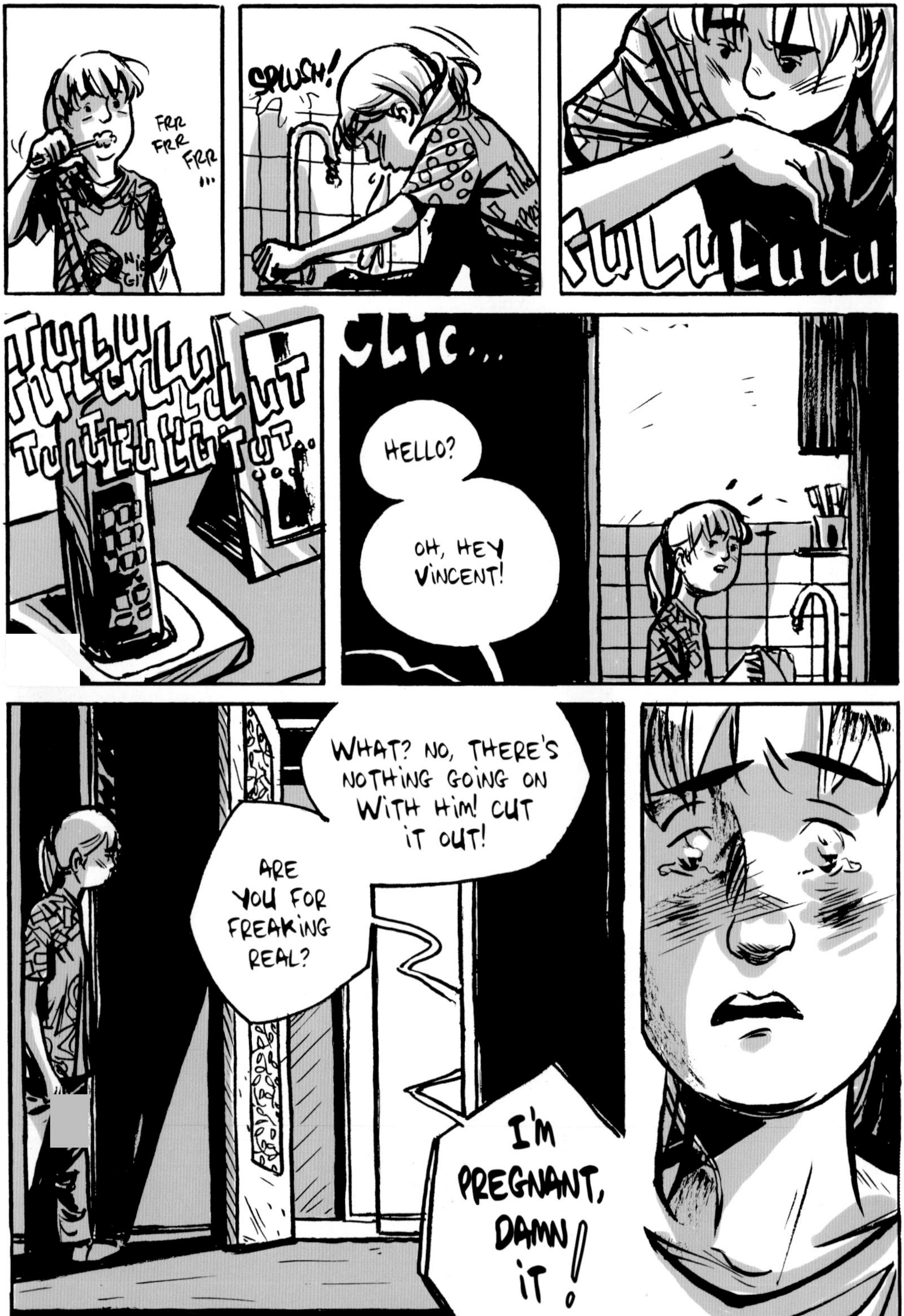
FRR
FRR
FRR
...
SPLUSH!
TULULULU
TULULULUT
TULULULUT
TULULULUT...
CLIC...
HELLO?
OH, HEY VINCENT!
WHAT? NO, THERE'S NOTHING GOING ON WITH HIM! CUT IT OUT!
ARE YOU FOR FREAKING REAL?
I'M PREGNANT, DAMN IT!

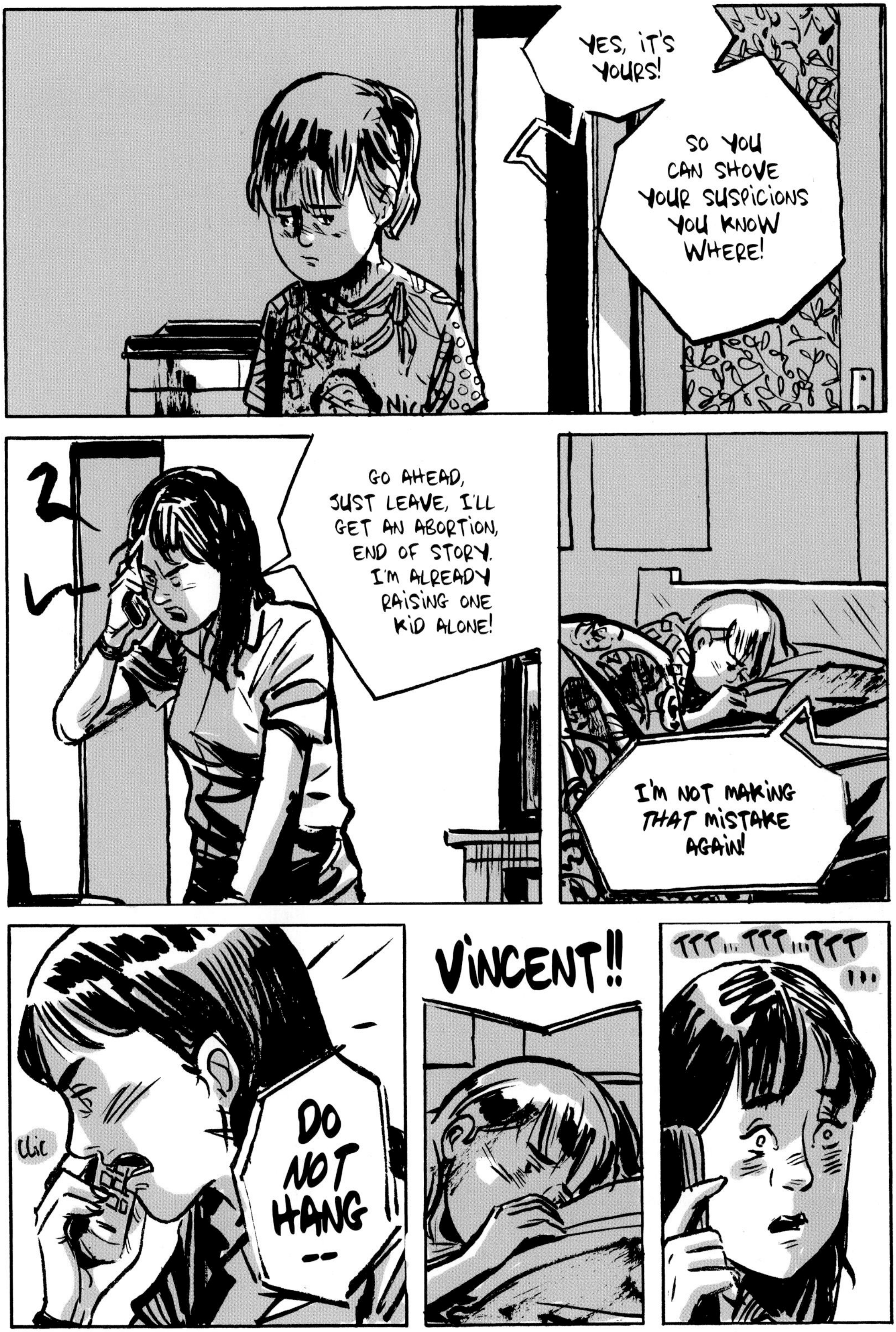
YES, IT'S YOURS!
SO YOU CAN SHOVE YOUR SUSPICIONS YOU KNOW WHERE!
GO AHEAD, JUST LEAVE, I'LL GET AN ABORTION, END OF STORY. I'M ALREADY RAISING ONE KID ALONE!
I'M NOT MAKING *THAT* MISTAKE AGAIN!
Clic
DO NOT HANG --
VINCENT!!
TTT... TTT... TTT ...

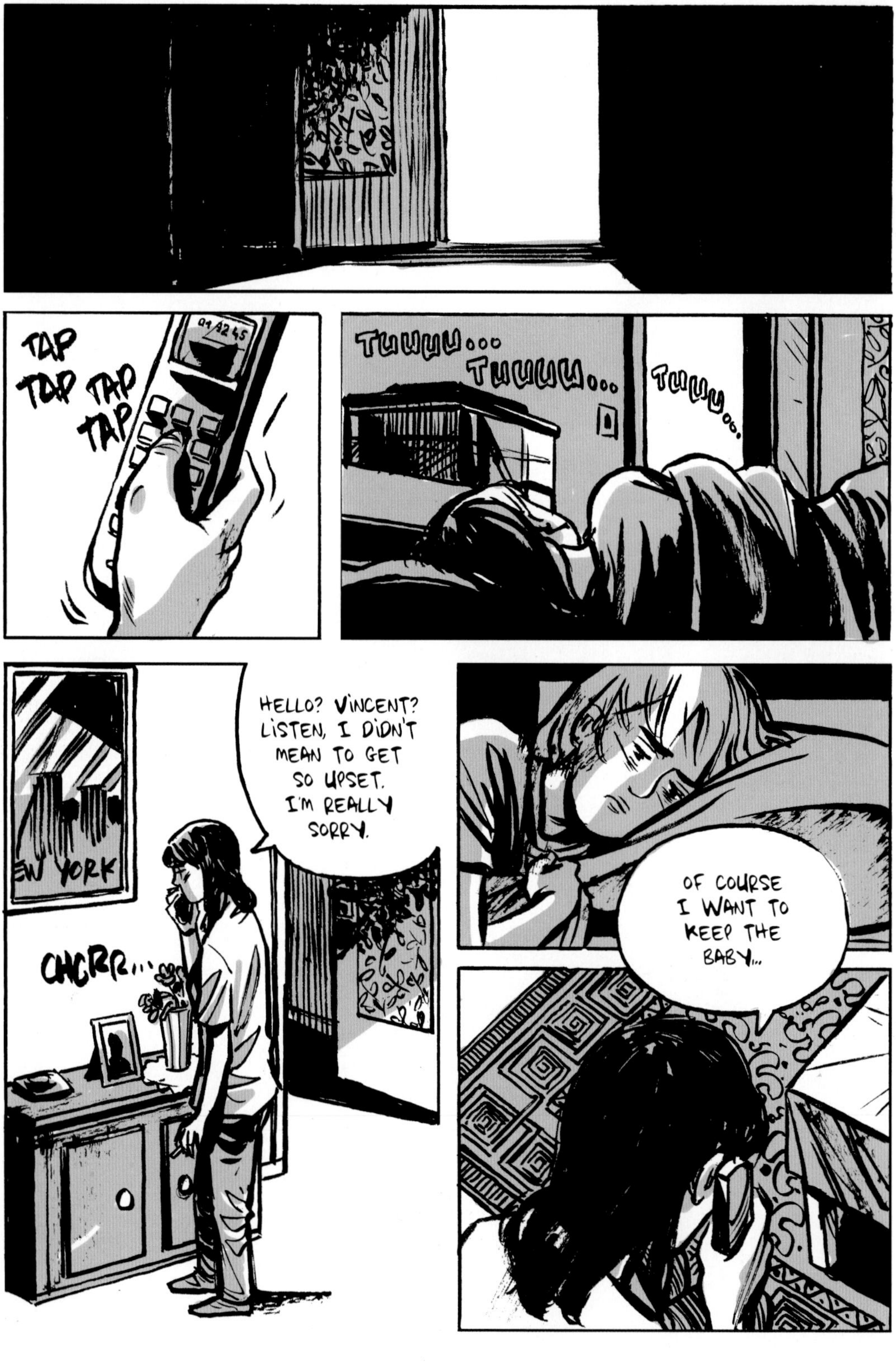
TAP
TAP TAP
TAP
TUUUU...
TUUUU...
TUUU...
HELLO? VINCENT? LISTEN, I DIDN'T MEAN TO GET SO UPSET. I'M REALLY SORRY.
CHCRR...
OF COURSE I WANT TO KEEP THE BABY...

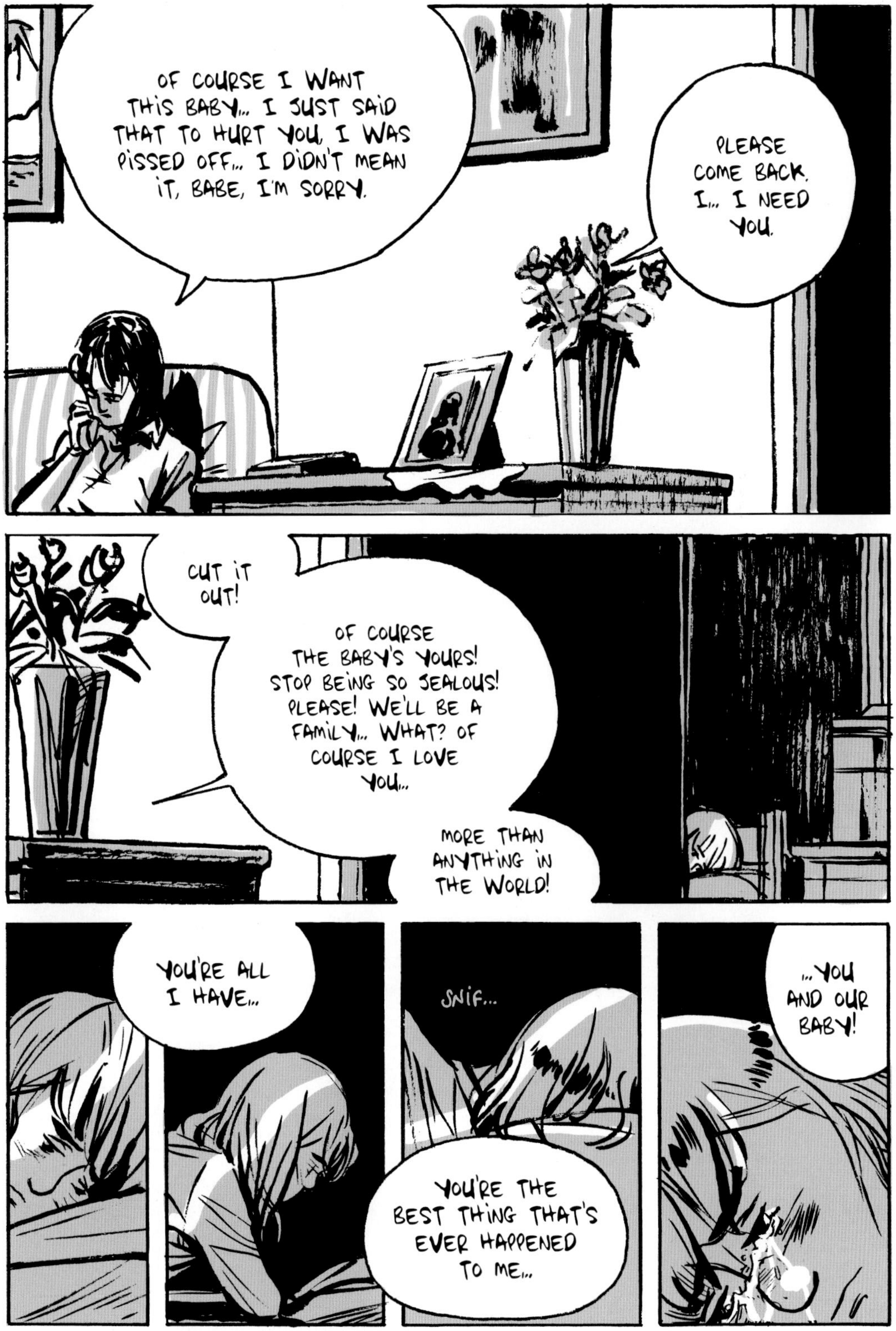

OF COURSE I WANT THIS BABY... I JUST SAID THAT TO HURT YOU, I WAS PISSED OFF... I DIDN'T MEAN IT, BABE, I'M SORRY.
PLEASE COME BACK. I... I NEED YOU.
CUT IT OUT!
OF COURSE THE BABY'S YOURS! STOP BEING SO JEALOUS! PLEASE! WE'LL BE A FAMILY... WHAT? OF COURSE I LOVE YOU...
MORE THAN ANYTHING IN THE WORLD!
YOU'RE ALL I HAVE...
SNIF...
YOU'RE THE BEST THING THAT'S EVER HAPPENED TO ME...
...YOU AND OUR BABY!

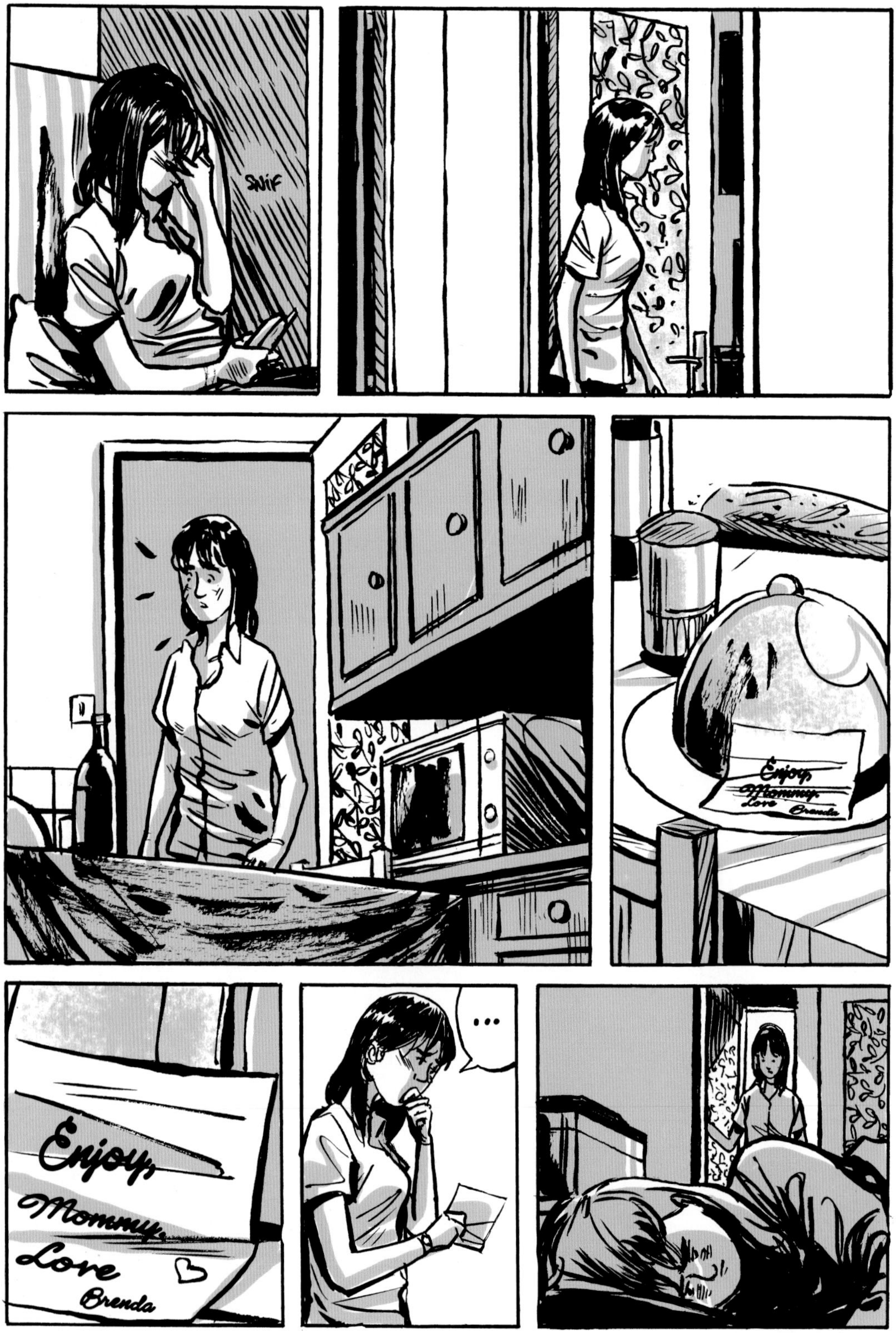
SNIF
Enjoy,
Mommy.
Love
Brenda
Enjoy,
Mommy.
Love
Brenda
...

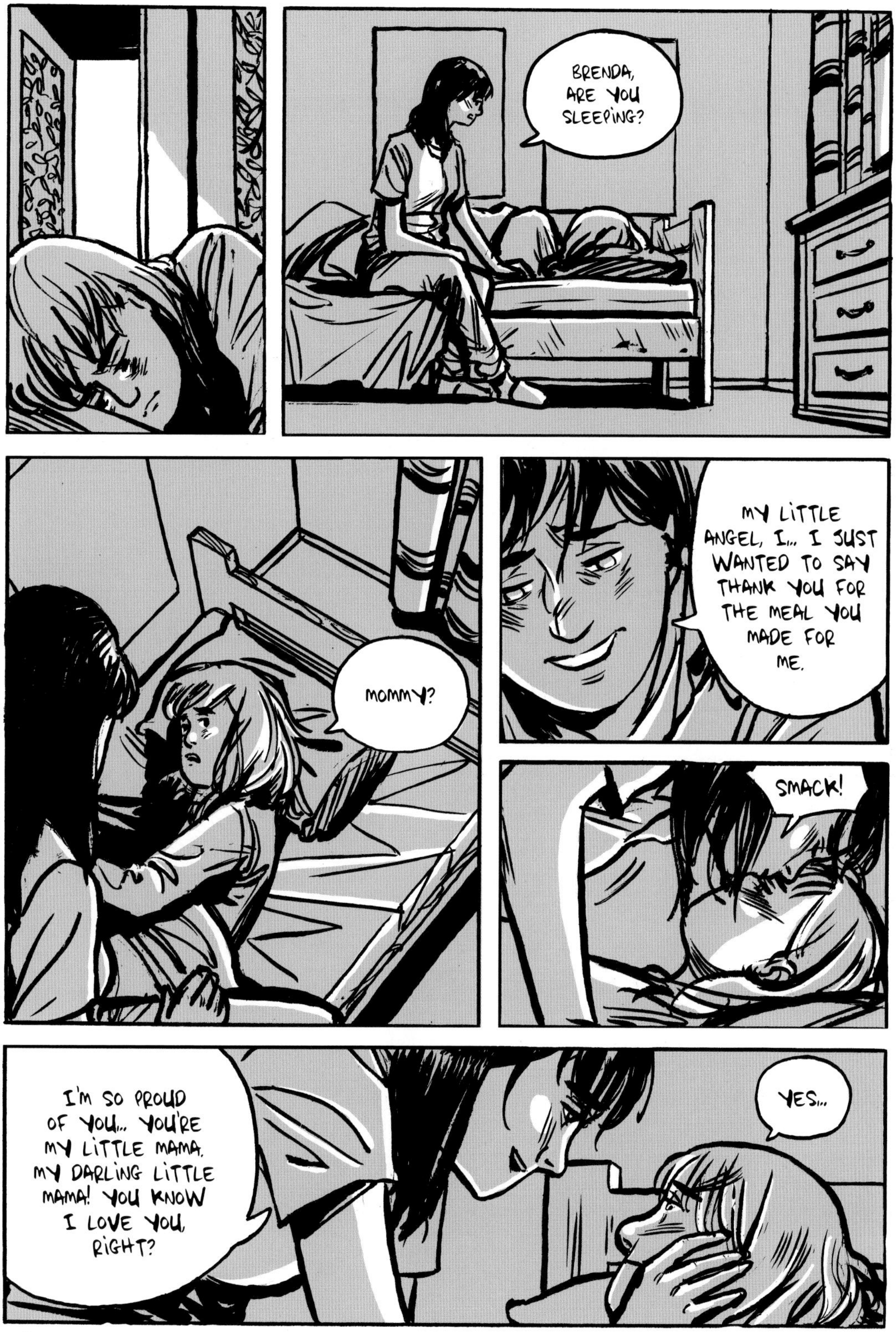
BRENDA, ARE YOU SLEEPING?
MOMMY?
MY LITTLE ANGEL, I... I JUST WANTED TO SAY THANK YOU FOR THE MEAL YOU MADE FOR ME.
SMACK!
I'M SO PROUD OF YOU... YOU'RE MY LITTLE MAMA. MY DARLING LITTLE MAMA! YOU KNOW I LOVE YOU, RIGHT?
YES...

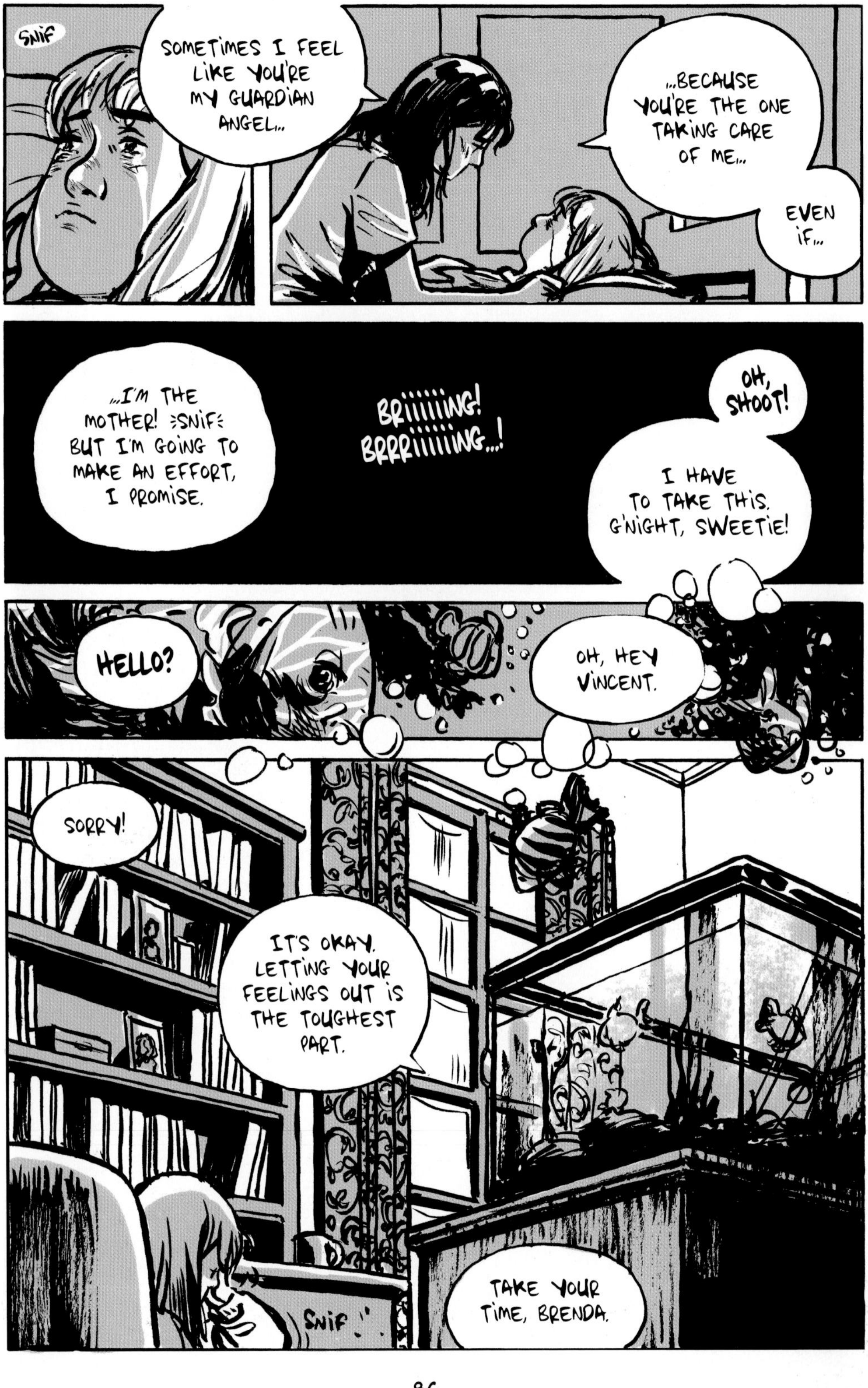
SNIF
SOMETIMES I FEEL LIKE YOU'RE MY GUARDIAN ANGEL...
...BECAUSE YOU'RE THE ONE TAKING CARE OF ME...
EVEN IF...
...I'M THE MOTHER! SNIF BUT I'M GOING TO MAKE AN EFFORT, I PROMISE.
BRIIIIIING! BRRRIIIIIING...!
OH, SHOOT!
I HAVE TO TAKE THIS. G'NIGHT, SWEETIE!
HELLO?
OH, HEY VINCENT.
SORRY!
IT'S OKAY. LETTING YOUR FEELINGS OUT IS THE TOUGHEST PART.
SNIF !
TAKE YOUR TIME, BRENDA.

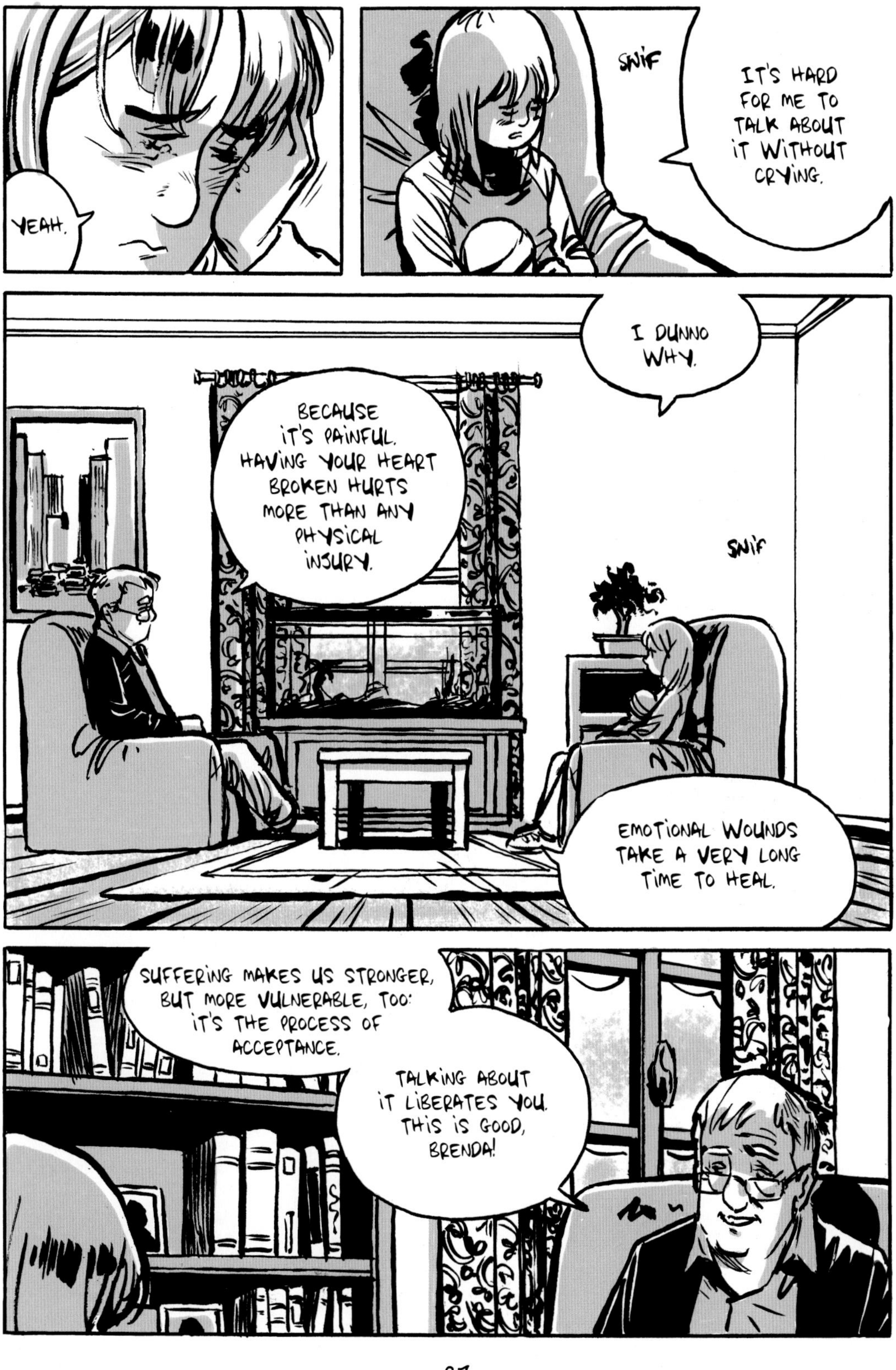

YEAH.
SNIF
IT'S HARD FOR ME TO TALK ABOUT IT WITHOUT CRYING.
I DUNNO WHY.
BECAUSE IT'S PAINFUL. HAVING YOUR HEART BROKEN HURTS MORE THAN ANY PHYSICAL INJURY.
SNIF
EMOTIONAL WOUNDS TAKE A VERY LONG TIME TO HEAL.
SUFFERING MAKES US STRONGER, BUT MORE VULNERABLE, TOO: IT'S THE PROCESS OF ACCEPTANCE.
TALKING ABOUT IT LIBERATES YOU. THIS IS GOOD, BRENDA!

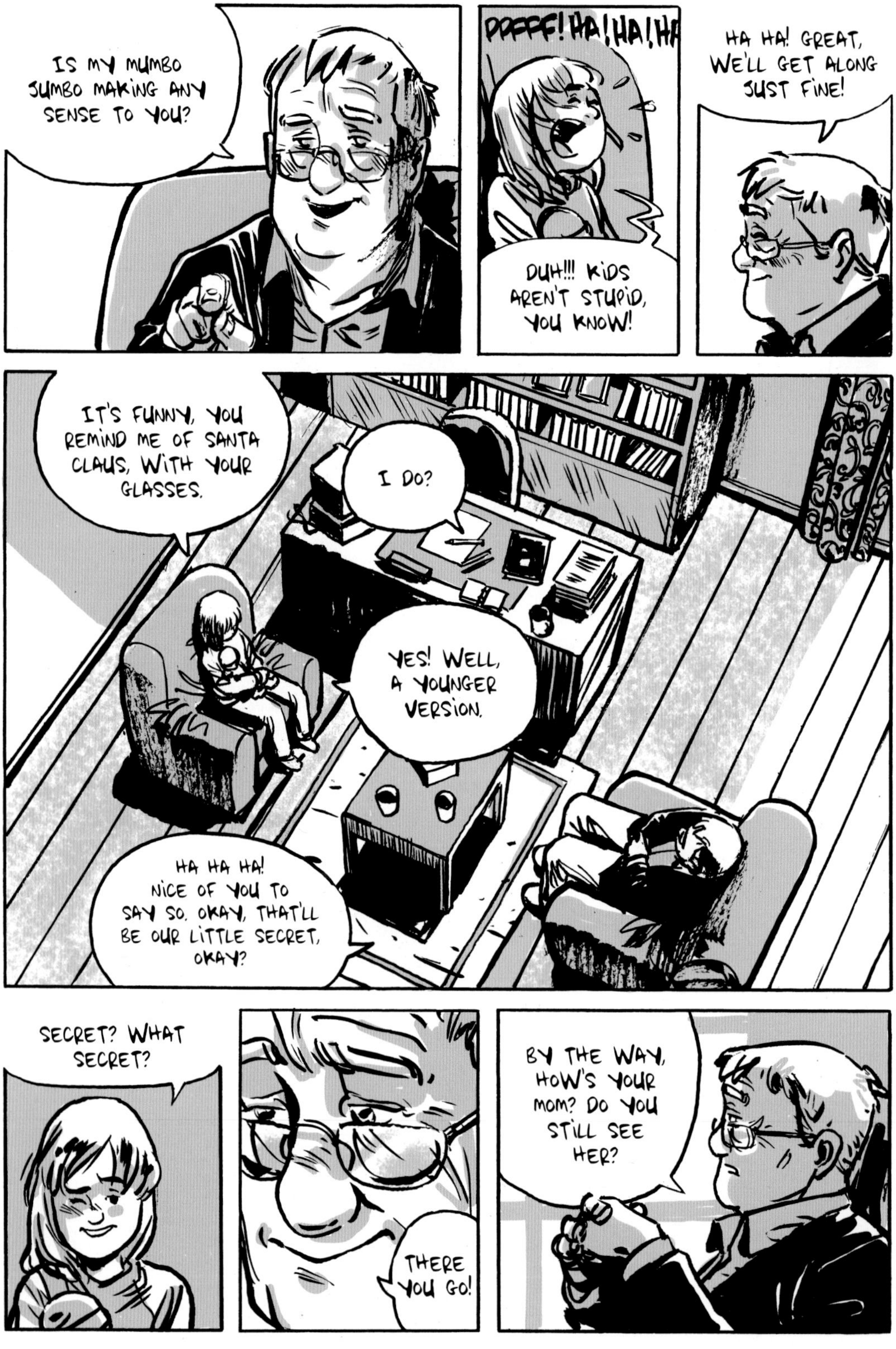
IS MY MUMBO JUMBO MAKING ANY SENSE TO YOU?
PRFFF! HA! HA! HA
DUH!!! KIDS AREN'T STUPID, YOU KNOW!
HA HA! GREAT, WE'LL GET ALONG JUST FINE!
IT'S FUNNY, YOU REMIND ME OF SANTA CLAUS, WITH YOUR GLASSES.
I DO?
YES! WELL, A YOUNGER VERSION.
HA HA HA! NICE OF YOU TO SAY SO. OKAY, THAT'LL BE OUR LITTLE SECRET, OKAY?
SECRET? WHAT SECRET?
THERE YOU GO!
BY THE WAY, HOW'S YOUR MOM? DO YOU STILL SEE HER?

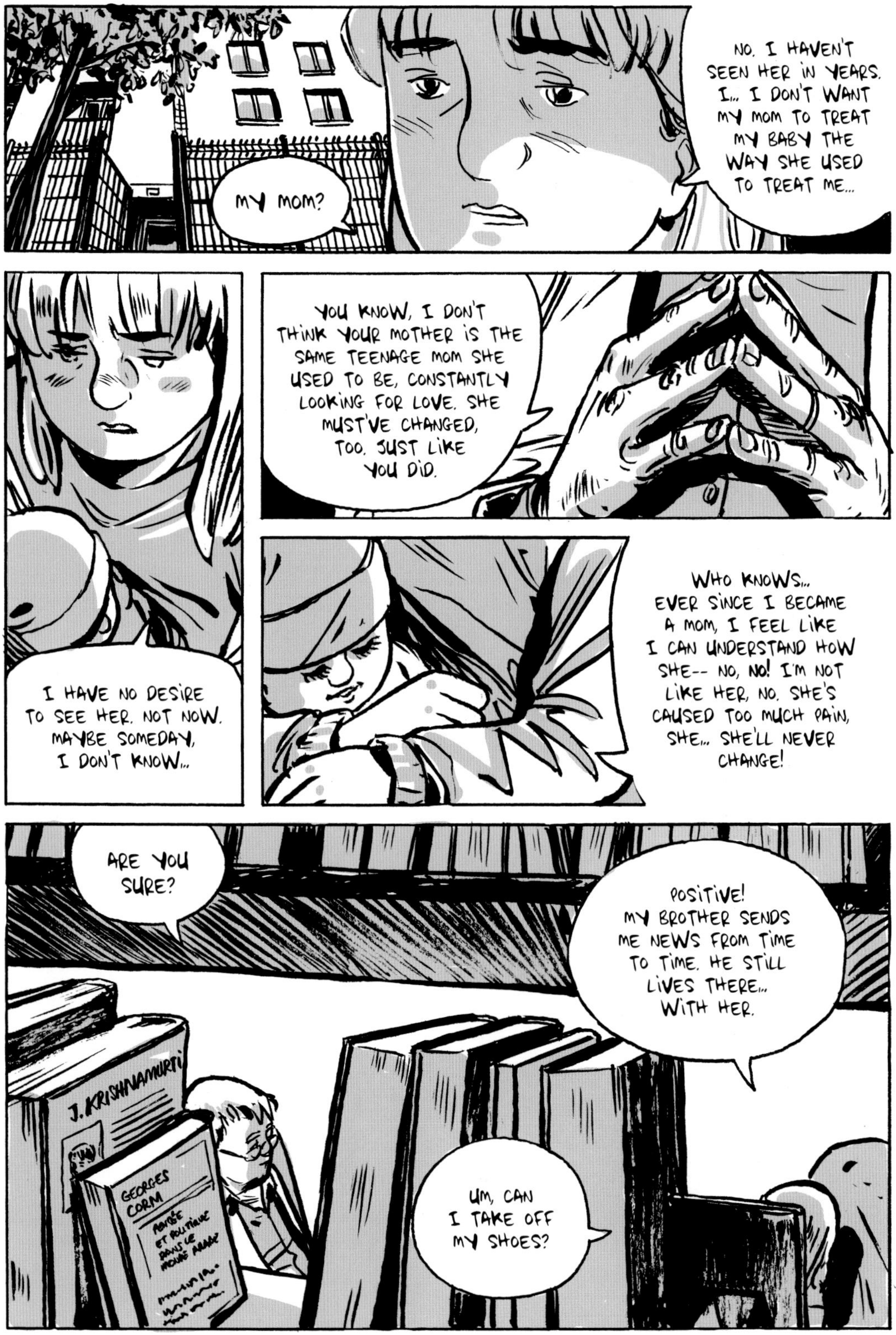
MY MOM?
NO. I HAVEN'T SEEN HER IN YEARS. I... I DON'T WANT MY MOM TO TREAT MY BABY THE WAY SHE USED TO TREAT ME...
YOU KNOW, I DON'T THINK YOUR MOTHER IS THE SAME TEENAGE MOM SHE USED TO BE, CONSTANTLY LOOKING FOR LOVE. SHE MUST'VE CHANGED, TOO. JUST LIKE YOU DID.
I HAVE NO DESIRE TO SEE HER. NOT NOW. MAYBE SOMEDAY, I DON'T KNOW...
WHO KNOWS... EVER SINCE I BECAME A MOM, I FEEL LIKE I CAN UNDERSTAND HOW SHE-- NO, NO! I'M NOT LIKE HER, NO. SHE'S CAUSED TOO MUCH PAIN, SHE... SHE'LL NEVER CHANGE!
ARE YOU SURE?
POSITIVE! MY BROTHER SENDS ME NEWS FROM TIME TO TIME. HE STILL LIVES THERE... WITH HER.
J. KRISHNAMURTI
GEORGES CORM
UM, CAN I TAKE OFF MY SHOES?

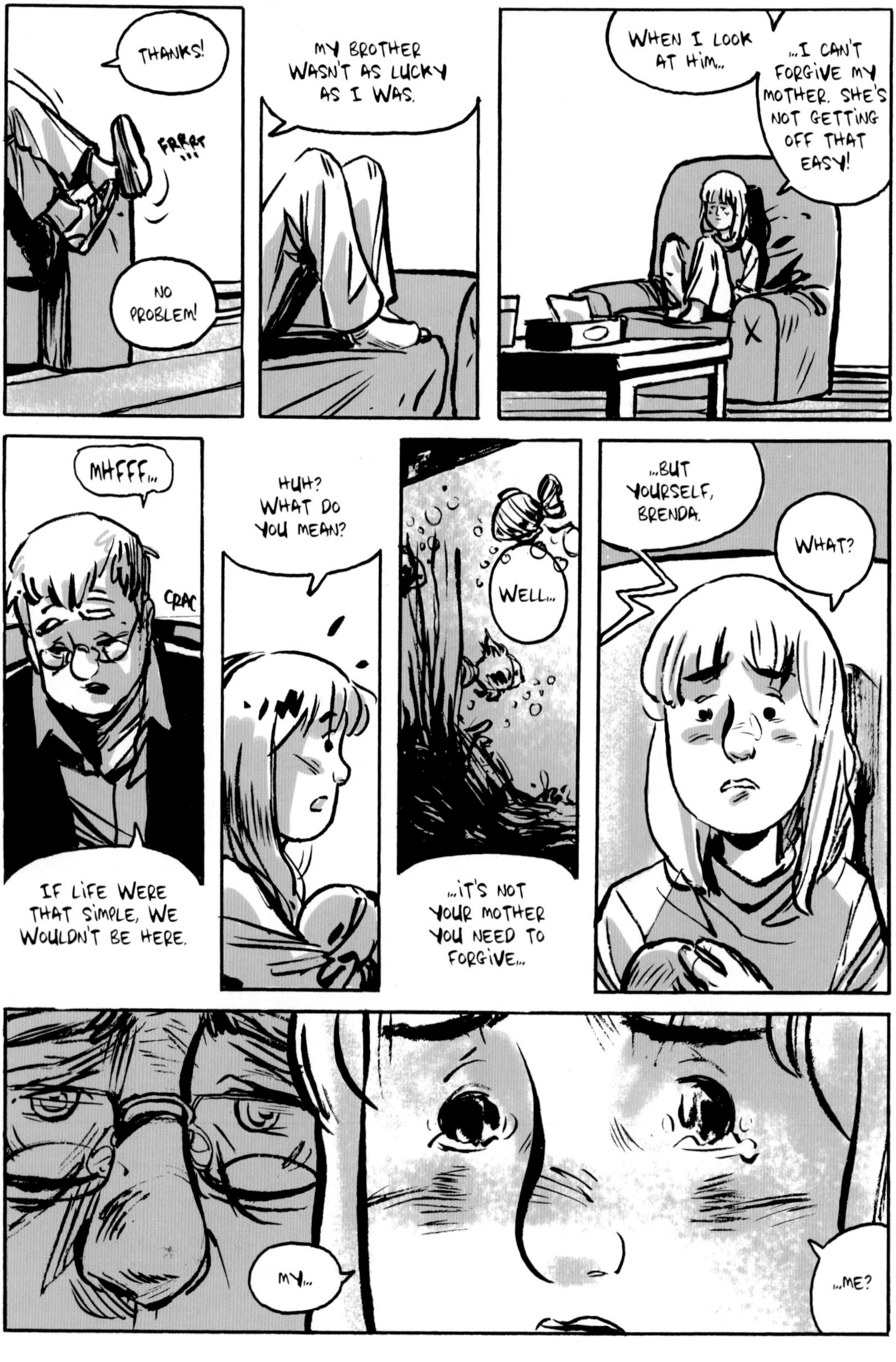
THANKS!
FRRRT
NO PROBLEM!
MY BROTHER WASN'T AS LUCKY AS I WAS.
WHEN I LOOK AT HIM...
...I CAN'T FORGIVE MY MOTHER. SHE'S NOT GETTING OFF THAT EASY!
MHFFF...
CRAC
IF LIFE WERE THAT SIMPLE, WE WOULDN'T BE HERE.
HUH? WHAT DO YOU MEAN?
WELL...
...IT'S NOT YOUR MOTHER YOU NEED TO FORGIVE...
...BUT YOURSELF, BRENDA.
WHAT?
MY...
...ME?

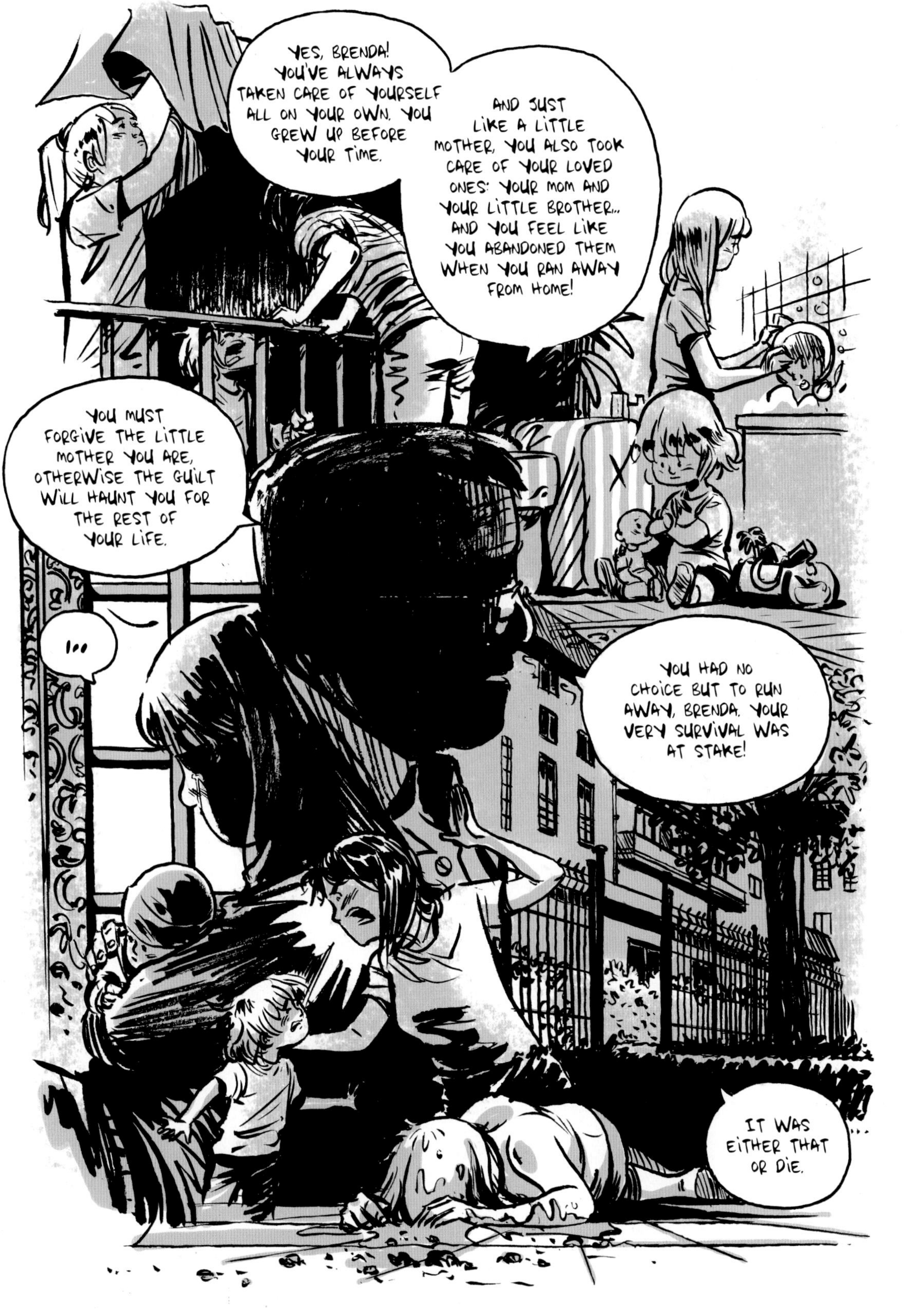
YES, BRENDA! YOU'VE ALWAYS TAKEN CARE OF YOURSELF ALL ON YOUR OWN. YOU GREW UP BEFORE YOUR TIME.
AND JUST LIKE A LITTLE MOTHER, YOU ALSO TOOK CARE OF YOUR LOVED ONES: YOUR MOM AND YOUR LITTLE BROTHER... AND YOU FEEL LIKE YOU ABANDONED THEM WHEN YOU RAN AWAY FROM HOME!
YOU MUST FORGIVE THE LITTLE MOTHER YOU ARE, OTHERWISE THE GUILT WILL HAUNT YOU FOR THE REST OF YOUR LIFE.
...
YOU HAD NO CHOICE BUT TO RUN AWAY, BRENDA. YOUR VERY SURVIVAL WAS AT STAKE!
IT WAS EITHER THAT OR DIE.

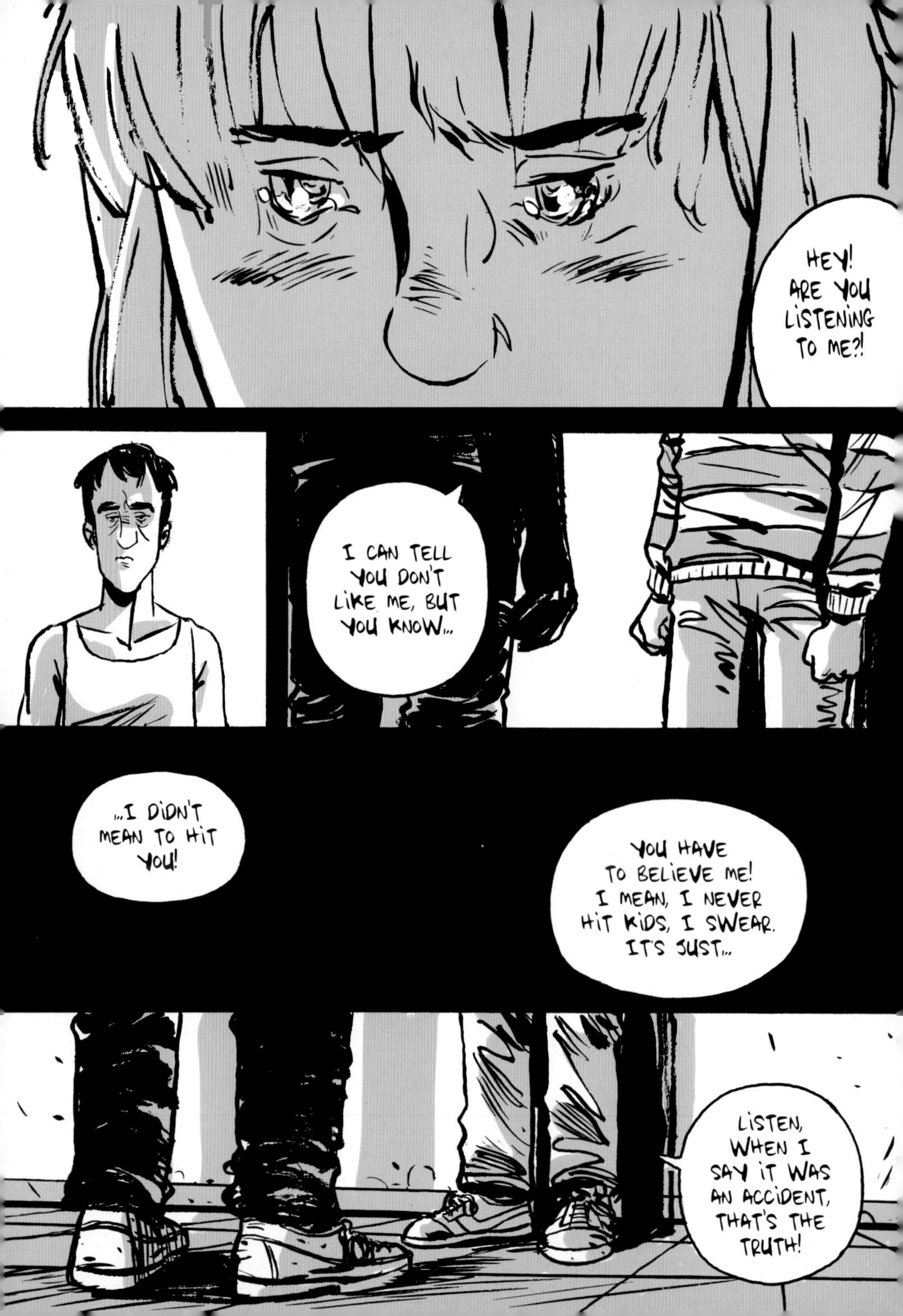
HEY! ARE YOU LISTENING TO ME?!
I CAN TELL YOU DON'T LIKE ME, BUT YOU KNOW...
...I DIDN'T MEAN TO HIT YOU!
YOU HAVE TO BELIEVE ME! I MEAN, I NEVER HIT KIDS, I SWEAR. IT'S JUST...
LISTEN, WHEN I SAY IT WAS AN ACCIDENT, THAT'S THE TRUTH!

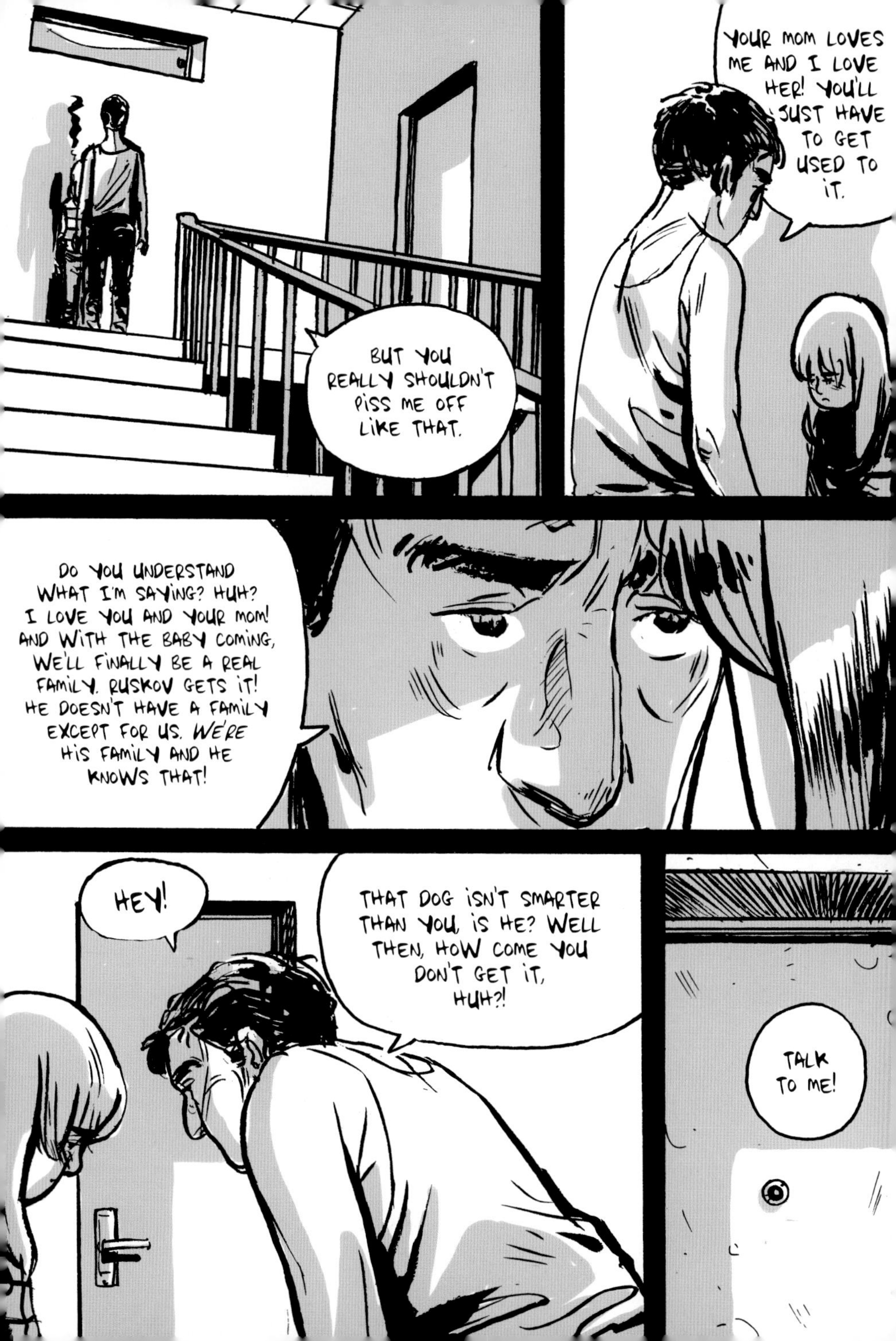
BUT YOU REALLY SHOULDN'T PISS ME OFF LIKE THAT.
YOUR MOM LOVES ME AND I LOVE HER! YOU'LL JUST HAVE TO GET USED TO IT.
DO YOU UNDERSTAND WHAT I'M SAYING? HUH? I LOVE YOU AND YOUR MOM! AND WITH THE BABY COMING, WE'LL FINALLY BE A REAL FAMILY. RUSKOV GETS IT! HE DOESN'T HAVE A FAMILY EXCEPT FOR US. *WE'RE* HIS FAMILY AND HE KNOWS THAT!
HEY!
THAT DOG ISN'T SMARTER THAN YOU, IS HE? WELL THEN, HOW COME YOU DON'T GET IT, HUH?!
TALK TO ME!

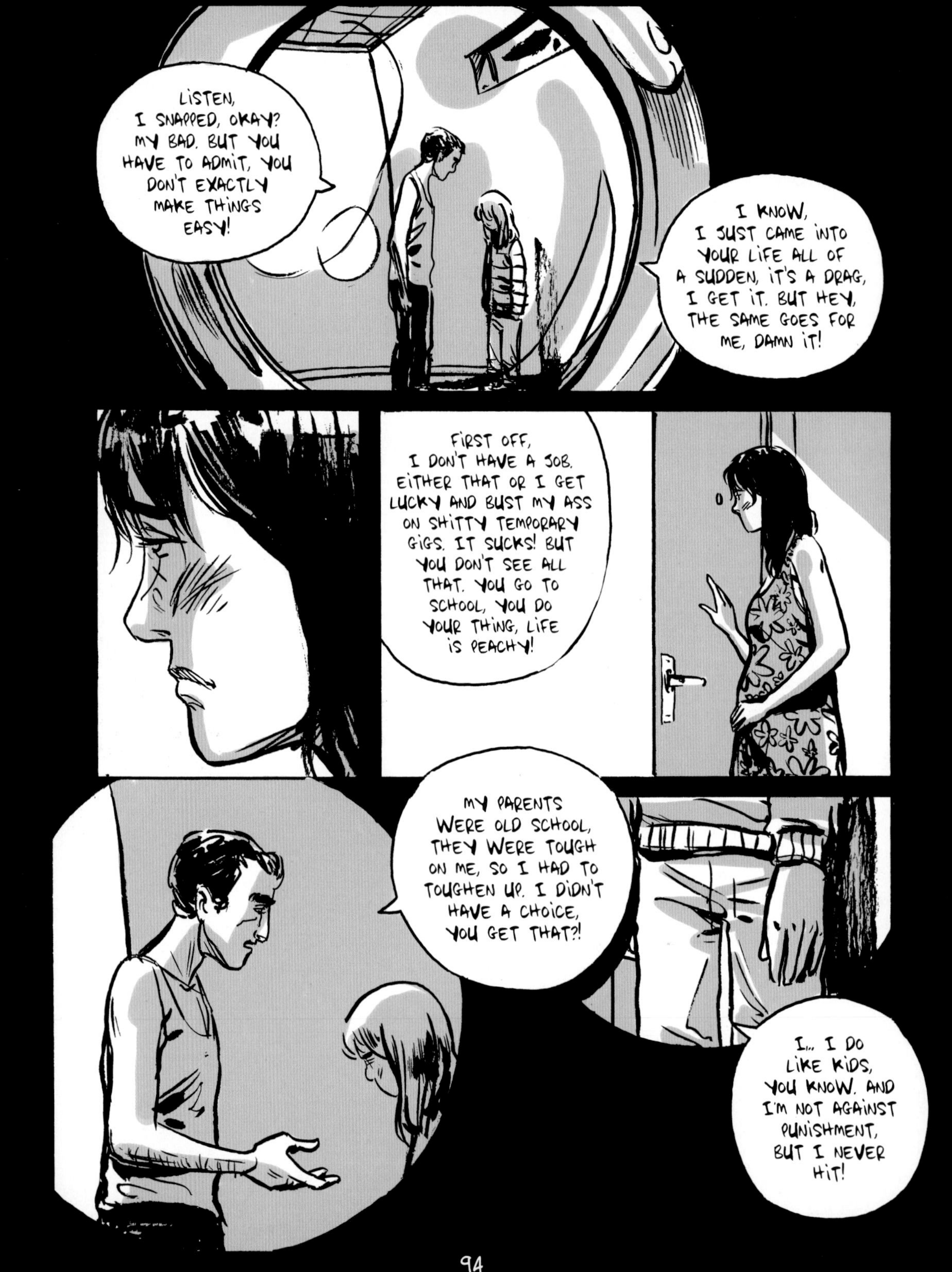
LISTEN, I SNAPPED, OKAY? MY BAD. BUT YOU HAVE TO ADMIT, YOU DON'T EXACTLY MAKE THINGS EASY!
I KNOW, I JUST CAME INTO YOUR LIFE ALL OF A SUDDEN, IT'S A DRAG, I GET IT. BUT HEY, THE SAME GOES FOR ME, DAMN IT!
FIRST OFF, I DON'T HAVE A JOB. EITHER THAT OR I GET LUCKY AND BUST MY ASS ON SHITTY TEMPORARY GIGS. IT SUCKS! BUT YOU DON'T SEE ALL THAT. YOU GO TO SCHOOL, YOU DO YOUR THING, LIFE IS PEACHY!
MY PARENTS WERE OLD SCHOOL, THEY WERE TOUGH ON ME, SO I HAD TO TOUGHEN UP. I DIDN'T HAVE A CHOICE, YOU GET THAT?!
I... I DO LIKE KIDS, YOU KNOW. AND I'M NOT AGAINST PUNISHMENT, BUT I NEVER HIT!

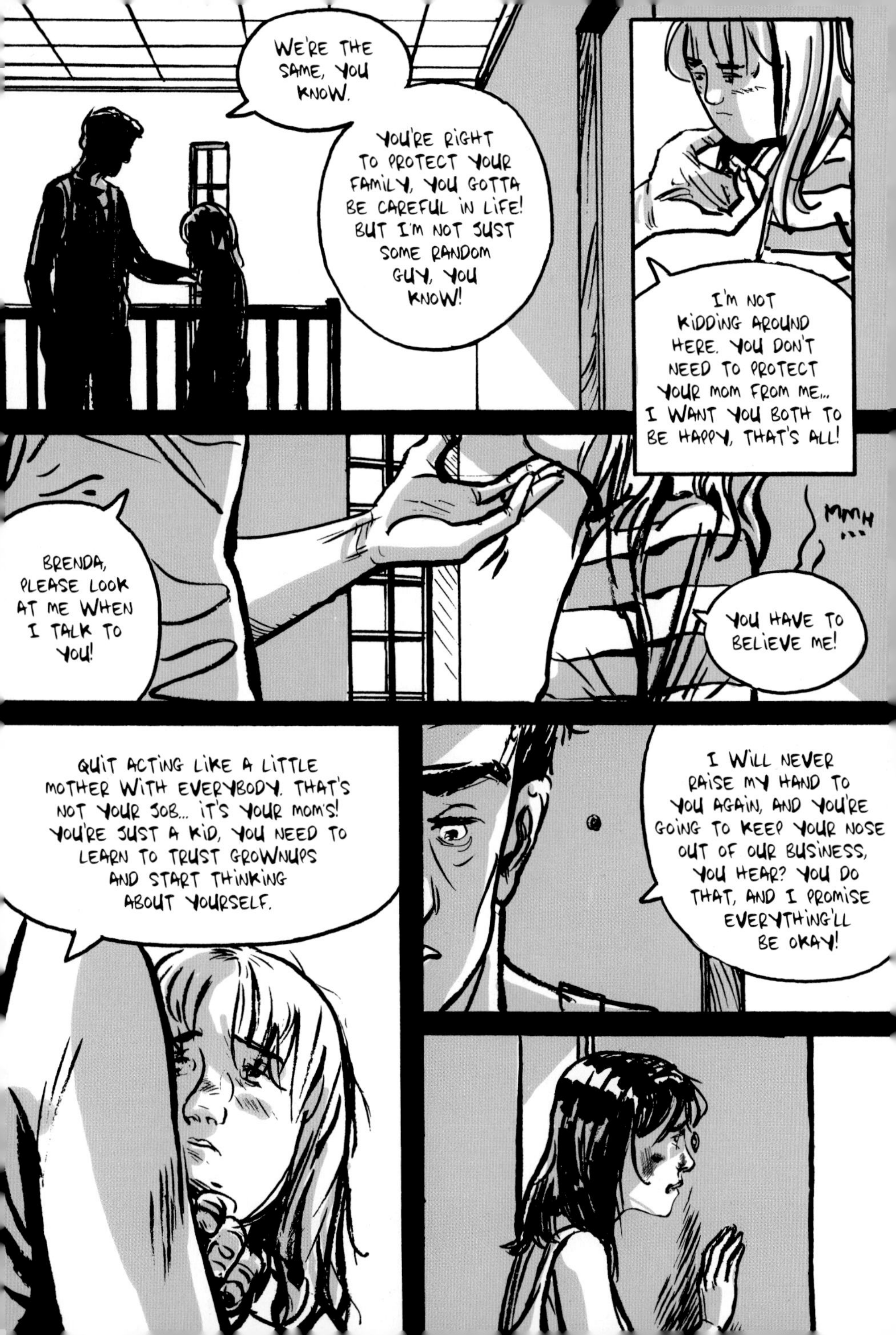
WE'RE THE SAME, YOU KNOW.
YOU'RE RIGHT TO PROTECT YOUR FAMILY, YOU GOTTA BE CAREFUL IN LIFE! BUT I'M NOT JUST SOME RANDOM GUY, YOU KNOW!
I'M NOT KIDDING AROUND HERE. YOU DON'T NEED TO PROTECT YOUR MOM FROM ME... I WANT YOU BOTH TO BE HAPPY, THAT'S ALL!
BRENDA, PLEASE LOOK AT ME WHEN I TALK TO YOU!
MMH...
YOU HAVE TO BELIEVE ME!
QUIT ACTING LIKE A LITTLE MOTHER WITH EVERYBODY. THAT'S NOT YOUR JOB... IT'S YOUR MOM'S! YOU'RE JUST A KID, YOU NEED TO LEARN TO TRUST GROWNUPS AND START THINKING ABOUT YOURSELF.
I WILL NEVER RAISE MY HAND TO YOU AGAIN, AND YOU'RE GOING TO KEEP YOUR NOSE OUT OF OUR BUSINESS, YOU HEAR? YOU DO THAT, AND I PROMISE EVERYTHING'LL BE OKAY!

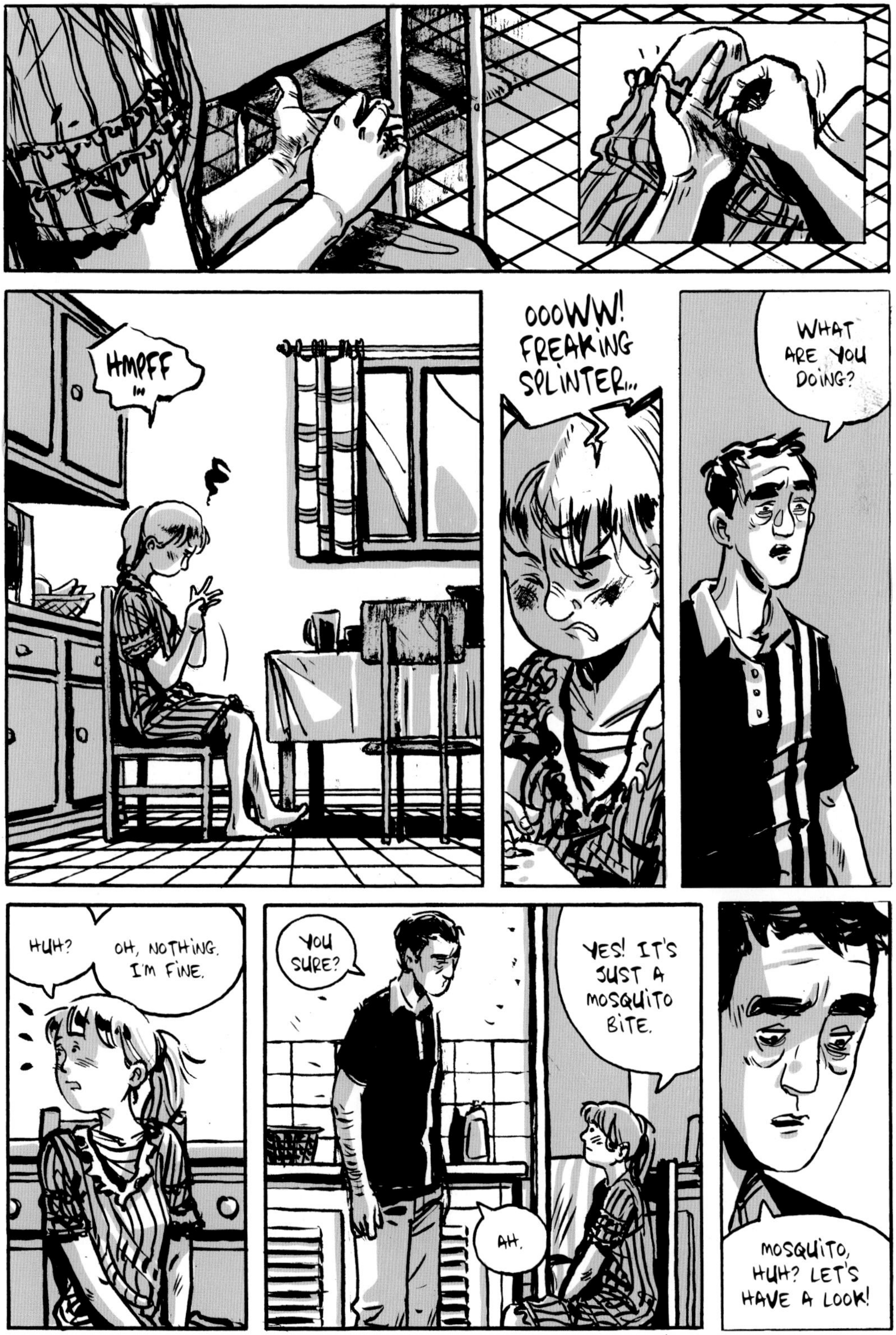
HMPFF ...
OOOWW! FREAKING SPLINTER...
WHAT ARE YOU DOING?
HUH?
OH, NOTHING. I'M FINE.
YOU SURE?
YES! IT'S JUST A MOSQUITO BITE.
AH.
MOSQUITO, HUH? LET'S HAVE A LOOK!

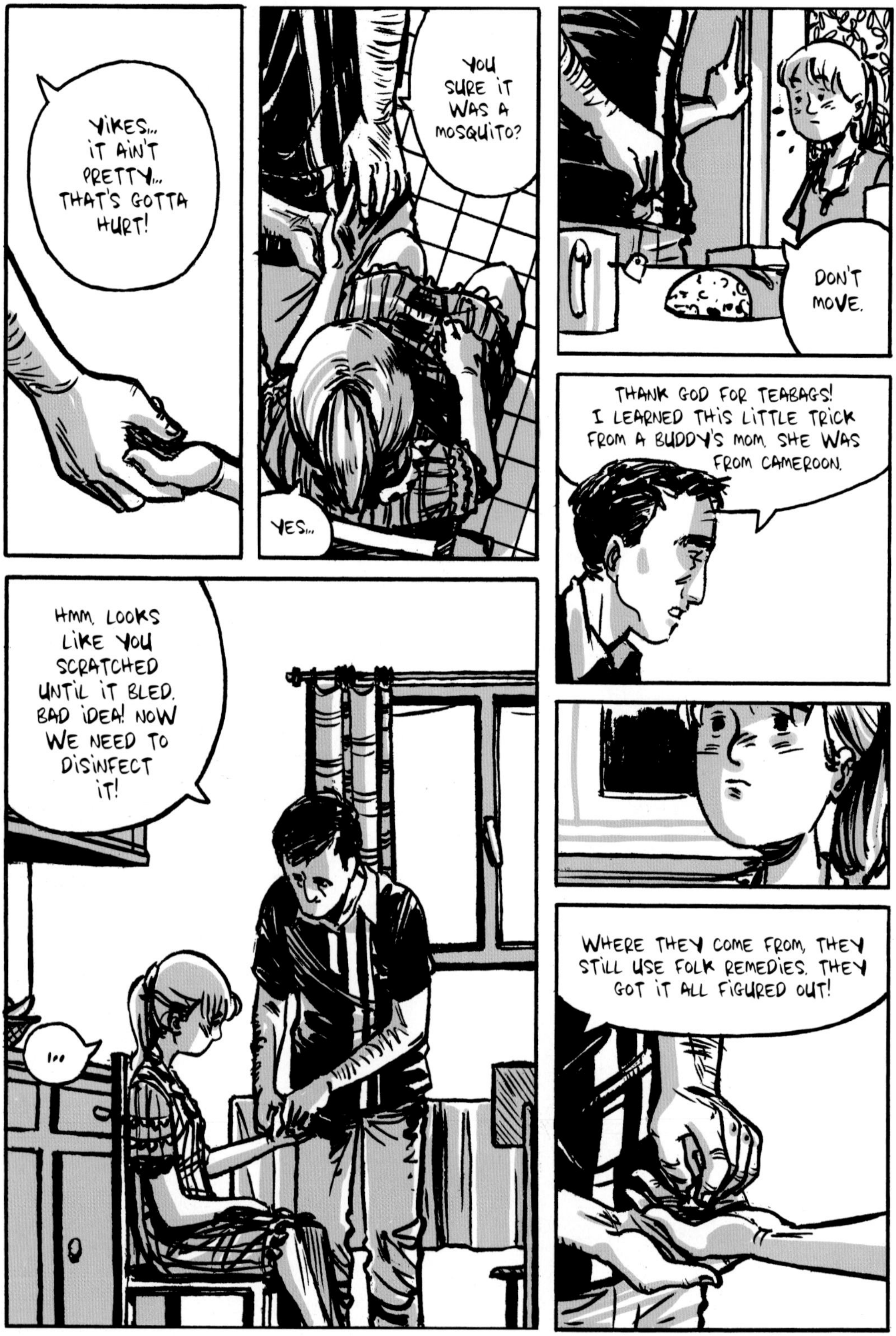

YIKES... IT AIN'T PRETTY... THAT'S GOTTA HURT!
YOU SURE IT WAS A MOSQUITO?
YES...
DON'T MOVE.
THANK GOD FOR TEABAGS! I LEARNED THIS LITTLE TRICK FROM A BUDDY'S MOM. SHE WAS FROM CAMEROON.
HMM. LOOKS LIKE YOU SCRATCHED UNTIL IT BLED. BAD IDEA! NOW WE NEED TO DISINFECT IT!
...
WHERE THEY COME FROM, THEY STILL USE FOLK REMEDIES. THEY GOT IT ALL FIGURED OUT!

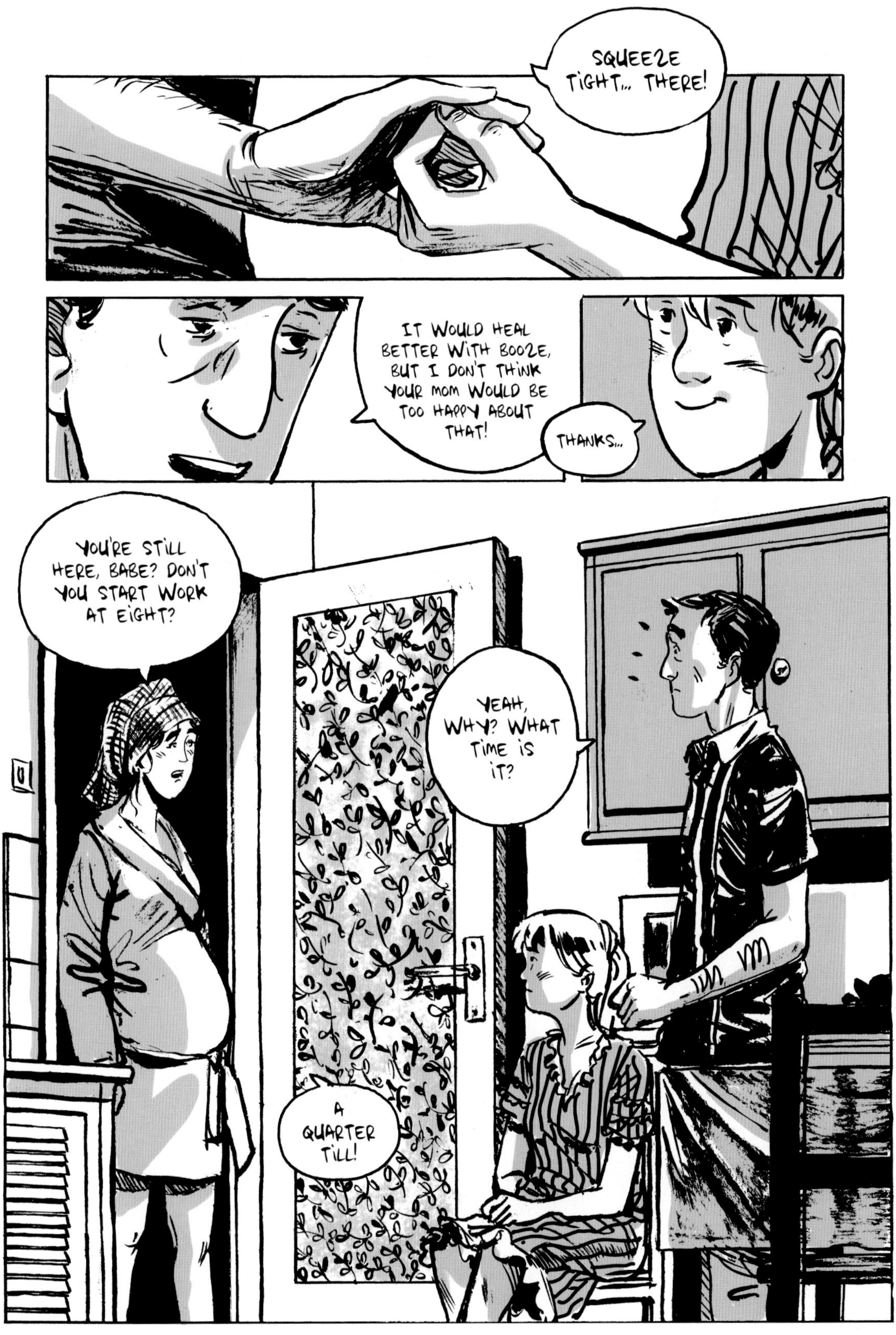
SQUEEZE TIGHT... THERE!
IT WOULD HEAL BETTER WITH BOOZE, BUT I DON'T THINK YOUR MOM WOULD BE TOO HAPPY ABOUT THAT!
THANKS...
YOU'RE STILL HERE, BABE? DON'T YOU START WORK AT EIGHT?
YEAH, WHY? WHAT TIME IS IT?
A QUARTER TILL!

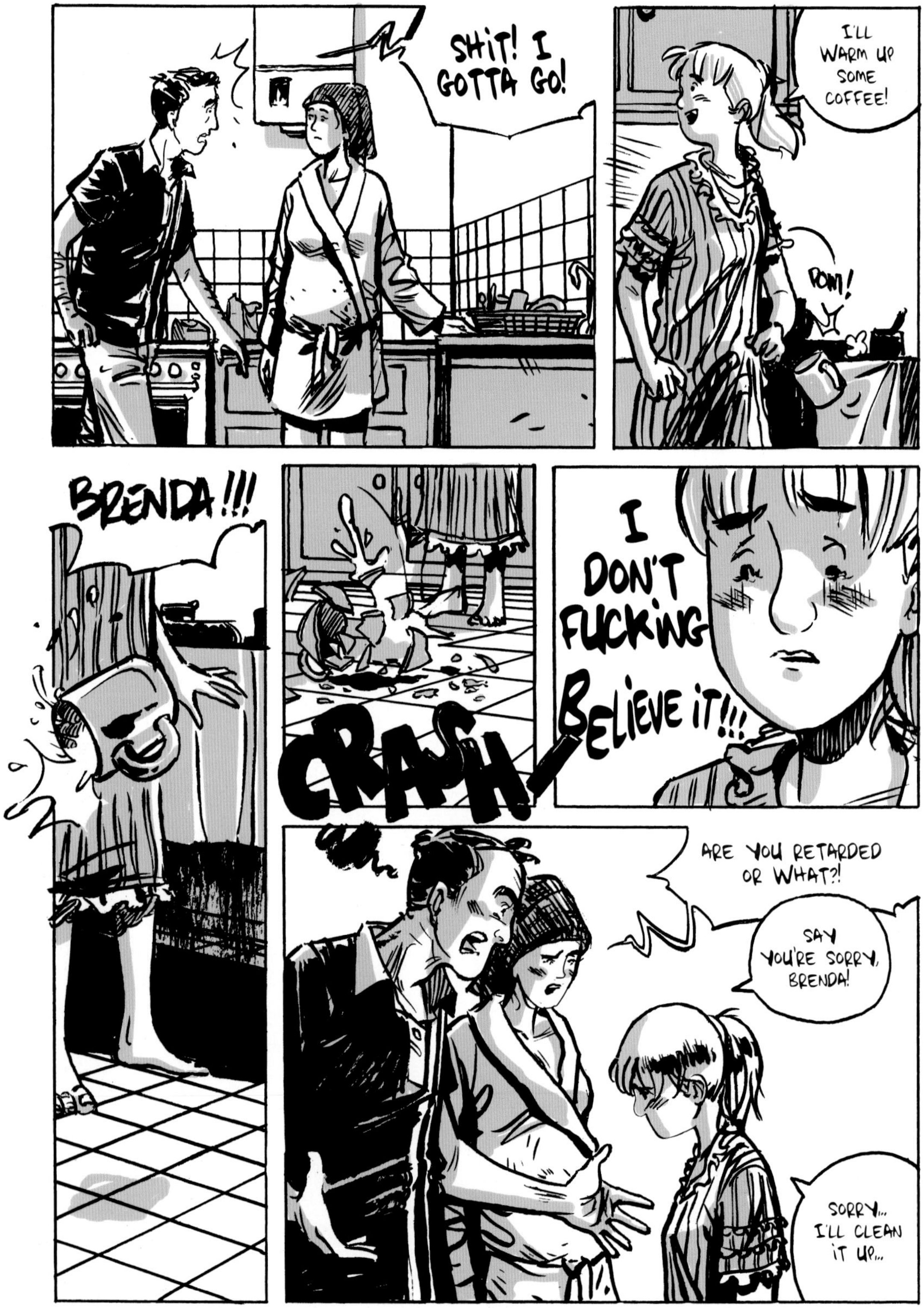
SHIT! I GOTTA GO!
I'LL WARM UP SOME COFFEE!
POW!
BRENDA!!!
CRASH!
I DON'T FUCKING BELIEVE IT!!!
ARE YOU RETARDED OR WHAT?!
SAY YOU'RE SORRY, BRENDA!
SORRY... I'LL CLEAN IT UP...

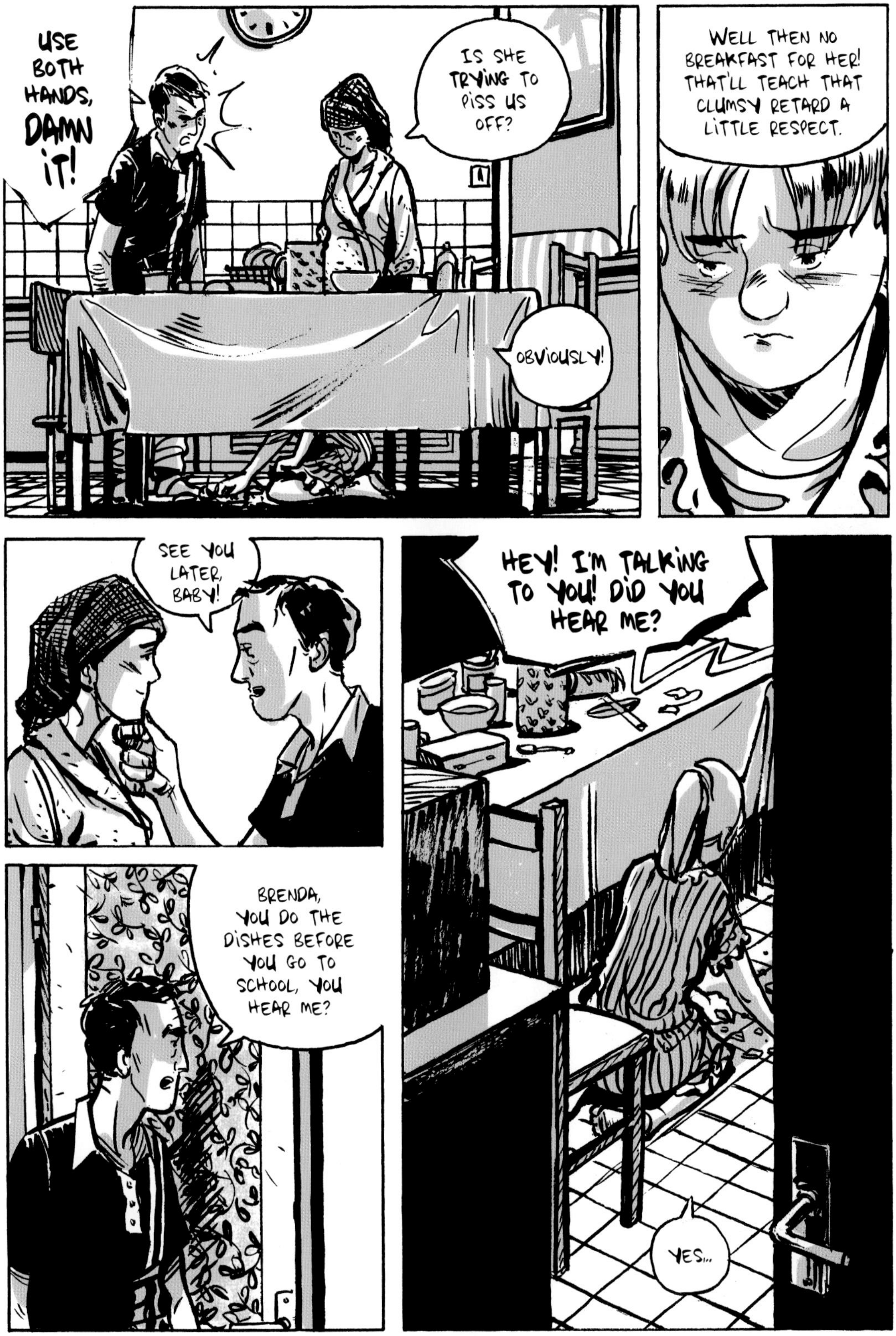
USE BOTH HANDS, DAMN IT!
IS SHE TRYING TO PISS US OFF?
OBVIOUSLY!
WELL THEN NO BREAKFAST FOR HER! THAT'LL TEACH THAT CLUMSY RETARD A LITTLE RESPECT.
SEE YOU LATER, BABY!
BRENDA, YOU DO THE DISHES BEFORE YOU GO TO SCHOOL, YOU HEAR ME?
HEY! I'M TALKING TO YOU! DID YOU HEAR ME?
YES...

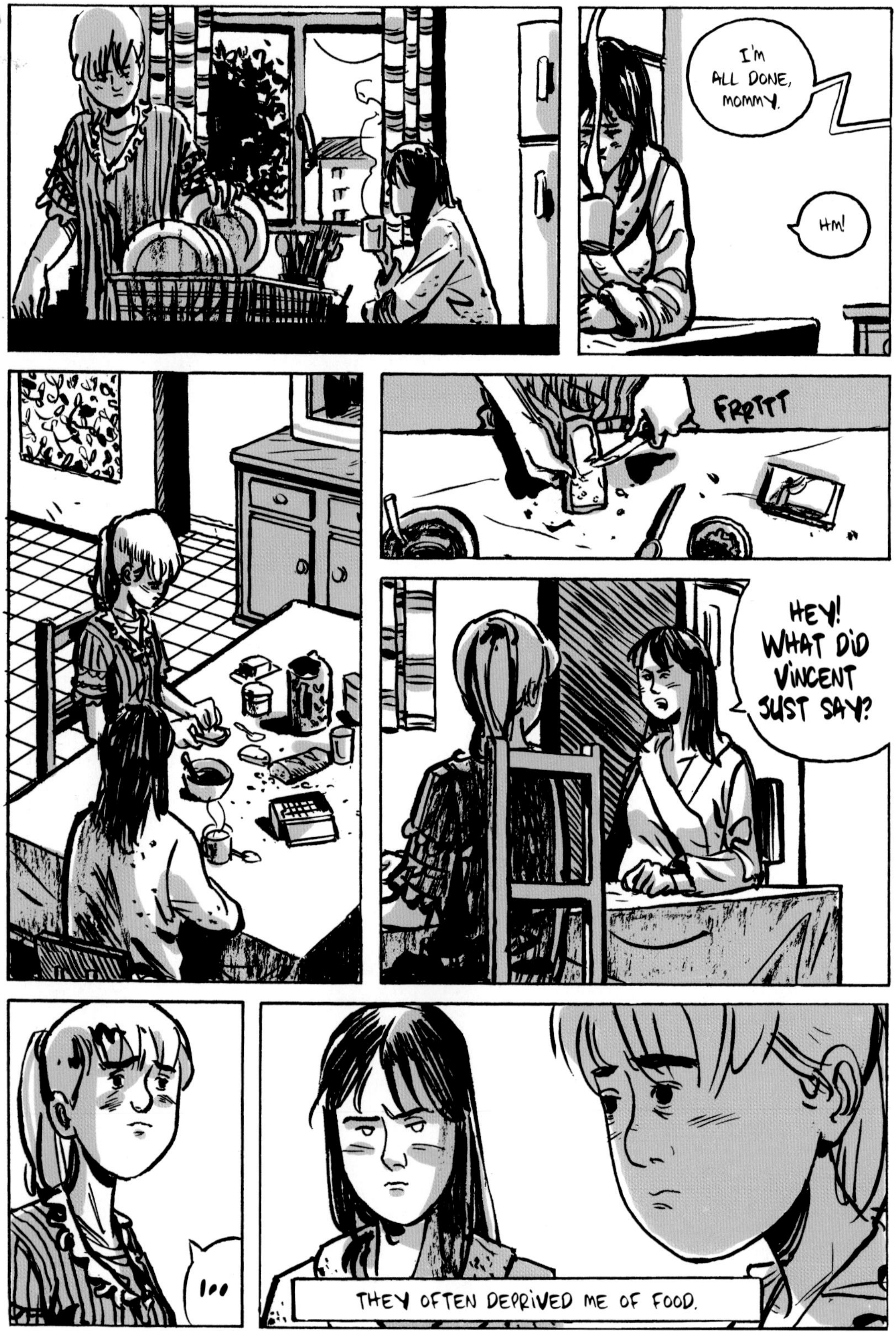
I'M ALL DONE, MOMMY.
HM!
FRTTT
HEY! WHAT DID VINCENT JUST SAY?
...
THEY OFTEN DEPRIVED ME OF FOOD.

SO I USED TO STEAL IT.

SOMETIMES I WAS SO HUNGRY, I COULDN'T SLEEP AT NIGHT.

SO I'D GET UP TO GO GET FOOD.

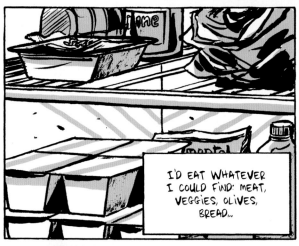

I'D EAT WHATEVER I COULD FIND: MEAT, VEGGIES, OLIVES, BREAD...

I AVOIDED SWEET THINGS SO THEY WOULDN'T SUSPECT ME.

BRENDA!

I WAS SO AFRAID OF GETTING CAUGHT, IT GAVE ME TERRIBLE STOMACH CRAMPS.

BRENDA!

I ASKED YOU A QUESTION, DAMN IT! NOW GIVE ME THAT PIECE OF TOAST AND GET OUT OF MY SIGHT!

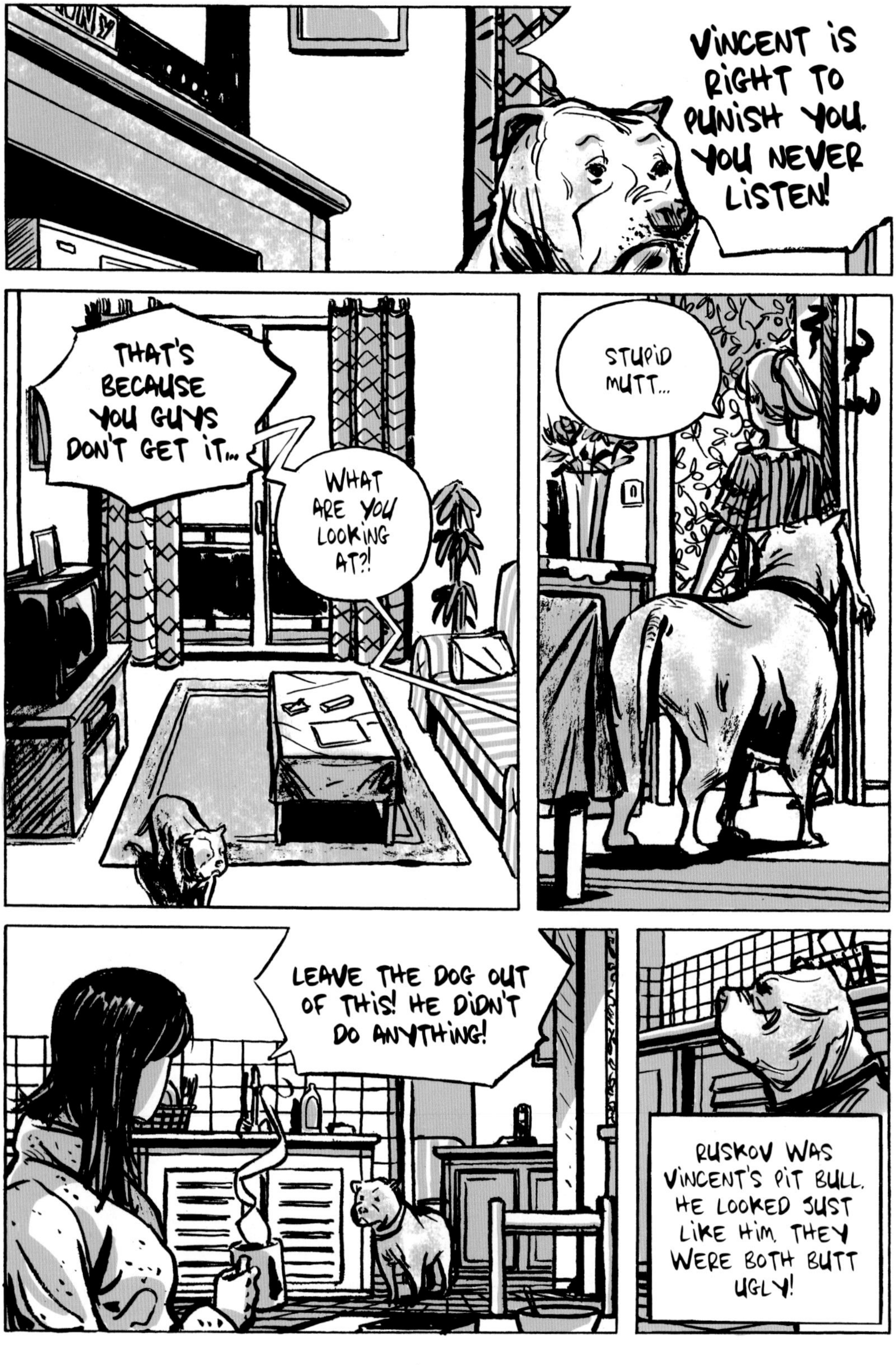
VINCENT IS RIGHT TO PUNISH YOU. YOU NEVER LISTEN!
THAT'S BECAUSE YOU GUYS DON'T GET IT...
WHAT ARE YOU LOOKING AT?!
STUPID MUTT...
LEAVE THE DOG OUT OF THIS! HE DIDN'T DO ANYTHING!
RUSKOV WAS VINCENT'S PIT BULL. HE LOOKED JUST LIKE HIM. THEY WERE BOTH BUTT UGLY!

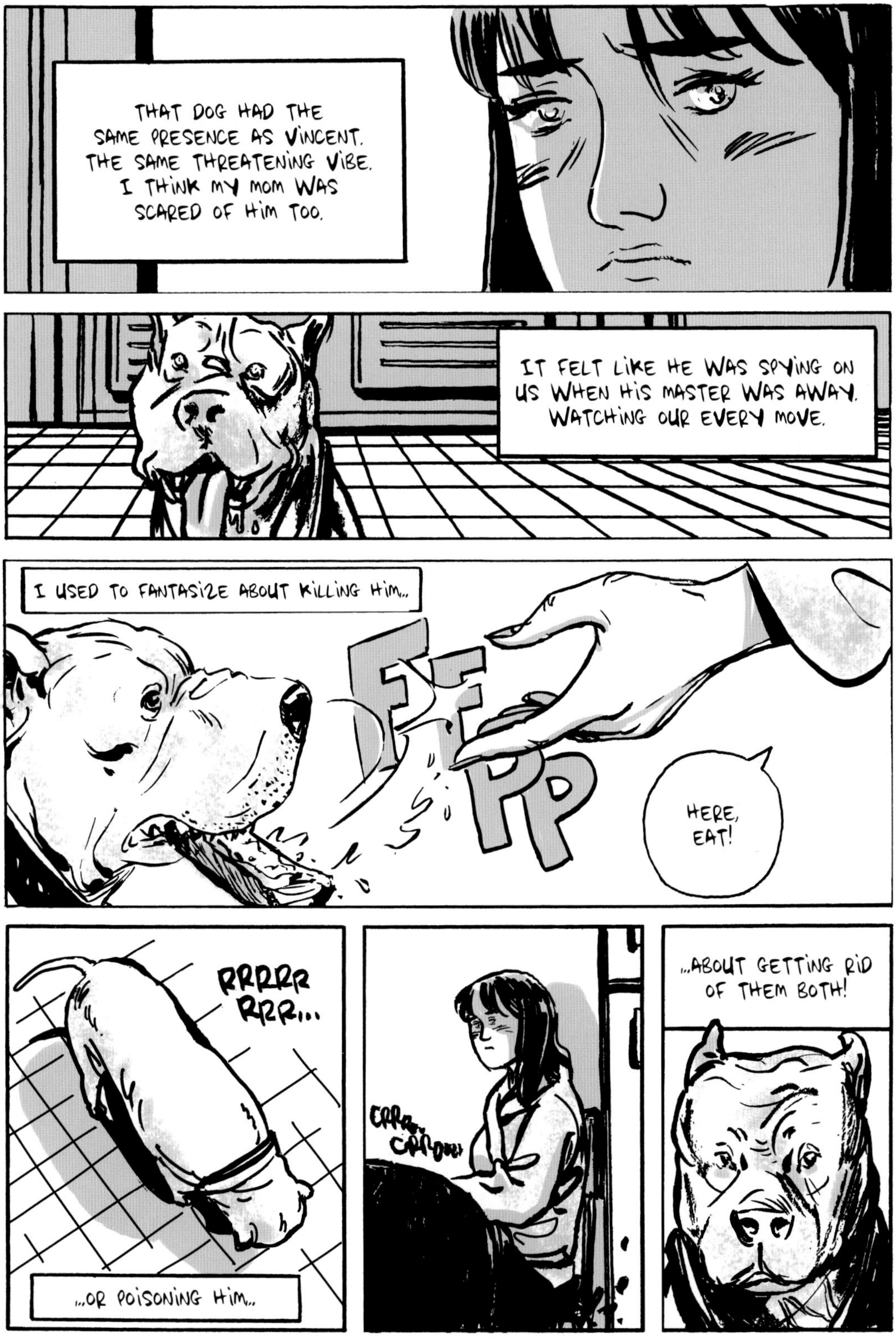
THAT DOG HAD THE SAME PRESENCE AS VINCENT. THE SAME THREATENING VIBE. I THINK MY MOM WAS SCARED OF HIM TOO.
IT FELT LIKE HE WAS SPYING ON US WHEN HIS MASTER WAS AWAY. WATCHING OUR EVERY MOVE.
I USED TO FANTASIZE ABOUT KILLING HIM...
HERE, EAT!
RRRRR RRR...
...OR POISONING HIM...
...ABOUT GETTING RID OF THEM BOTH!

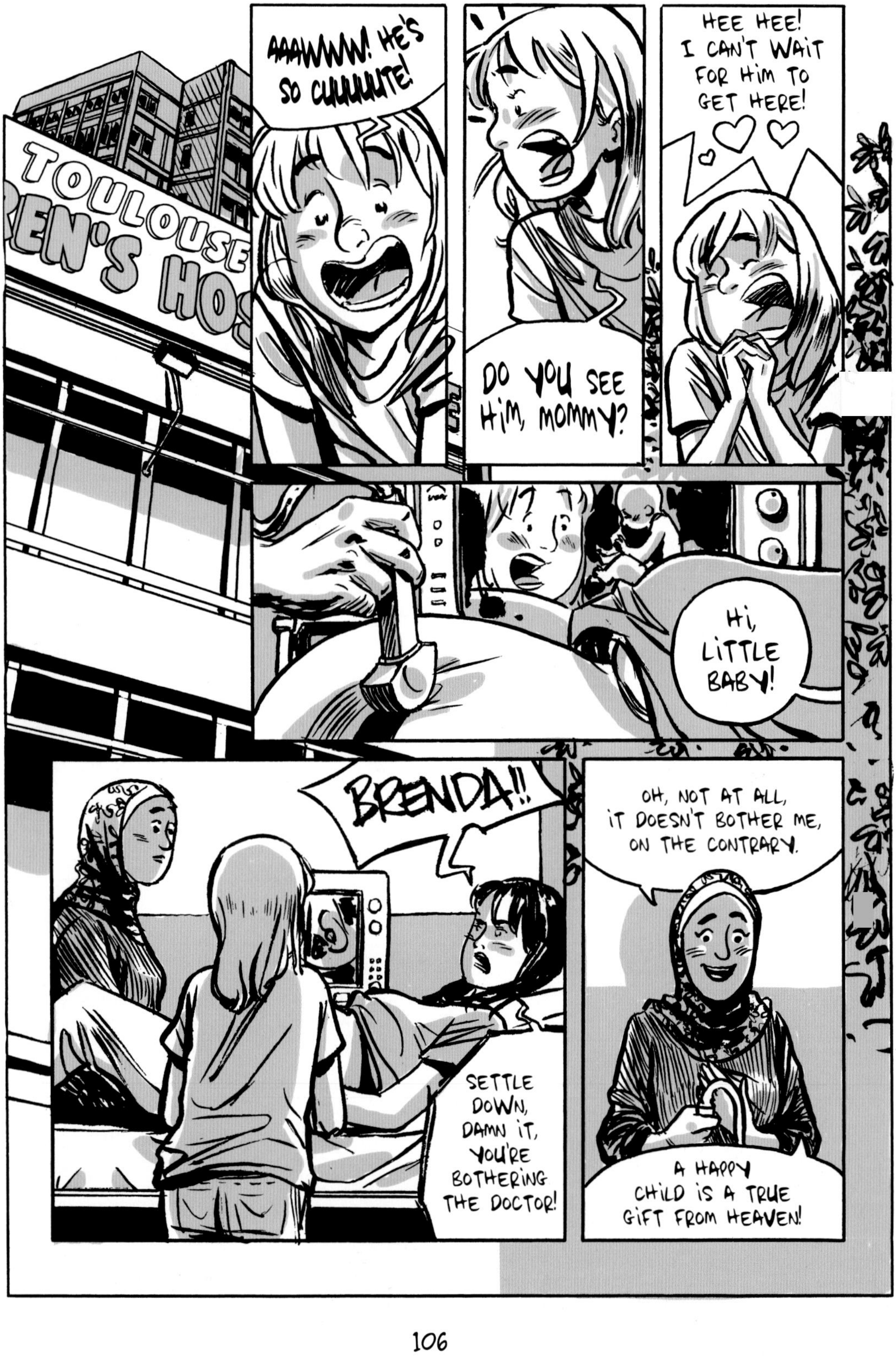

TOULOUSE
REN'S HOS
AAAWWW! HE'S SO CUUUUUTE!
DO YOU SEE HIM, MOMMY?
HEE HEE! I CAN'T WAIT FOR HIM TO GET HERE!
HI, LITTLE BABY!
BRENDA!!
SETTLE DOWN, DAMN IT, YOU'RE BOTHERING THE DOCTOR!
OH, NOT AT ALL, IT DOESN'T BOTHER ME, ON THE CONTRARY.
A HAPPY CHILD IS A TRUE GIFT FROM HEAVEN!

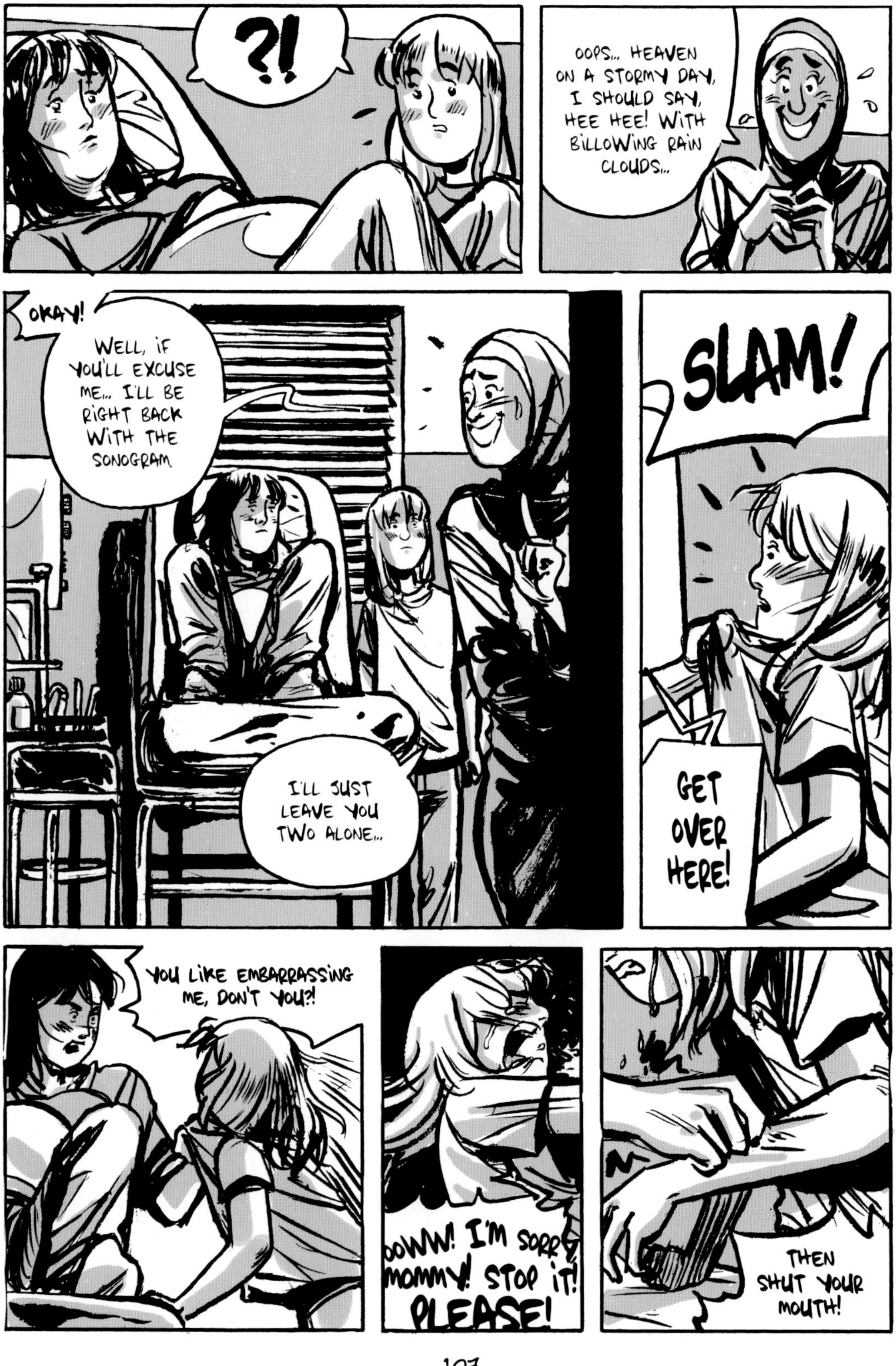
?!
OOPS... HEAVEN ON A STORMY DAY, I SHOULD SAY, HEE HEE! WITH BILLOWING RAIN CLOUDS...
OKAY!
WELL, IF YOU'LL EXCUSE ME... I'LL BE RIGHT BACK WITH THE SONOGRAM.
I'LL JUST LEAVE YOU TWO ALONE...
SLAM!
GET OVER HERE!
YOU LIKE EMBARRASSING ME, DON'T YOU?!
OWW! I'M SORRY MOMMY! STOP IT! PLEASE!
THEN SHUT YOUR MOUTH!

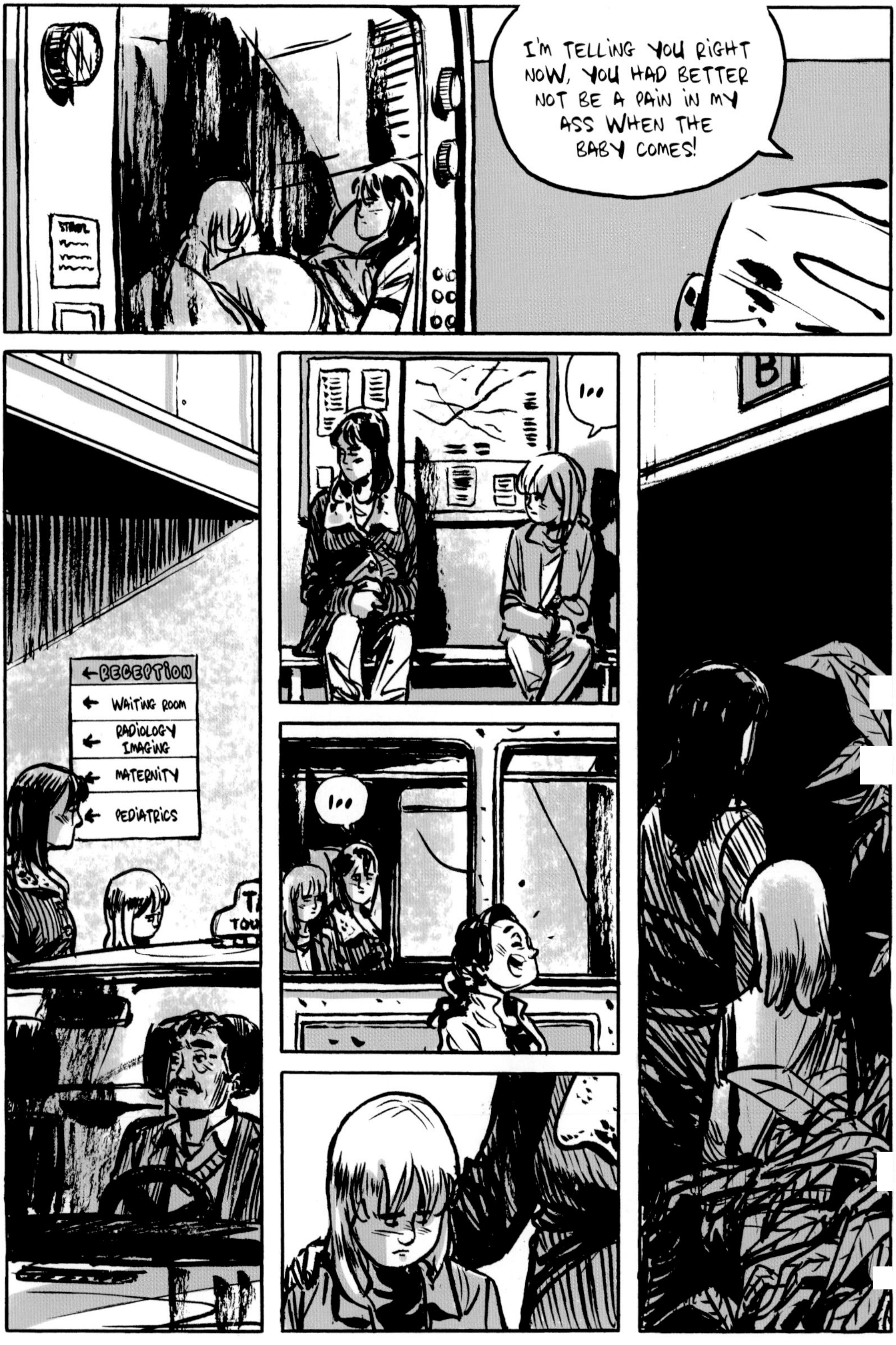
I'M TELLING YOU RIGHT NOW, YOU HAD BETTER NOT BE A PAIN IN MY ASS WHEN THE BABY COMES!
←RECEPTION
← WAITING ROOM
← RADIOLOGY IMAGING
← MATERNITY
← PEDIATRICS
...
...
B

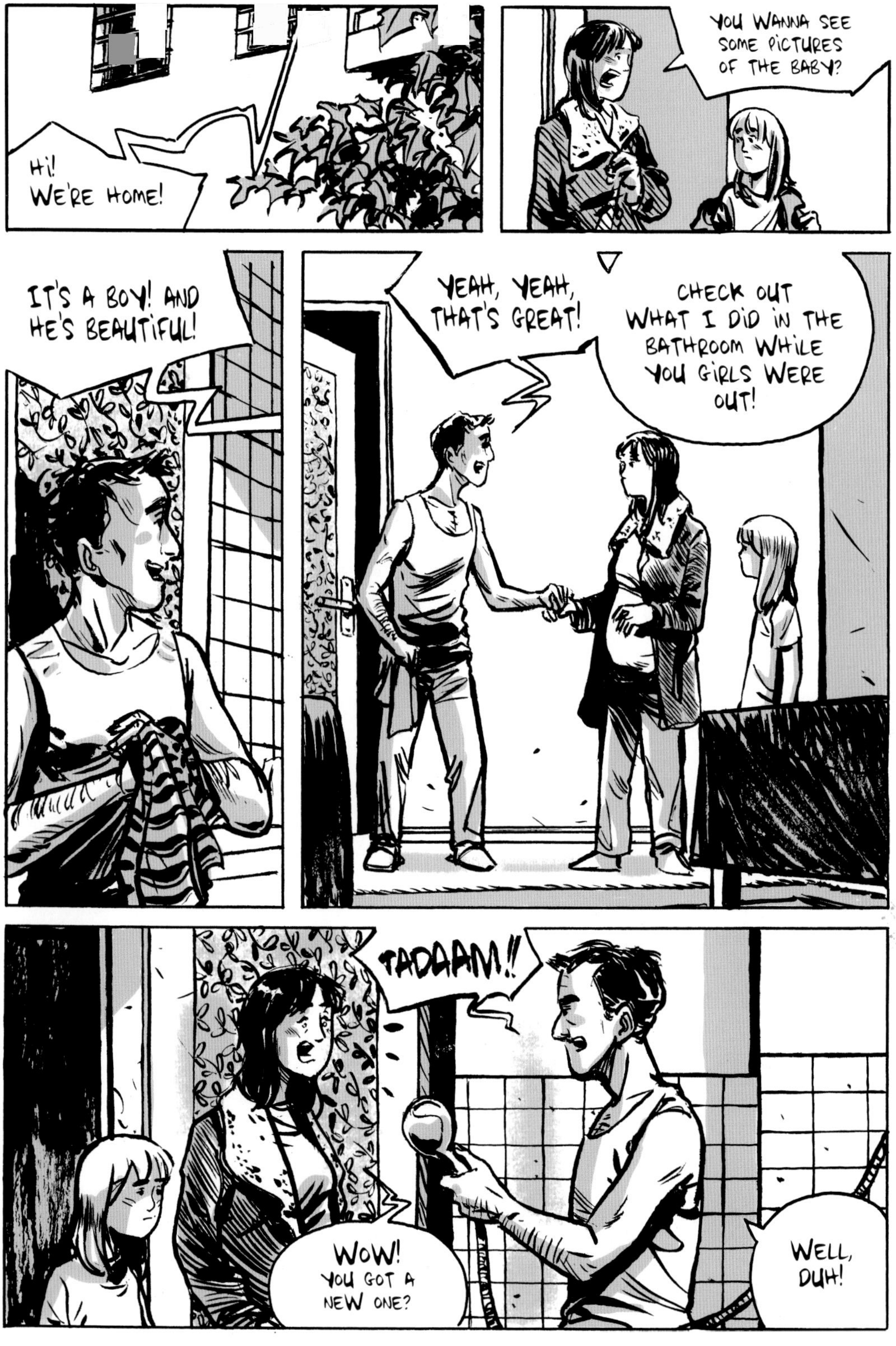
Hi!
WE'RE HOME!
YOU WANNA SEE SOME PICTURES OF THE BABY?
IT'S A BOY! AND HE'S BEAUTIFUL!
YEAH, YEAH, THAT'S GREAT!
CHECK OUT WHAT I DID IN THE BATHROOM WHILE YOU GIRLS WERE OUT!
TADAAM!!
WOW! YOU GOT A NEW ONE?
WELL, DUH!

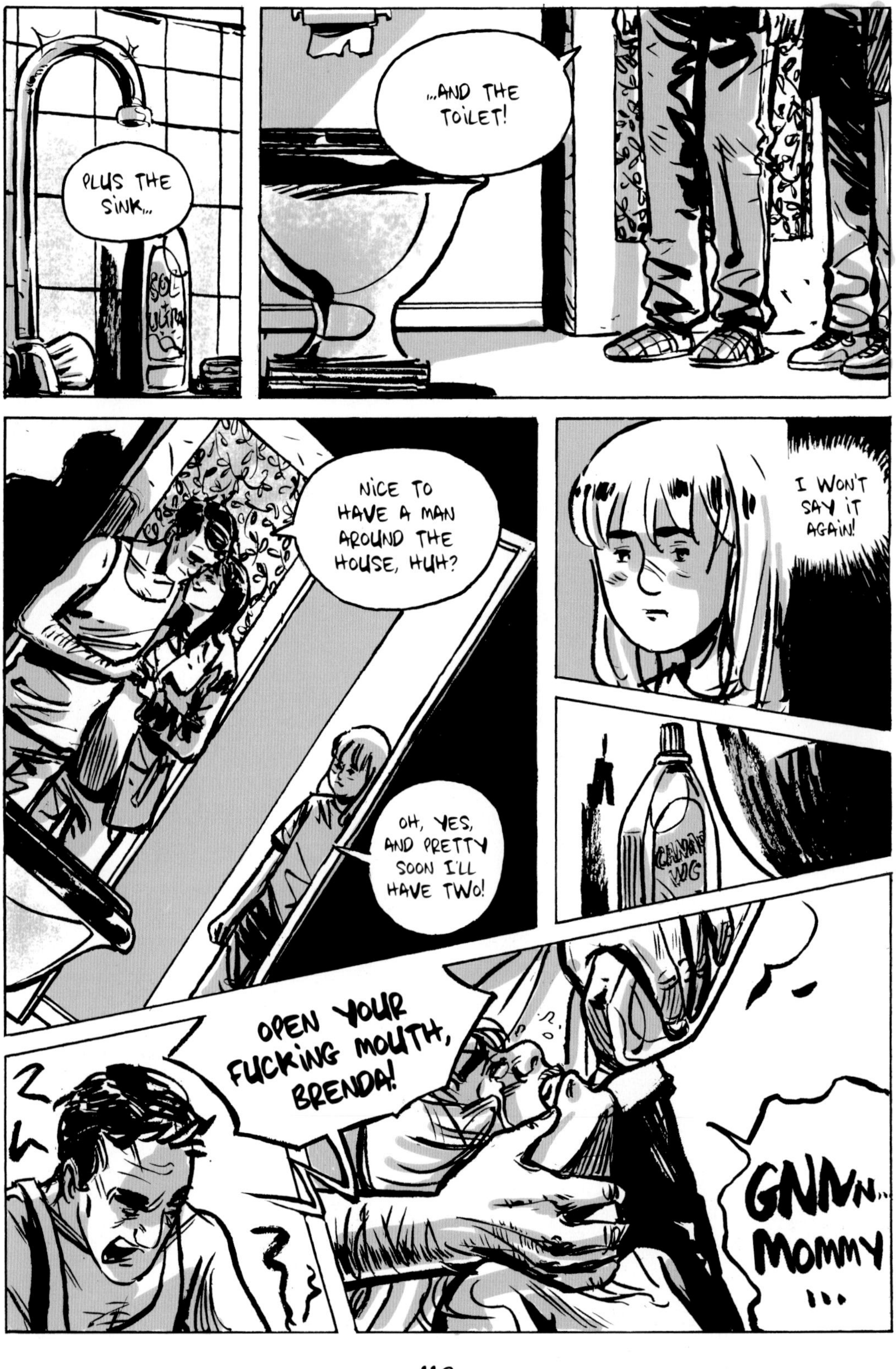
PLUS THE SINK...
...AND THE TOILET!
NICE TO HAVE A MAN AROUND THE HOUSE, HUH?
OH, YES, AND PRETTY SOON I'LL HAVE TWO!
I WON'T SAY IT AGAIN!
OPEN YOUR FUCKING MOUTH, BRENDA!
GNNn... MOMMY ...

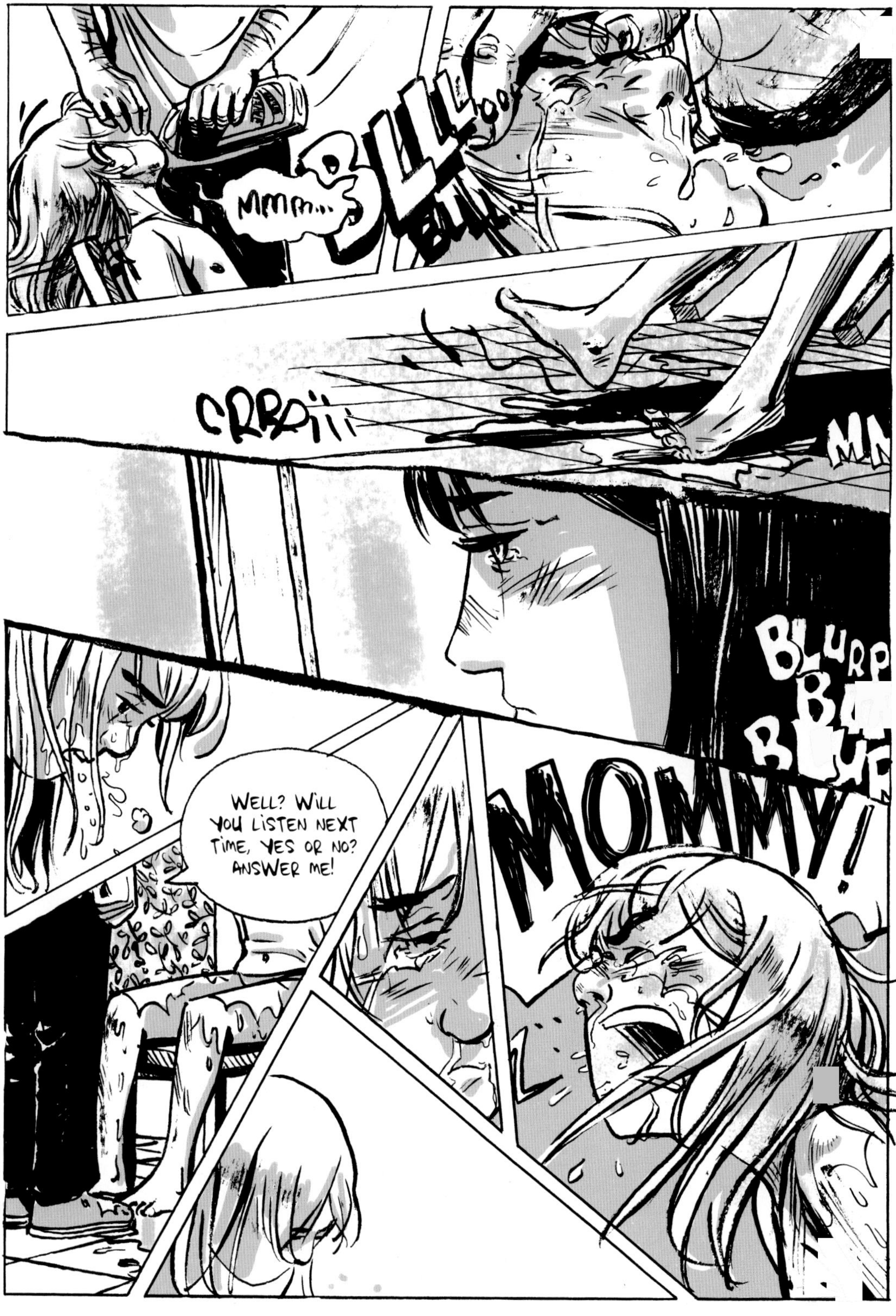
MMM...
BLLL...
BLL
CRRRiii
MM
BLURP
WELL? WILL YOU LISTEN NEXT TIME, YES OR NO? ANSWER ME!
MOMMY!

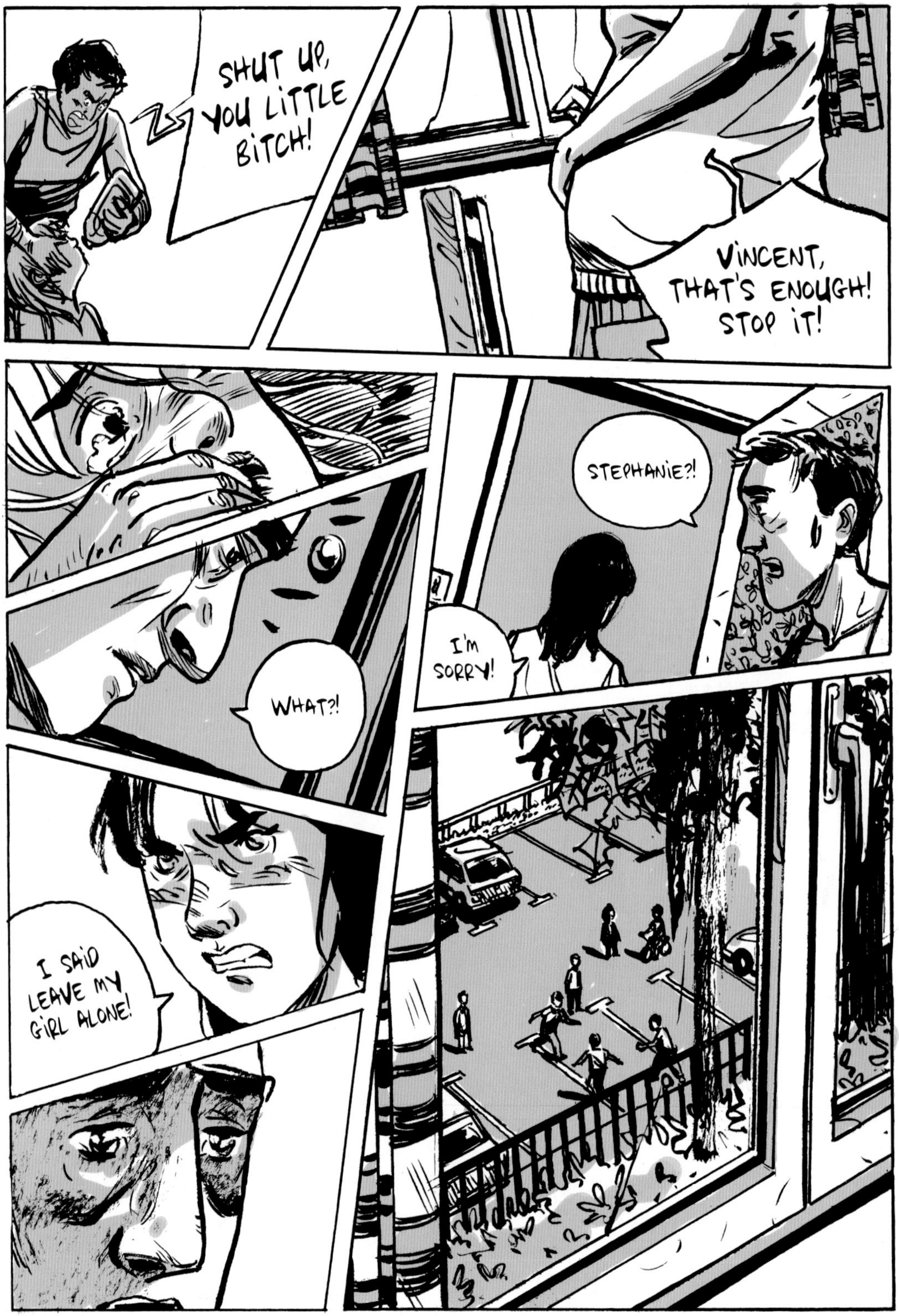
SHUT UP, YOU LITTLE BITCH!
VINCENT, THAT'S ENOUGH! STOP IT!
STEPHANIE?!
WHAT?!
I'M SORRY!
I SAID LEAVE MY GIRL ALONE!

WHENEVER MY MOM CAME TO MY DEFENSE, HE'D HIT HER LATER THAT NIGHT.
VINCENT, NOOOO, AAAAH!
BAM!!!
SHUT UP!
WHIMPER WHIMPER WHIMPER
BAF BAF
NEVER CONTRADICT ME IN FRONT OF YOUR KID, YOU HEAR?!
WHIMPER WHIMPER
OOOW
STOP

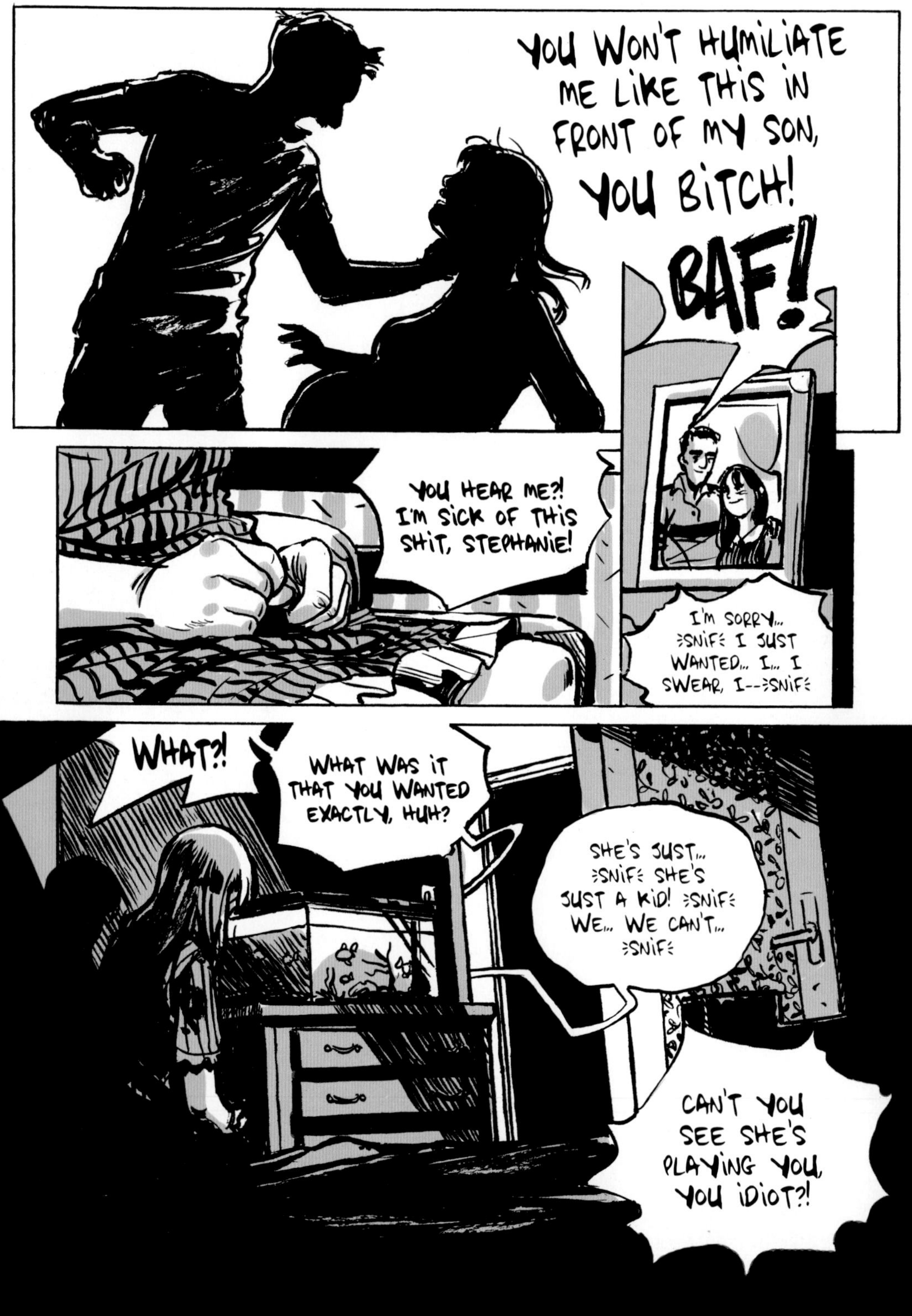
YOU WON'T HUMILIATE ME LIKE THIS IN FRONT OF MY SON, YOU BITCH!
BAF!
YOU HEAR ME?! I'M SICK OF THIS SHIT, STEPHANIE!
I'M SORRY... ≶SNIF≷ I JUST WANTED... I... I SWEAR, I-- ≶SNIF≷
WHAT?!
WHAT WAS IT THAT YOU WANTED EXACTLY, HUH?
SHE'S JUST... ≶SNIF≷ SHE'S JUST A KID! ≶SNIF≷ WE... WE CAN'T... ≶SNIF≷
CAN'T YOU SEE SHE'S PLAYING YOU, YOU IDIOT?!

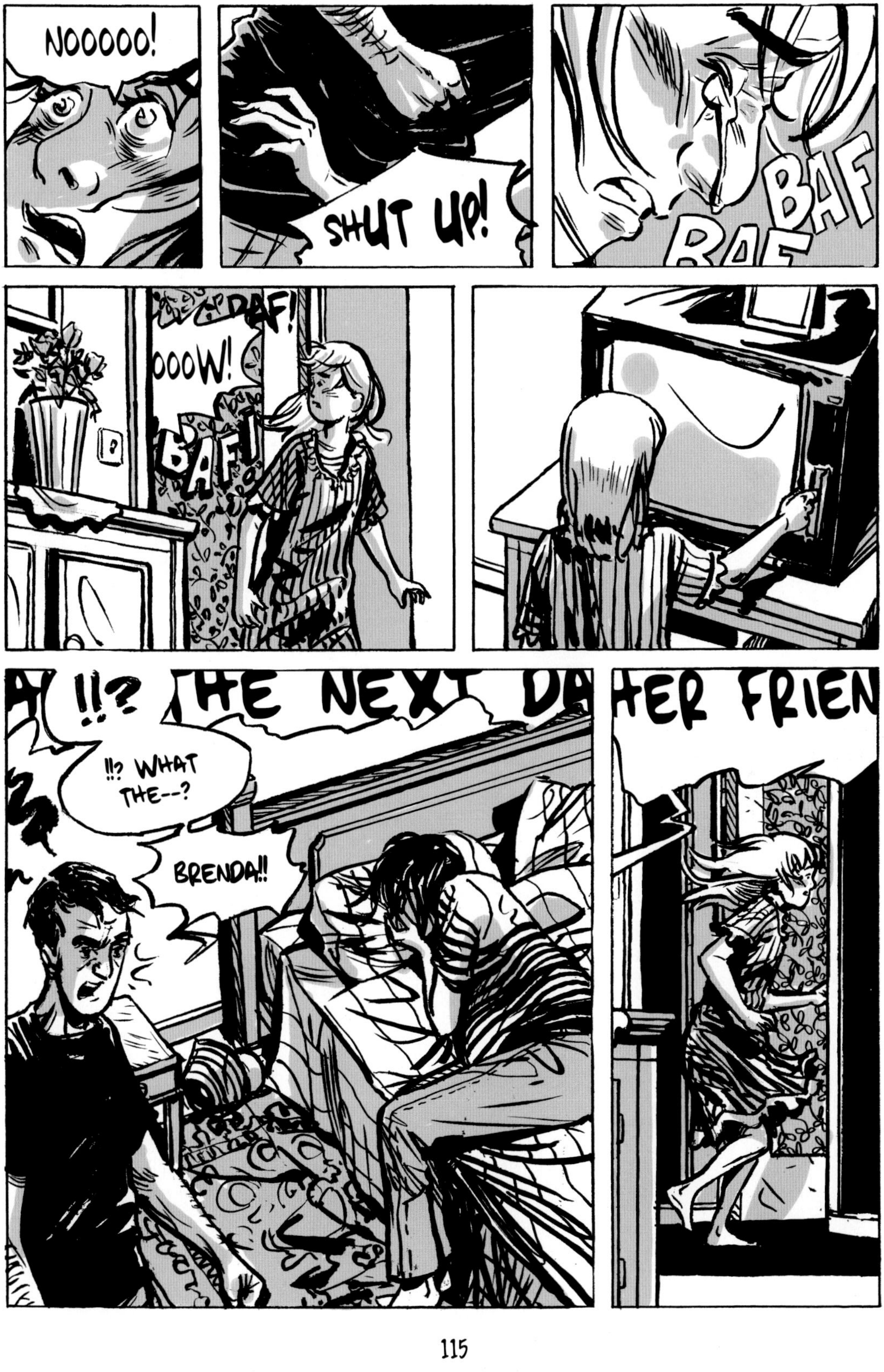
NOOOOO!
SHUT UP!
BAF
DAF!
OOOW!
BAF!
!!?
THE NEXT DA
HER FRIEN
!!? WHAT THE--?
BRENDA!!

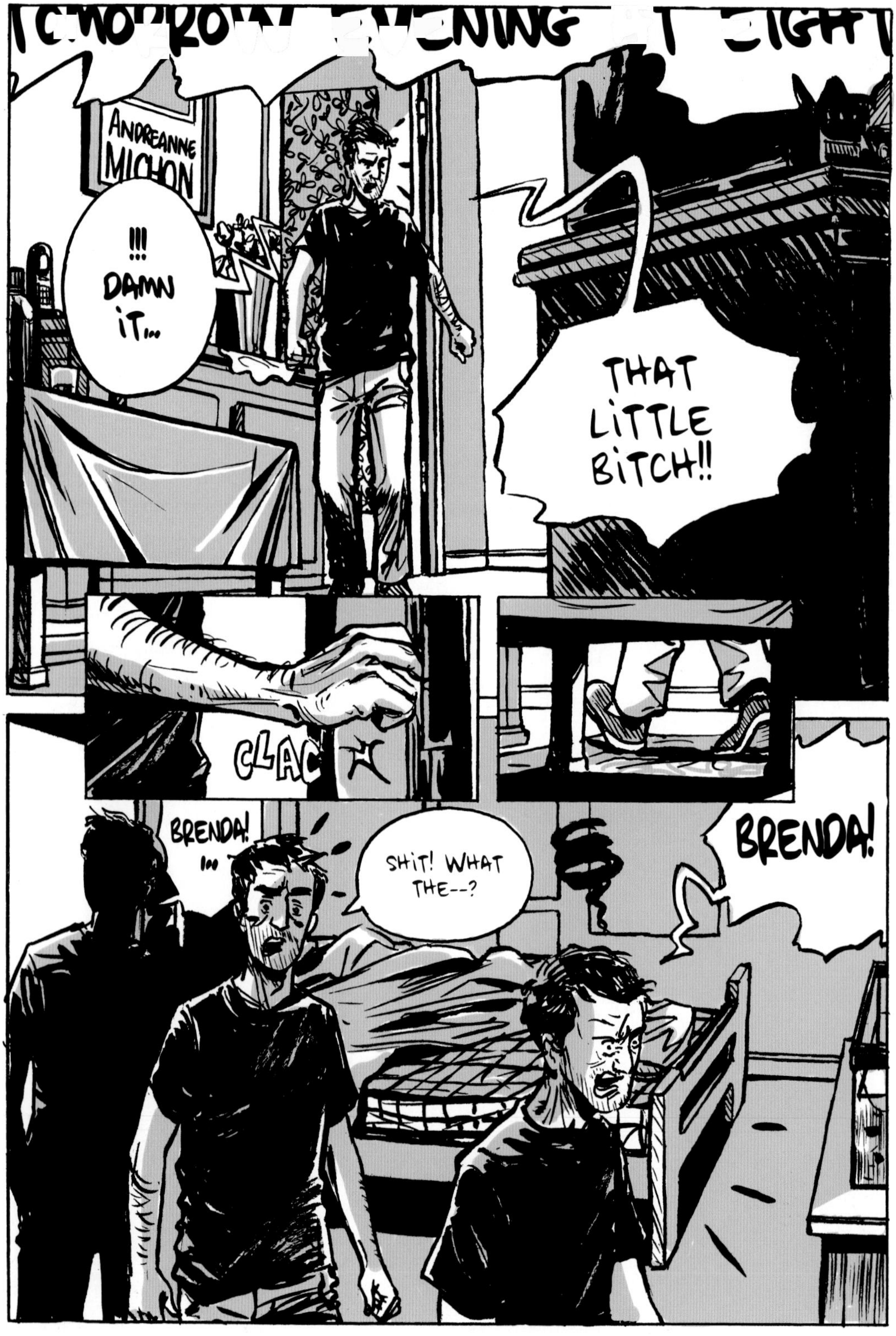
ANDREANNE MICHON
!!! DAMN IT...
THAT LITTLE BITCH!!
CLAC
BRENDA! ...
SHIT! WHAT THE--?
BRENDA!

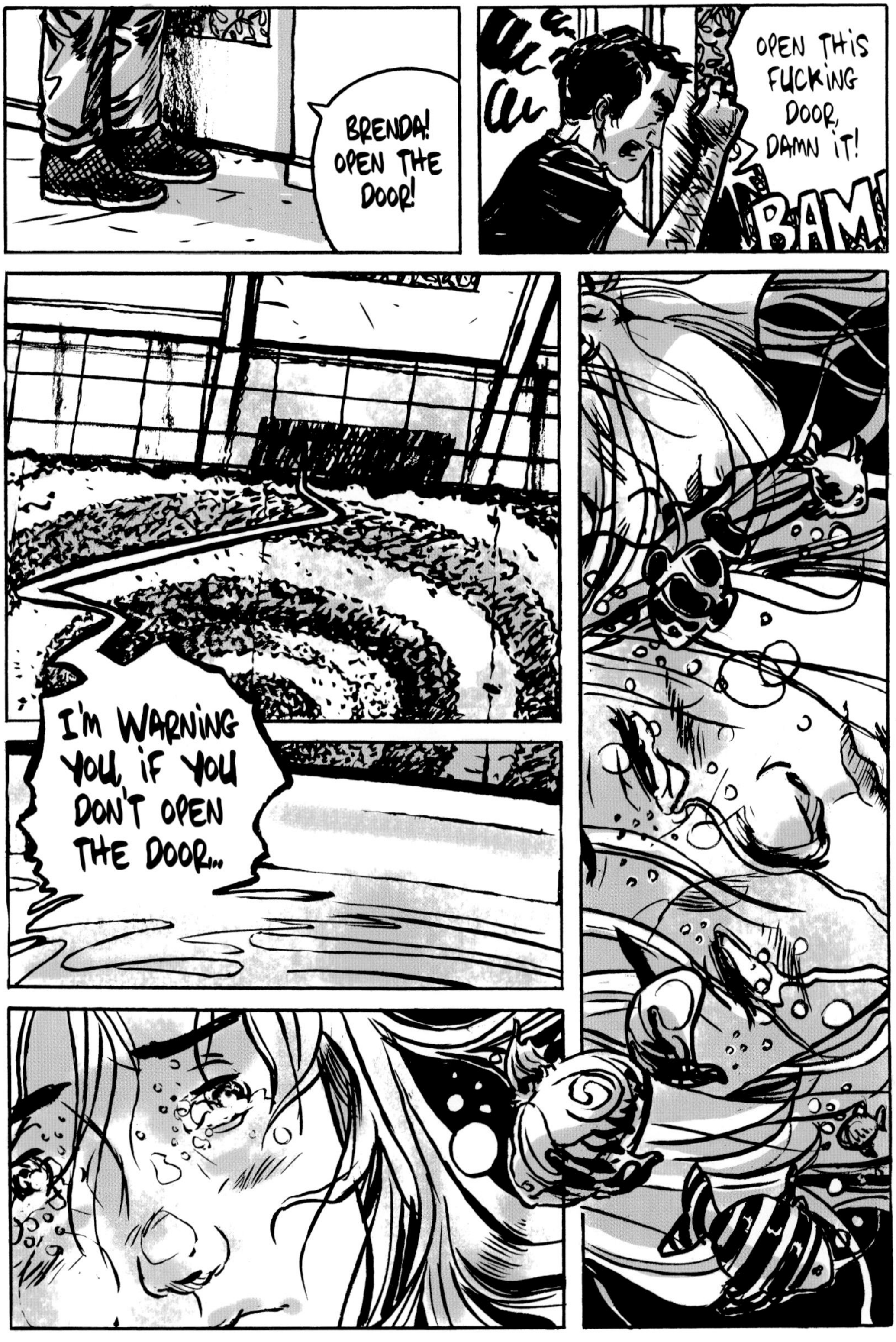
BRENDA! OPEN THE DOOR!
OPEN THIS FUCKING DOOR, DAMN IT!
BAM
I'M WARNING YOU, IF YOU DON'T OPEN THE DOOR...

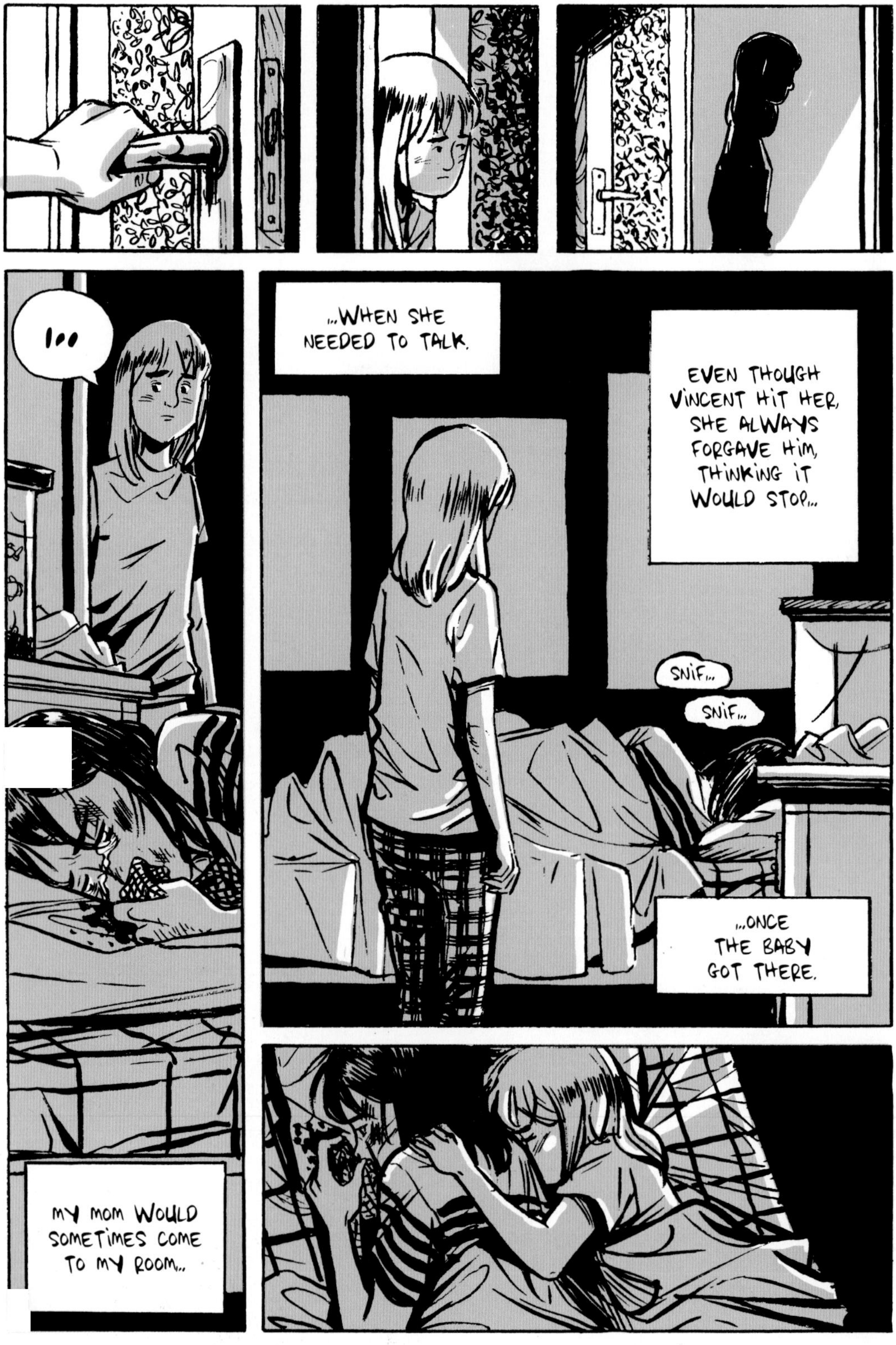
I...
...WHEN SHE NEEDED TO TALK.
EVEN THOUGH VINCENT HIT HER, SHE ALWAYS FORGAVE HIM, THINKING IT WOULD STOP...
SNIF...
SNIF...
...ONCE THE BABY GOT THERE.
MY MOM WOULD SOMETIMES COME TO MY ROOM...

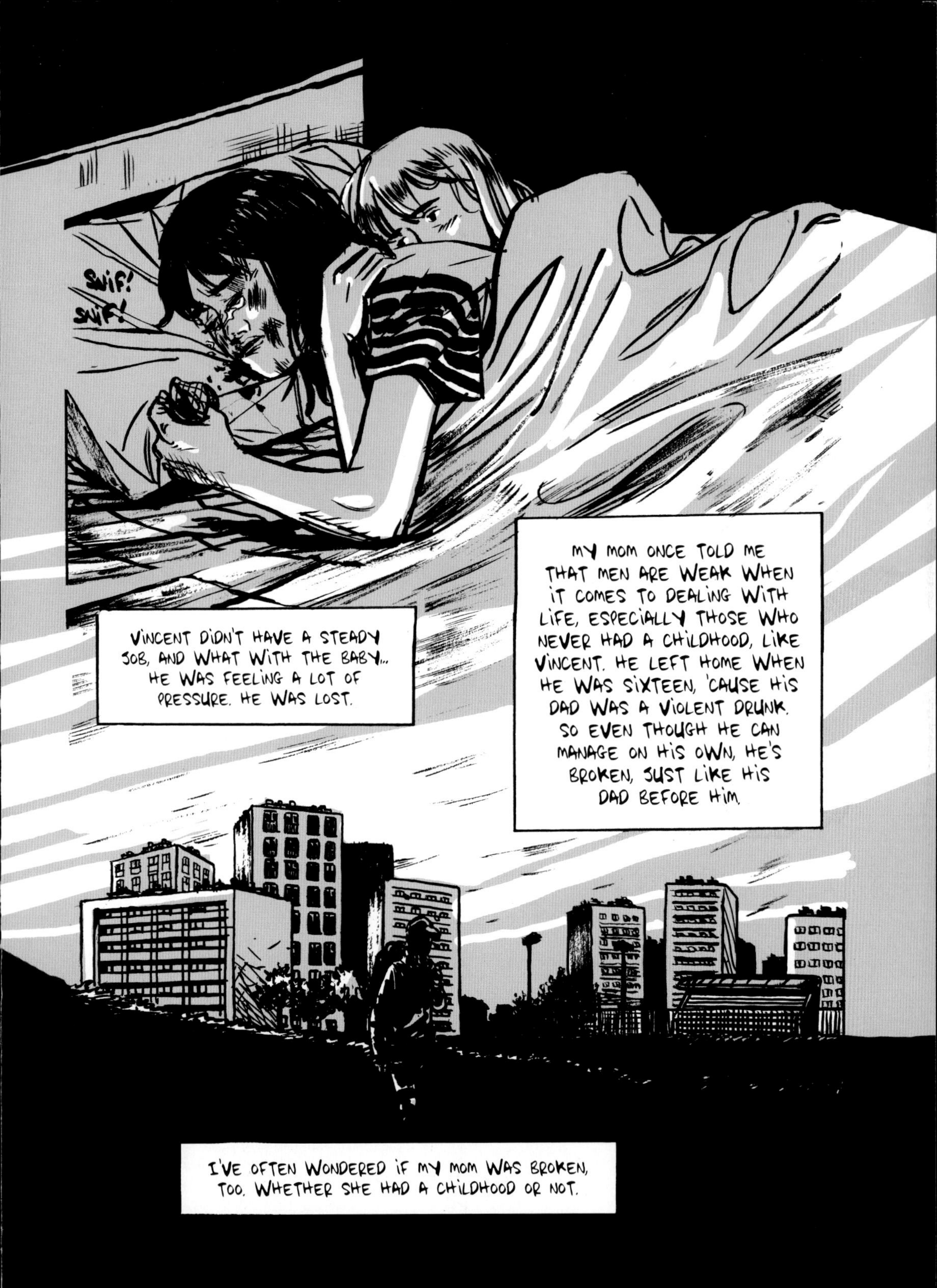
SNIF!
SNIF!
VINCENT DIDN'T HAVE A STEADY JOB, AND WHAT WITH THE BABY... HE WAS FEELING A LOT OF PRESSURE. HE WAS LOST.
MY MOM ONCE TOLD ME THAT MEN ARE WEAK WHEN IT COMES TO DEALING WITH LIFE, ESPECIALLY THOSE WHO NEVER HAD A CHILDHOOD, LIKE VINCENT. HE LEFT HOME WHEN HE WAS SIXTEEN, 'CAUSE HIS DAD WAS A VIOLENT DRUNK. SO EVEN THOUGH HE CAN MANAGE ON HIS OWN, HE'S BROKEN, JUST LIKE HIS DAD BEFORE HIM.
I'VE OFTEN WONDERED IF MY MOM WAS BROKEN, TOO. WHETHER SHE HAD A CHILDHOOD OR NOT.

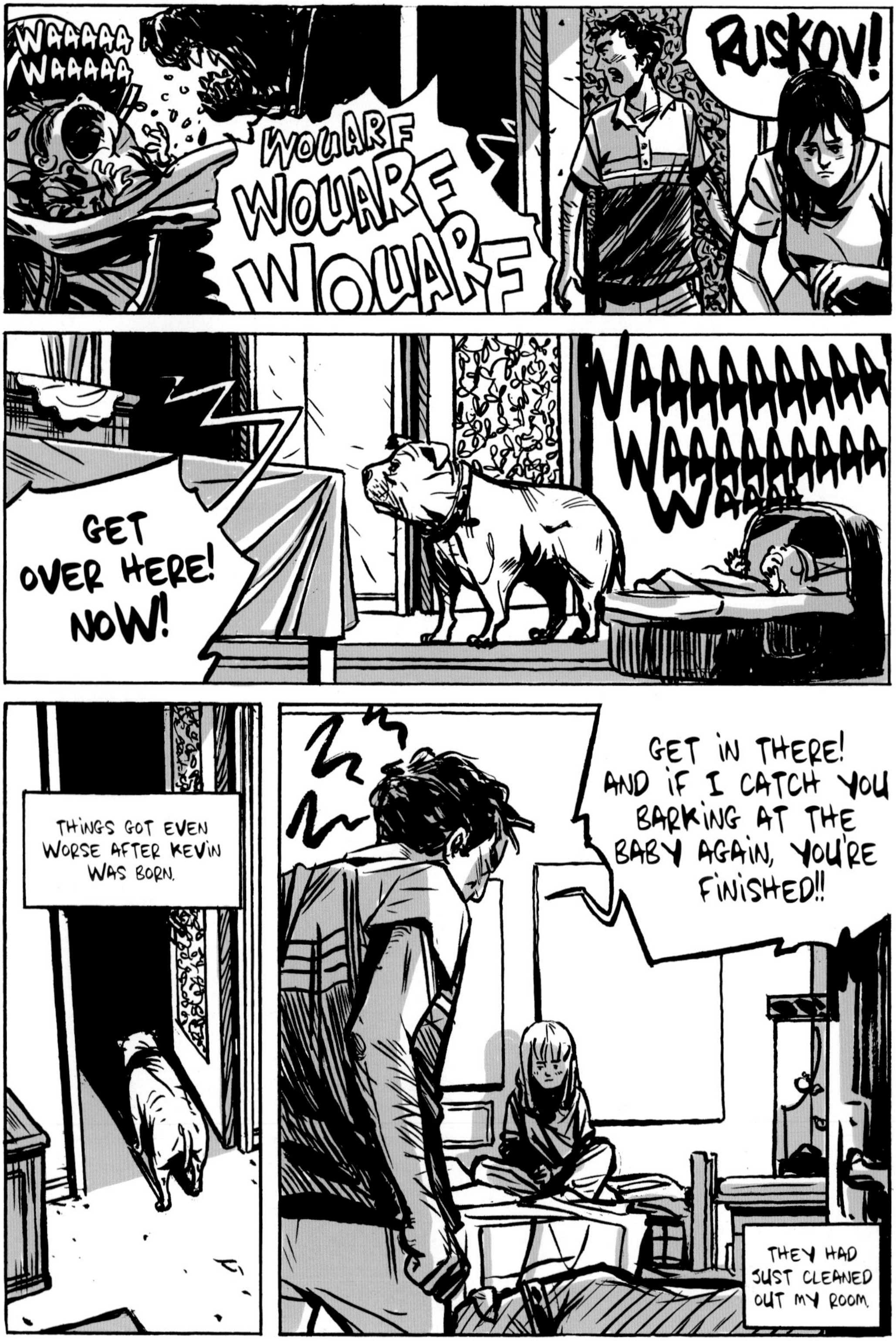
WAAAAA
WAAAAA
WOUARF
WOUARF
WOUARF
RUSKOV!
WAAAAAAAAA
WAAAAAAAAA
GET OVER HERE! NOW!
THINGS GOT EVEN WORSE AFTER KEVIN WAS BORN.
GET IN THERE! AND IF I CATCH YOU BARKING AT THE BABY AGAIN, YOU'RE FINISHED!!
THEY HAD JUST CLEANED OUT MY ROOM.

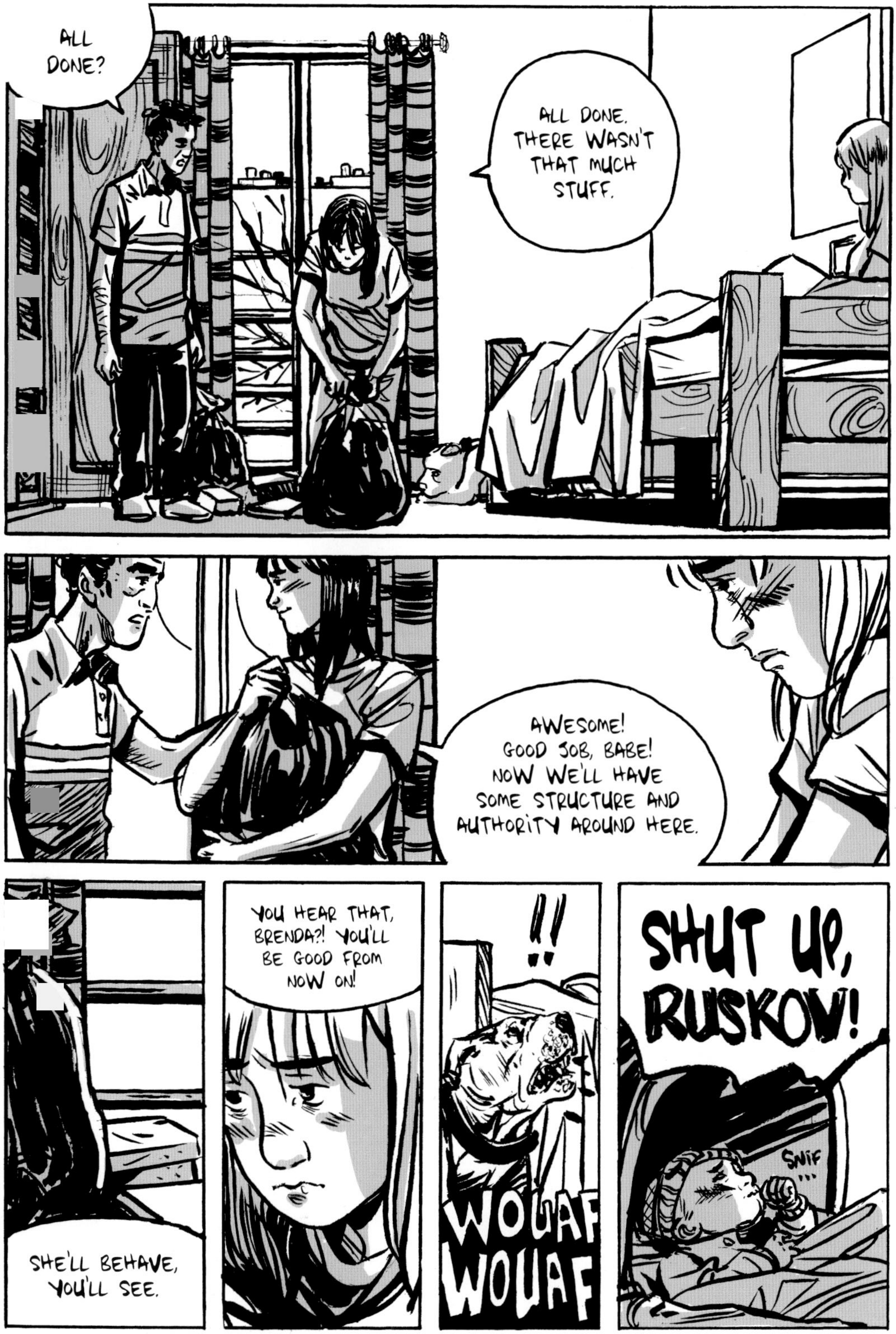
ALL DONE?
ALL DONE. THERE WASN'T THAT MUCH STUFF.
AWESOME! GOOD JOB, BABE! NOW WE'LL HAVE SOME STRUCTURE AND AUTHORITY AROUND HERE.
SHE'LL BEHAVE, YOU'LL SEE.
YOU HEAR THAT, BRENDA?! YOU'LL BE GOOD FROM NOW ON!
!!
WOUAF WOUAF
SHUT UP, RUSKOV!
SNIF...

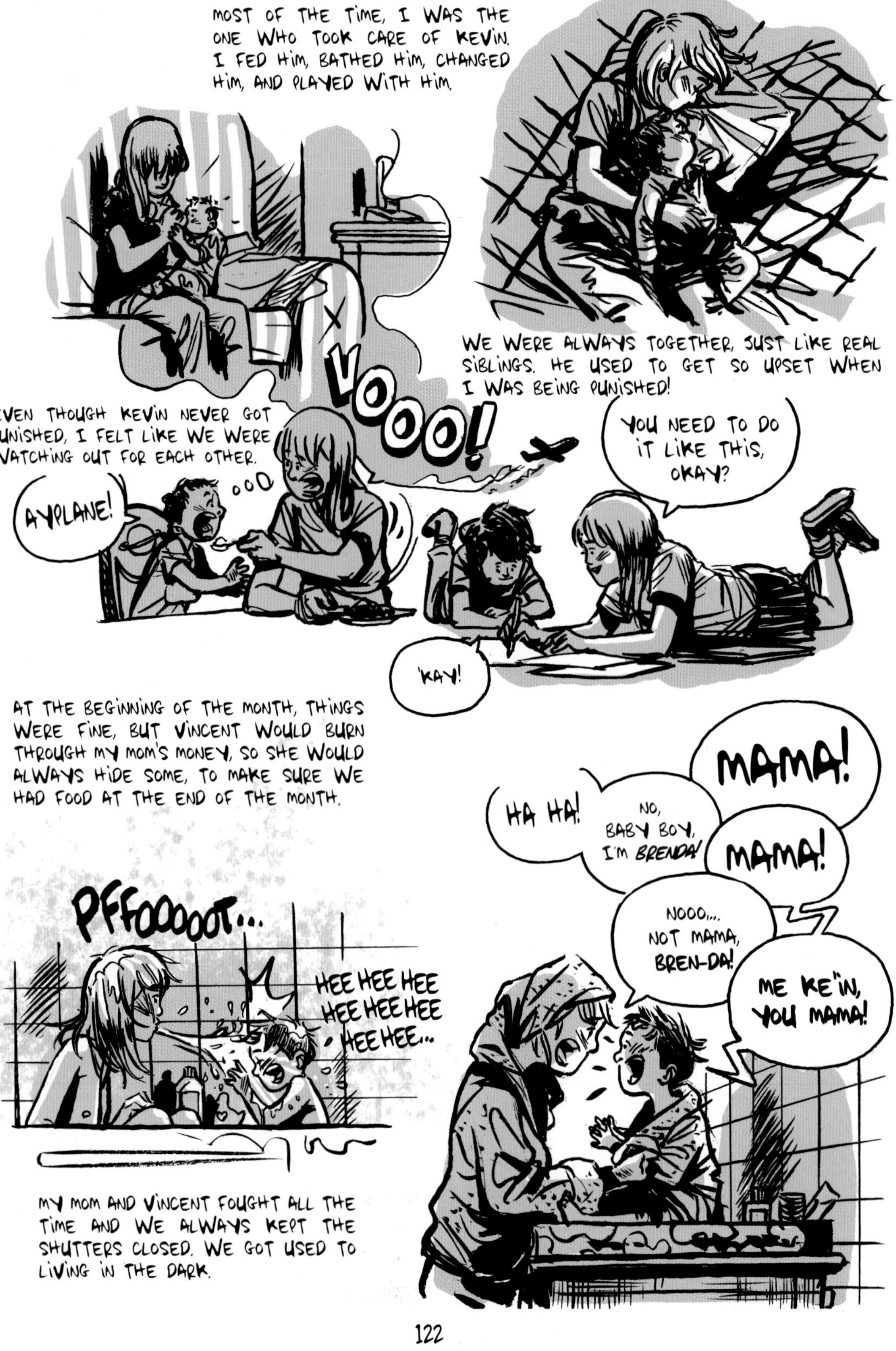
MOST OF THE TIME, I WAS THE ONE WHO TOOK CARE OF KEVIN. I FED HIM, BATHED HIM, CHANGED HIM, AND PLAYED WITH HIM.
WE WERE ALWAYS TOGETHER, JUST LIKE REAL SIBLINGS. HE USED TO GET SO UPSET WHEN I WAS BEING PUNISHED!
EVEN THOUGH KEVIN NEVER GOT PUNISHED, I FELT LIKE WE WERE WATCHING OUT FOR EACH OTHER.
VOOOO!
AYPLANE!
OOO
YOU NEED TO DO IT LIKE THIS, OKAY?
'KAY!
AT THE BEGINNING OF THE MONTH, THINGS WERE FINE, BUT VINCENT WOULD BURN THROUGH MY MOM'S MONEY, SO SHE WOULD ALWAYS HIDE SOME, TO MAKE SURE WE HAD FOOD AT THE END OF THE MONTH.
PFFOOOOOOT...
HEE HEE HEE HEE HEE HEE HEE HEE...
MY MOM AND VINCENT FOUGHT ALL THE TIME AND WE ALWAYS KEPT THE SHUTTERS CLOSED. WE GOT USED TO LIVING IN THE DARK.
HA HA!
MAMA!
NO, BABY BOY, I'M BRENDA!
MAMA!
NOOO... NOT MAMA, BREN-DA!
ME KE'IN, YOU MAMA!

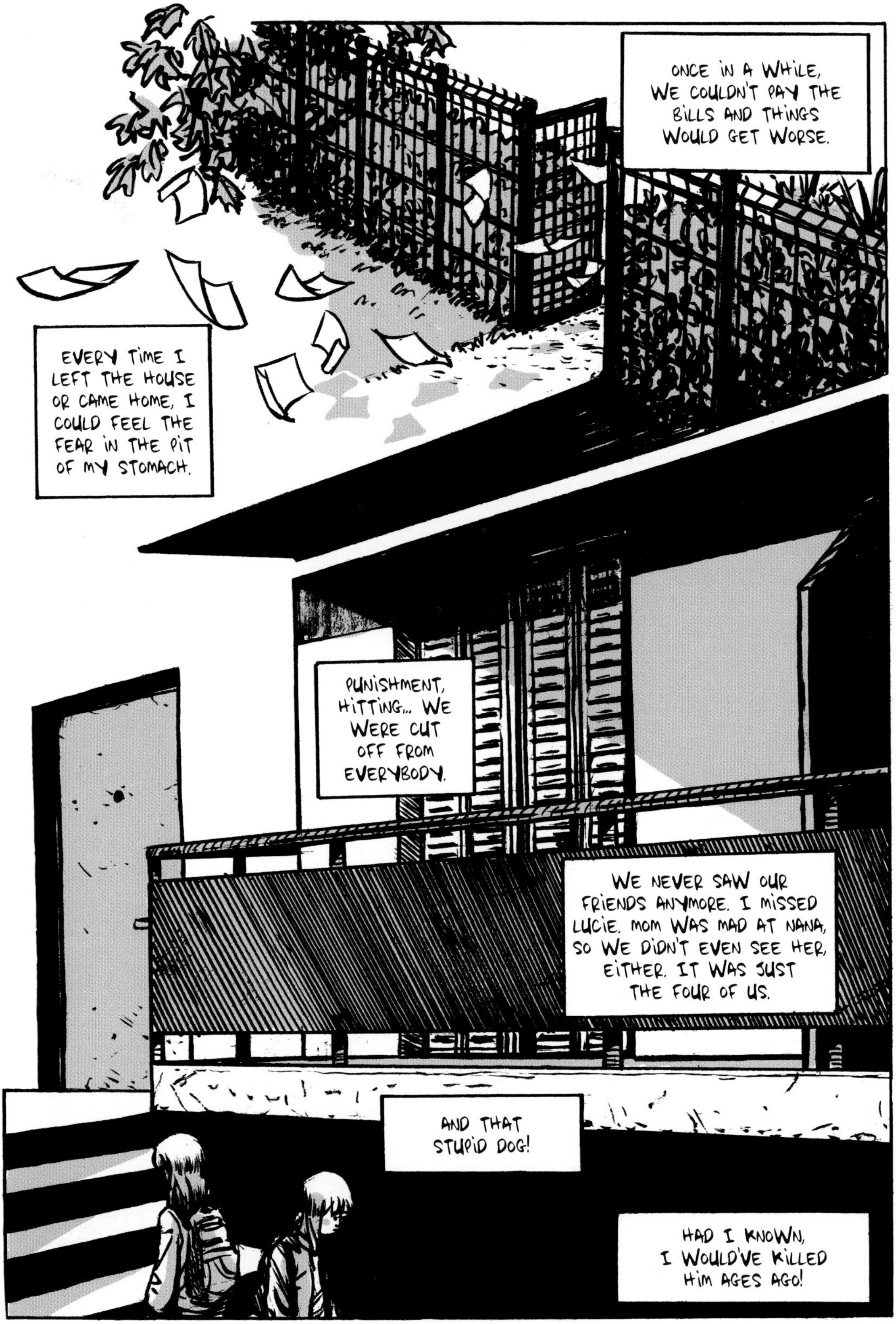
ONCE IN A WHILE, WE COULDN'T PAY THE BILLS AND THINGS WOULD GET WORSE.
EVERY TIME I LEFT THE HOUSE OR CAME HOME, I COULD FEEL THE FEAR IN THE PIT OF MY STOMACH.
PUNISHMENT, HITTING... WE WERE CUT OFF FROM EVERYBODY.
WE NEVER SAW OUR FRIENDS ANYMORE. I MISSED LUCIE. MOM WAS MAD AT NANA, SO WE DIDN'T EVEN SEE HER, EITHER. IT WAS JUST THE FOUR OF US.
AND THAT STUPID DOG!
HAD I KNOWN, I WOULD'VE KILLED HIM AGES AGO!

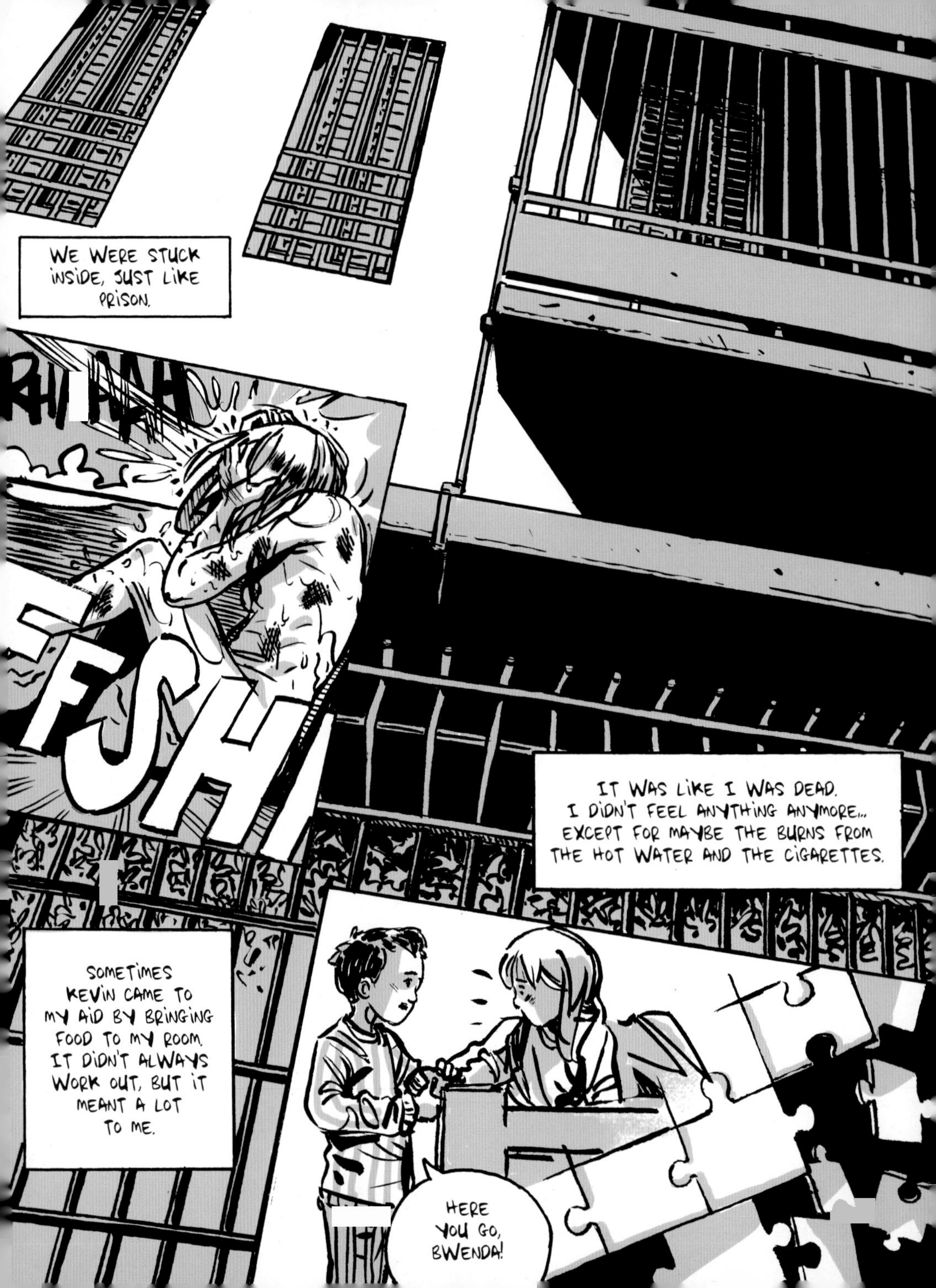
WE WERE STUCK INSIDE, JUST LIKE PRISON.
FSH
IT WAS LIKE I WAS DEAD. I DIDN'T FEEL ANYTHING ANYMORE... EXCEPT FOR MAYBE THE BURNS FROM THE HOT WATER AND THE CIGARETTES.
SOMETIMES KEVIN CAME TO MY AID BY BRINGING FOOD TO MY ROOM. IT DIDN'T ALWAYS WORK OUT, BUT IT MEANT A LOT TO ME.
HERE YOU GO, BWENDA!

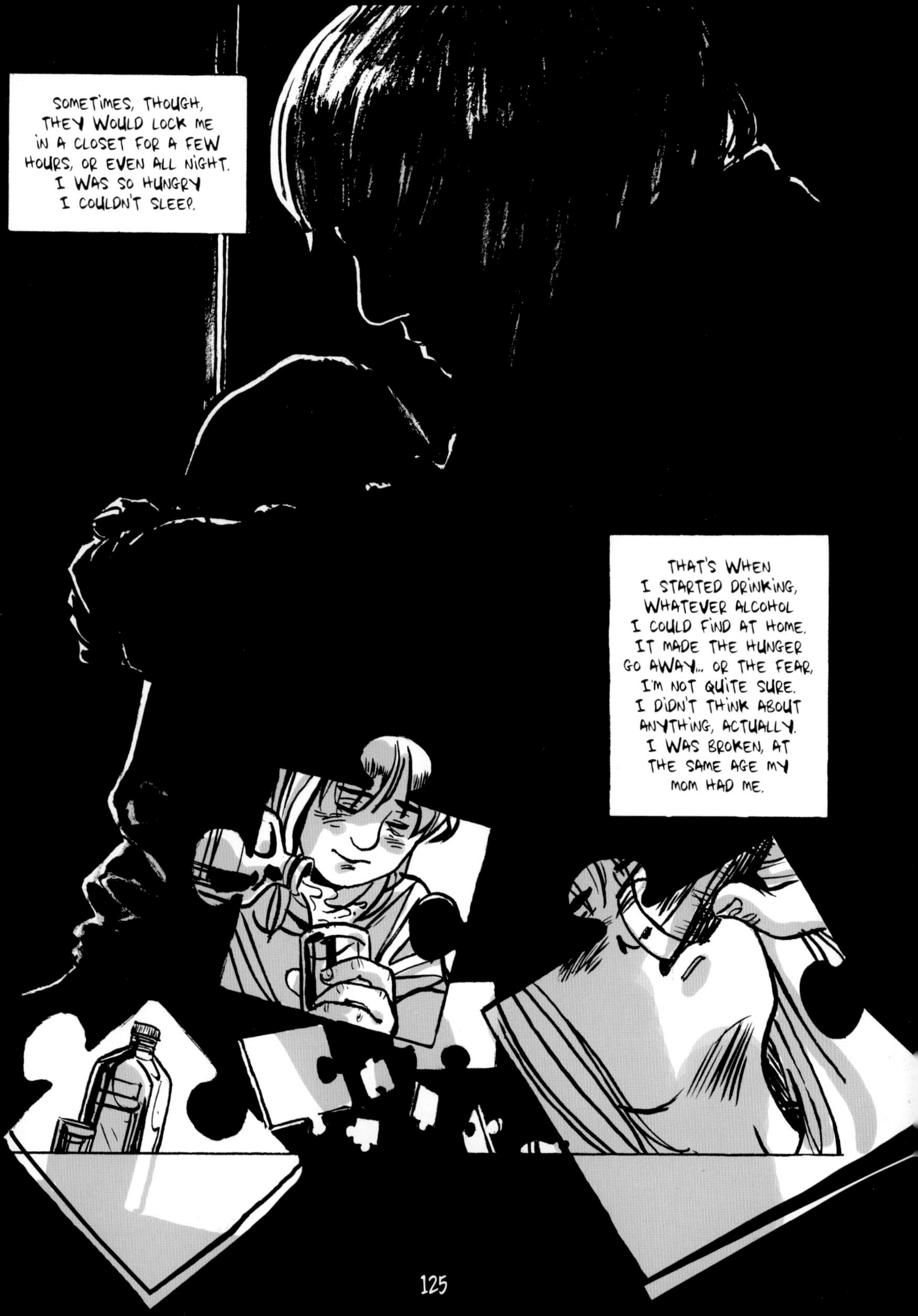
SOMETIMES, THOUGH, THEY WOULD LOCK ME IN A CLOSET FOR A FEW HOURS, OR EVEN ALL NIGHT. I WAS SO HUNGRY I COULDN'T SLEEP.
THAT'S WHEN I STARTED DRINKING, WHATEVER ALCOHOL I COULD FIND AT HOME. IT MADE THE HUNGER GO AWAY... OR THE FEAR, I'M NOT QUITE SURE. I DIDN'T THINK ABOUT ANYTHING, ACTUALLY. I WAS BROKEN, AT THE SAME AGE MY MOM HAD ME.

I LOVED ALCOHOL...

IT HELPED ME ENDURE VINCENT'S FAVORITE SONG... ABSOLUTE TORTURE!!

OH HOW I LOVE YOU! OH HOW I LOVE YOU, OH...*

THAT IDIOT WOULD OPEN THE WINDOW SO HE COULD POLLUTE THE WHOLE TOWN WITH HIS TALENTLESS SHIT!

OH HOW

SNIF!...

OH HOW I LOOOVE

AND HE'D SING THAT CRAPPY SONG TO MY MOM TO APOLOGIZE FOR BEING SUCH AN ASSHOLE!

*TRANSLATION OF LYRICS FROM "QUE JE T'AIME" PERFORMED BY JOHNNY HALLYDAY.

126

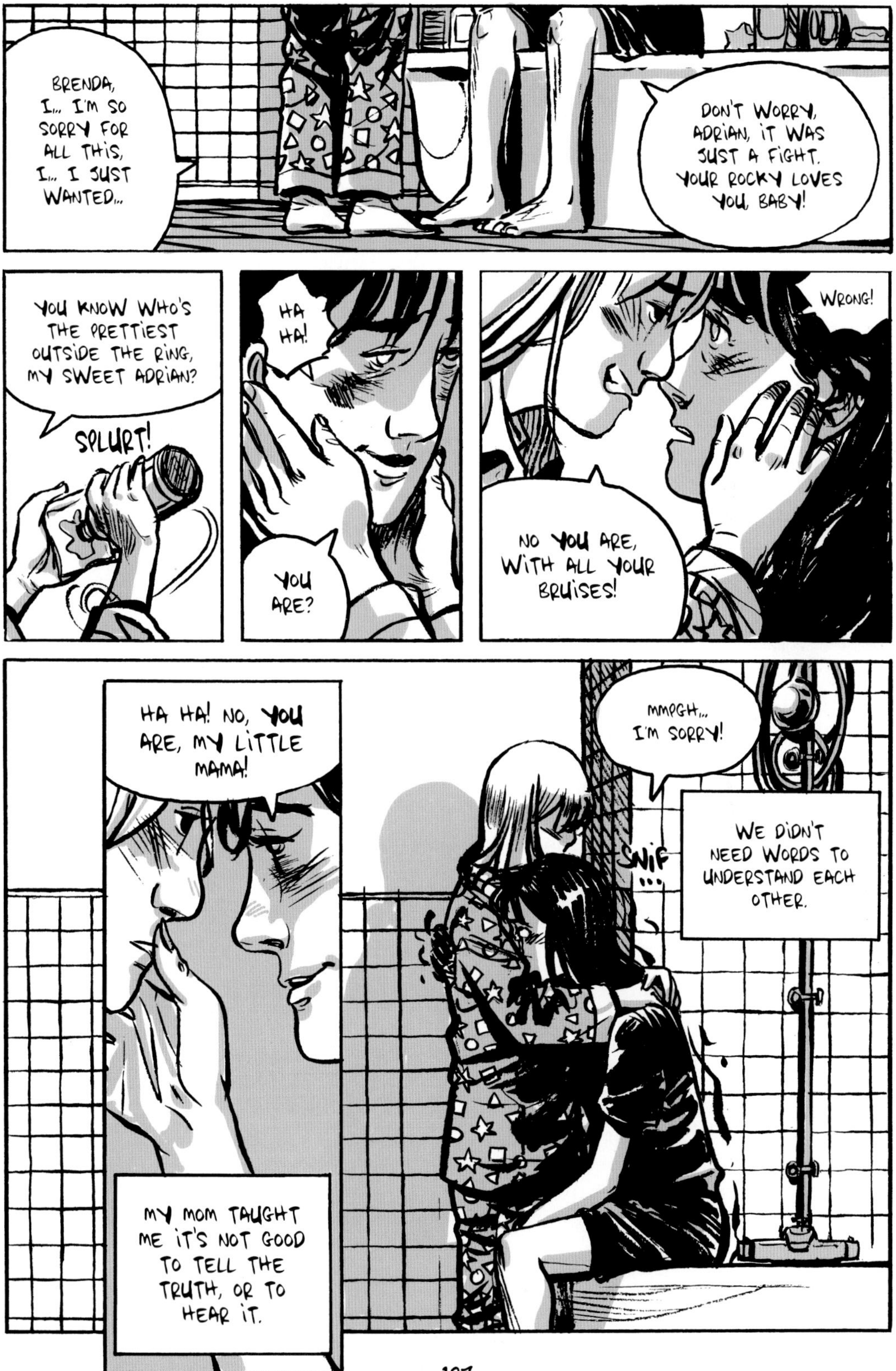

BRENDA, I... I'M SO SORRY FOR ALL THIS, I... I JUST WANTED...
DON'T WORRY, ADRIAN, IT WAS JUST A FIGHT. YOUR ROCKY LOVES YOU, BABY!
YOU KNOW WHO'S THE PRETTIEST OUTSIDE THE RING, MY SWEET ADRIAN?
SPLURT!
HA HA!
YOU ARE?
WRONG!
NO YOU ARE, WITH ALL YOUR BRUISES!
HA HA! NO, YOU ARE, MY LITTLE MAMA!
MMPGH... I'M SORRY!
SNIF...
WE DIDN'T NEED WORDS TO UNDERSTAND EACH OTHER.
MY MOM TAUGHT ME IT'S NOT GOOD TO TELL THE TRUTH, OR TO HEAR IT.

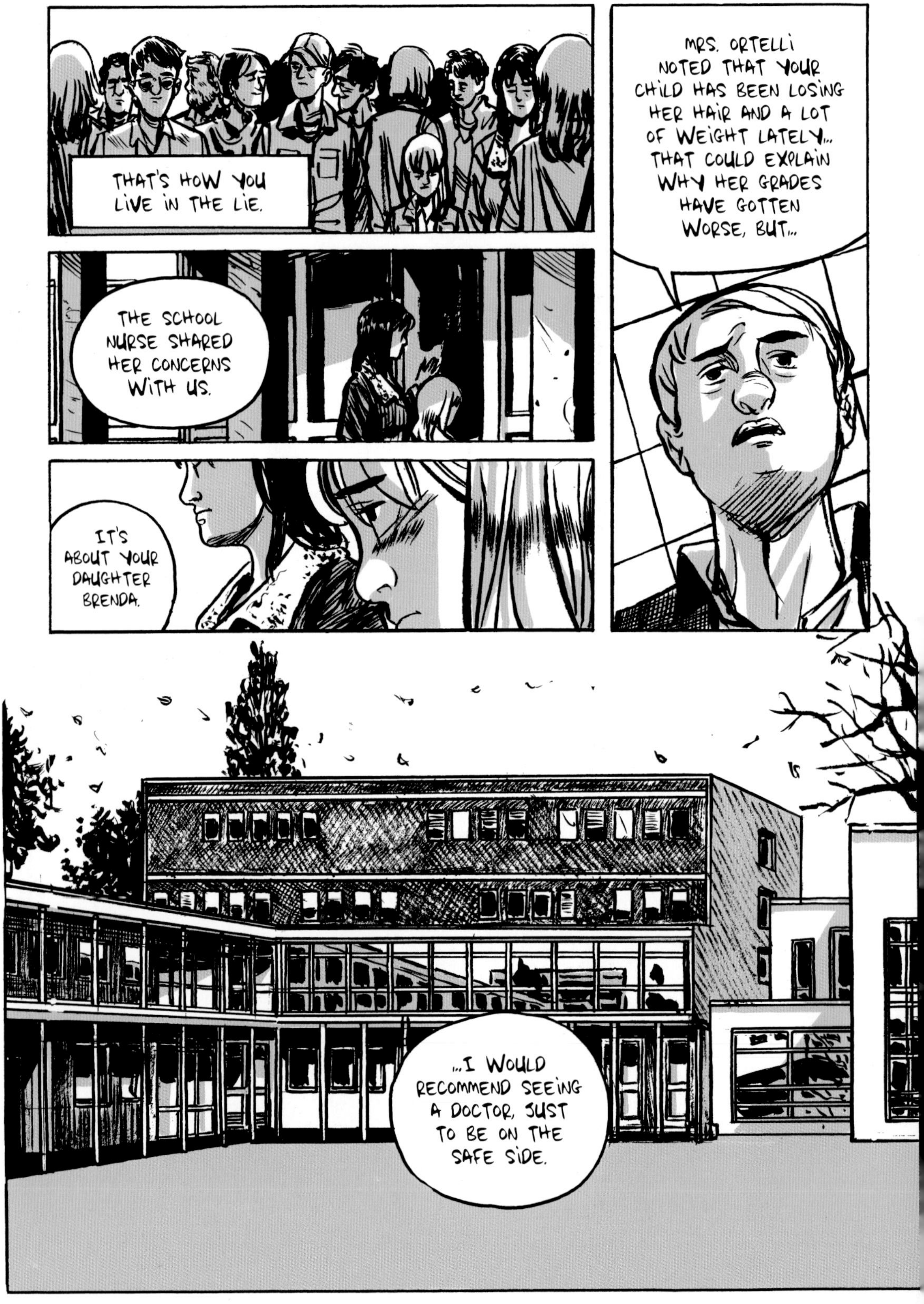
THAT'S HOW YOU LIVE IN THE LIE.
THE SCHOOL NURSE SHARED HER CONCERNS WITH US.
IT'S ABOUT YOUR DAUGHTER BRENDA.
MRS. ORTELLI NOTED THAT YOUR CHILD HAS BEEN LOSING HER HAIR AND A LOT OF WEIGHT LATELY... THAT COULD EXPLAIN WHY HER GRADES HAVE GOTTEN WORSE, BUT...
...I WOULD RECOMMEND SEEING A DOCTOR, JUST TO BE ON THE SAFE SIDE.

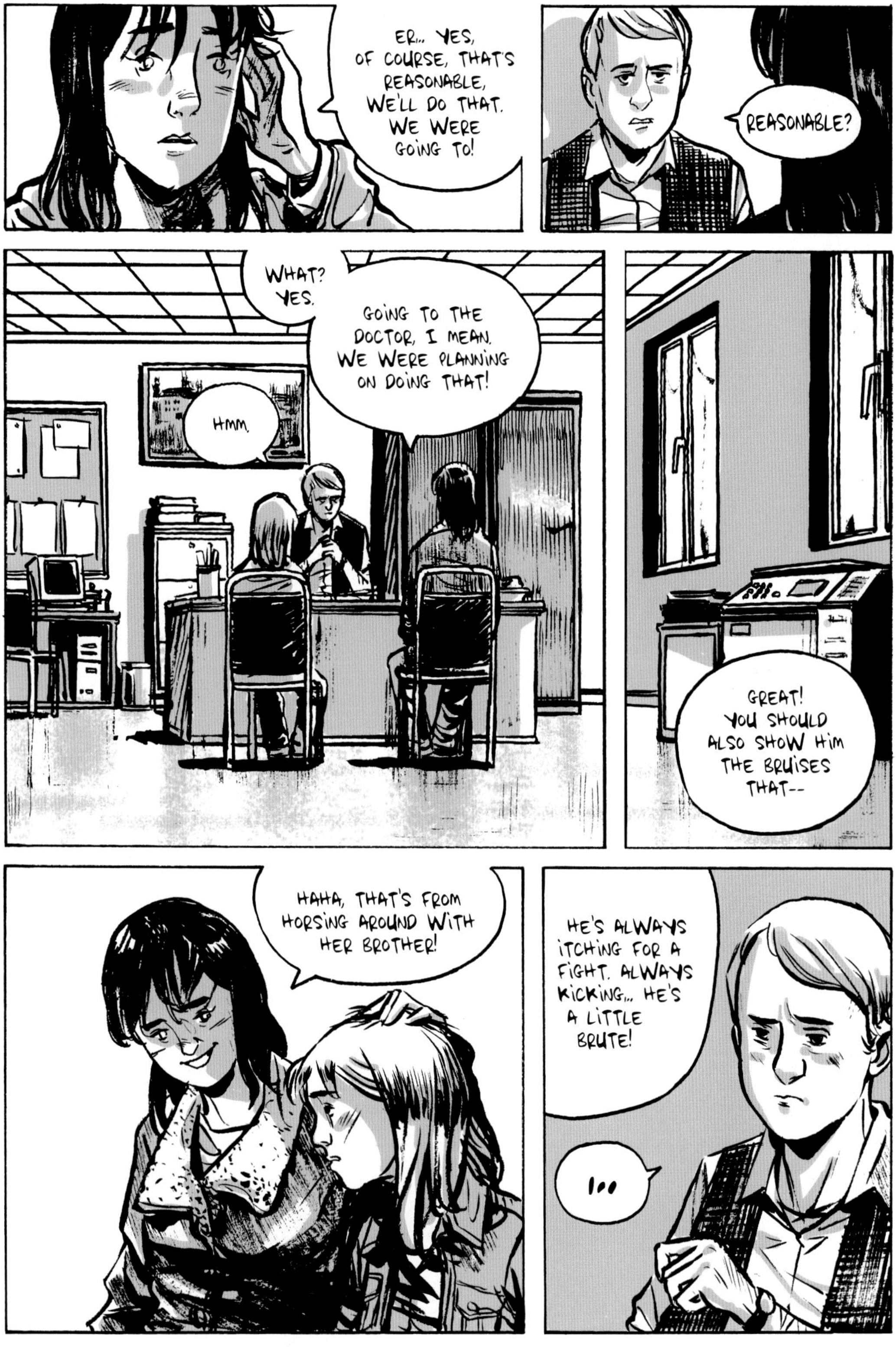
ER... YES, OF COURSE, THAT'S REASONABLE, WE'LL DO THAT. WE WERE GOING TO!
REASONABLE?
WHAT? YES.
GOING TO THE DOCTOR, I MEAN. WE WERE PLANNING ON DOING THAT!
HMM.
GREAT! YOU SHOULD ALSO SHOW HIM THE BRUISES THAT--
HAHA, THAT'S FROM HORSING AROUND WITH HER BROTHER!
HE'S ALWAYS ITCHING FOR A FIGHT. ALWAYS KICKING... HE'S A LITTLE BRUTE!
...

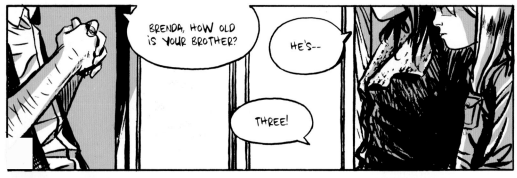

BRENDA, HOW OLD IS YOUR BROTHER?

HE'S--

THREE!

BUT HE LOOKS SIX... HE'S A BIG BOY!

WHAT!?

WAIT... WHAT ARE YOU TRYING TO SAY?

SO BIG HE LEAVES BRUISES EVERY-WHERE...

ARE YOU INSINUATING THAT I BEAT MY DAUGHTER?!

NO, I JUST--

I'VE HAD IT, WE'RE DONE! LET'S GO, BRENDA.

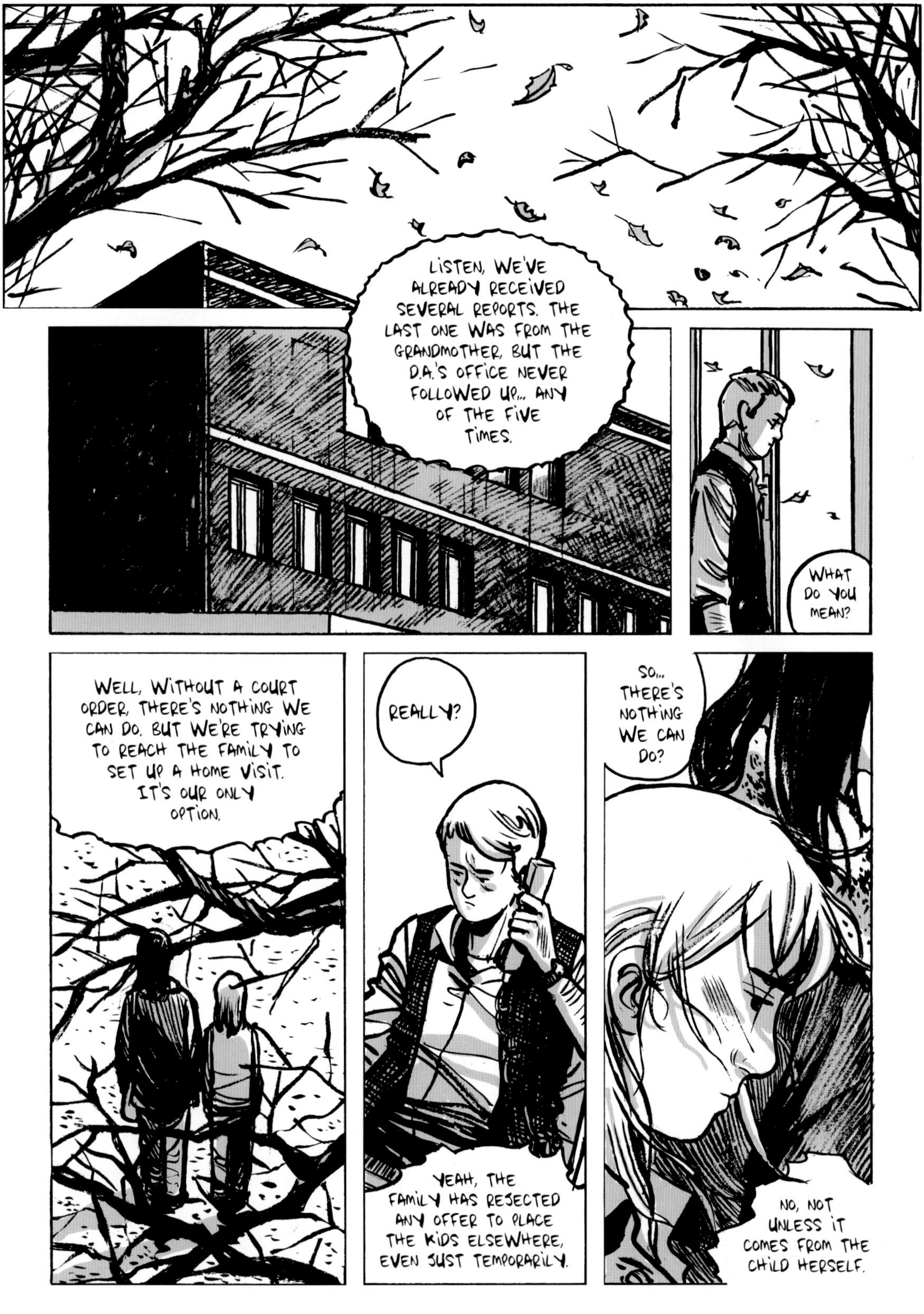
LISTEN, WE'VE ALREADY RECEIVED SEVERAL REPORTS. THE LAST ONE WAS FROM THE GRANDMOTHER, BUT THE D.A.'S OFFICE NEVER FOLLOWED UP... ANY OF THE FIVE TIMES.
WHAT DO YOU MEAN?
WELL, WITHOUT A COURT ORDER, THERE'S NOTHING WE CAN DO. BUT WE'RE TRYING TO REACH THE FAMILY TO SET UP A HOME VISIT. IT'S OUR ONLY OPTION.
REALLY?
YEAH, THE FAMILY HAS REJECTED ANY OFFER TO PLACE THE KIDS ELSEWHERE, EVEN JUST TEMPORARILY.
SO... THERE'S NOTHING WE CAN DO?
NO, NOT UNLESS IT COMES FROM THE CHILD HERSELF.

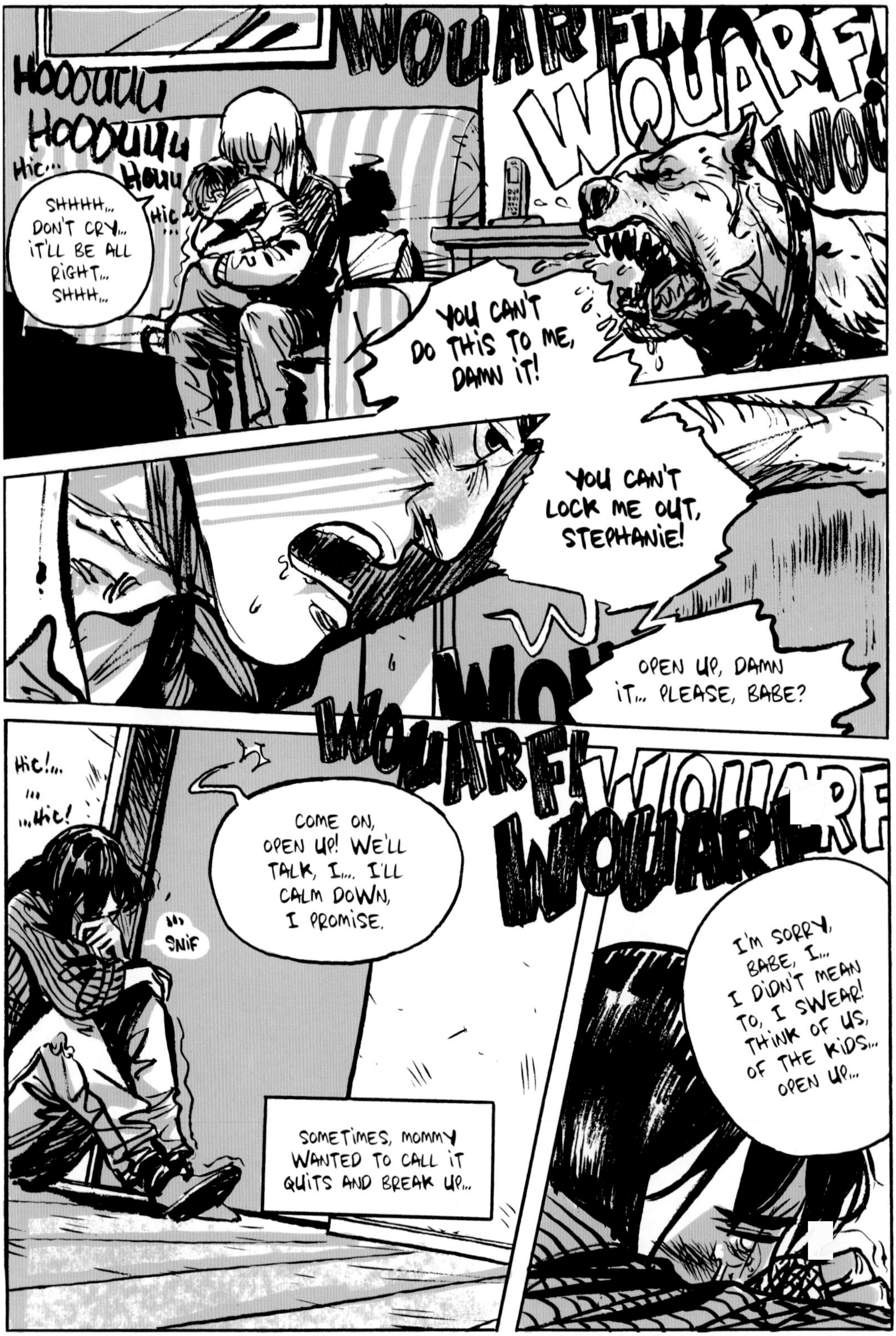

HOOOUUUU
HOOOUUUU
HIC...
HOUU
HIC
SHHHH... DON'T CRY... IT'LL BE ALL RIGHT... SHHH...
WOUARF!
WOUARF!
YOU CAN'T DO THIS TO ME, DAMN IT!
YOU CAN'T LOCK ME OUT, STEPHANIE!
OPEN UP, DAMN IT... PLEASE, BABE?
WOUARF!
HIC!...
...
...HIC!
COME ON, OPEN UP! WE'LL TALK, I... I'LL CALM DOWN, I PROMISE.
... SNIF
I'M SORRY, BABE, I... I DIDN'T MEAN TO, I SWEAR! THINK OF US, OF THE KIDS... OPEN UP...
SOMETIMES, MOMMY WANTED TO CALL IT QUITS AND BREAK UP...

...BUT SHE ALWAYS ENDED UP FORGIVING HIM...

...EVEN THOUGH HE WAS HURTING HER!

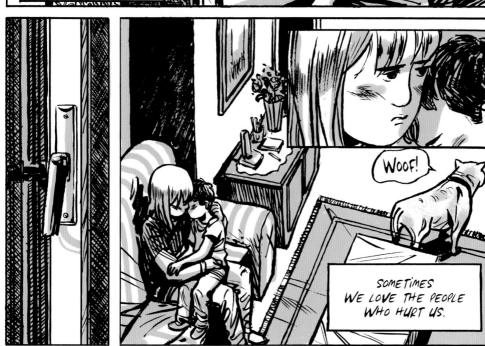

WOOF!

SOMETIMES WE LOVE THE PEOPLE WHO HURT US.

WHEN I SAY NOOO, YOU'RE THE ONE WHO SAYS YEEESSS, OH HOW I LOVE YOU, OH HOW I LOVE YOU, OH HOW I LOOOOVE YOU

MAYBE SO, BUT PEOPLE CAN'T HURT THE PEOPLE THEY LOVE, THOUGH, RIGHT?

UNFORTUNATELY... THEY CAN...

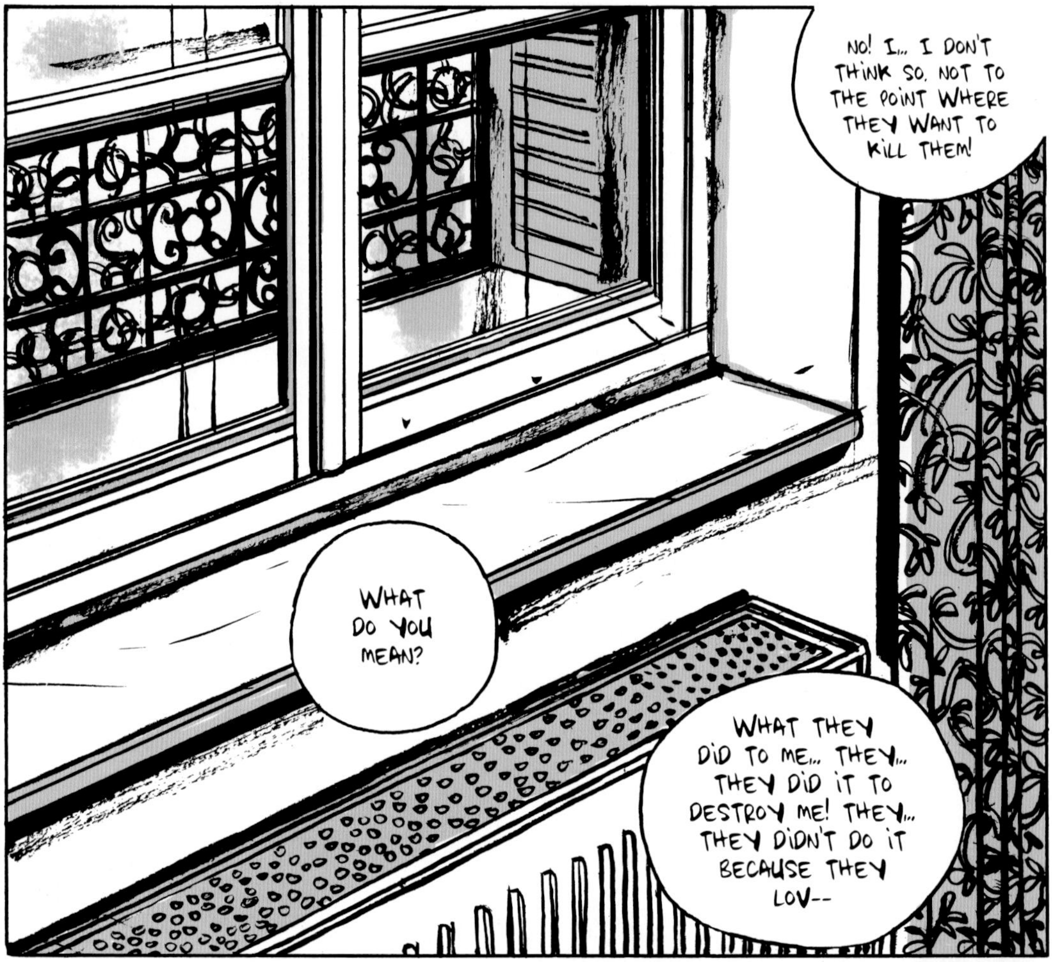
NO! I... I DON'T THINK SO. NOT TO THE POINT WHERE THEY WANT TO KILL THEM!
WHAT DO YOU MEAN?
WHAT THEY DID TO ME... THEY... THEY DID IT TO DESTROY ME! THEY... THEY DIDN'T DO IT BECAUSE THEY LOV--

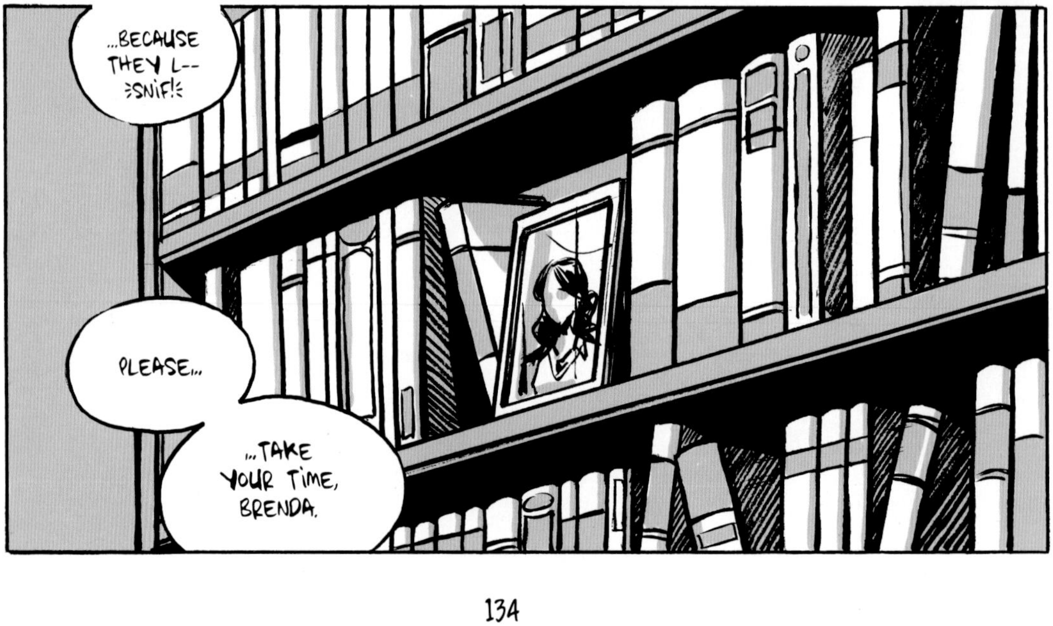
...BECAUSE THEY L-- SNIF!
PLEASE...
...TAKE YOUR TIME, BRENDA.

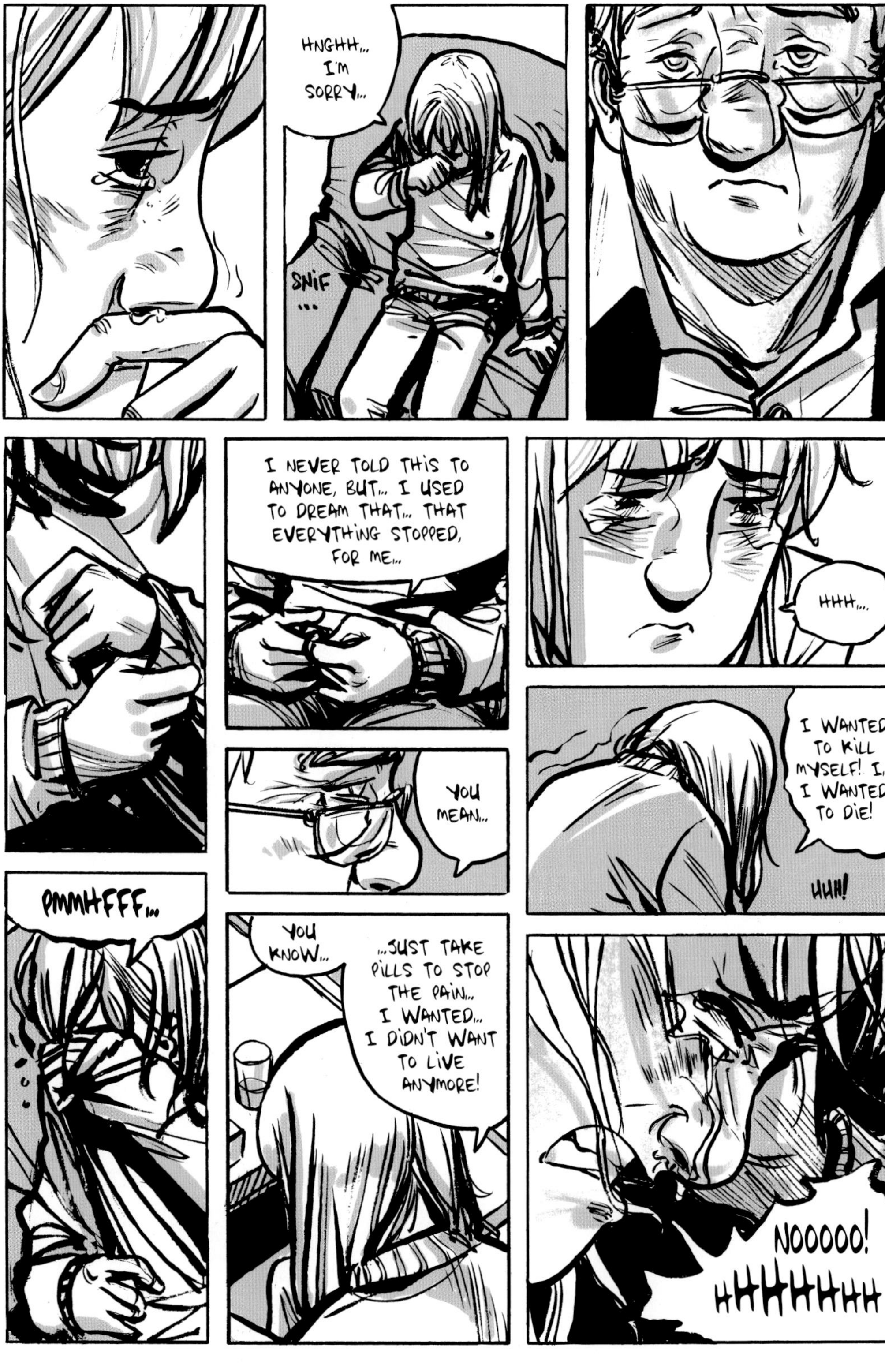

HNGHH... I'M SORRY...
SNIF ...
I NEVER TOLD THIS TO ANYONE, BUT... I USED TO DREAM THAT... THAT EVERYTHING STOPPED, FOR ME...
HHH....
YOU MEAN...
I WANTED TO KILL MYSELF! I... I WANTED TO DIE!
HUH!
PMMHFFF...
YOU KNOW...
...JUST TAKE PILLS TO STOP THE PAIN... I WANTED... I DIDN'T WANT TO LIVE ANYMORE!
NOOOOO! HHHHHHHH

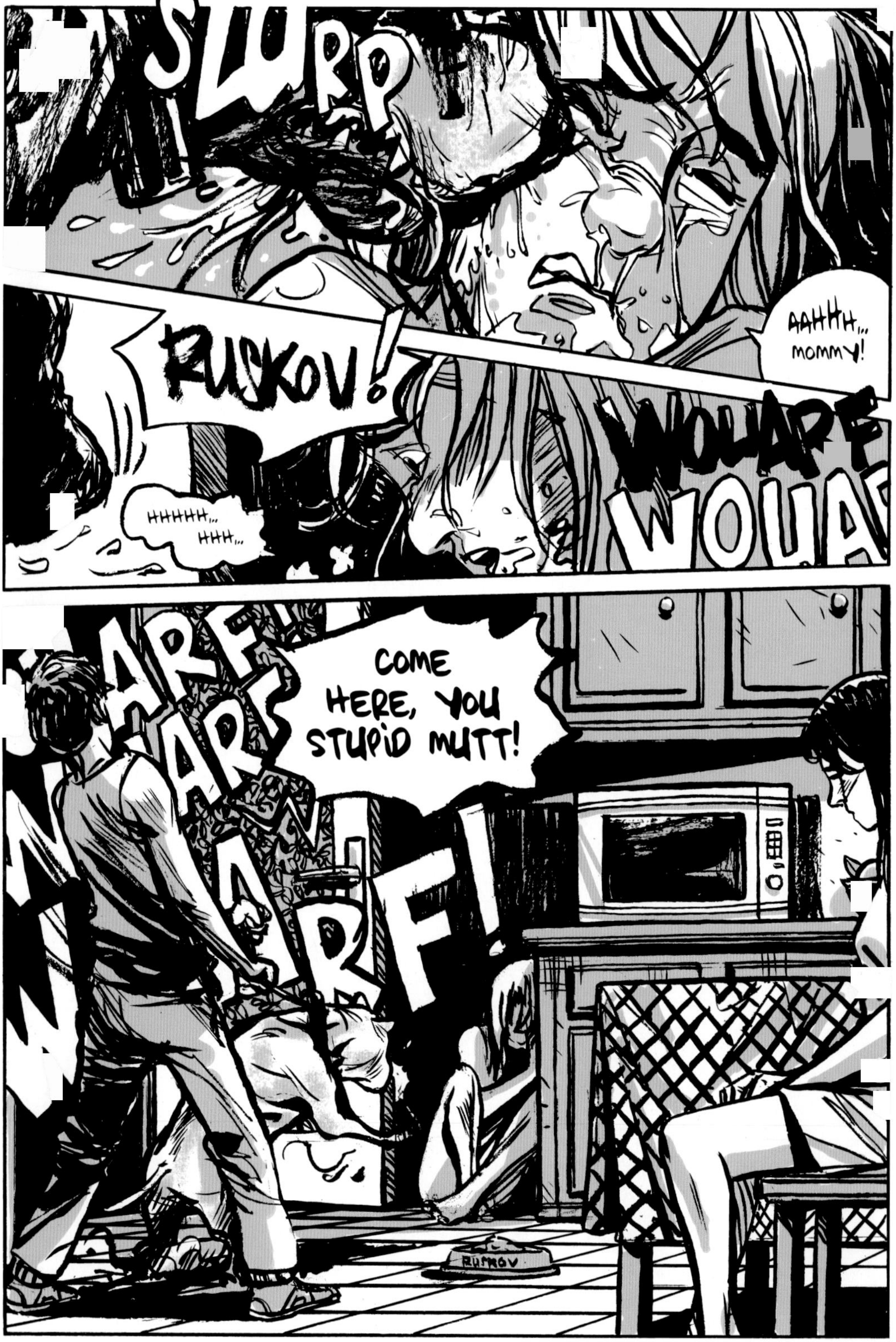
SLURP
RUSKOV!
AAHHH... MOMMY!
HHHHH... HHH...
WOUARF
COME HERE, YOU STUPID MUTT!
ARF!
RUSKOV

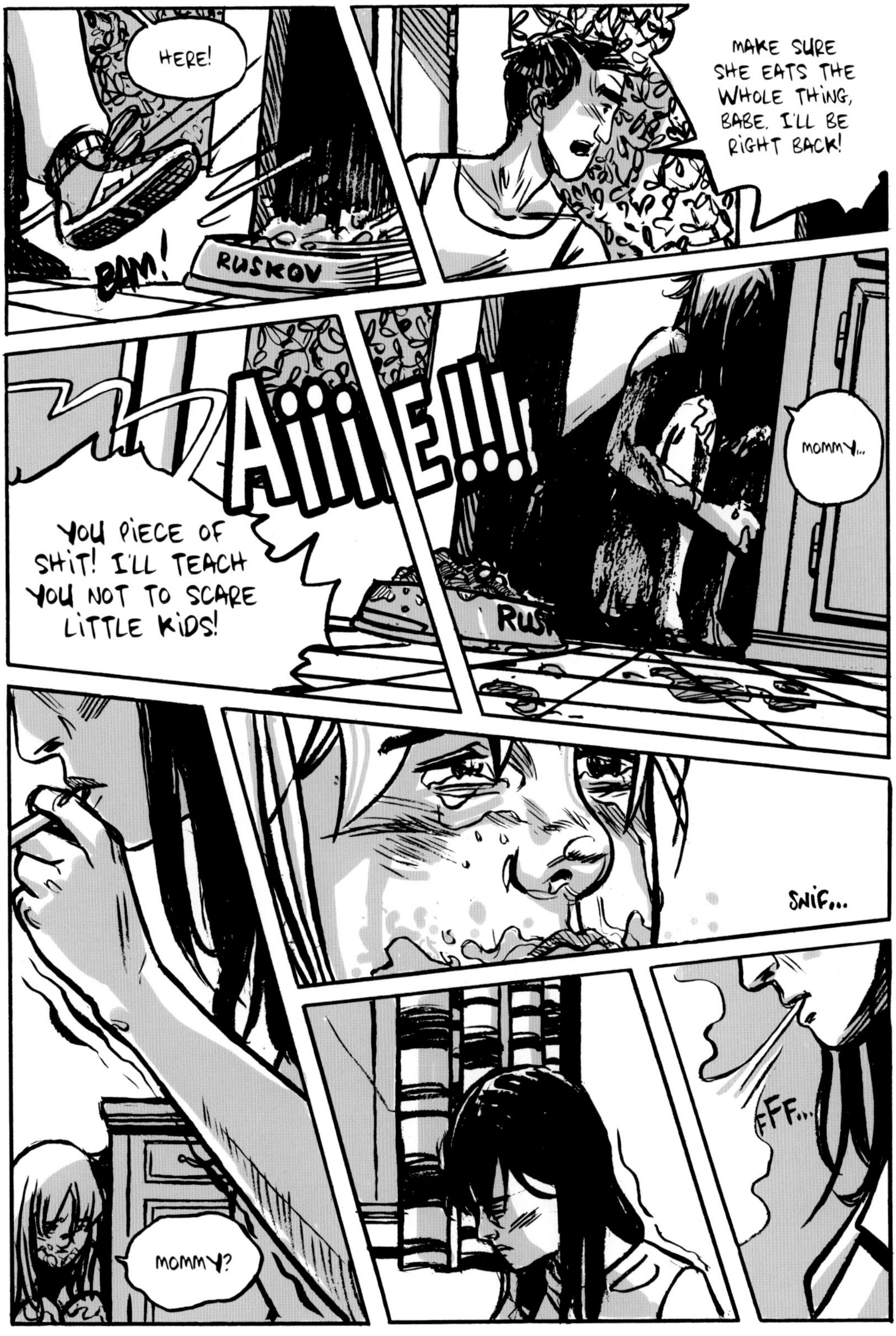
HERE!
BAM!
RUSKOV
MAKE SURE SHE EATS THE WHOLE THING, BABE. I'LL BE RIGHT BACK!
AiiiE!!!
YOU PIECE OF SHIT! I'LL TEACH YOU NOT TO SCARE LITTLE KIDS!
MOMMY...
SNIF...
MOMMY?
FFF...

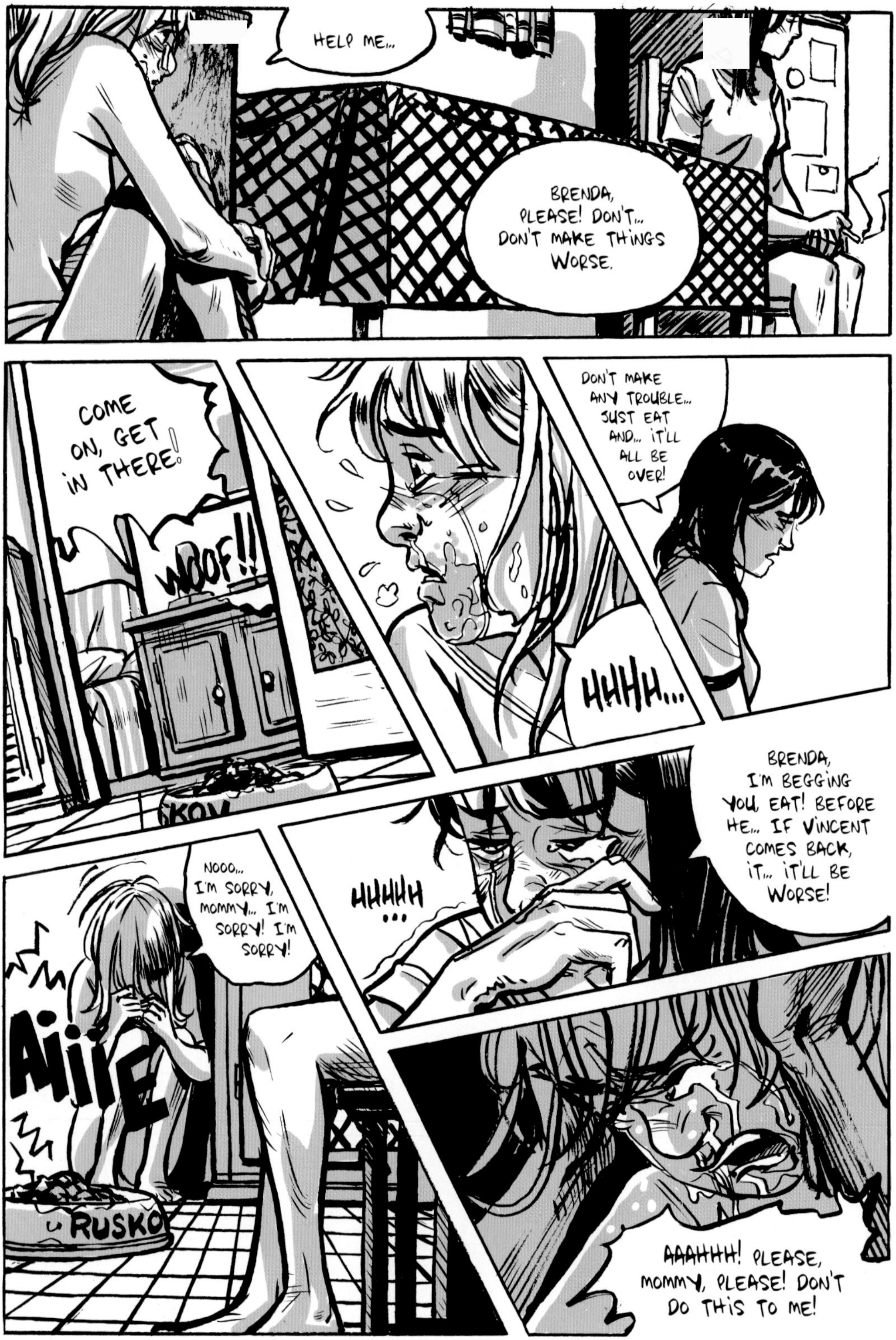
HELP ME...
BRENDA, PLEASE! DON'T... DON'T MAKE THINGS WORSE.
COME ON, GET IN THERE!
WOOF!!
RUSKO
HHHH...
DON'T MAKE ANY TROUBLE... JUST EAT AND... IT'LL ALL BE OVER!
NOOO... I'M SORRY, MOMMY... I'M SORRY! I'M SORRY!
AIIIE
RUSKO
HHHHH...
BRENDA, I'M BEGGING YOU, EAT! BEFORE HE... IF VINCENT COMES BACK, IT... IT'LL BE WORSE!
AAAHHH! PLEASE, MOMMY, PLEASE! DON'T DO THIS TO ME!

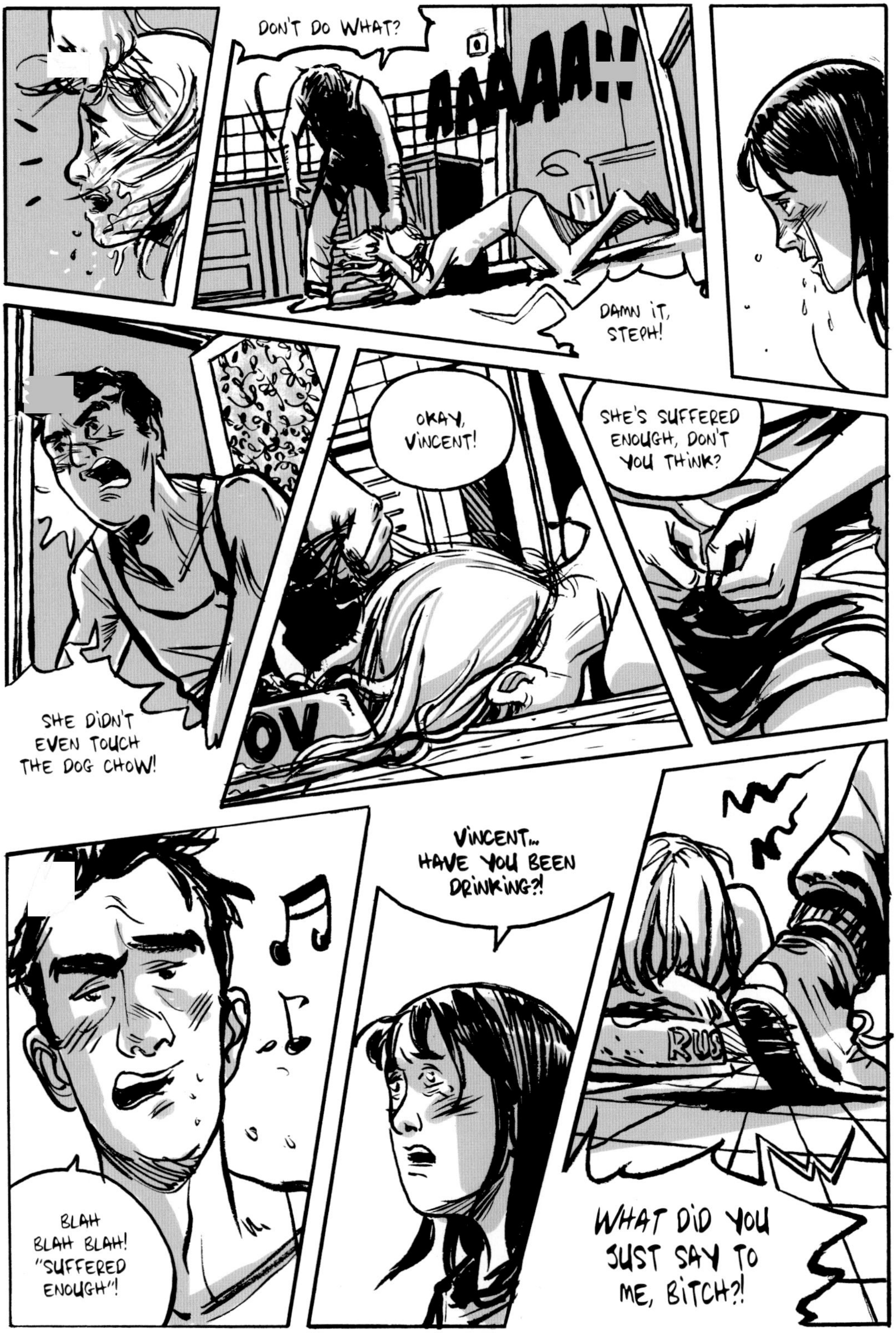
DON'T DO WHAT?
AAAAA!!
DAMN IT, STEPH!
SHE DIDN'T EVEN TOUCH THE DOG CHOW!
OKAY, VINCENT!
SHE'S SUFFERED ENOUGH, DON'T YOU THINK?
BLAH BLAH BLAH! "SUFFERED ENOUGH"!
VINCENT... HAVE YOU BEEN DRINKING?!
WHAT DID YOU JUST SAY TO ME, BITCH?!

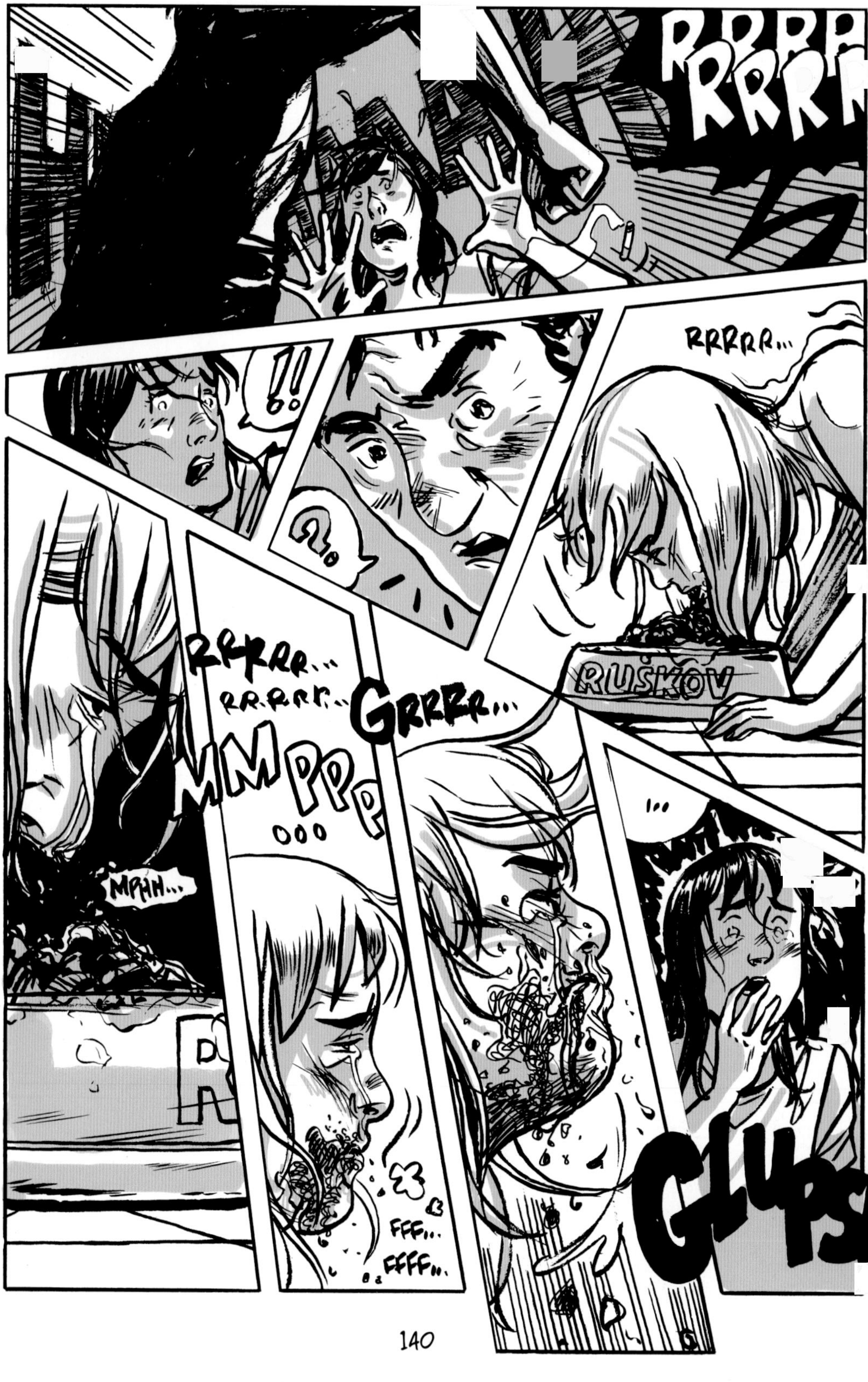
RRRR
RRRR
!!
?
RRRRR...
RUSKOV
RRRRR...
RRRRRR...
GRRRR...
MMPPP
OOO
MPHH...
...
FFF...
FFFF...
GLUPS!

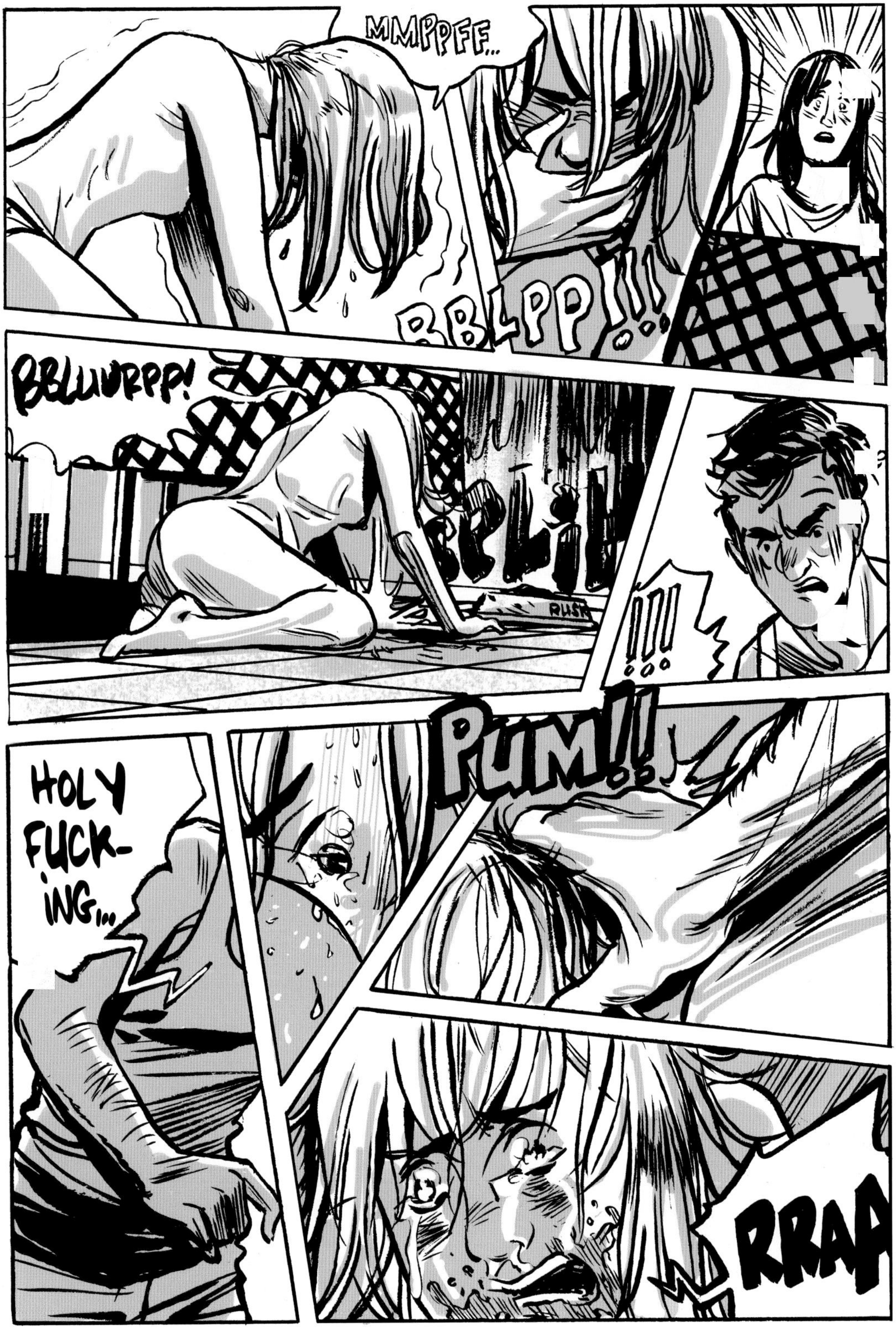
MMPPFF...
BBLPP!!!
BBLLURPP!
RUSH
!!!
PUM!!
HOLY FUCKING...
RRAP

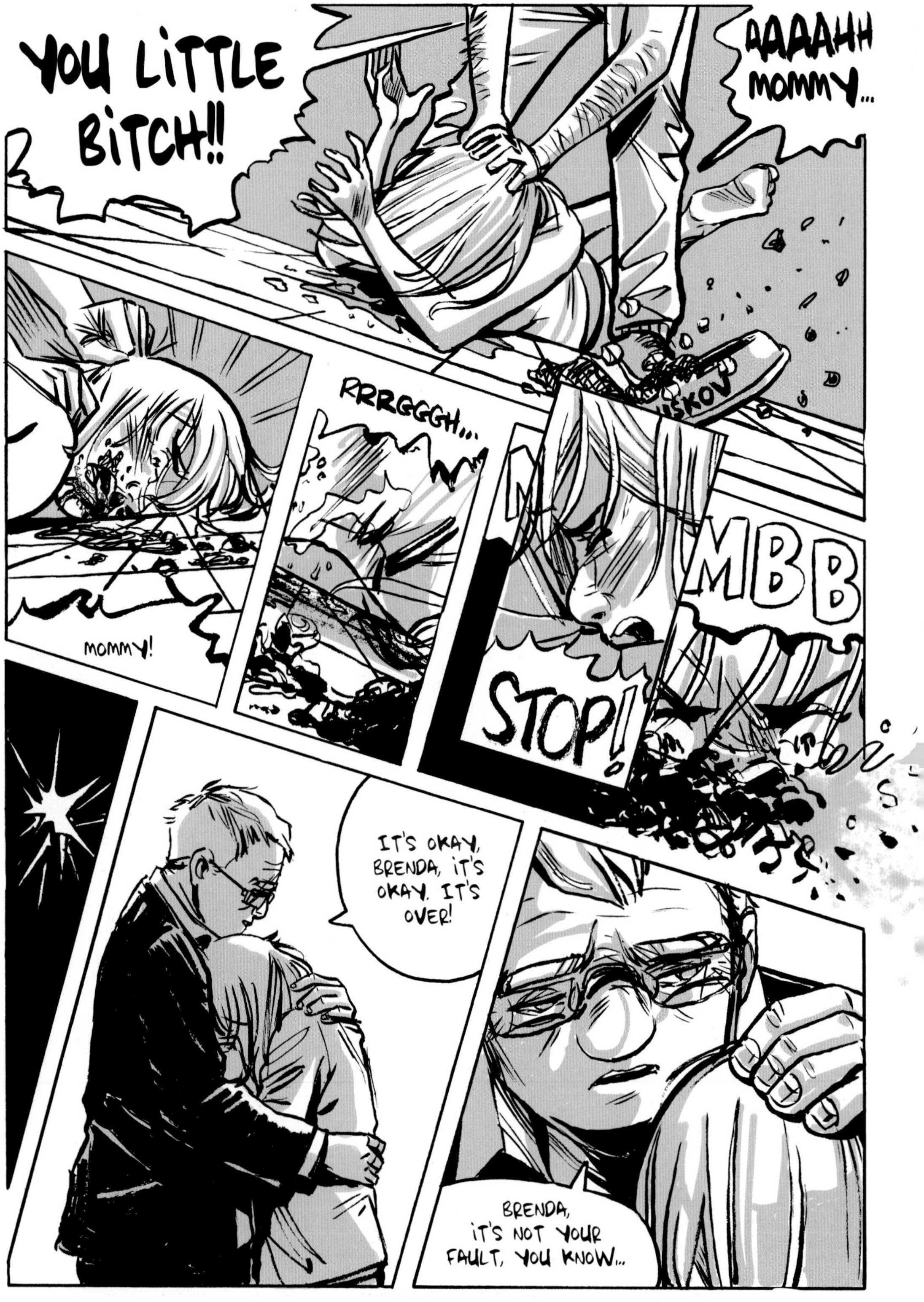
YOU LITTLE BITCH!!
AAAAHH MOMMY...
ISKOV
MOMMY!
RRRGGGH...
MBB
STOP!
IT'S OKAY, BRENDA, IT'S OKAY. IT'S OVER!
BRENDA, IT'S NOT YOUR FAULT, YOU KNOW...

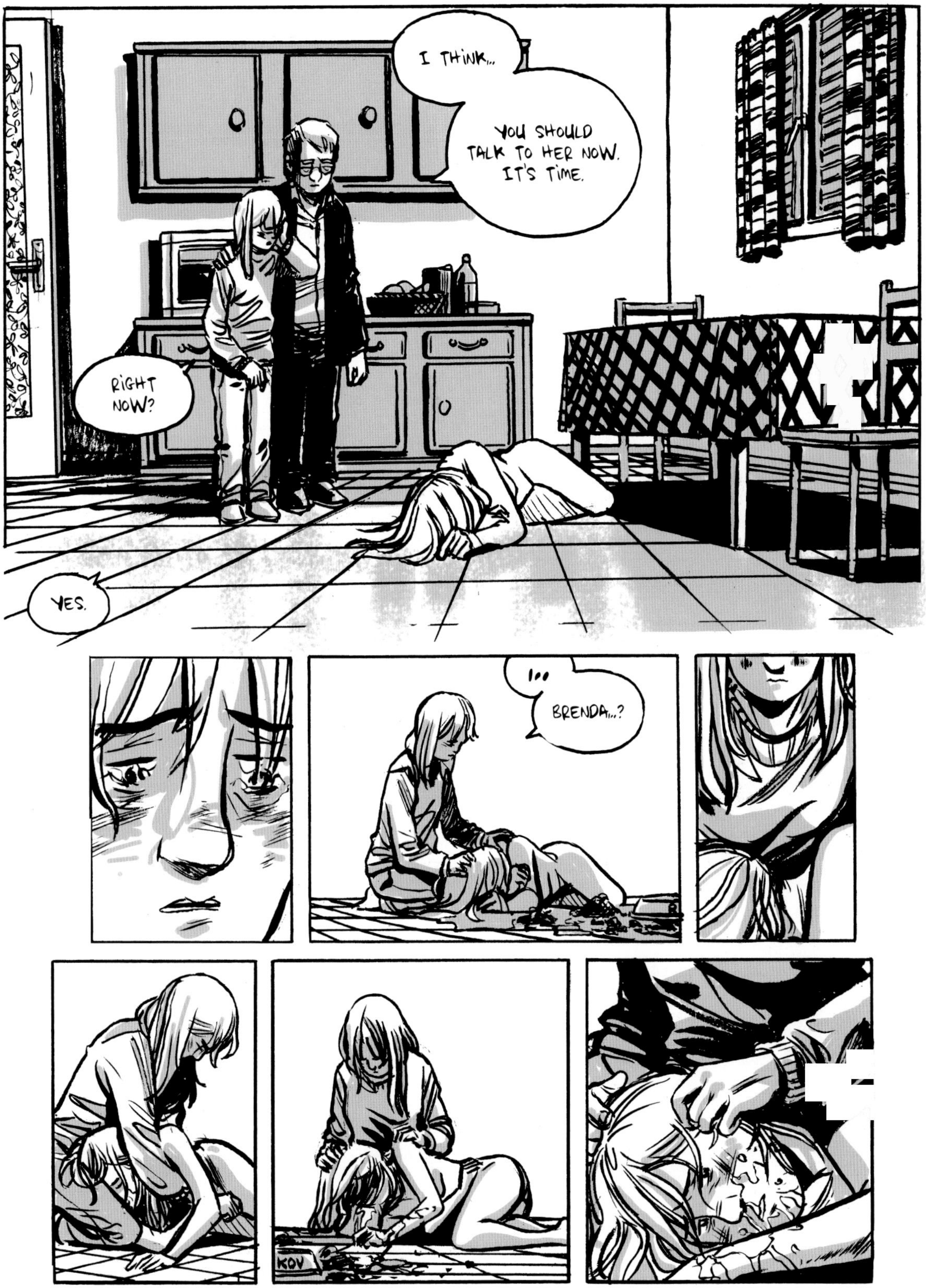
I THINK...
YOU SHOULD TALK TO HER NOW. IT'S TIME.
RIGHT NOW?
YES.
I...
BRENDA...?
KOV

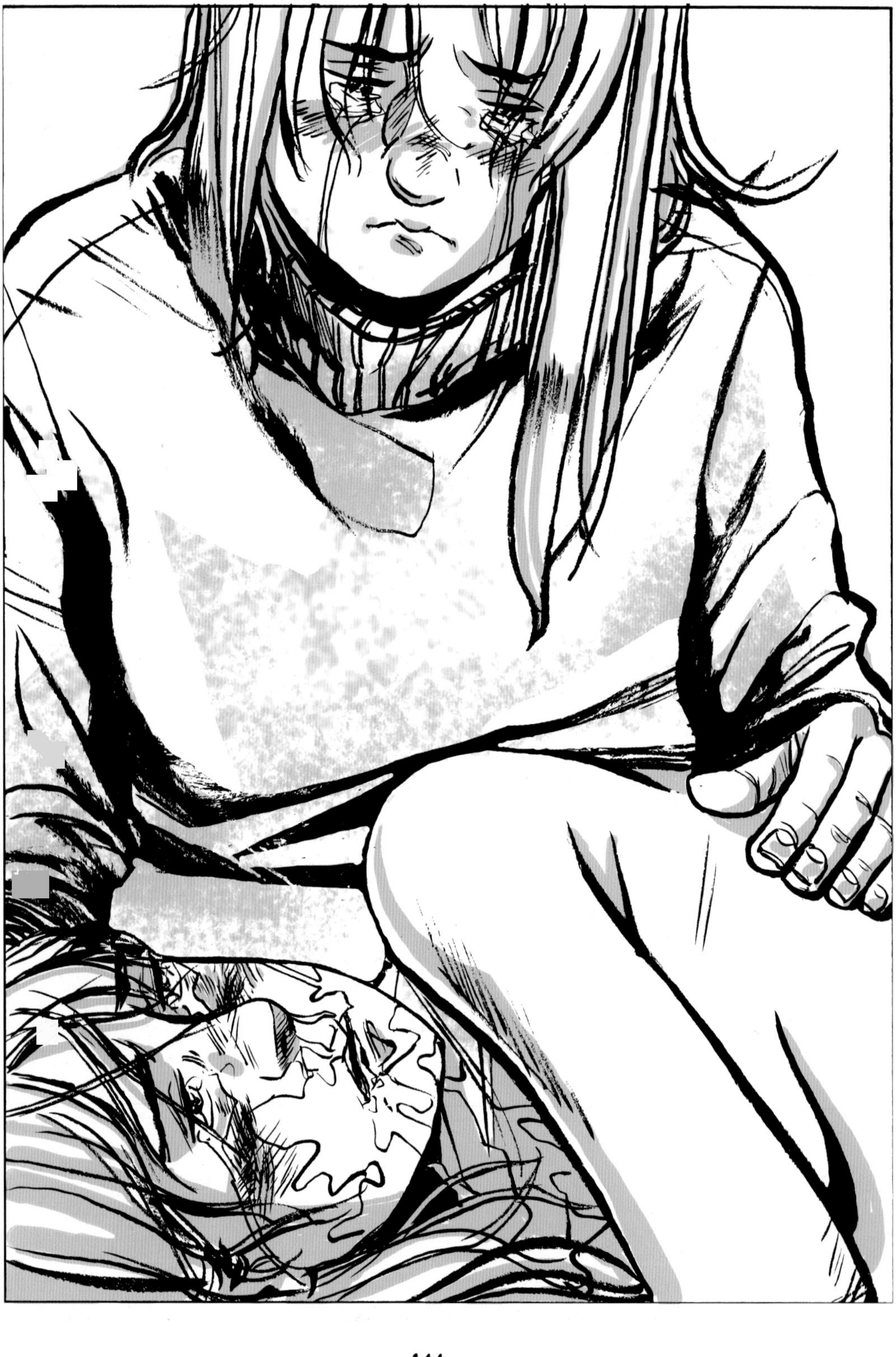

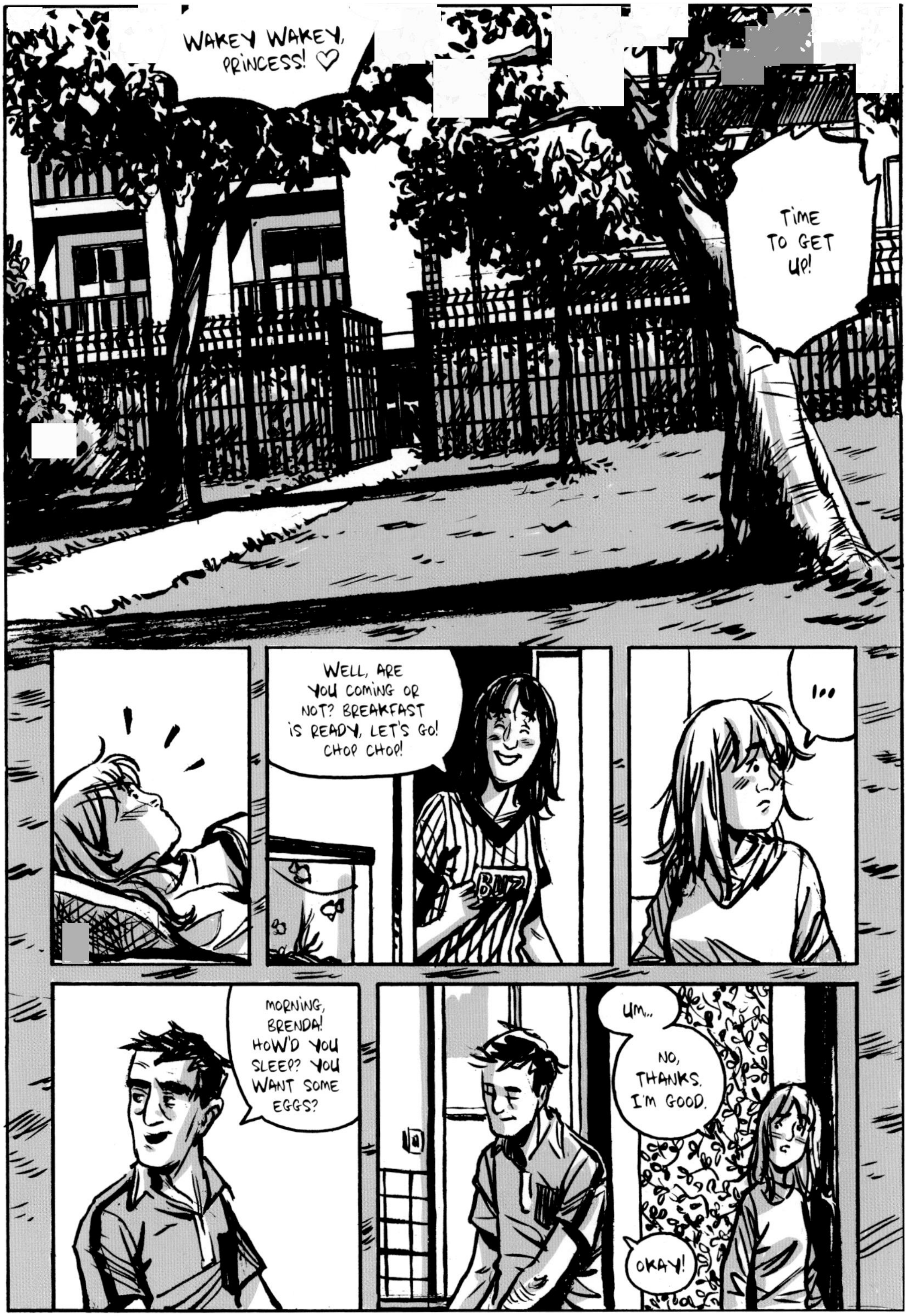
WAKEY WAKEY, PRINCESS! ♡
TIME TO GET UP!
!
WELL, ARE YOU COMING OR NOT? BREAKFAST IS READY, LET'S GO! CHOP CHOP!
...
MORNING, BRENDA! HOW'D YOU SLEEP? YOU WANT SOME EGGS?
UM..
NO, THANKS. I'M GOOD.
OKAY!

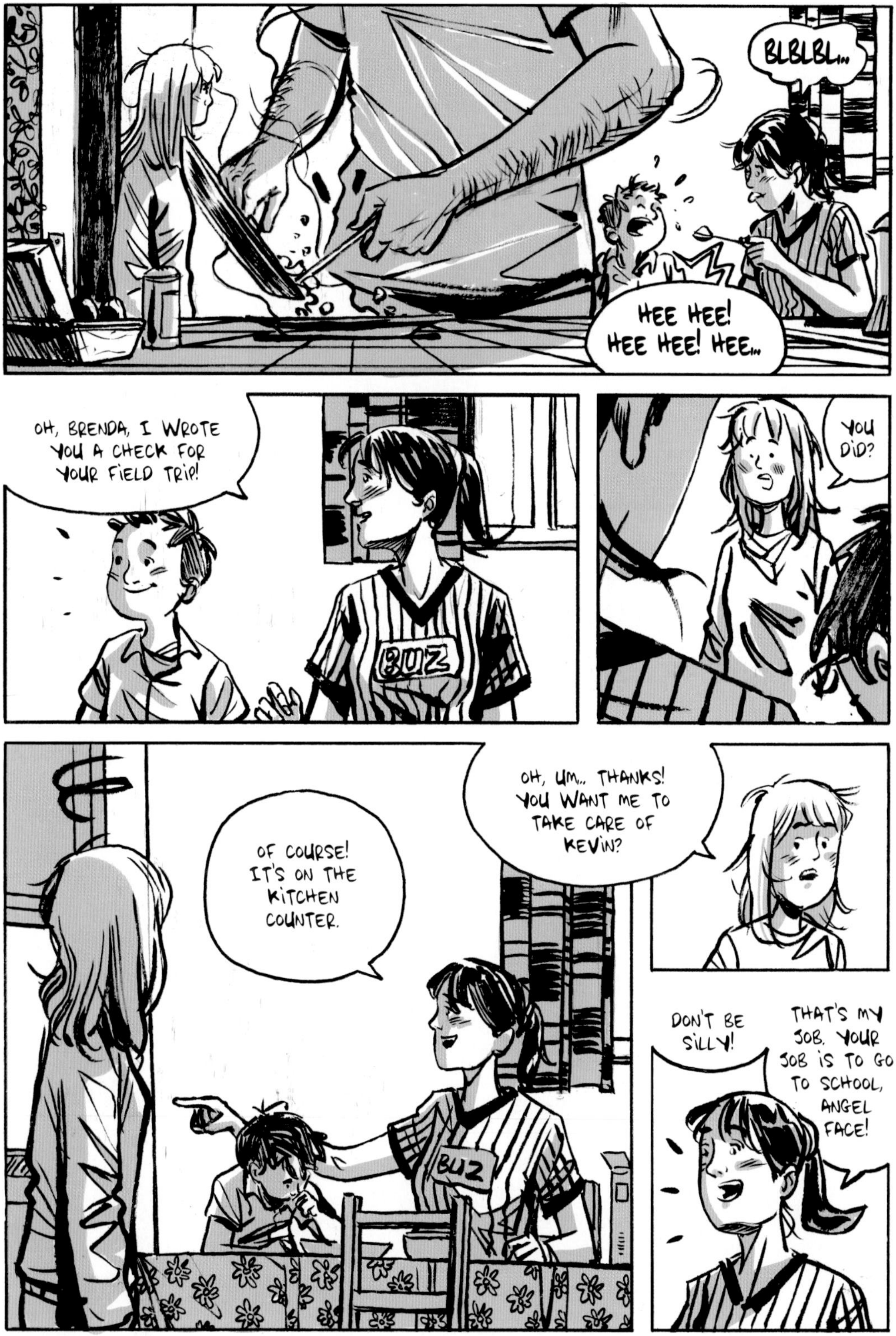
BLBLBL...
HEE HEE! HEE HEE! HEE...
OH, BRENDA, I WROTE YOU A CHECK FOR YOUR FIELD TRIP!
YOU DID?
OF COURSE! IT'S ON THE KITCHEN COUNTER.
OH, UM... THANKS! YOU WANT ME TO TAKE CARE OF KEVIN?
DON'T BE SILLY!
THAT'S MY JOB. YOUR JOB IS TO GO TO SCHOOL, ANGEL FACE!

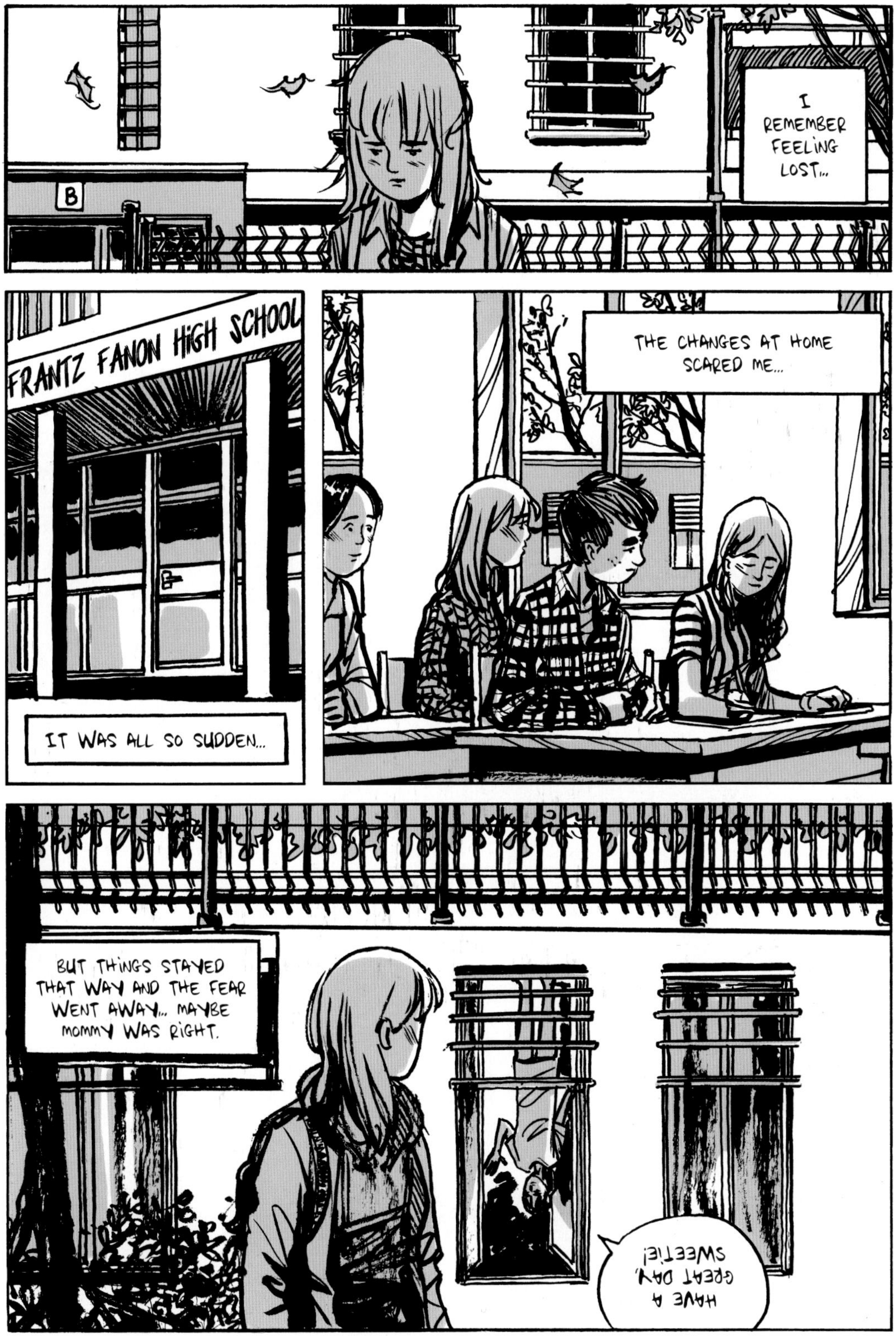
B
I REMEMBER FEELING LOST...
FRANTZ FANON HIGH SCHOOL
IT WAS ALL SO SUDDEN...
THE CHANGES AT HOME SCARED ME...
BUT THINGS STAYED THAT WAY AND THE FEAR WENT AWAY... MAYBE MOMMY WAS RIGHT.
HAVE A GREAT DAY, SWEETIE!

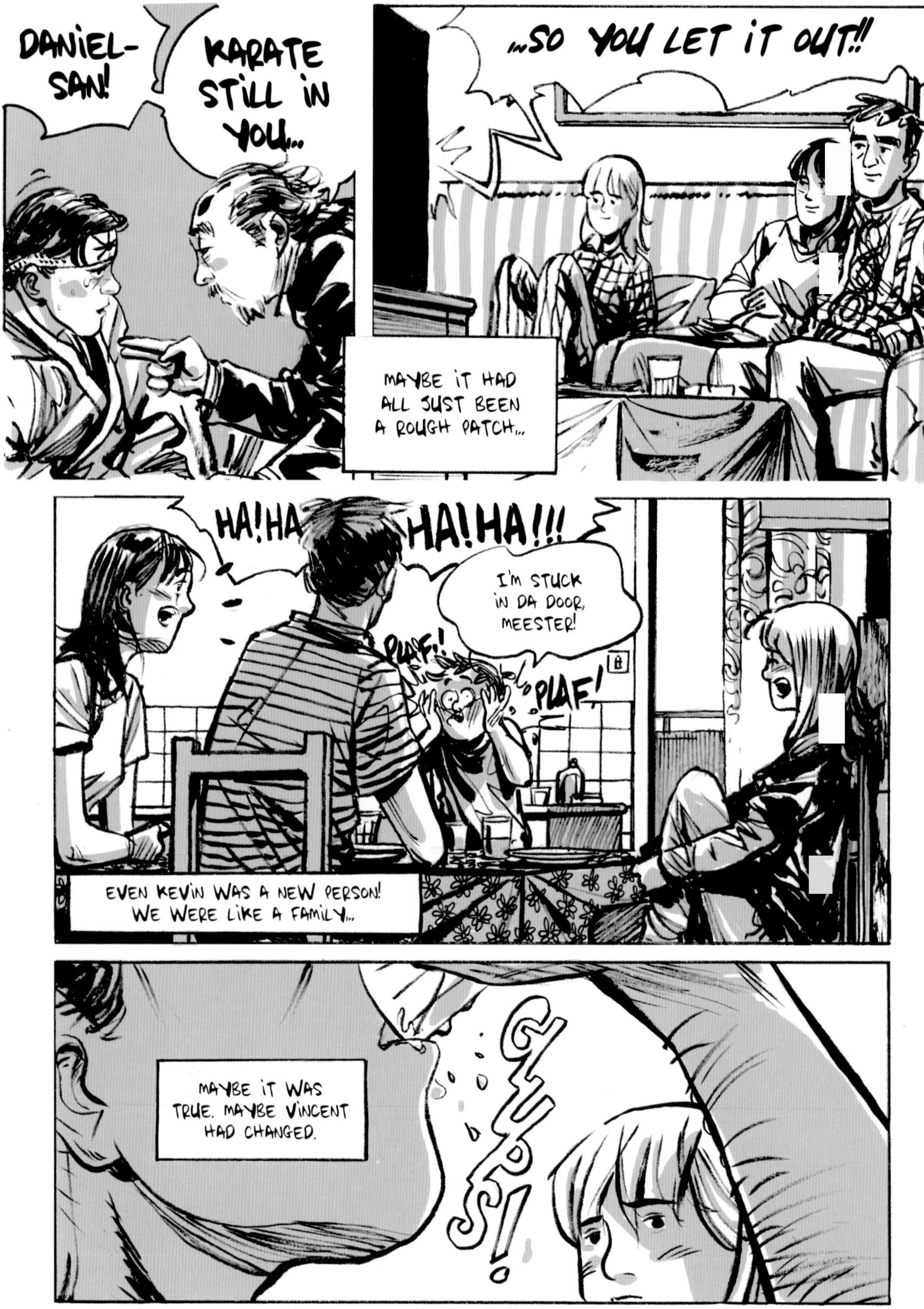
DANIEL-SAN!
KARATE STILL IN YOU...
...SO YOU LET IT OUT!!
MAYBE IT HAD ALL JUST BEEN A ROUGH PATCH...
HA!HA HA!HA!!!
I'M STUCK IN DA DOOR, MEESTER!
PLAF!
PLAF!
EVEN KEVIN WAS A NEW PERSON! WE WERE LIKE A FAMILY...
MAYBE IT WAS TRUE. MAYBE VINCENT HAD CHANGED.
GLUPS!

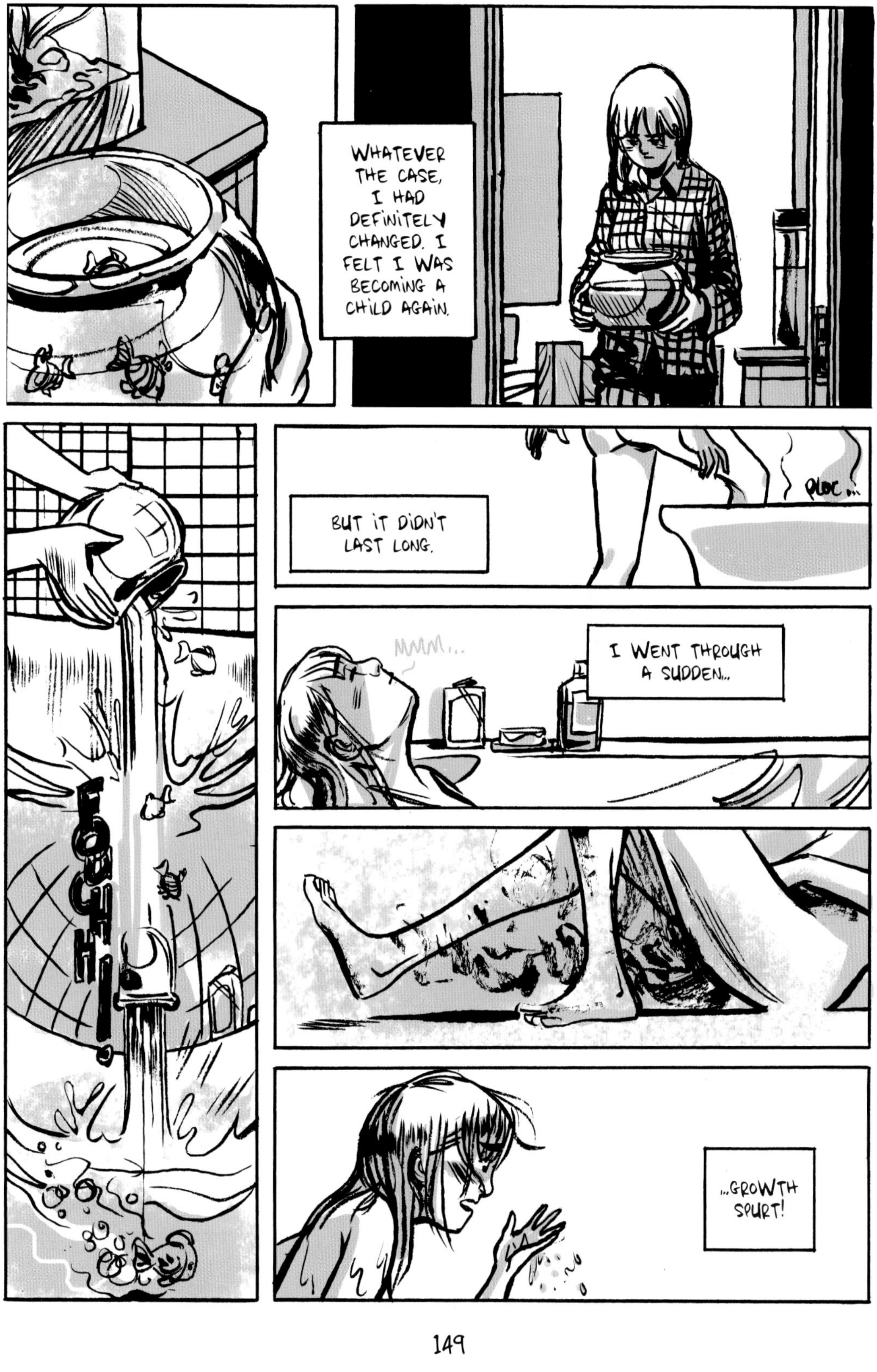
WHATEVER THE CASE, I HAD DEFINITELY CHANGED. I FELT I WAS BECOMING A CHILD AGAIN.
BUT IT DIDN'T LAST LONG.
PLOC...
MMM...
I WENT THROUGH A SUDDEN...
...GROWTH SPURT!

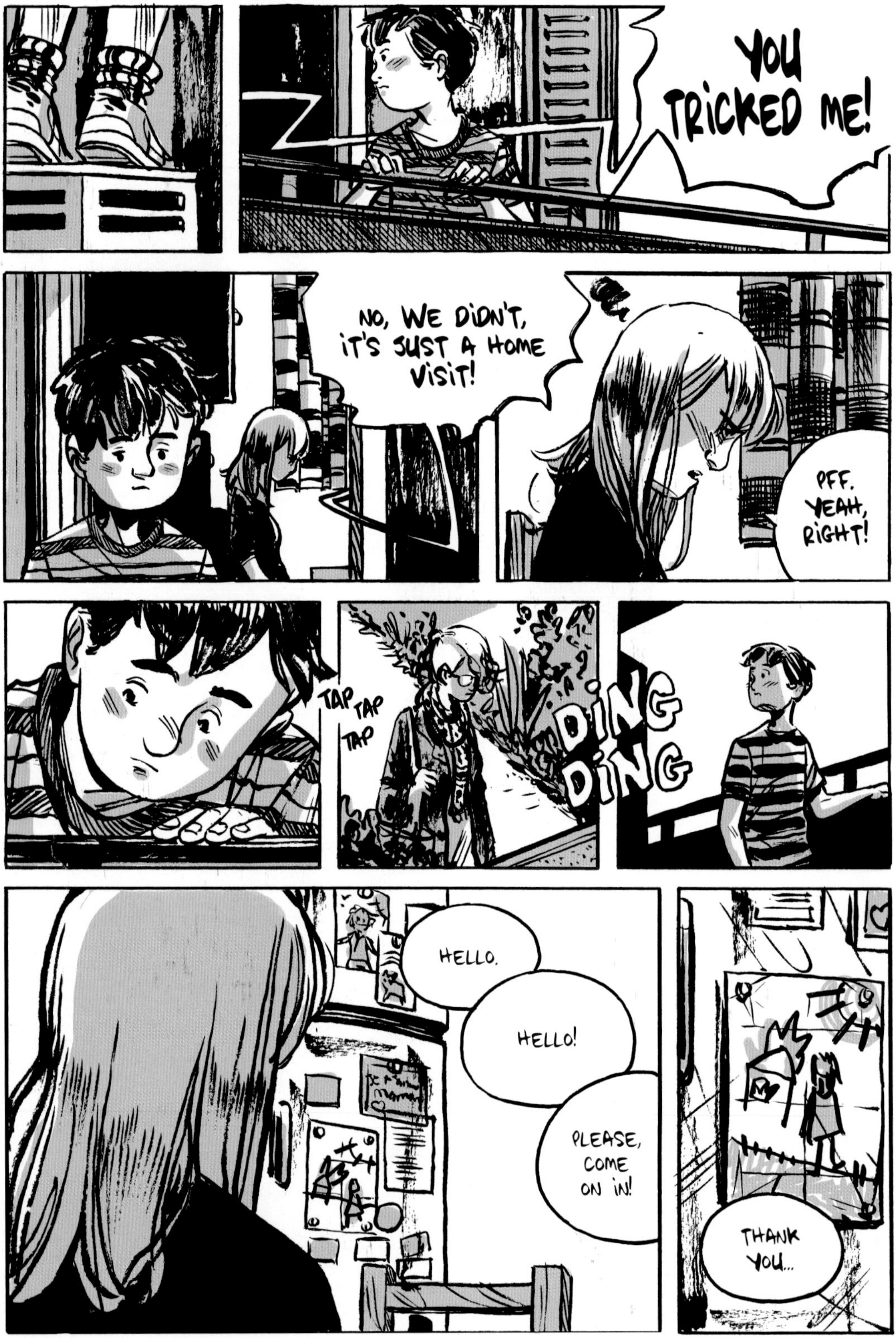

YOU TRICKED ME!
NO, WE DIDN'T, IT'S JUST A HOME VISIT!
PFF. YEAH, RIGHT!
TAP TAP TAP
DING DING
HELLO.
HELLO!
PLEASE, COME ON IN!
THANK YOU...

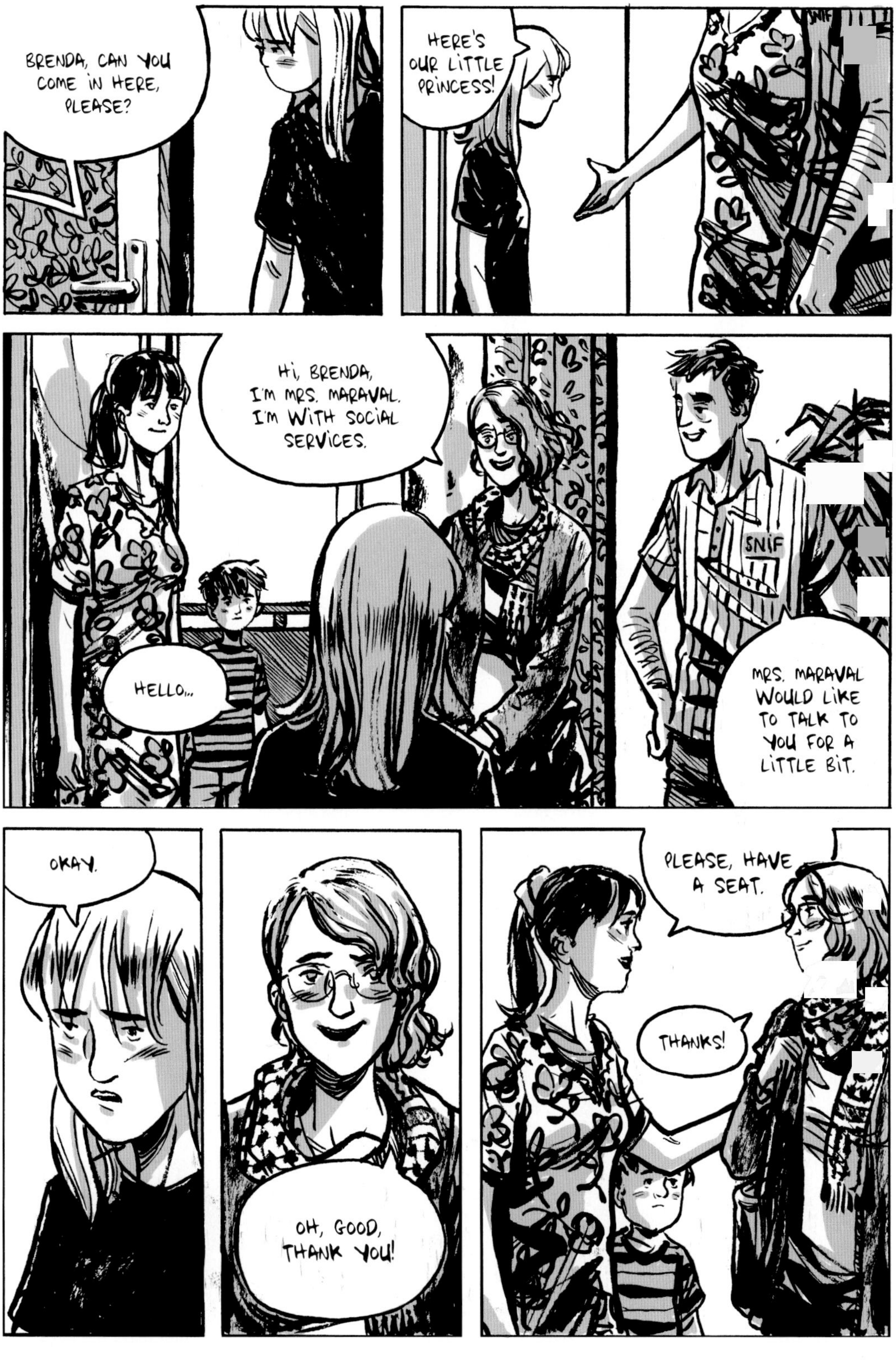
BRENDA, CAN YOU COME IN HERE, PLEASE?
HERE'S OUR LITTLE PRINCESS!
SNIF
HI, BRENDA, I'M MRS. MARAVAL. I'M WITH SOCIAL SERVICES.
HELLO...
SNIF
MRS. MARAVAL WOULD LIKE TO TALK TO YOU FOR A LITTLE BIT.
OKAY.
OH, GOOD, THANK YOU!
PLEASE, HAVE A SEAT.
THANKS!

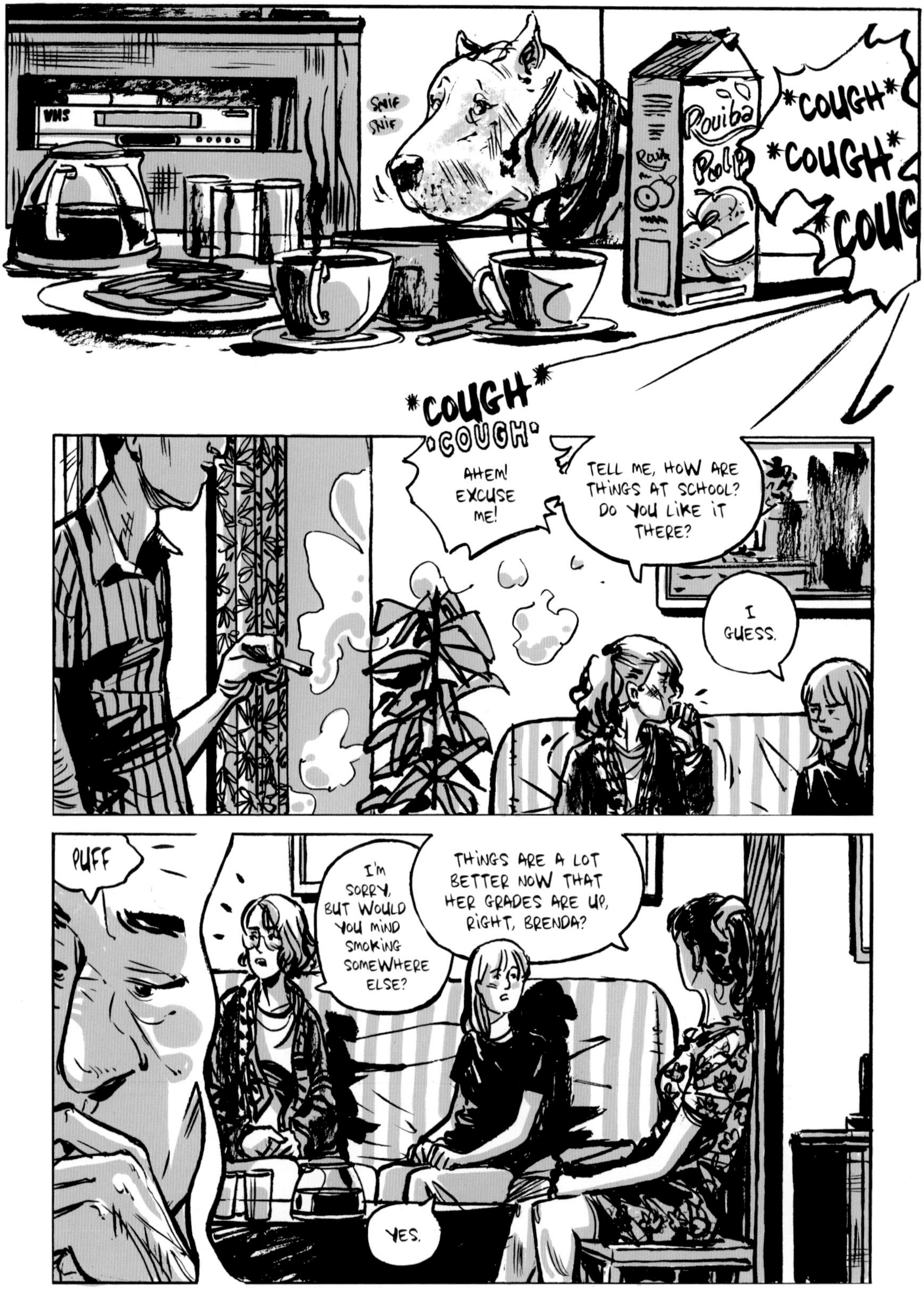

SNIF SNIF
Rouiba
Pulp
COUGH
COUGH
COUG
COUGH
COUGH
AHEM! EXCUSE ME!
TELL ME, HOW ARE THINGS AT SCHOOL? DO YOU LIKE IT THERE?
I GUESS.
PUFF
I'M SORRY, BUT WOULD YOU MIND SMOKING SOMEWHERE ELSE?
THINGS ARE A LOT BETTER NOW THAT HER GRADES ARE UP, RIGHT, BRENDA?
YES.

IS THAT RIGHT?

THAT'S GREAT TO HEAR!

WAY TO GO, BRENDA!

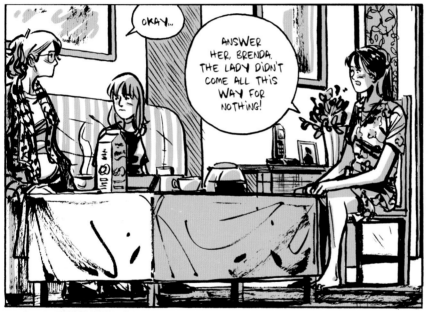

OKAY...

ANSWER HER, BRENDA. THE LADY DIDN'T COME ALL THIS WAY FOR NOTHING!

YOU'LL HAVE TO EXCUSE HER...

WE TOLD HER YOU WERE COMING, BUT SHE WAS INTIMIDATED!

OH.

153

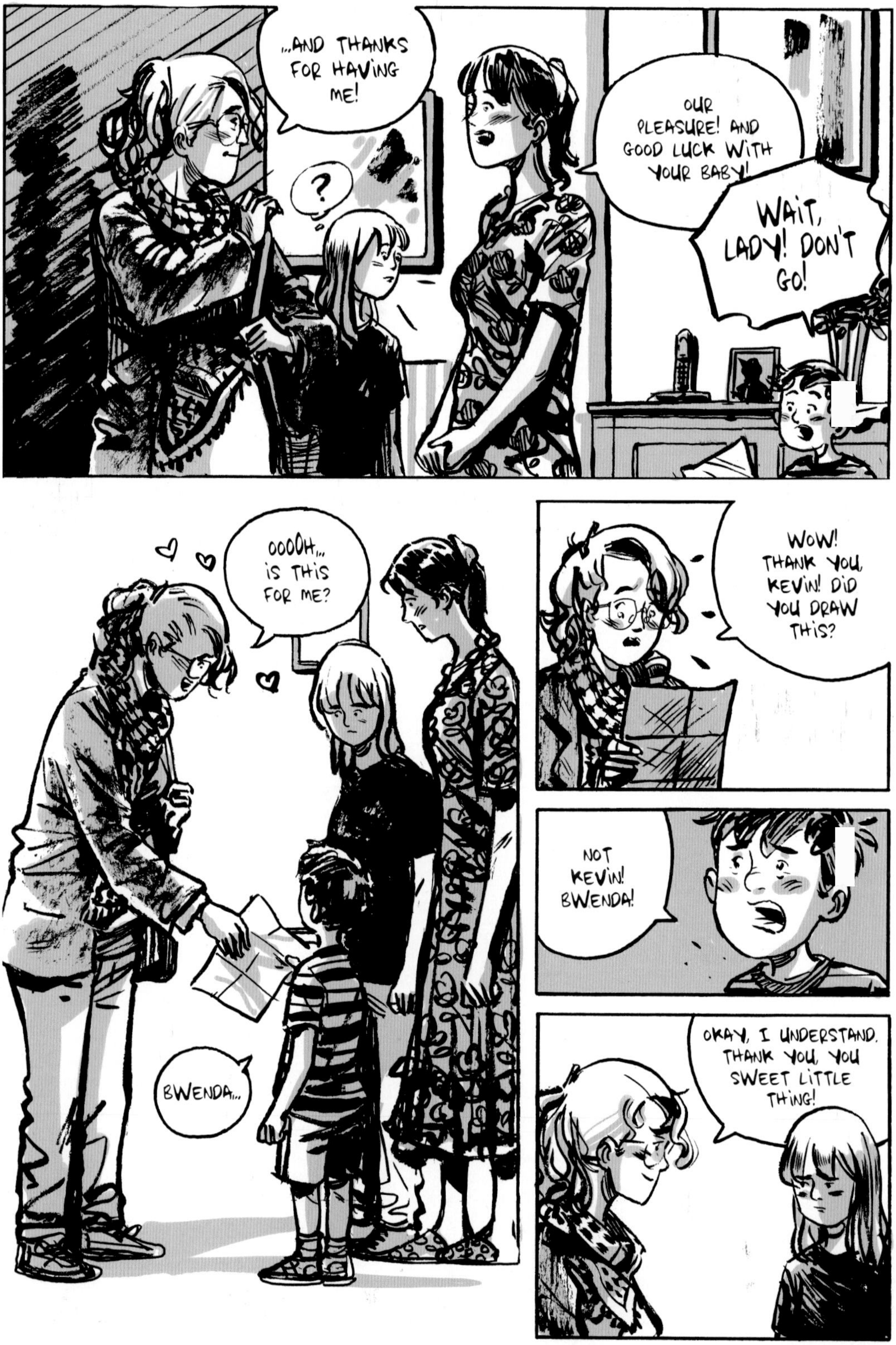
...AND THANKS FOR HAVING ME!
?
OUR PLEASURE! AND GOOD LUCK WITH YOUR BABY!
WAIT, LADY! DON'T GO!
OOOOH... IS THIS FOR ME?
BWENDA...
WOW! THANK YOU, KEVIN! DID YOU DRAW THIS?
NOT KEVIN! BWENDA!
OKAY, I UNDERSTAND. THANK YOU, YOU SWEET LITTLE THING!

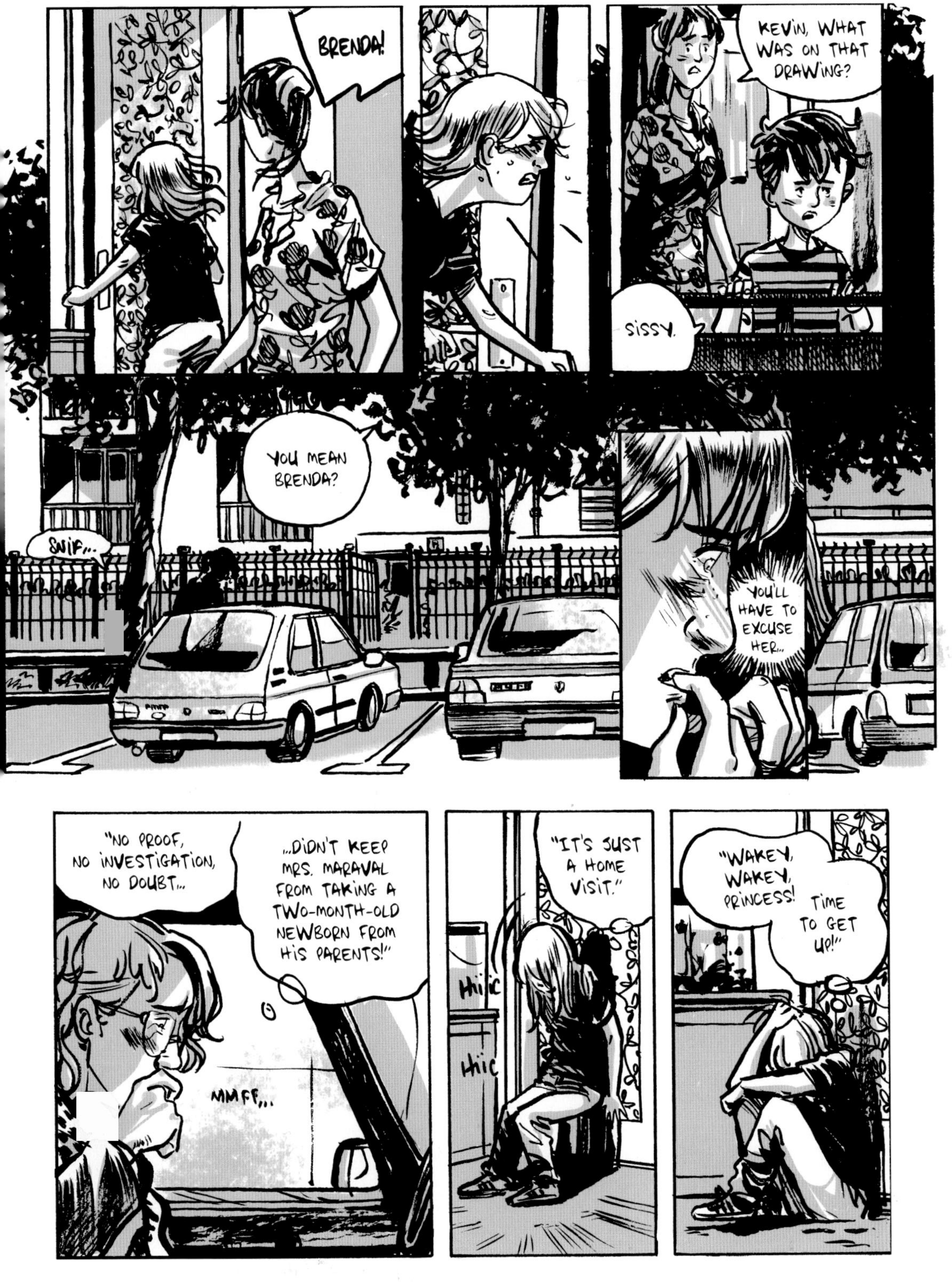
BRENDA!
KEVIN, WHAT WAS ON THAT DRAWING?
SISSY.
SNIF...
YOU MEAN BRENDA?
YOU'LL HAVE TO EXCUSE HER...
"NO PROOF, NO INVESTIGATION, NO DOUBT...
...DIDN'T KEEP MRS. MARAVAL FROM TAKING A TWO-MONTH-OLD NEWBORN FROM HIS PARENTS!"
MMFF...
"IT'S JUST A HOME VISIT."
HIIC
HIIC
"WAKEY, WAKEY, PRINCESS!
TIME TO GET UP!"

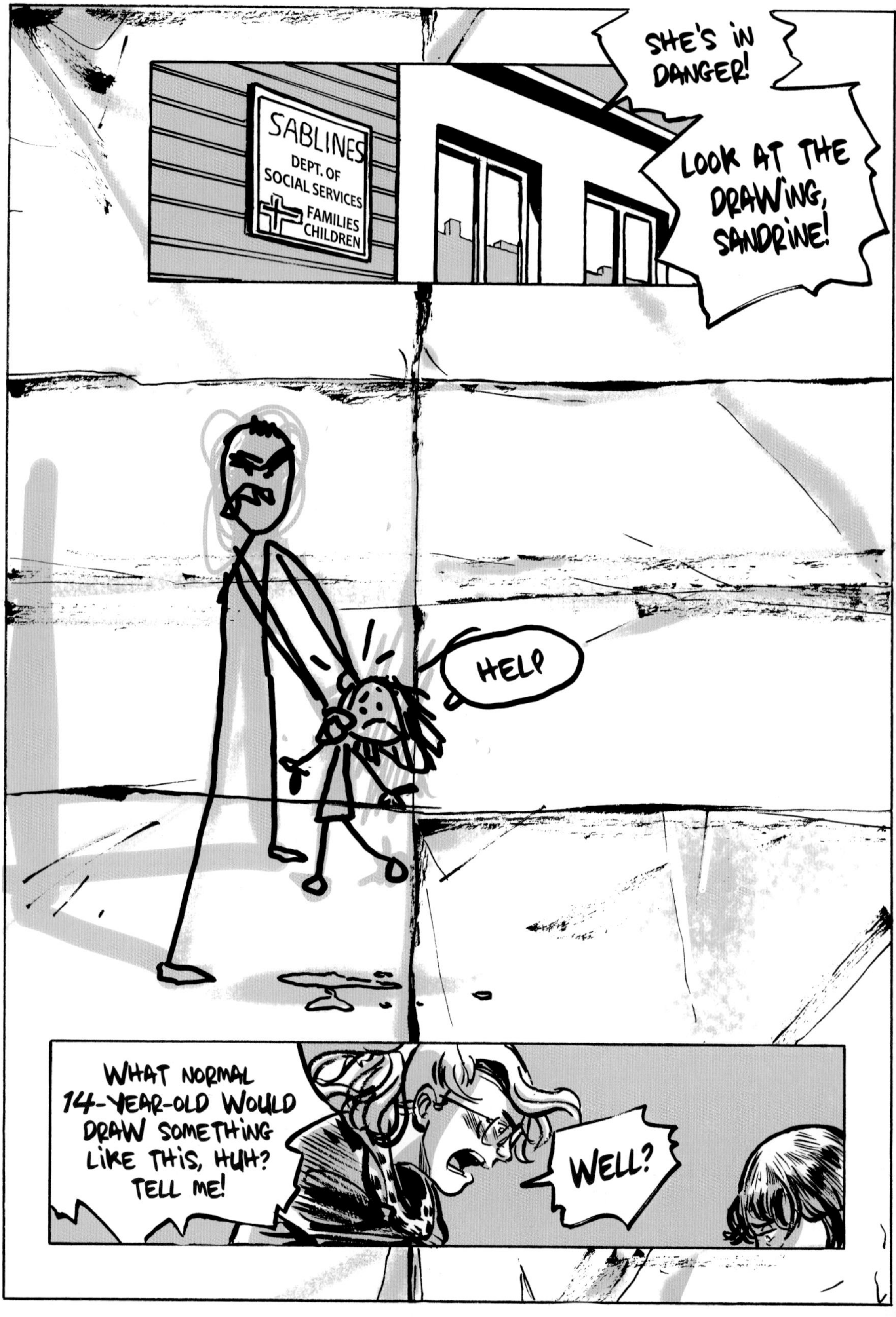
SABLINES
DEPT. OF SOCIAL SERVICES
FAMILIES CHILDREN
SHE'S IN DANGER!
LOOK AT THE DRAWING, SANDRINE!
HELP
WHAT NORMAL 14-YEAR-OLD WOULD DRAW SOMETHING LIKE THIS, HUH? TELL ME!
WELL?

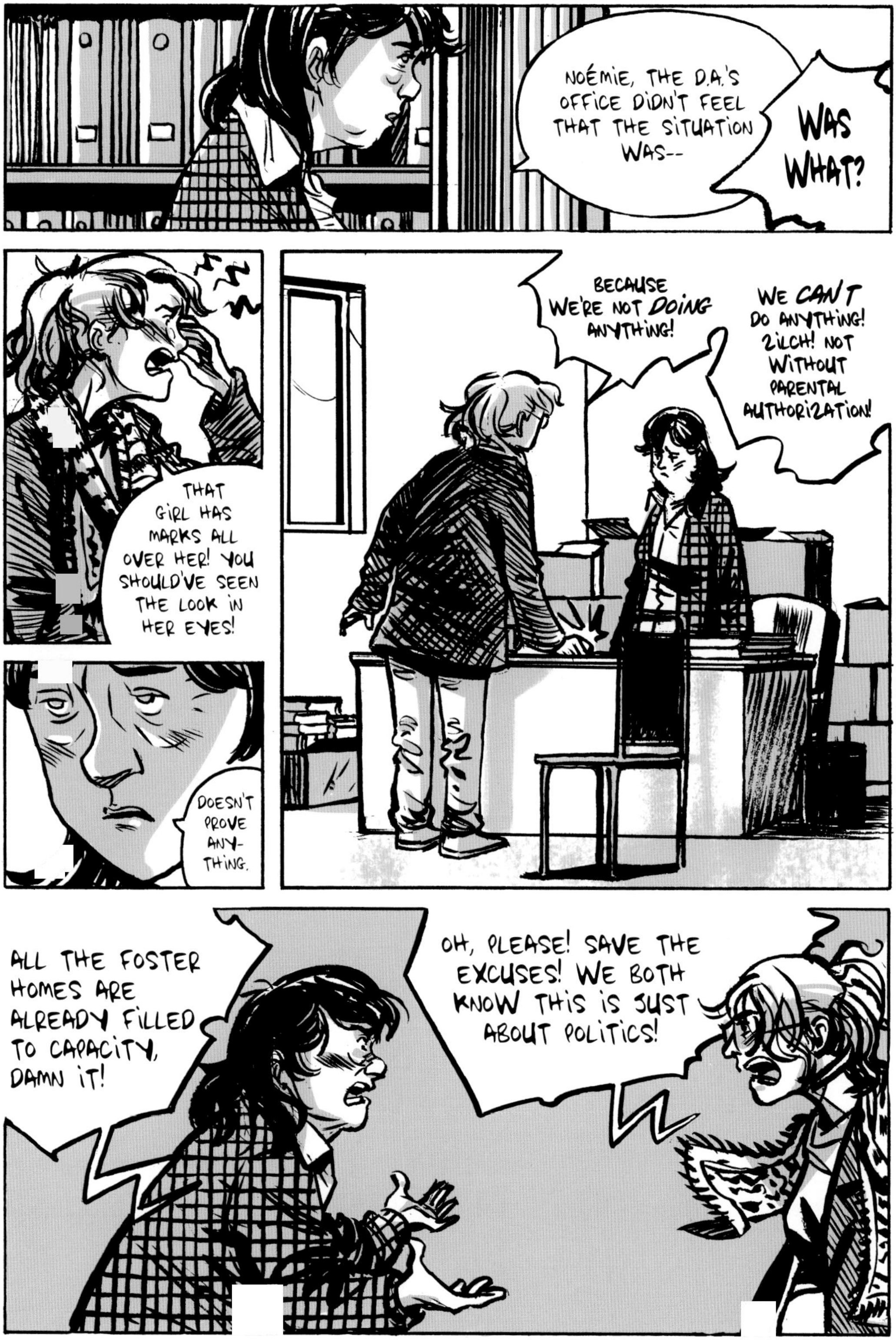
NOÉMIE, THE D.A.'S OFFICE DIDN'T FEEL THAT THE SITUATION WAS--
WAS WHAT?
THAT GIRL HAS MARKS ALL OVER HER! YOU SHOULD'VE SEEN THE LOOK IN HER EYES!
DOESN'T PROVE ANY-THING.
BECAUSE WE'RE NOT *DOING* ANYTHING!
WE *CAN'T* DO ANYTHING! ZILCH! NOT WITHOUT PARENTAL AUTHORIZATION!
ALL THE FOSTER HOMES ARE ALREADY FILLED TO CAPACITY, DAMN IT!
OH, PLEASE! SAVE THE EXCUSES! WE BOTH KNOW THIS IS JUST ABOUT POLITICS!

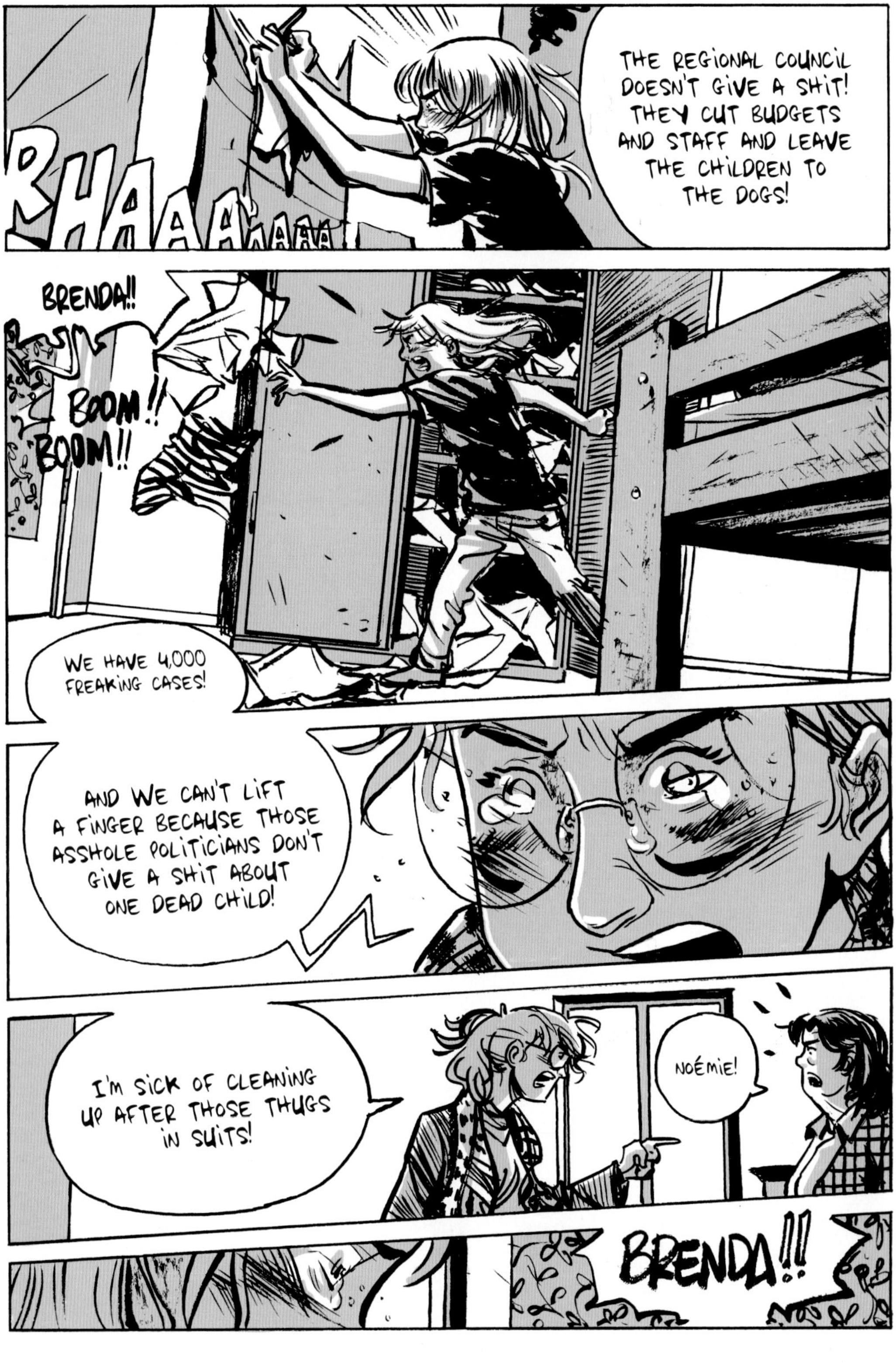
BHAAAAAAA
THE REGIONAL COUNCIL DOESN'T GIVE A SHIT! THEY CUT BUDGETS AND STAFF AND LEAVE THE CHILDREN TO THE DOGS!
BRENDA!!
BOOM!!
BOOM!!
WE HAVE 4,000 FREAKING CASES!
AND WE CAN'T LIFT A FINGER BECAUSE THOSE ASSHOLE POLITICIANS DON'T GIVE A SHIT ABOUT ONE DEAD CHILD!
I'M SICK OF CLEANING UP AFTER THOSE THUGS IN SUITS!
NOÉMIE!
BRENDA!!!

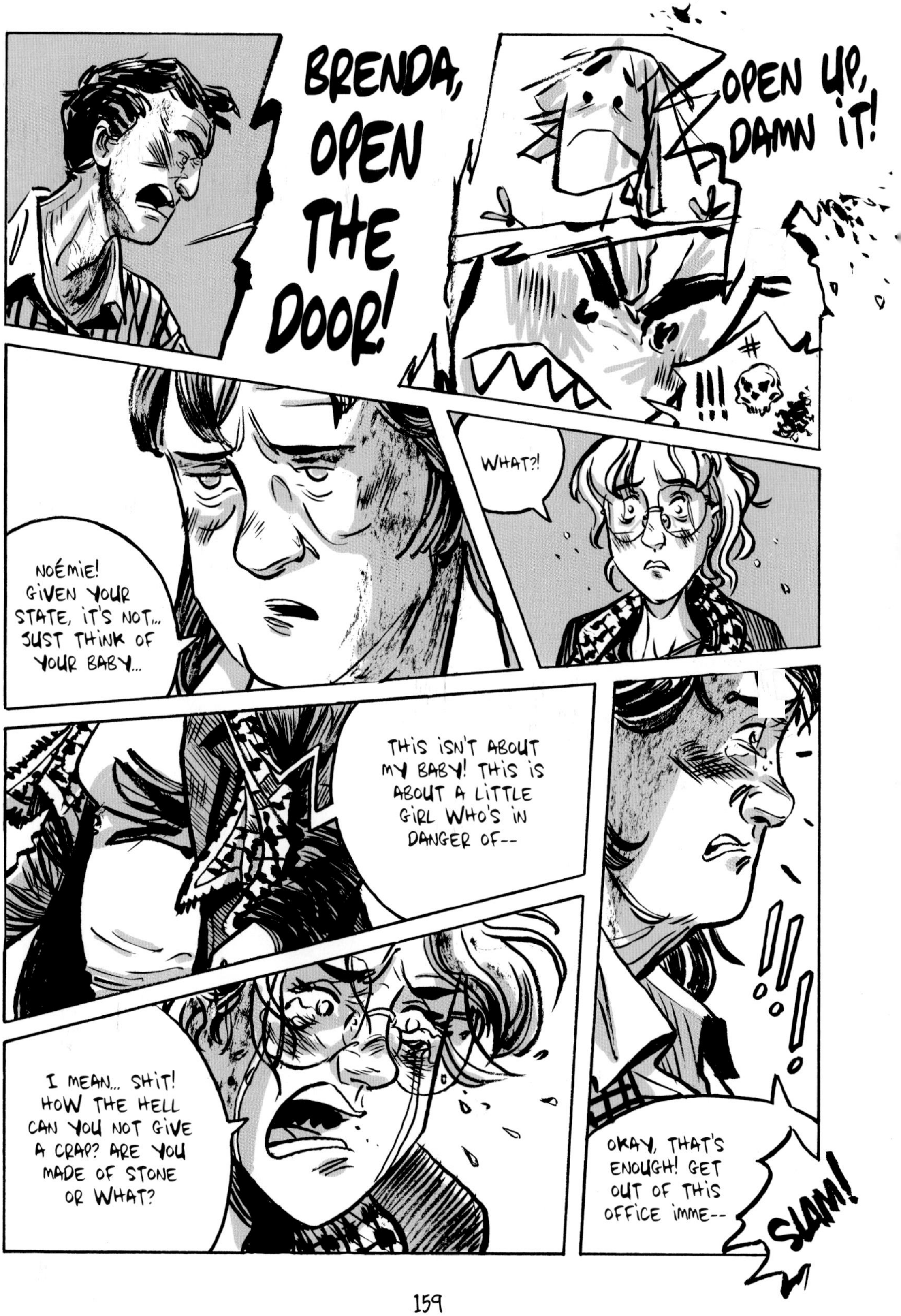
BRENDA, OPEN THE DOOR!
OPEN UP, DAMN IT!
!!!
WHAT?!
NOÉMIE! GIVEN YOUR STATE, IT'S NOT... JUST THINK OF YOUR BABY...
THIS ISN'T ABOUT MY BABY! THIS IS ABOUT A LITTLE GIRL WHO'S IN DANGER OF--
I MEAN... SHIT! HOW THE HELL CAN YOU NOT GIVE A CRAP? ARE YOU MADE OF STONE OR WHAT?
OKAY, THAT'S ENOUGH! GET OUT OF THIS OFFICE IMME--
SLAM!

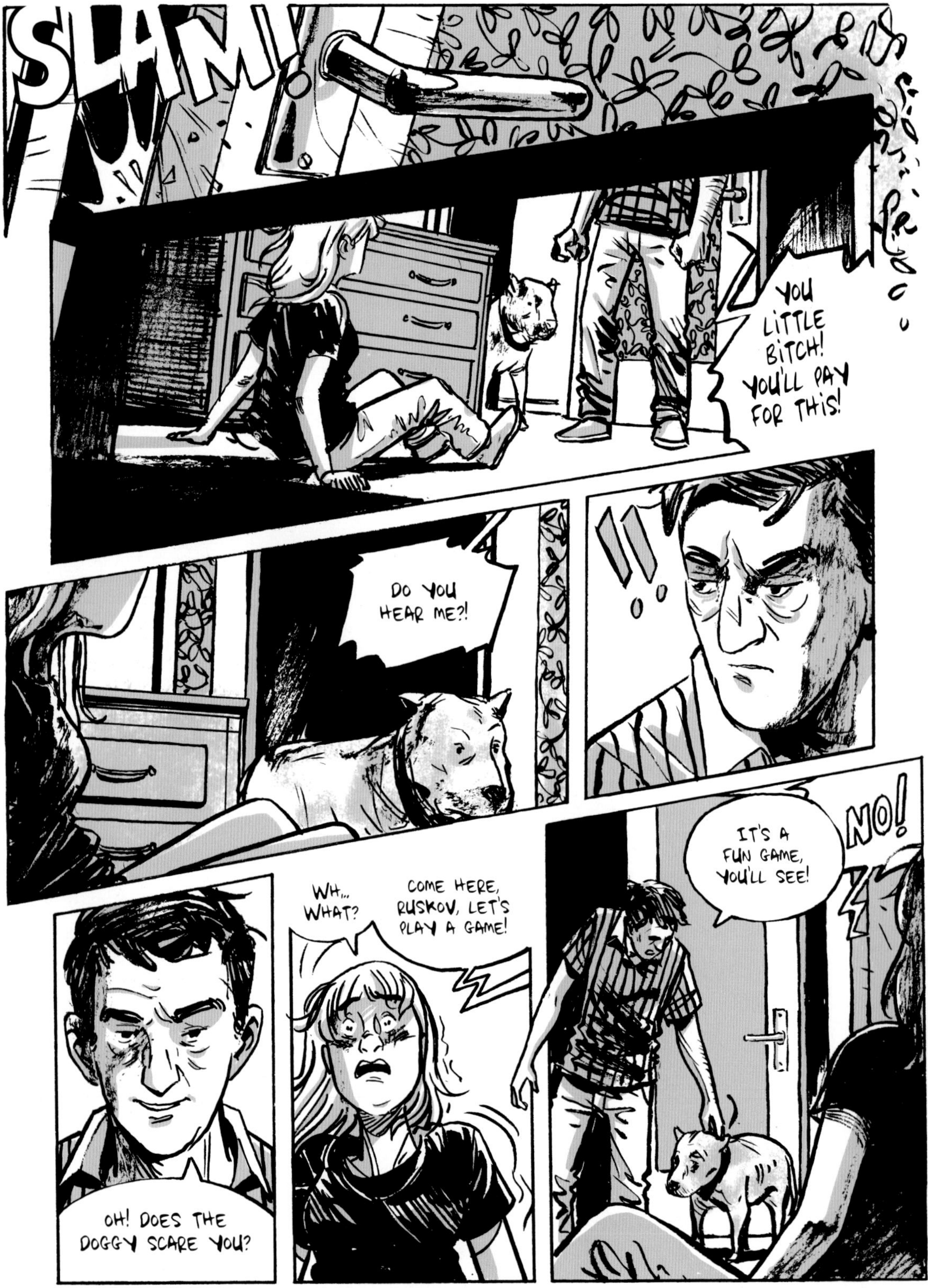
SLAM!
YOU LITTLE BITCH! YOU'LL PAY FOR THIS!
DO YOU HEAR ME?!
!!
OH! DOES THE DOGGY SCARE YOU?
WH... WHAT?
COME HERE, RUSKOV, LET'S PLAY A GAME!
IT'S A FUN GAME, YOU'LL SEE!
NO!

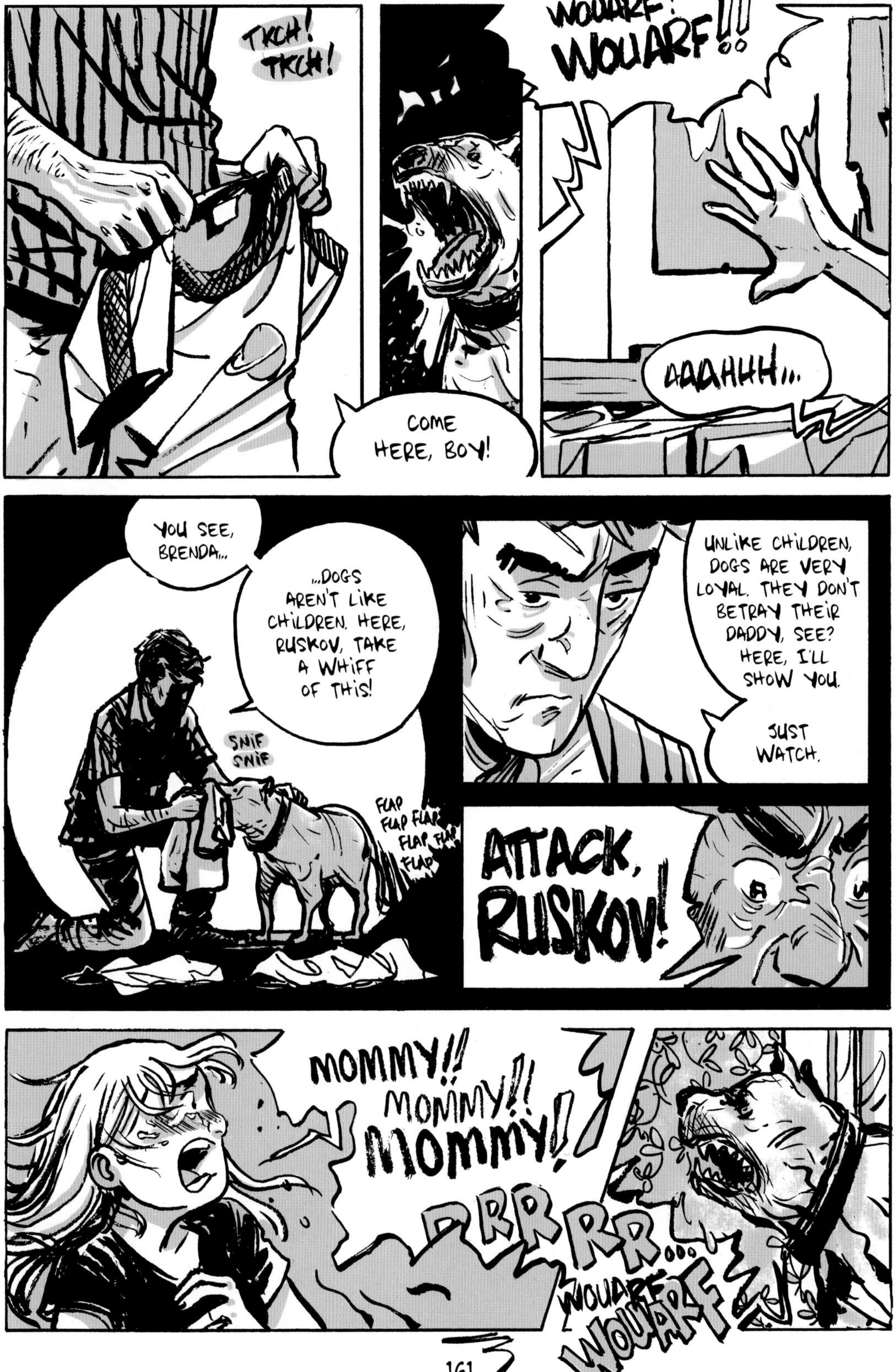
TKCH! TKCH!
WOUARF! WOUARF!!
AAAHHH...
COME HERE, BOY!
YOU SEE, BRENDA...
...DOGS AREN'T LIKE CHILDREN. HERE, RUSKOV, TAKE A WHIFF OF THIS!
SNIF SNIF
FLAP FLAP FLAP FLAP FLAP FLAP
UNLIKE CHILDREN, DOGS ARE VERY LOYAL. THEY DON'T BETRAY THEIR DADDY, SEE? HERE, I'LL SHOW YOU.
JUST WATCH.
ATTACK, RUSKOV!
MOMMY!! MOMMY!! MOMMY!!
RRRRR...
WOUARF WOUARF

SHIT!

WHAT THE HELL? ARE YOU SHITTING ME?

BEAT IT, YOU STUPID MUTT!

AIIIE

DAMN THAT DOG! HE NEVER LISTENS ANYMORE... I SWEAR, HE'S WORSE THAN YOU KIDS!

WHAT? WERE YOU SCARED?

SLAM!

I HAD HIM BY THE COLLAR, NO WORRIES!

EVEN IF HE WANTED TO, HE COULDN'T HAVE CHEWED OFF THAT UGLY MUG OF YOURS!

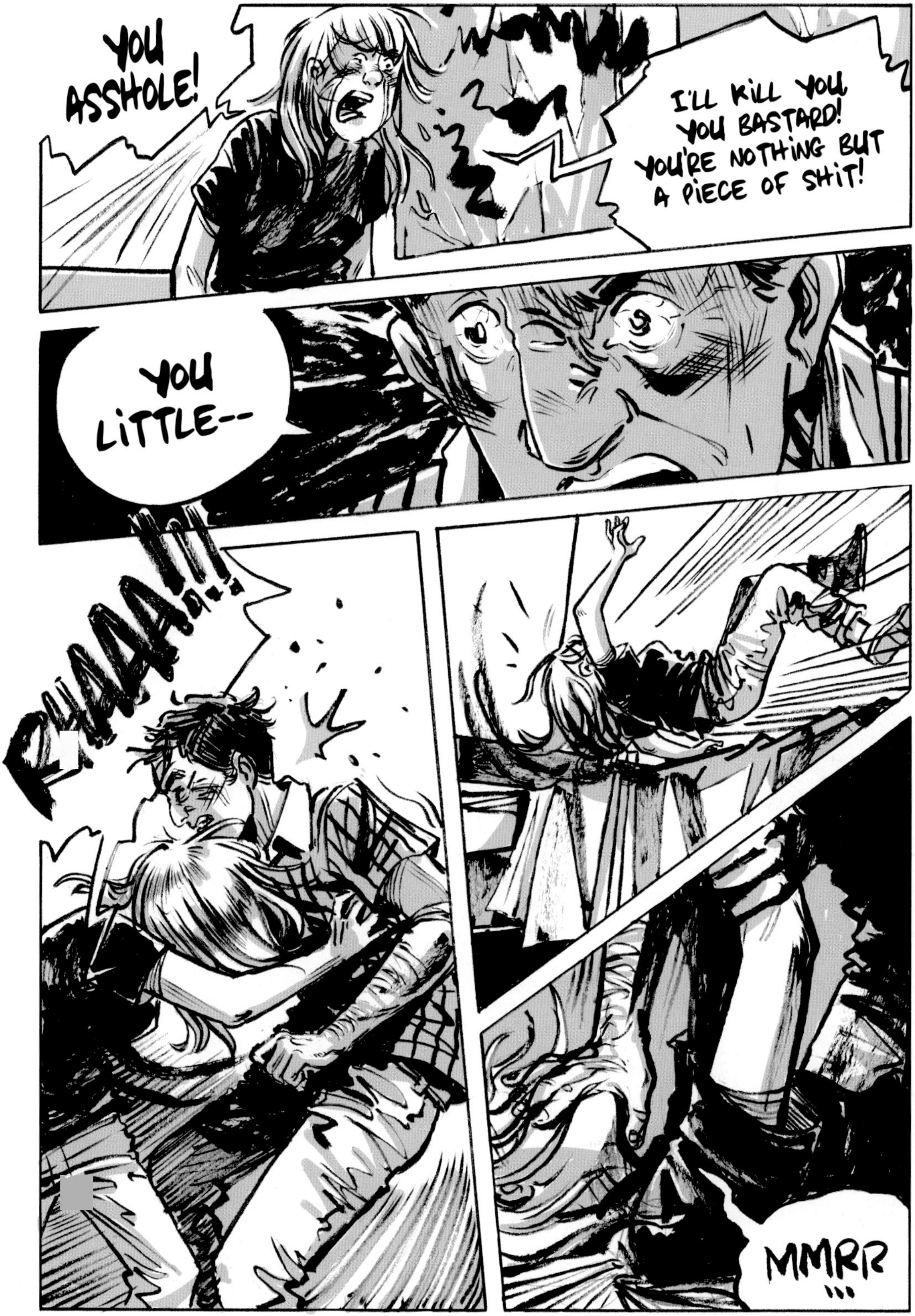
YOU ASSHOLE!
I'LL KILL YOU YOU BASTARD! YOU'RE NOTHING BUT A PIECE OF SHIT!
YOU LITTLE--
MMRR ...

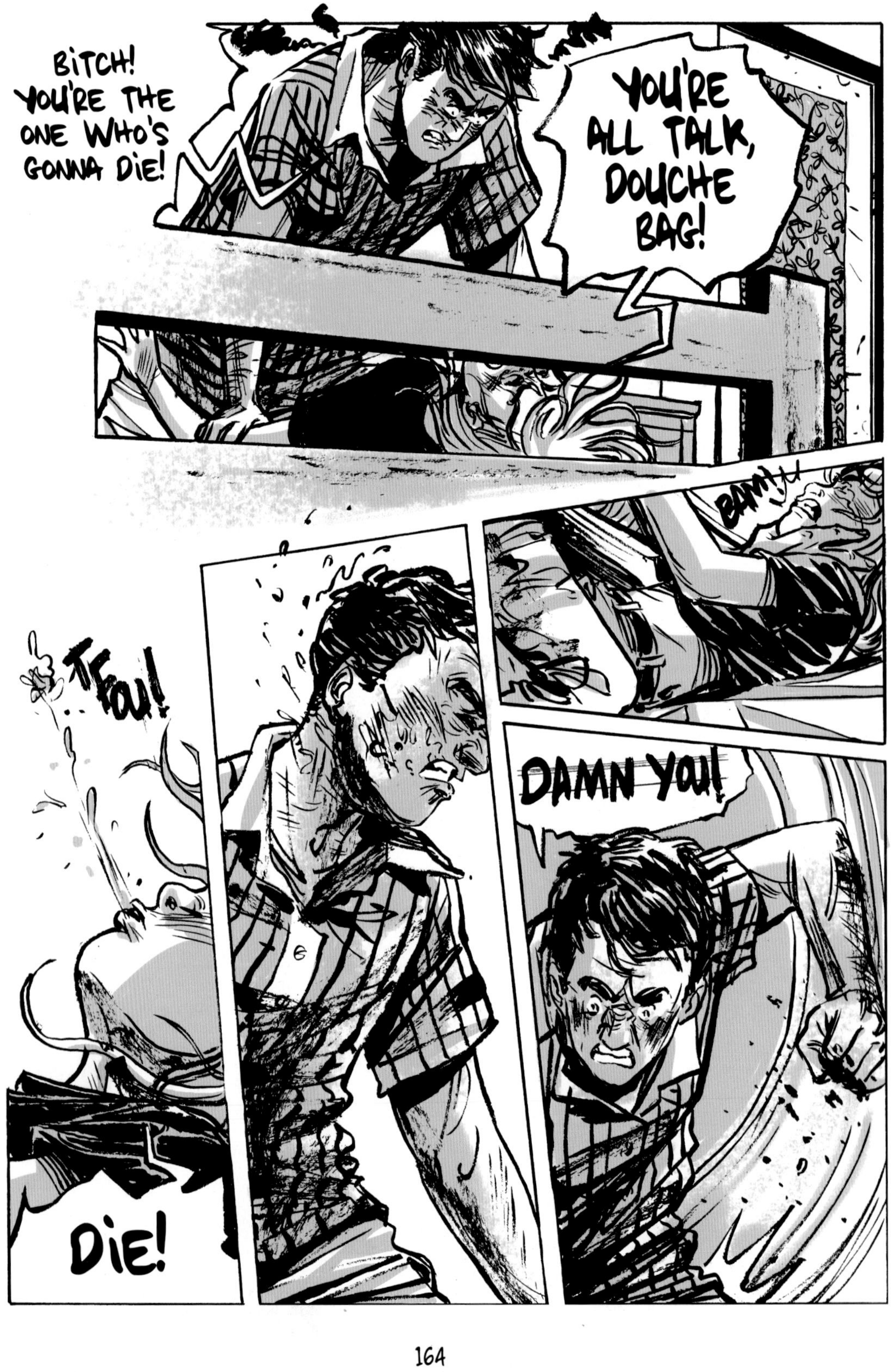
BITCH! YOU'RE THE ONE WHO'S GONNA DIE!
YOU'RE ALL TALK, DOUCHE BAG!
BAM!
TFOU!
DAMN YOU!
DIE!

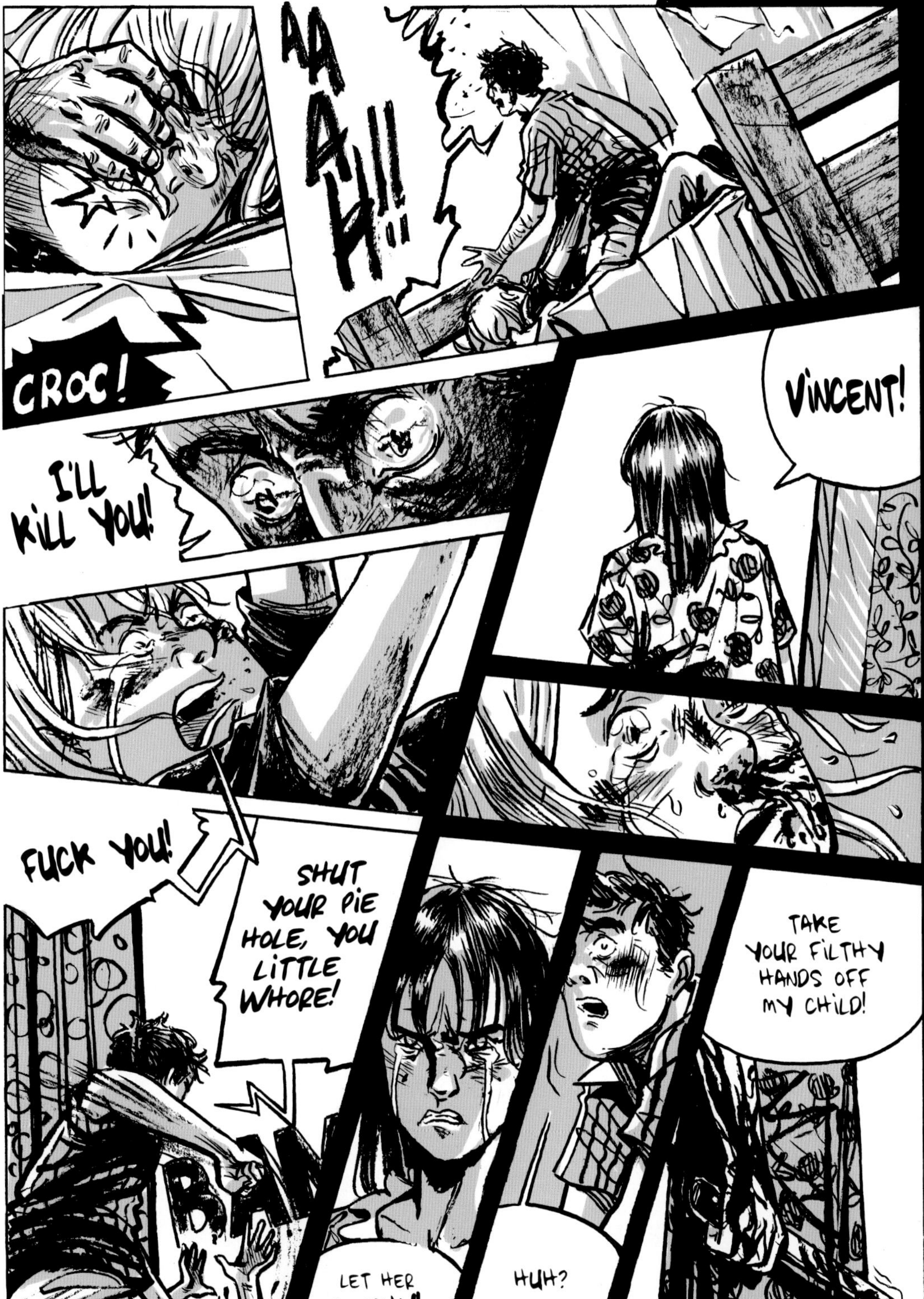
CROC!
AAAH!!!
I'LL KILL YOU!
VINCENT!
FUCK YOU!
SHUT YOUR PIE HOLE, YOU LITTLE WHORE!
TAKE YOUR FILTHY HANDS OFF MY CHILD!
LET HER GO. NOW!
HUH?

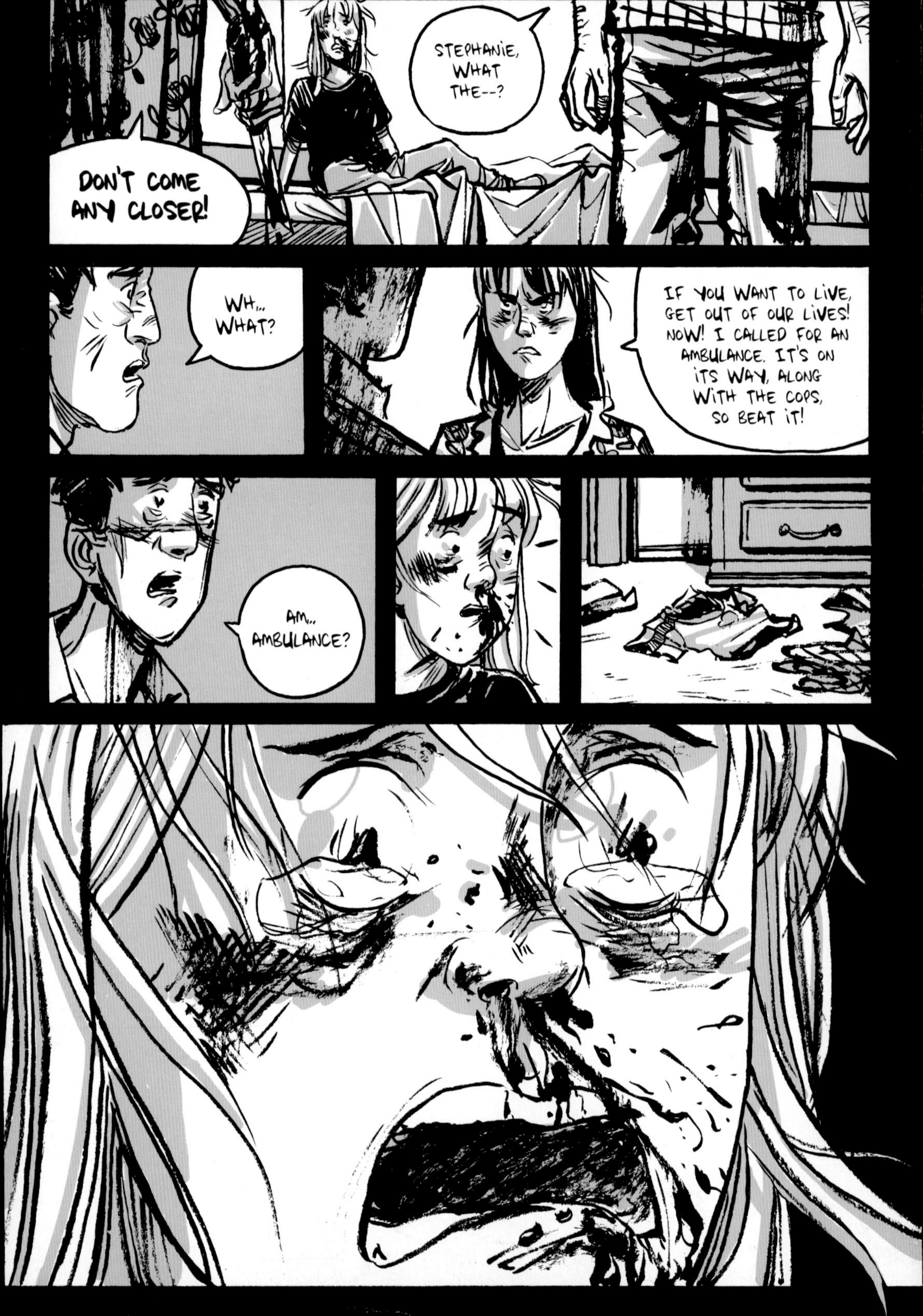
STEPHANIE, WHAT THE--?
DON'T COME ANY CLOSER!
WH... WHAT?
IF YOU WANT TO LIVE, GET OUT OF OUR LIVES! NOW! I CALLED FOR AN AMBULANCE. IT'S ON ITS WAY, ALONG WITH THE COPS, SO BEAT IT!
AM... AMBULANCE?

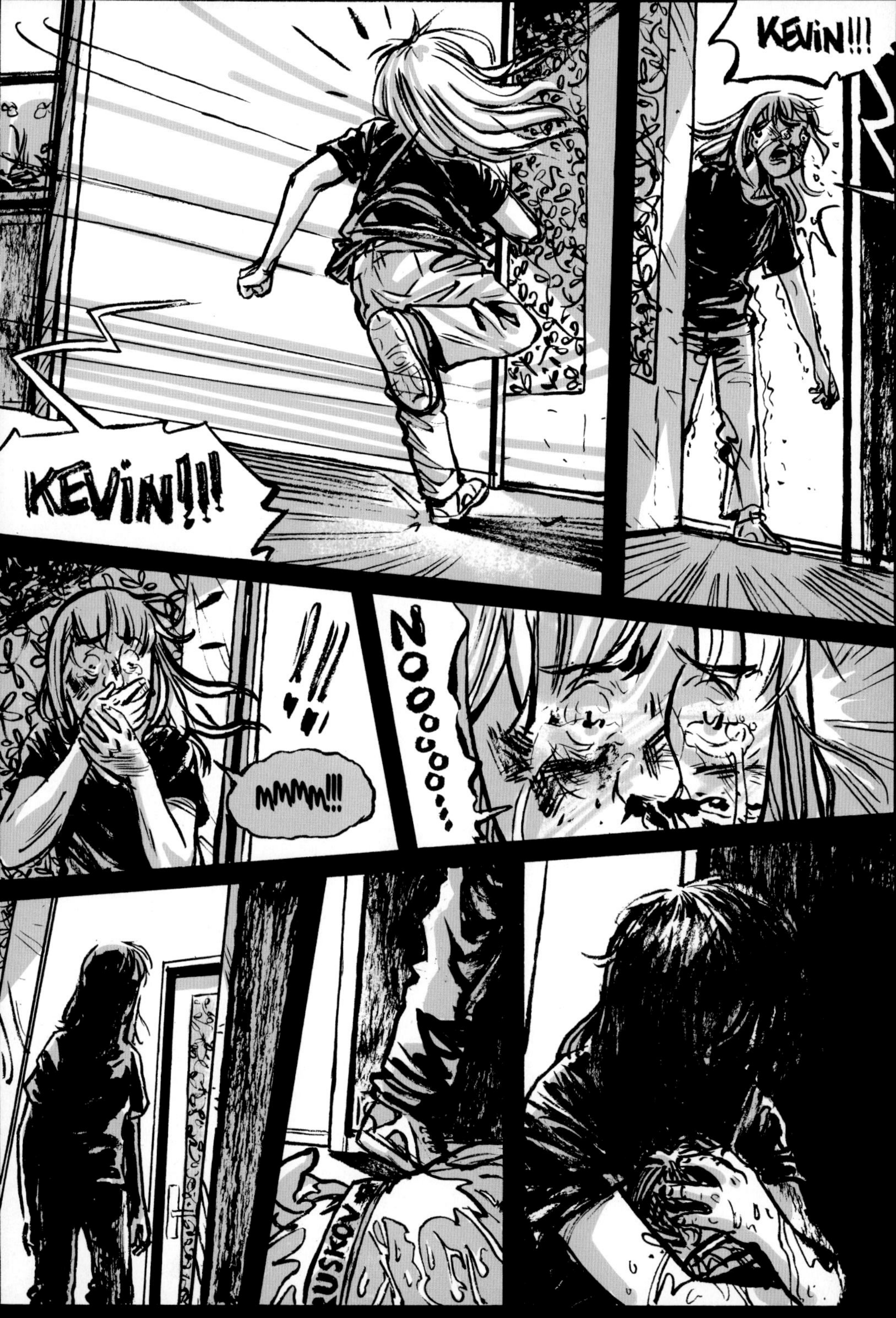
KEVIN!!!
KEVIN!!!
!!!
mmmm!!!
NOOOOOOO...
RUSKOV

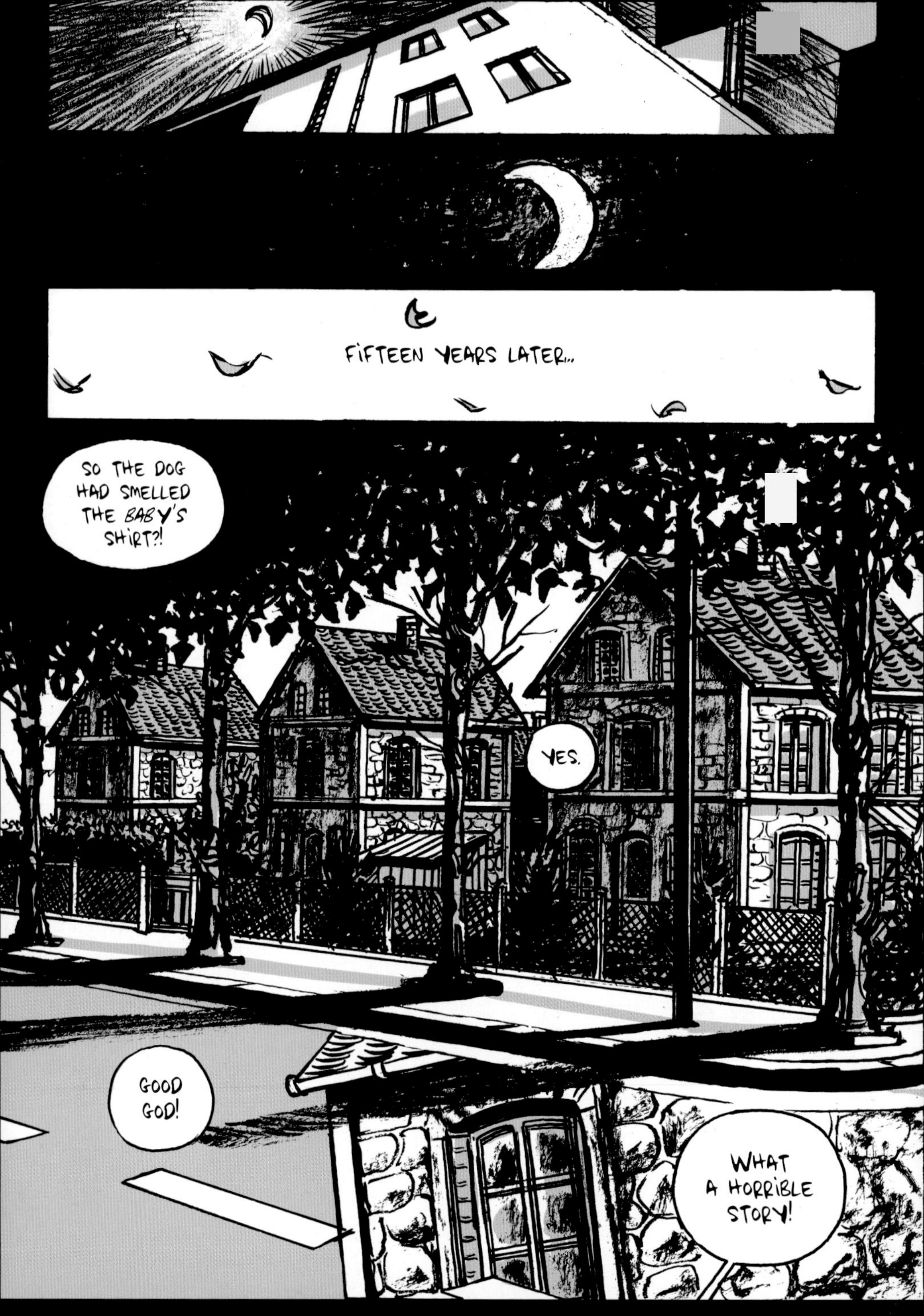
FIFTEEN YEARS LATER...
SO THE DOG HAD SMELLED THE BABY'S SHIRT?!
YES.
GOOD GOD!
WHAT A HORRIBLE STORY!

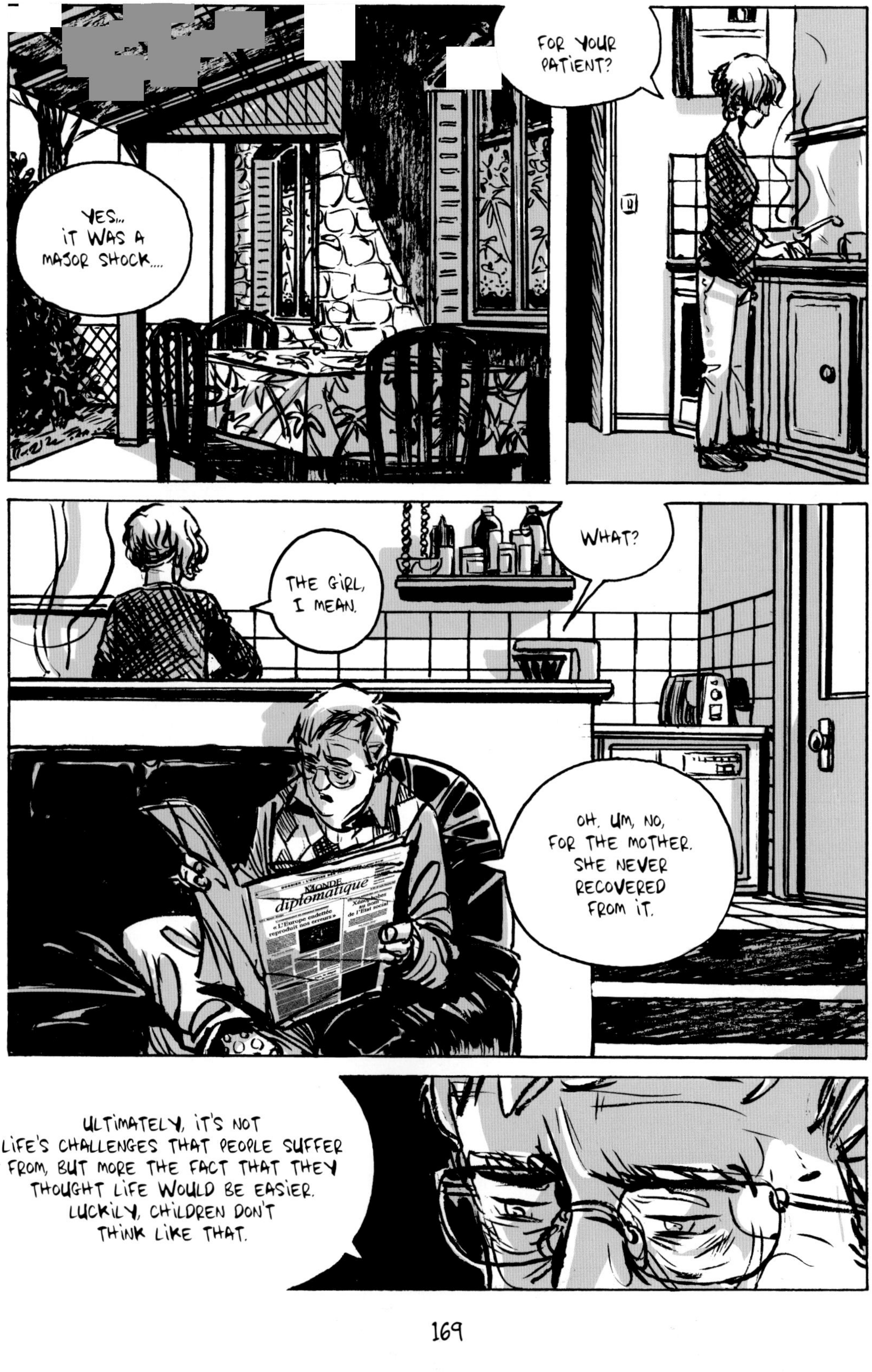
YES... IT WAS A MAJOR SHOCK....
FOR YOUR PATIENT?
THE GIRL, I MEAN.
WHAT?
OH. UM, NO, FOR THE MOTHER. SHE NEVER RECOVERED FROM IT.
ULTIMATELY, IT'S NOT LIFE'S CHALLENGES THAT PEOPLE SUFFER FROM, BUT MORE THE FACT THAT THEY THOUGHT LIFE WOULD BE EASIER. LUCKILY, CHILDREN DON'T THINK LIKE THAT.

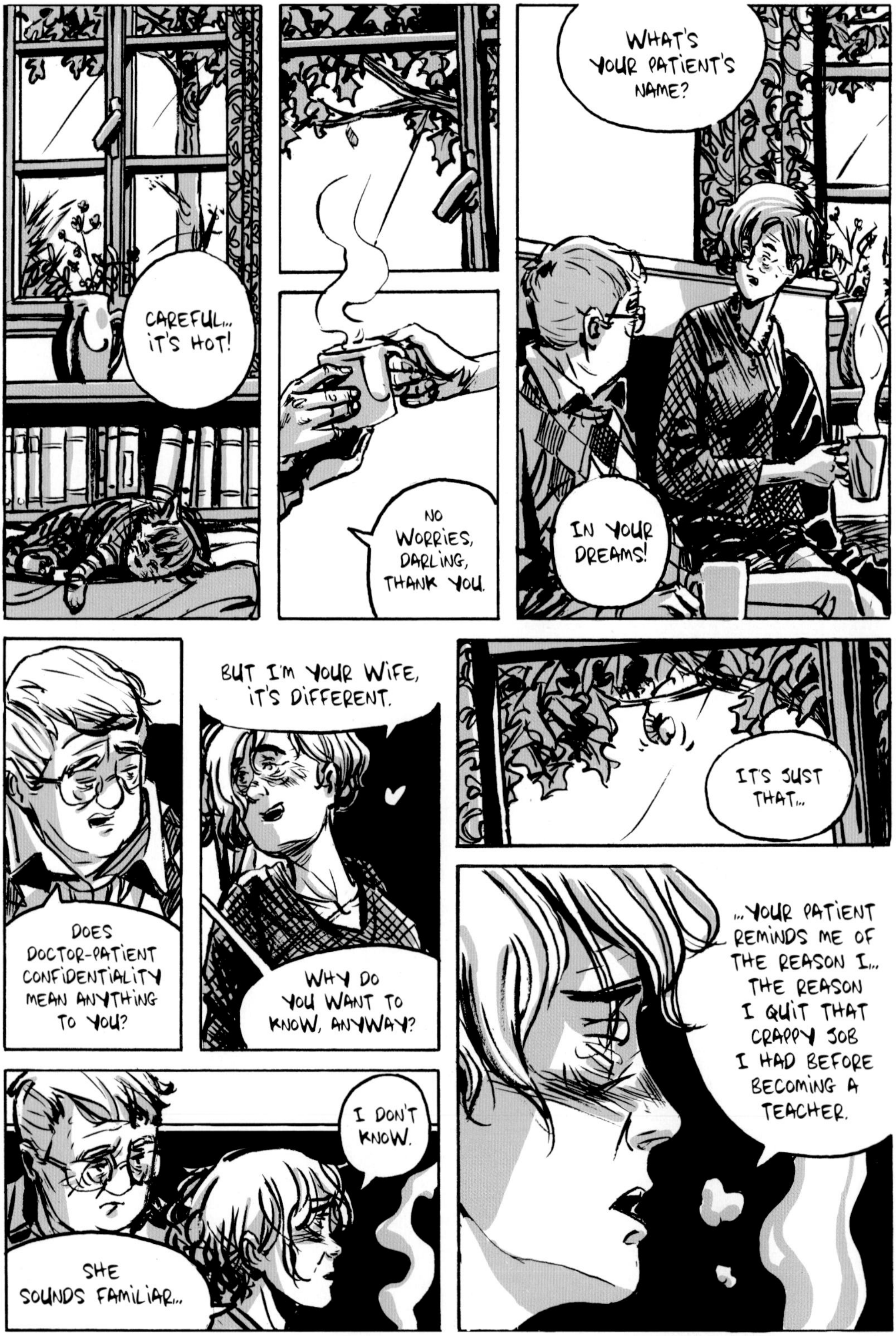
CAREFUL... IT'S HOT!
NO WORRIES, DARLING, THANK YOU.
WHAT'S YOUR PATIENT'S NAME?
IN YOUR DREAMS!
BUT I'M YOUR WIFE, IT'S DIFFERENT.
DOES DOCTOR-PATIENT CONFIDENTIALITY MEAN ANYTHING TO YOU?
WHY DO YOU WANT TO KNOW, ANYWAY?
I DON'T KNOW.
SHE SOUNDS FAMILIAR...
IT'S JUST THAT...
...YOUR PATIENT REMINDS ME OF THE REASON I... THE REASON I QUIT THAT CRAPPY JOB I HAD BEFORE BECOMING A TEACHER.

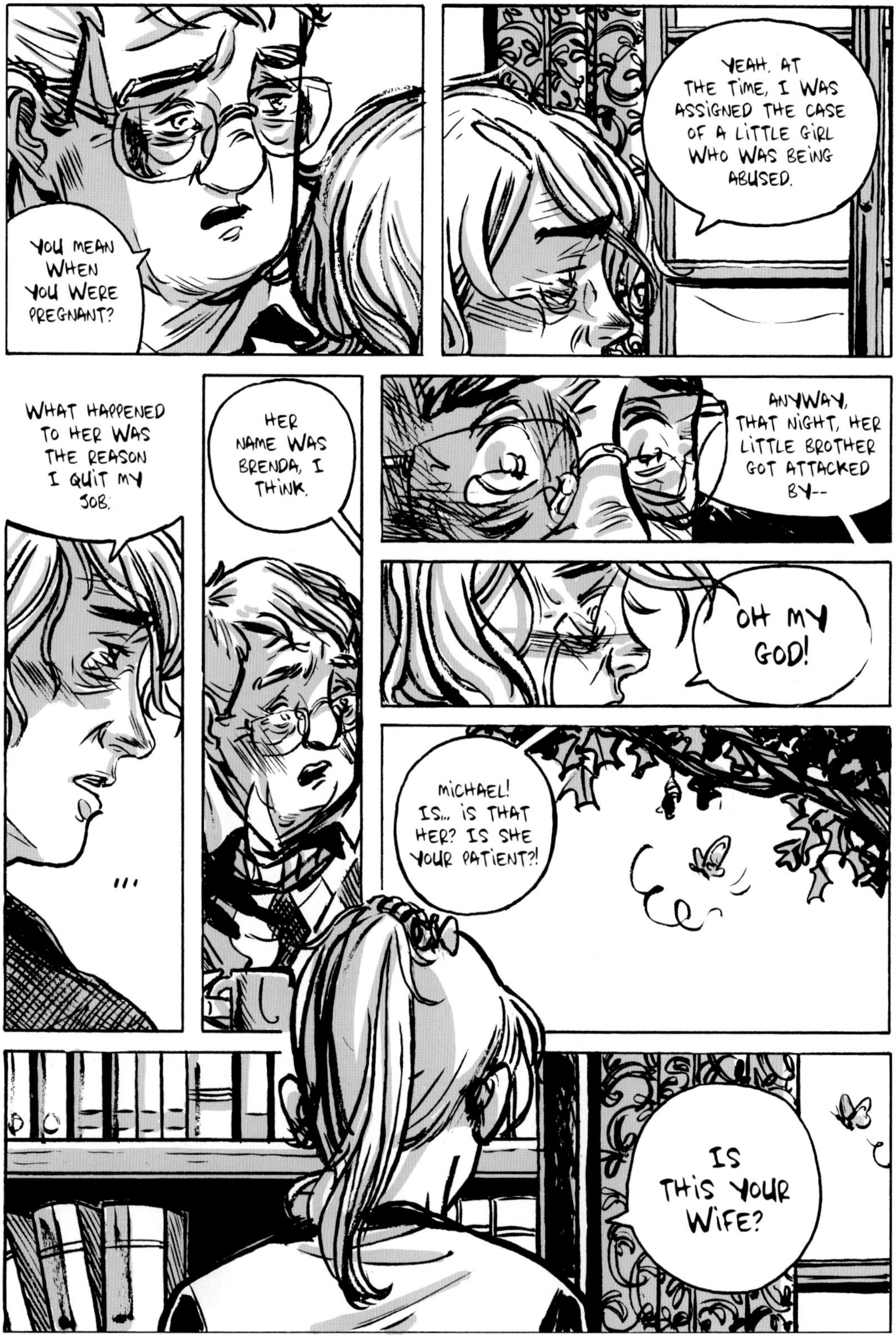
YEAH. AT THE TIME, I WAS ASSIGNED THE CASE OF A LITTLE GIRL WHO WAS BEING ABUSED.
YOU MEAN WHEN YOU WERE PREGNANT?
WHAT HAPPENED TO HER WAS THE REASON I QUIT MY JOB.
HER NAME WAS BRENDA, I THINK.
ANYWAY, THAT NIGHT, HER LITTLE BROTHER GOT ATTACKED BY--
OH MY GOD!
...
MICHAEL! IS... IS THAT HER? IS SHE YOUR PATIENT?!
IS THIS YOUR WIFE?

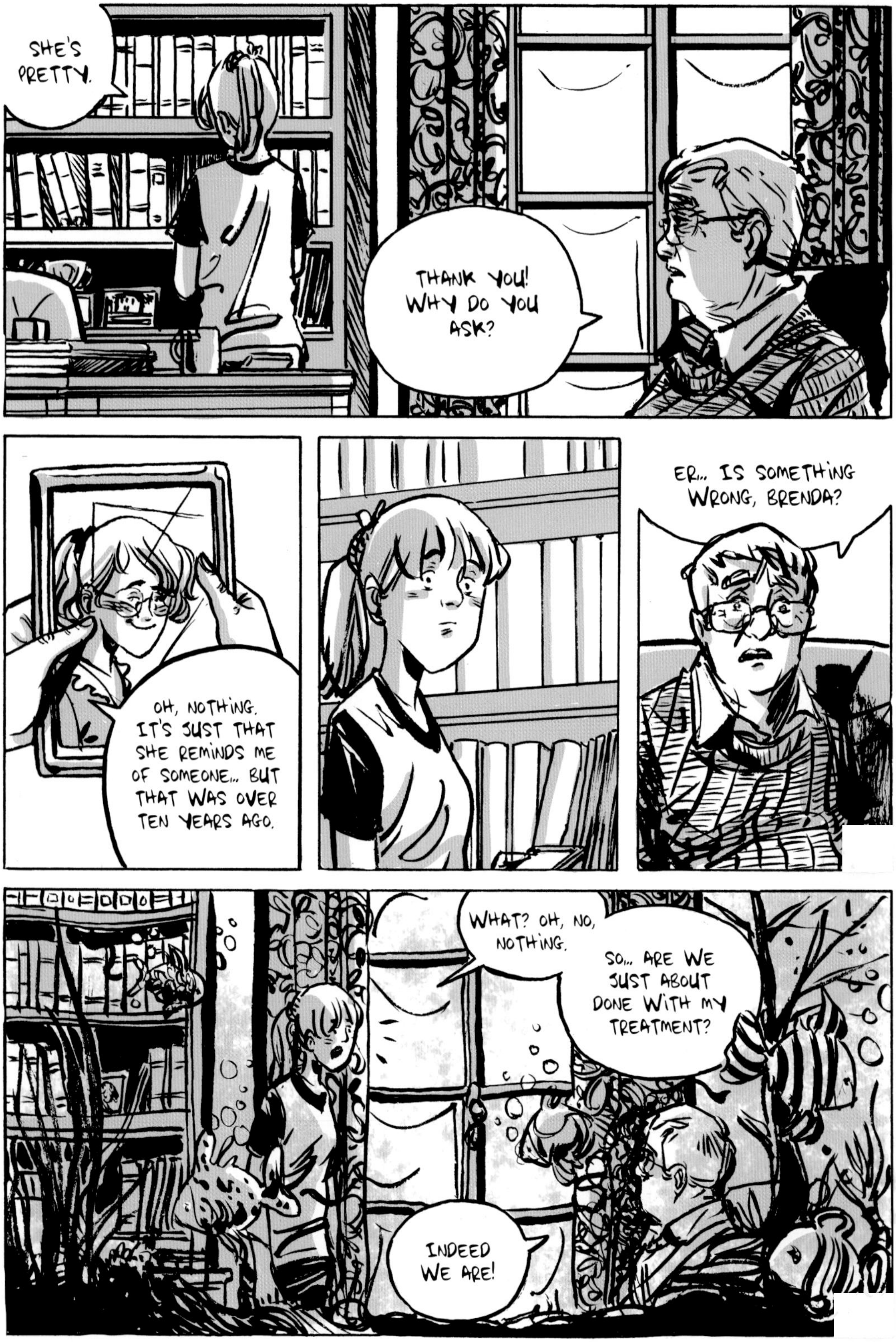
SHE'S PRETTY.
THANK YOU! WHY DO YOU ASK?
OH, NOTHING. IT'S JUST THAT SHE REMINDS ME OF SOMEONE... BUT THAT WAS OVER TEN YEARS AGO.
ER... IS SOMETHING WRONG, BRENDA?
WHAT? OH, NO, NOTHING.
SO... ARE WE JUST ABOUT DONE WITH MY TREATMENT?
INDEED WE ARE!

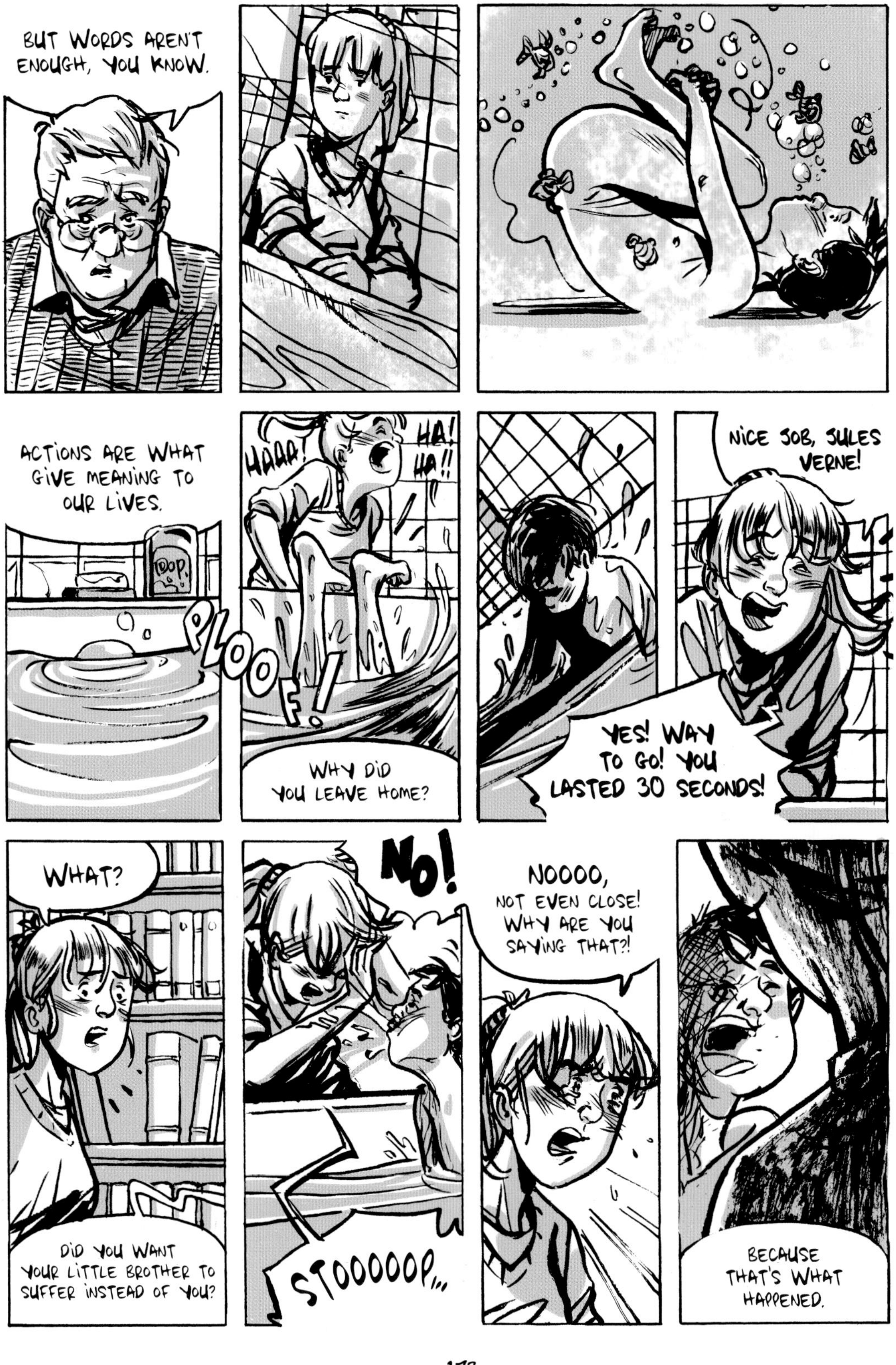
BUT WORDS AREN'T ENOUGH, YOU KNOW.
ACTIONS ARE WHAT GIVE MEANING TO OUR LIVES.
PLOOF!
HAAA!
HA! HA!!
WHY DID YOU LEAVE HOME?
NICE JOB, JULES VERNE!
YES! WAY TO GO! YOU LASTED 30 SECONDS!
WHAT?
DID YOU WANT YOUR LITTLE BROTHER TO SUFFER INSTEAD OF YOU?
NO!
STOOOOOP...
NOOOO, NOT EVEN CLOSE! WHY ARE YOU SAYING THAT?!
BECAUSE THAT'S WHAT HAPPENED.

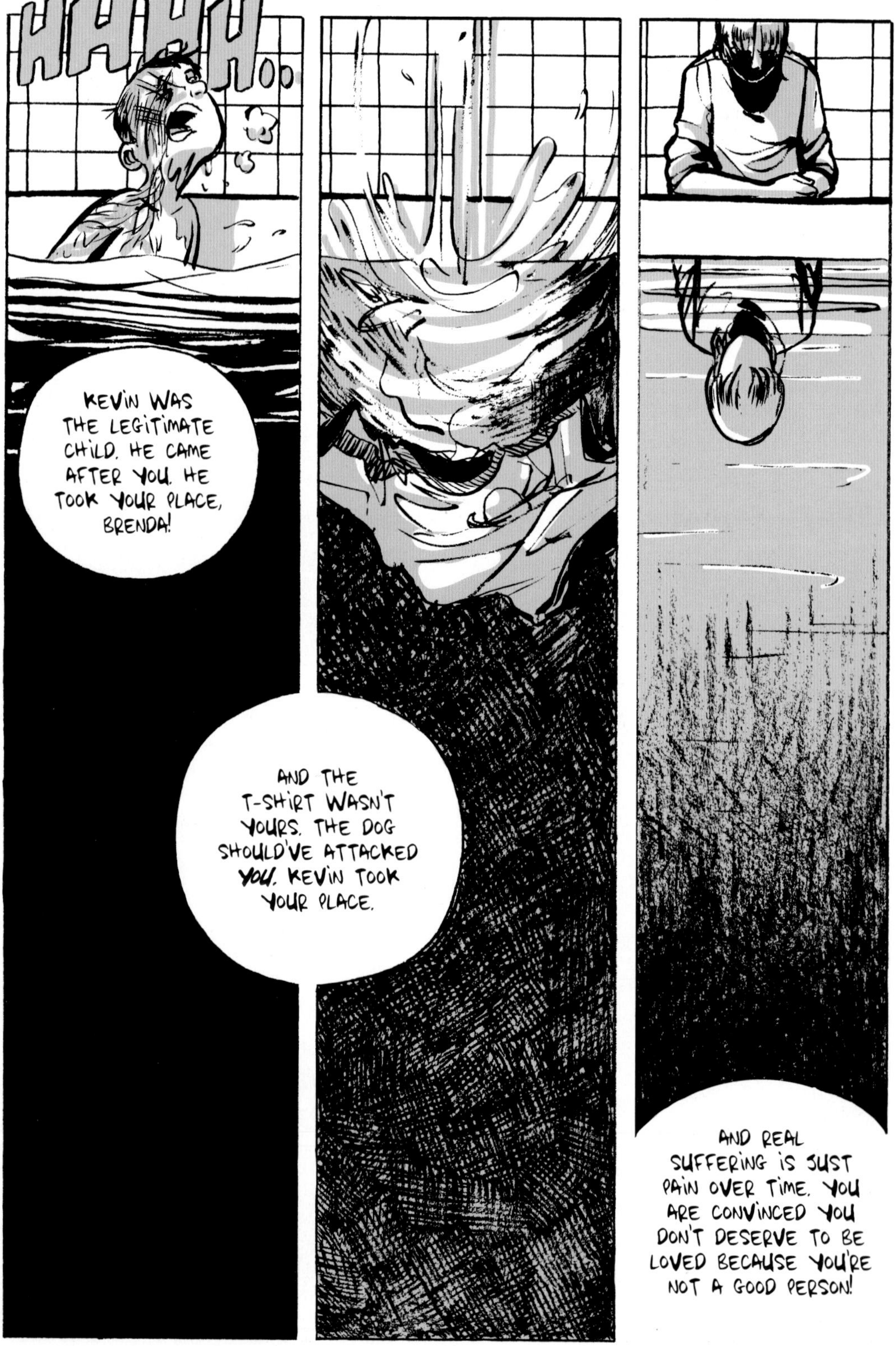
HHHHoo
KEVIN WAS THE LEGITIMATE CHILD. HE CAME AFTER YOU. HE TOOK YOUR PLACE, BRENDA!
AND THE T-SHIRT WASN'T YOURS. THE DOG SHOULD'VE ATTACKED YOU. KEVIN TOOK YOUR PLACE.
AND REAL SUFFERING IS JUST PAIN OVER TIME. YOU ARE CONVINCED YOU DON'T DESERVE TO BE LOVED BECAUSE YOU'RE NOT A GOOD PERSON!

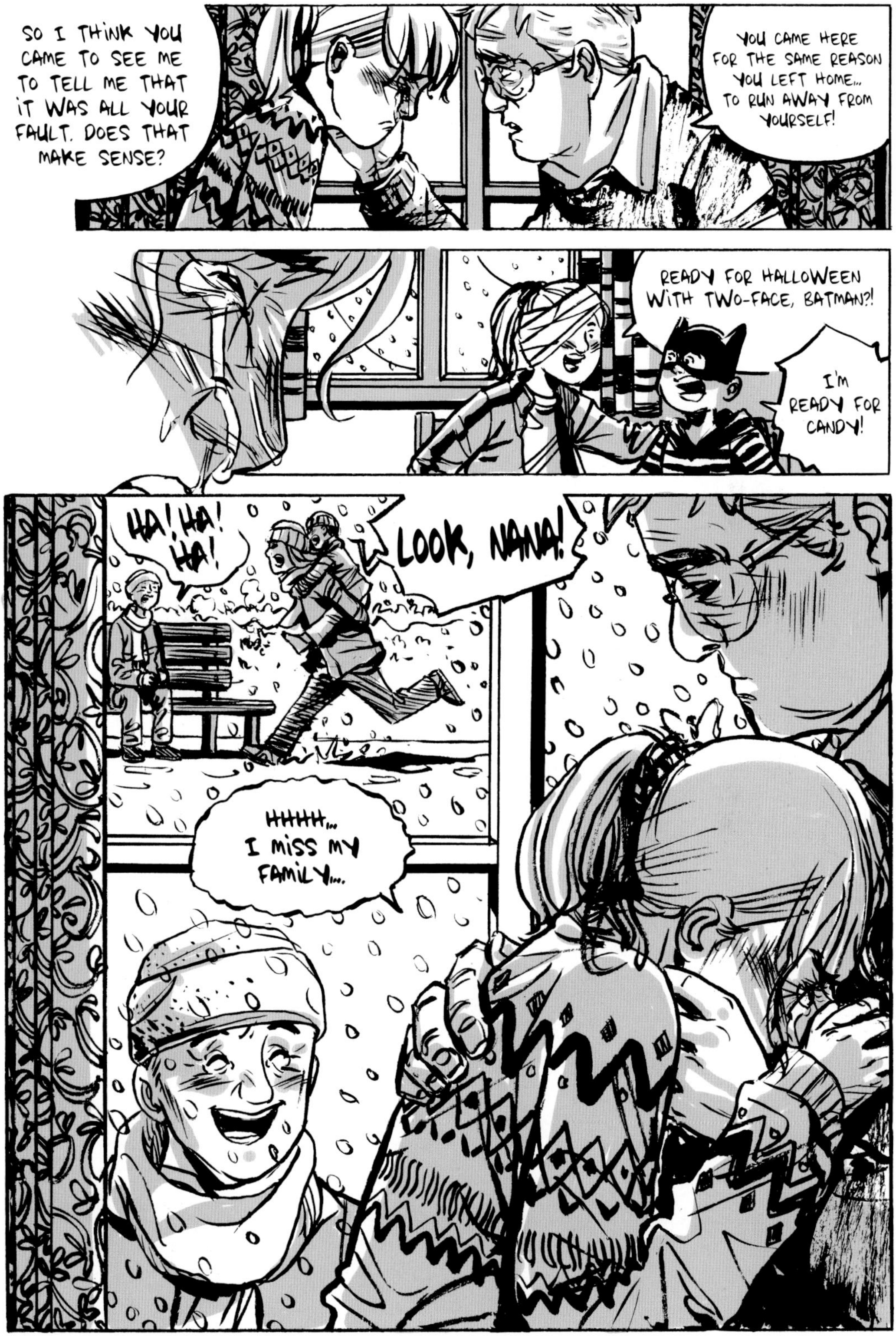
SO I THINK YOU CAME TO SEE ME TO TELL ME THAT IT WAS ALL YOUR FAULT. DOES THAT MAKE SENSE?
YOU CAME HERE FOR THE SAME REASON YOU LEFT HOME... TO RUN AWAY FROM YOURSELF!
READY FOR HALLOWEEN WITH TWO-FACE, BATMAN?!
I'M READY FOR CANDY!
HA! HA! HA!
LOOK, NANA!
HHHHH... I MISS MY FAMILY...

AFTER VINCENT LEFT, WE WENT BACK TO SEE NANA CATHY...

...MY GRANDMA.

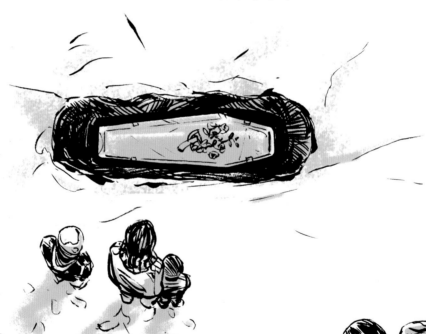

SHE WAS ALREADY VERY SICK, AND... AND THEN TWO YEARS LATER, SHE...

...SHE LEFT US.

176

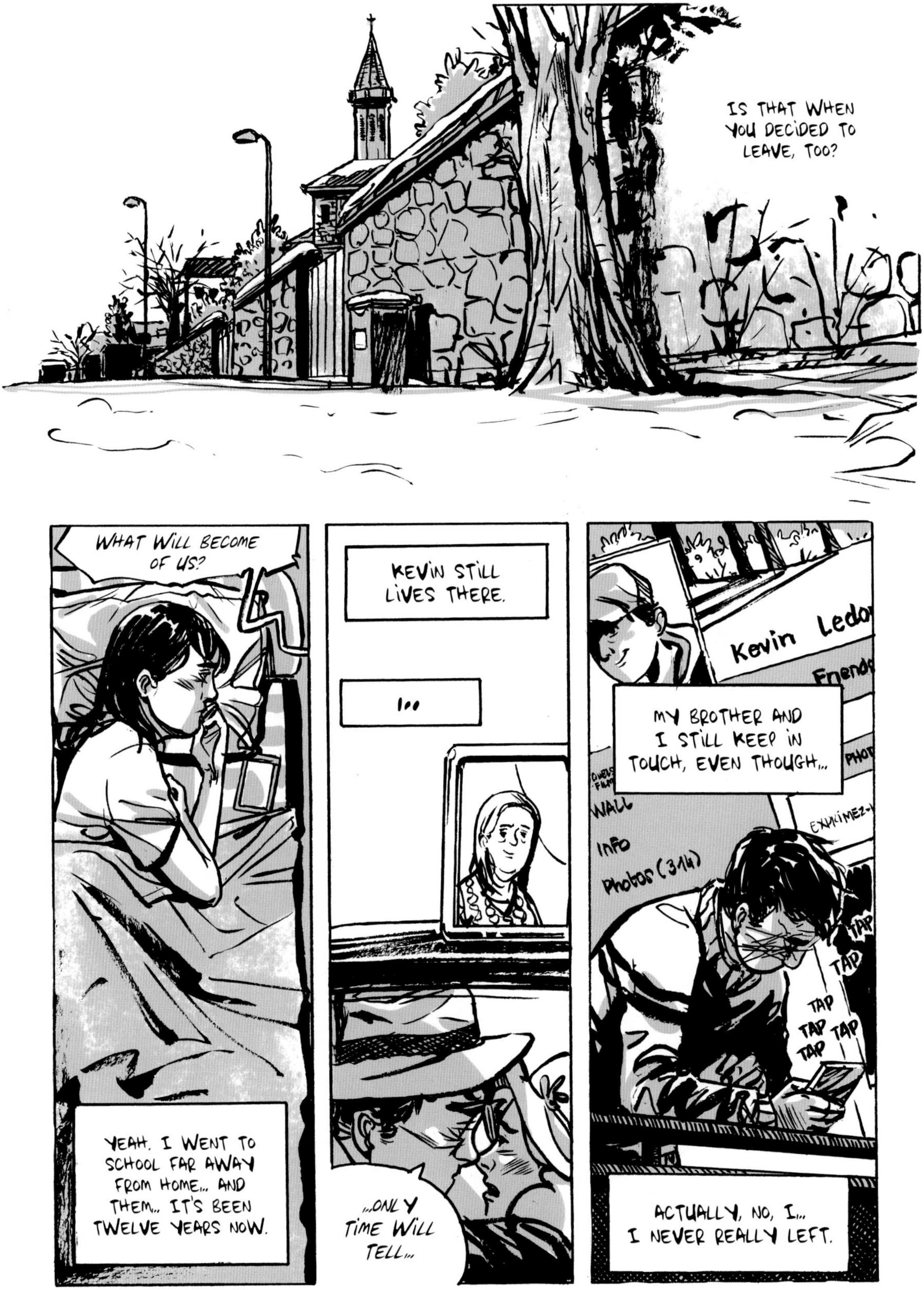
IS THAT WHEN YOU DECIDED TO LEAVE, TOO?
WHAT WILL BECOME OF US?
YEAH. I WENT TO SCHOOL FAR AWAY FROM HOME... AND THEM... IT'S BEEN TWELVE YEARS NOW.
KEVIN STILL LIVES THERE.
...
...ONLY TIME WILL TELL...
Kevin Ledo
Friends
MY BROTHER AND I STILL KEEP IN TOUCH, EVEN THOUGH...
Wall
Info
Photos (314)
TAP TAP TAP TAP TAP TAP
ACTUALLY, NO, I... I NEVER REALLY LEFT.

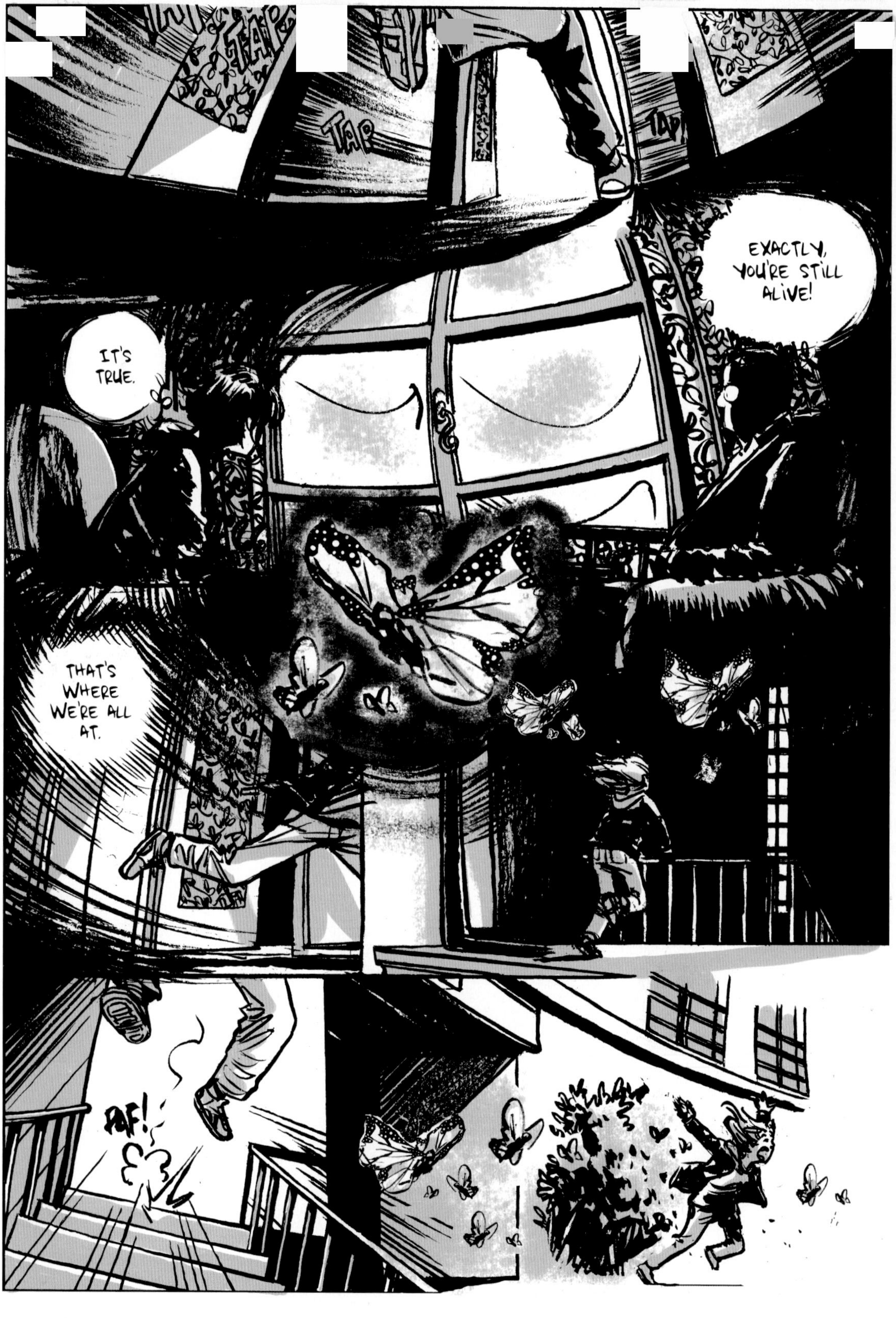
TAP
TAP
EXACTLY, YOU'RE STILL ALIVE!
IT'S TRUE.
THAT'S WHERE WE'RE ALL AT.
POF!

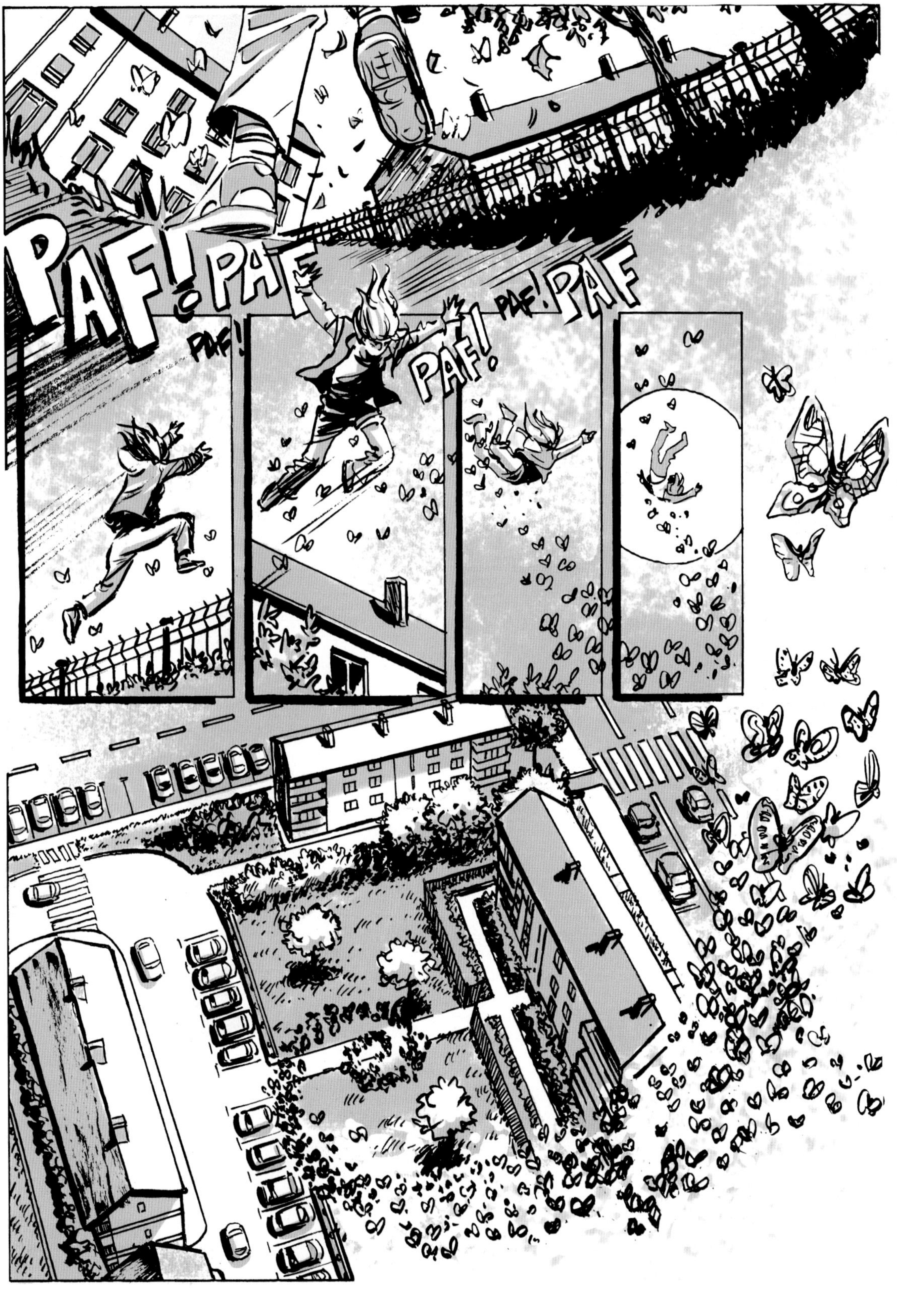

PAF!
PAF
PAF!
PAF!
PAF!
PAF

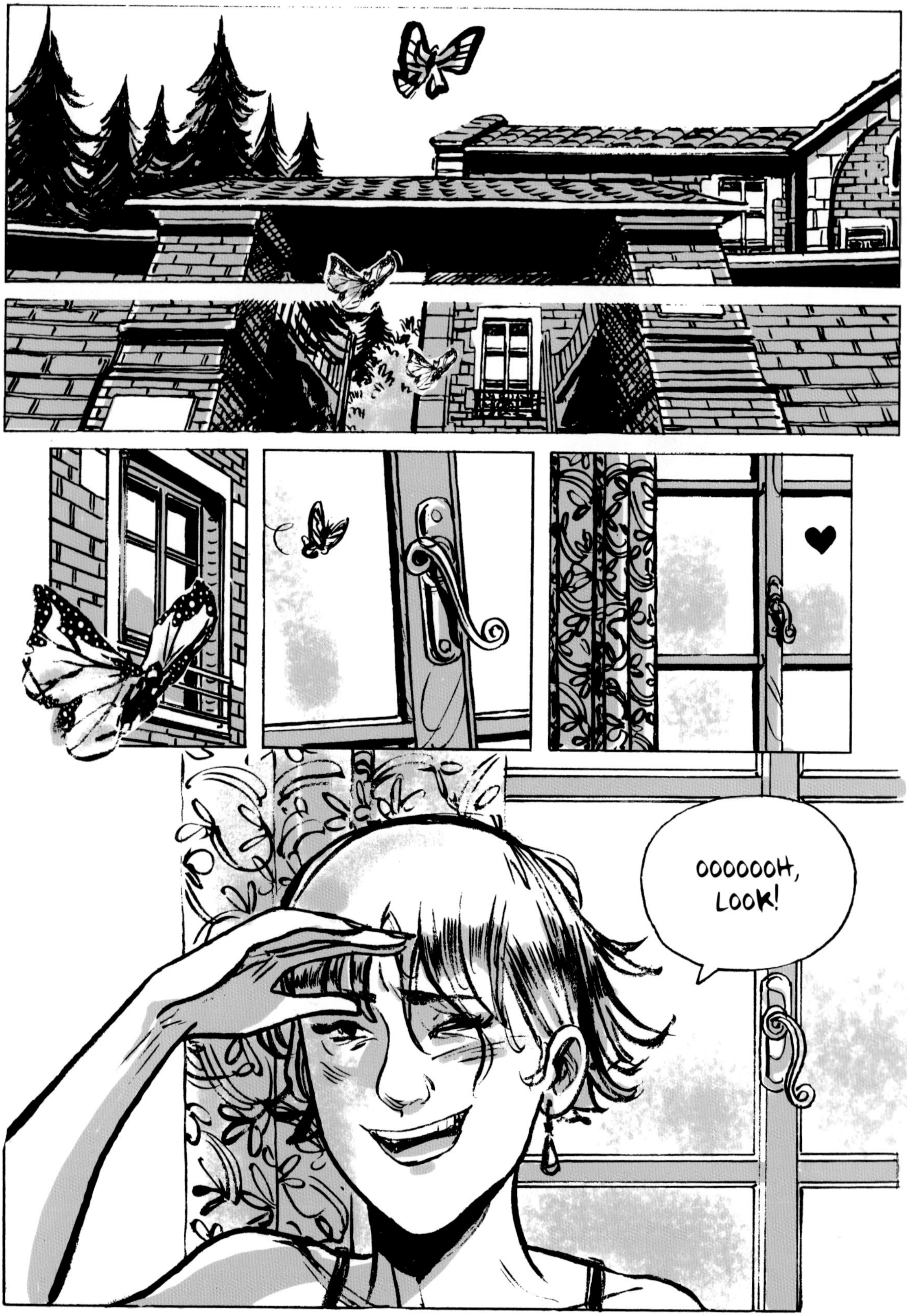
OOOOOOH, LOOK!

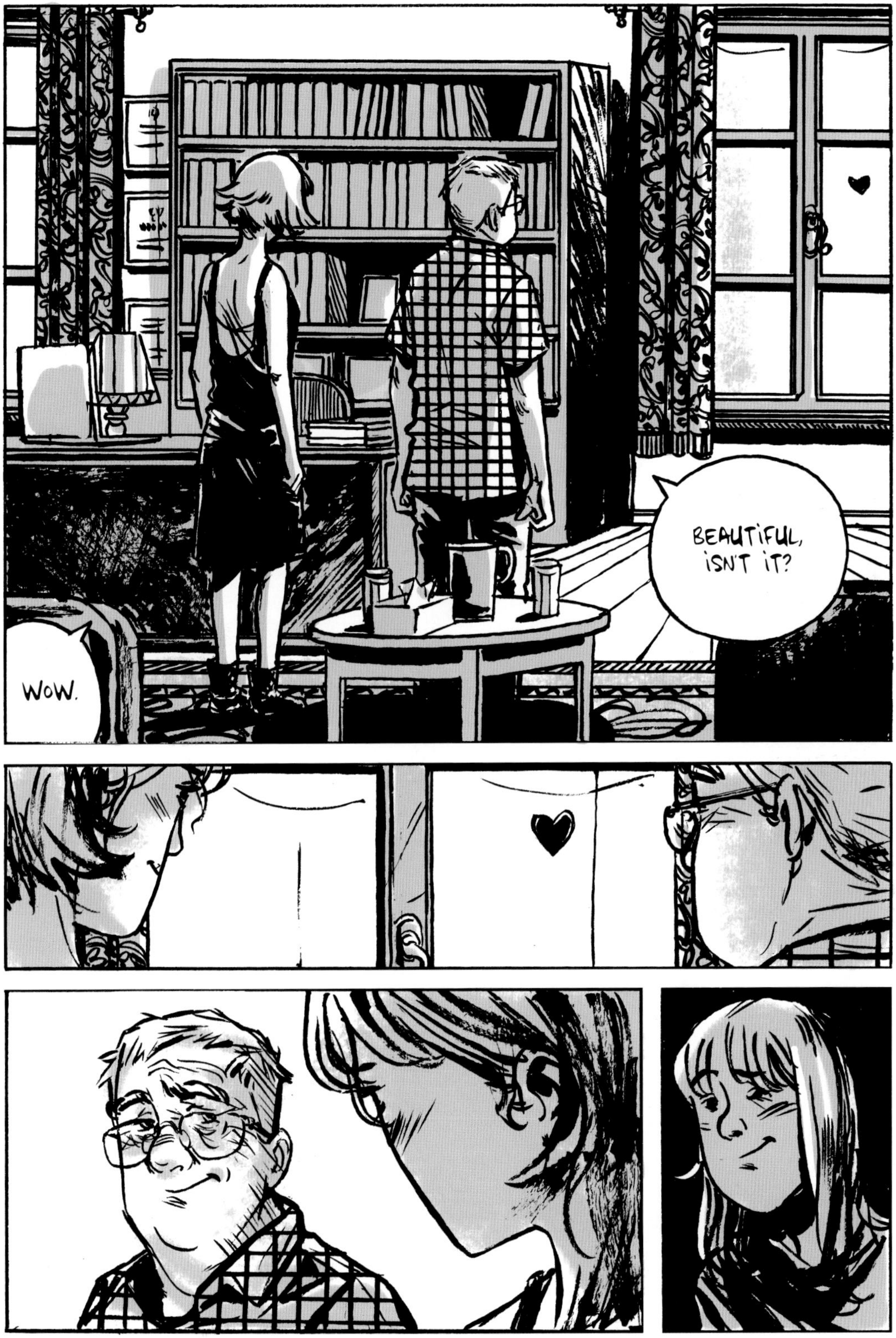
BEAUTIFUL, ISN'T IT?
WOW.

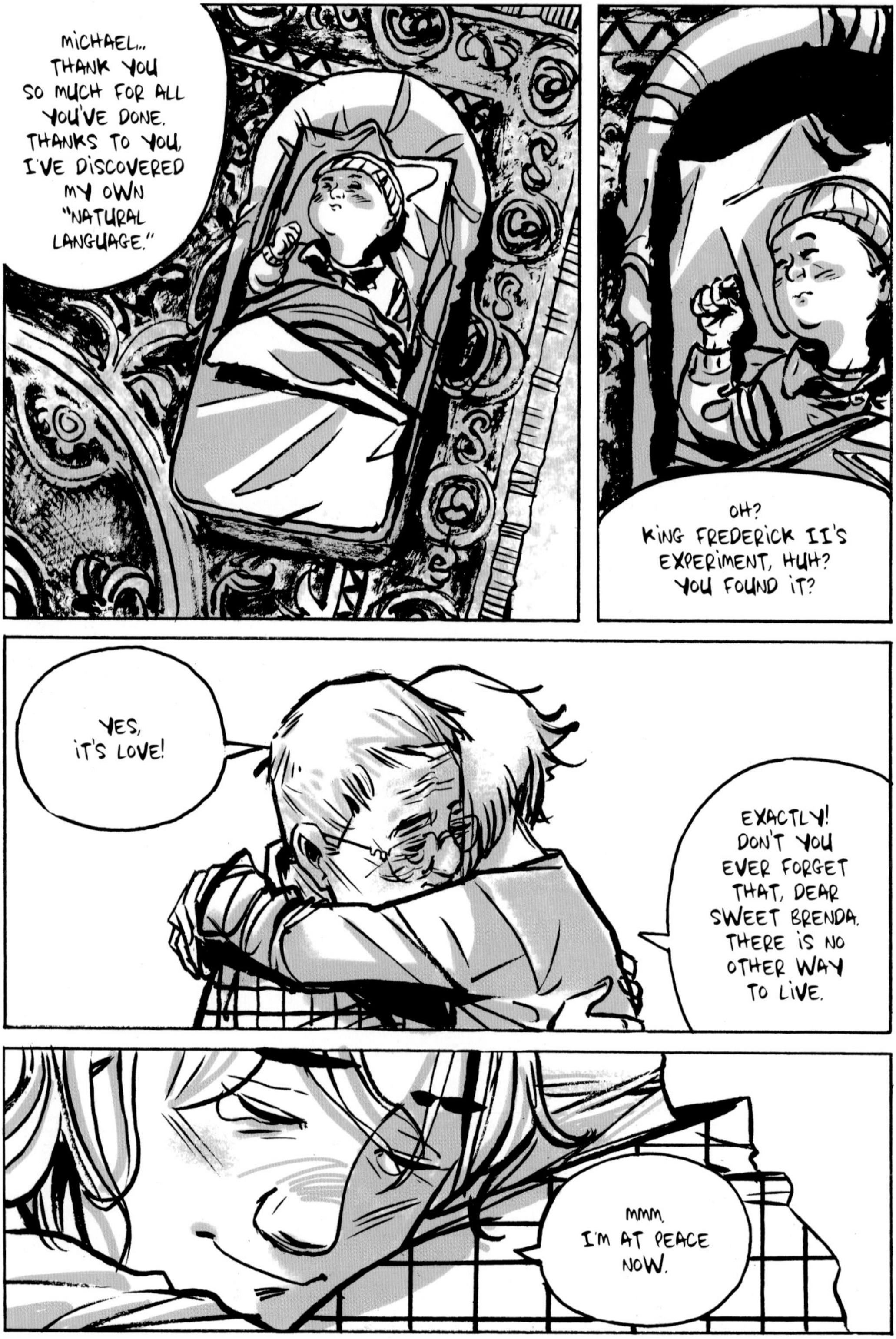
MICHAEL... THANK YOU SO MUCH FOR ALL YOU'VE DONE. THANKS TO YOU, I'VE DISCOVERED MY OWN "NATURAL LANGUAGE."
OH? KING FREDERICK II'S EXPERIMENT, HUH? YOU FOUND IT?
YES, IT'S LOVE!
EXACTLY! DON'T YOU EVER FORGET THAT, DEAR SWEET BRENDA. THERE IS NO OTHER WAY TO LIVE.
MMM. I'M AT PEACE NOW.

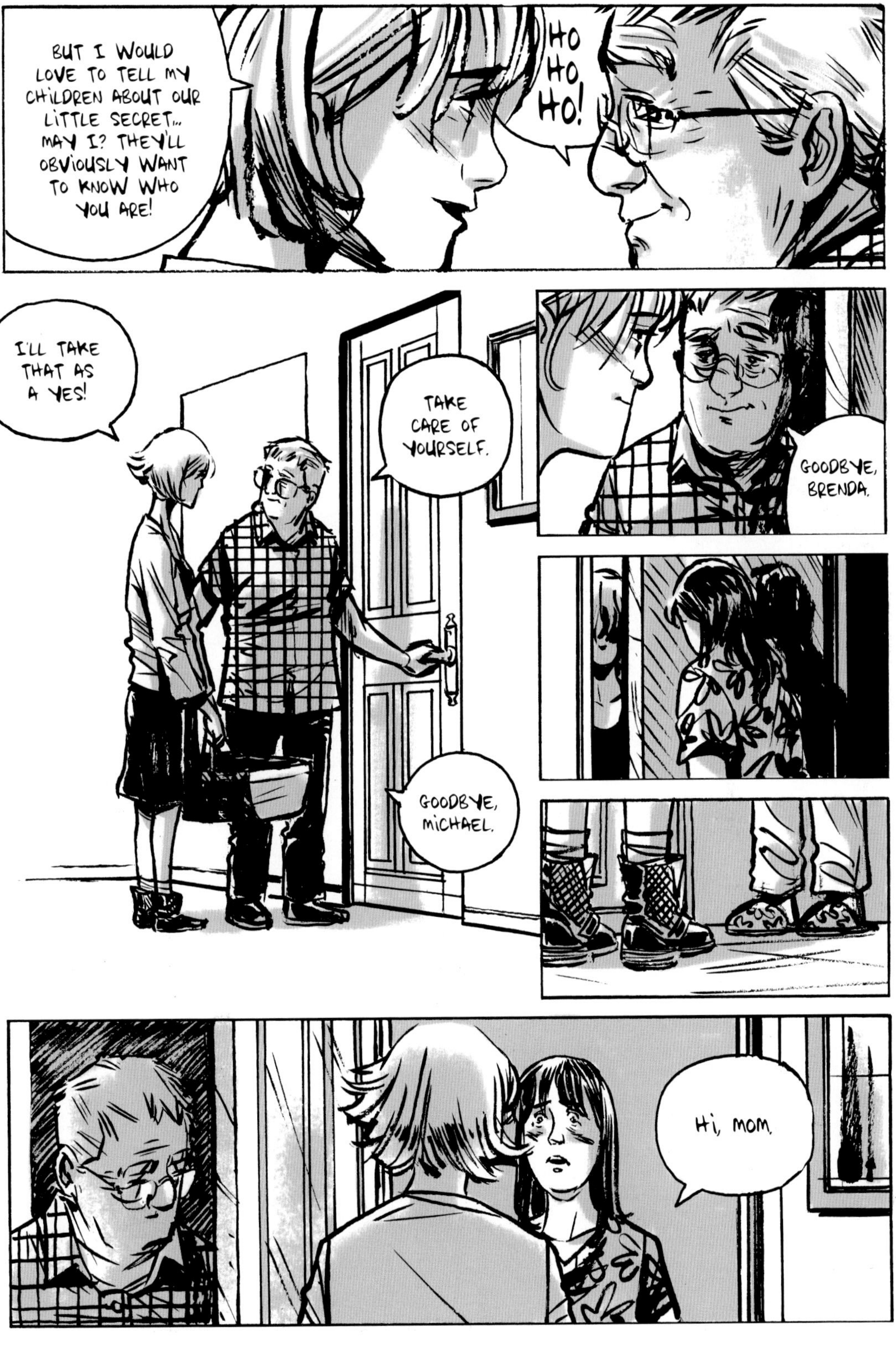
BUT I WOULD LOVE TO TELL MY CHILDREN ABOUT OUR LITTLE SECRET... MAY I? THEY'LL OBVIOUSLY WANT TO KNOW WHO YOU ARE!
HO HO HO!
I'LL TAKE THAT AS A YES!
TAKE CARE OF YOURSELF.
GOODBYE, BRENDA.
GOODBYE, MICHAEL.
Hi, MOM.

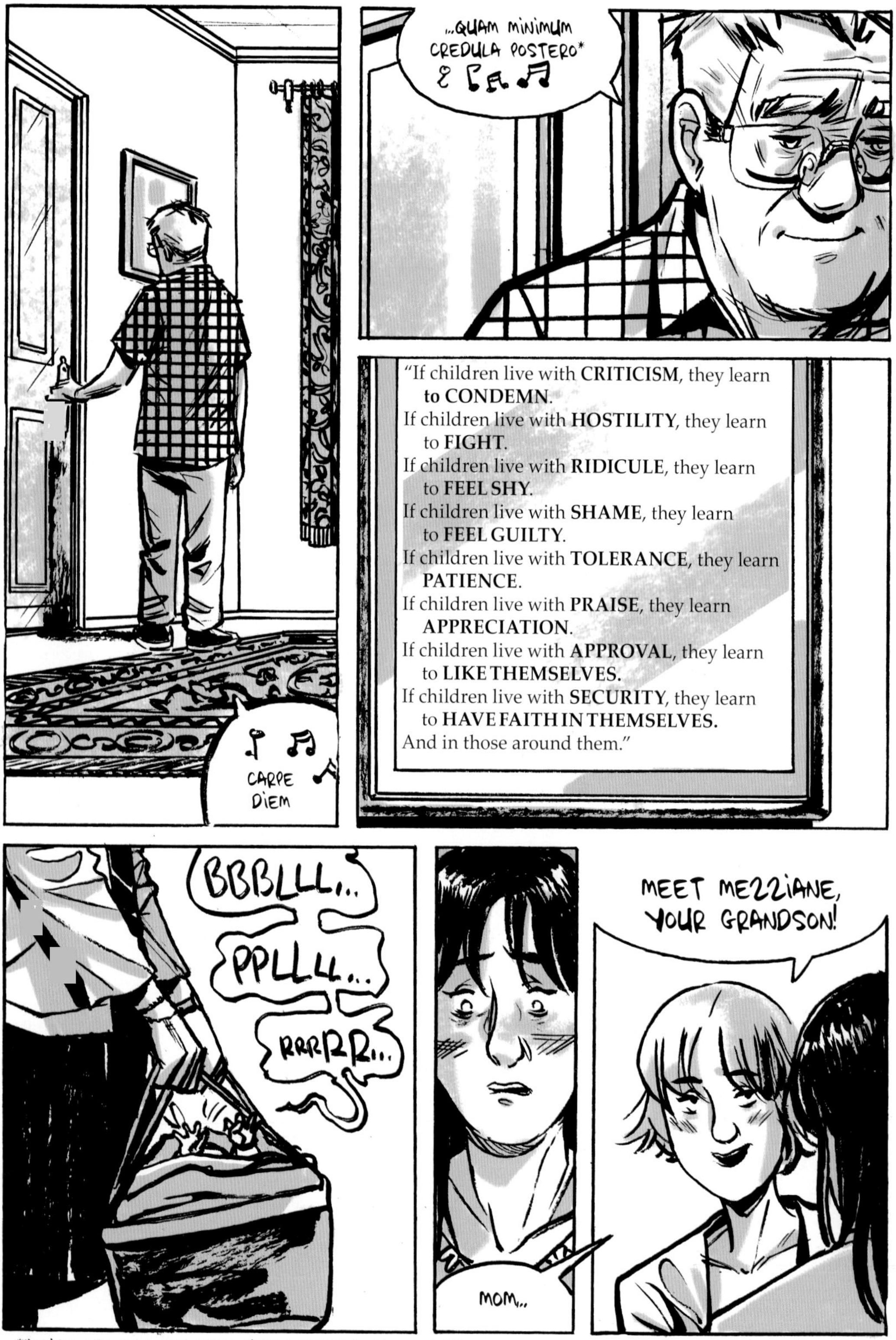
CARPE DIEM
...QUAM MINIMUM CREDULA POSTERO*
"If children live with CRITICISM, they learn to CONDEMN.
If children live with HOSTILITY, they learn to FIGHT.
If children live with RIDICULE, they learn to FEEL SHY.
If children live with SHAME, they learn to FEEL GUILTY.
If children live with TOLERANCE, they learn PATIENCE.
If children live with PRAISE, they learn APPRECIATION.
If children live with APPROVAL, they learn to LIKE THEMSELVES.
If children live with SECURITY, they learn to HAVE FAITH IN THEMSELVES.
And in those around them."
BBBLLL...
PPLLLL...
RRRRR...
MEET MEZZIANE, YOUR GRANDSON!
MOM...

*"SEIZE THE DAY, PUT VERY LITTLE TRUST IN TOMORROW." HORACE (*ODES*, 1.11).

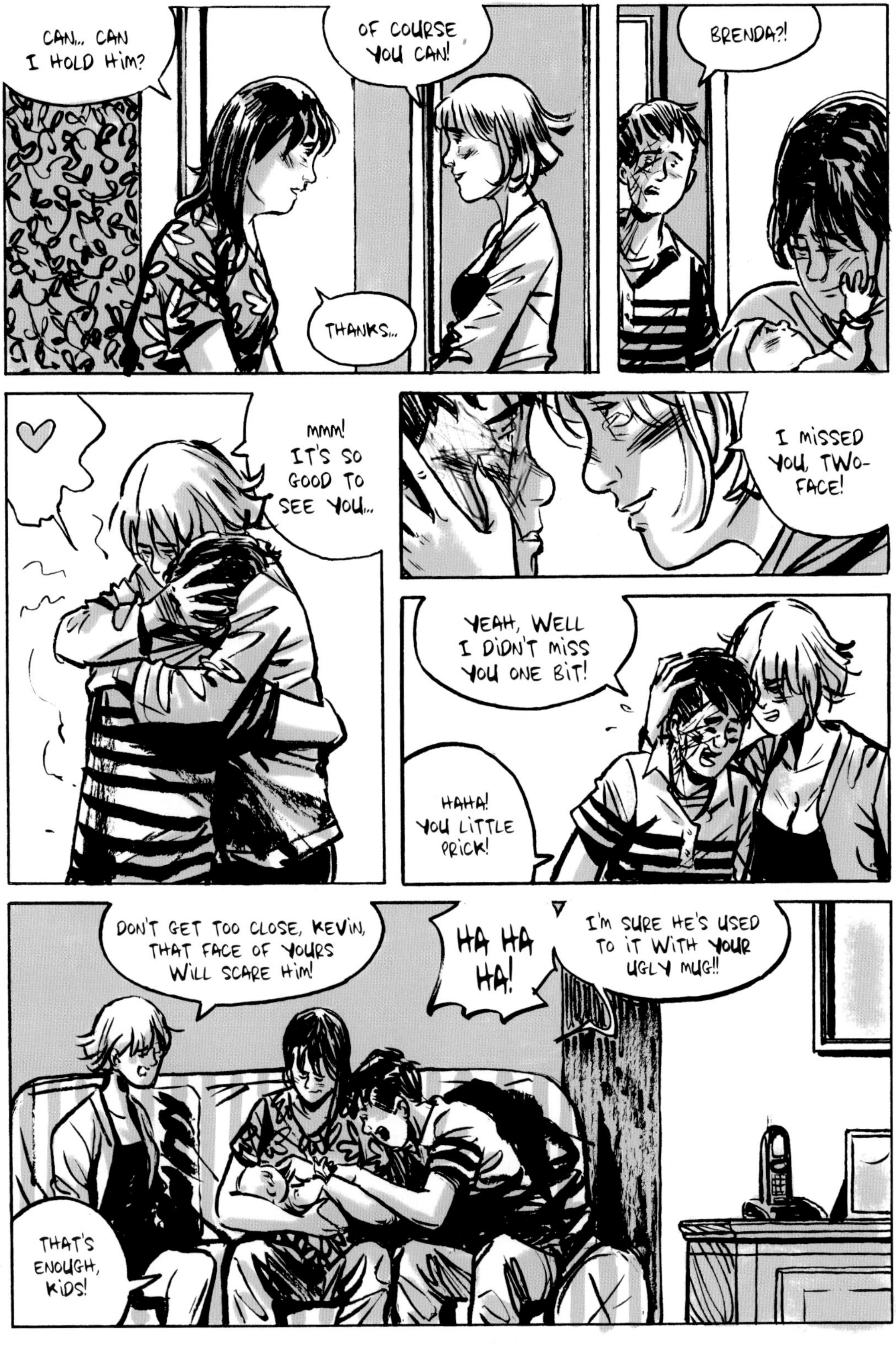
CAN... CAN I HOLD HIM?
OF COURSE YOU CAN!
THANKS...
BRENDA?!
MMM! IT'S SO GOOD TO SEE YOU...
I MISSED YOU, TWO-FACE!
YEAH, WELL I DIDN'T MISS YOU ONE BIT!
HAHA! YOU LITTLE PRICK!
DON'T GET TOO CLOSE, KEVIN, THAT FACE OF YOURS WILL SCARE HIM!
HA HA HA!
I'M SURE HE'S USED TO IT WITH YOUR UGLY MUG!!
THAT'S ENOUGH, KIDS!

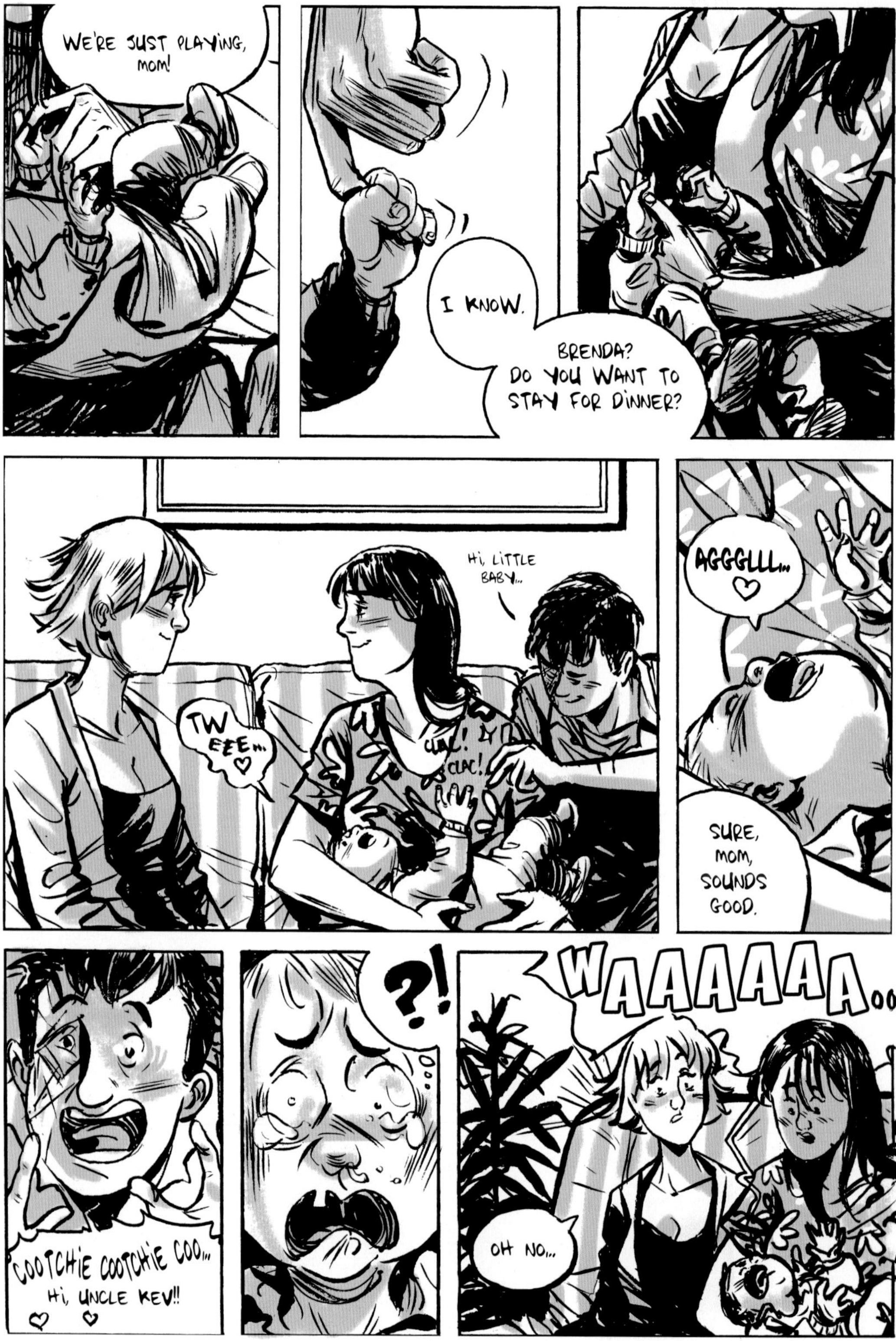

WE'RE JUST PLAYING, MOM!
I KNOW.
BRENDA? DO YOU WANT TO STAY FOR DINNER?
HI, LITTLE BABY...
TWEEE...♡
CLAC! CLAC!
AGGGLLL...♡
SURE, MOM, SOUNDS GOOD.
COOTCHIE COOTCHIE COO... HI, UNCLE KEV!!
?!
WAAAAAAooooo
OH NO...

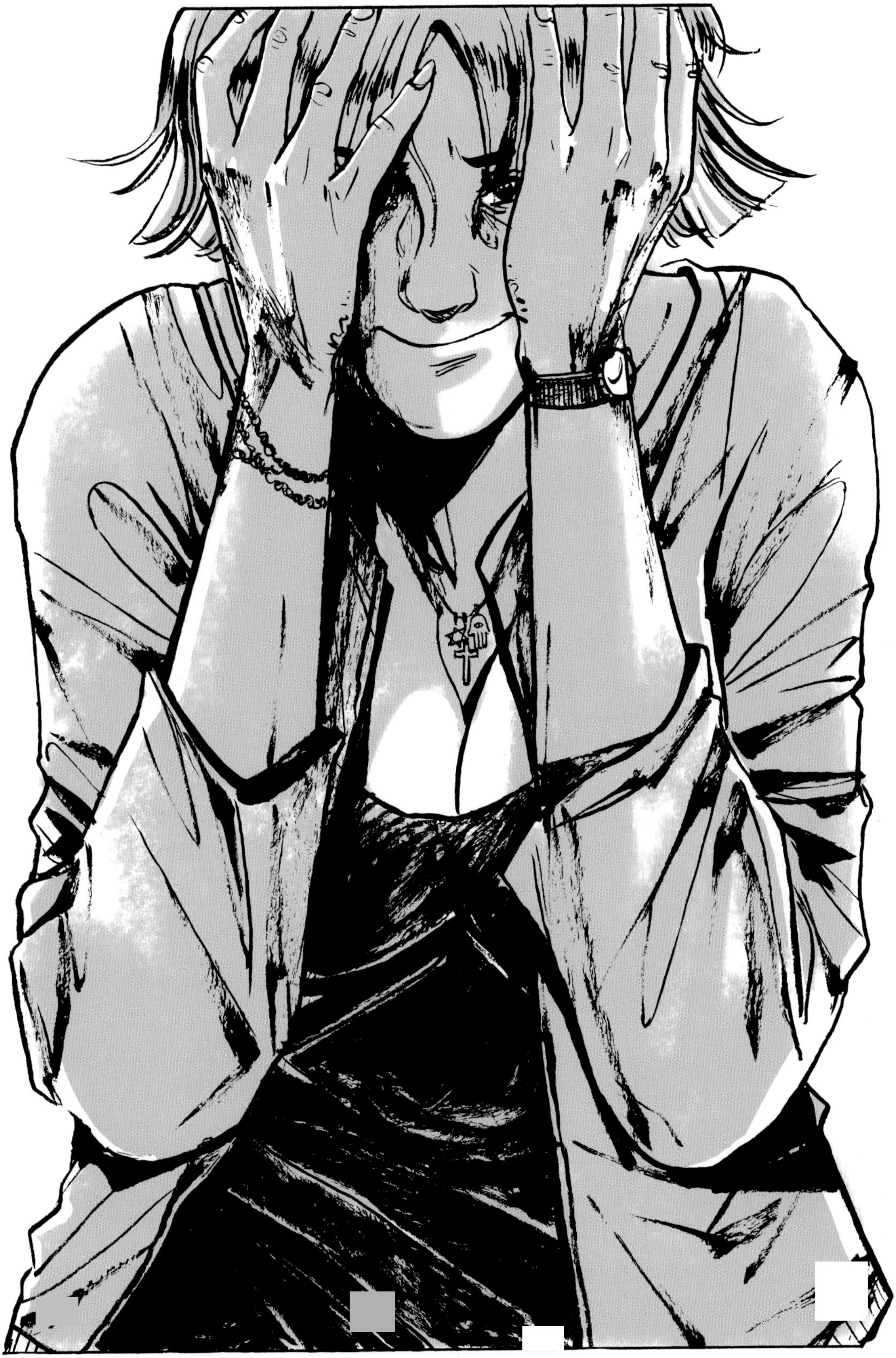

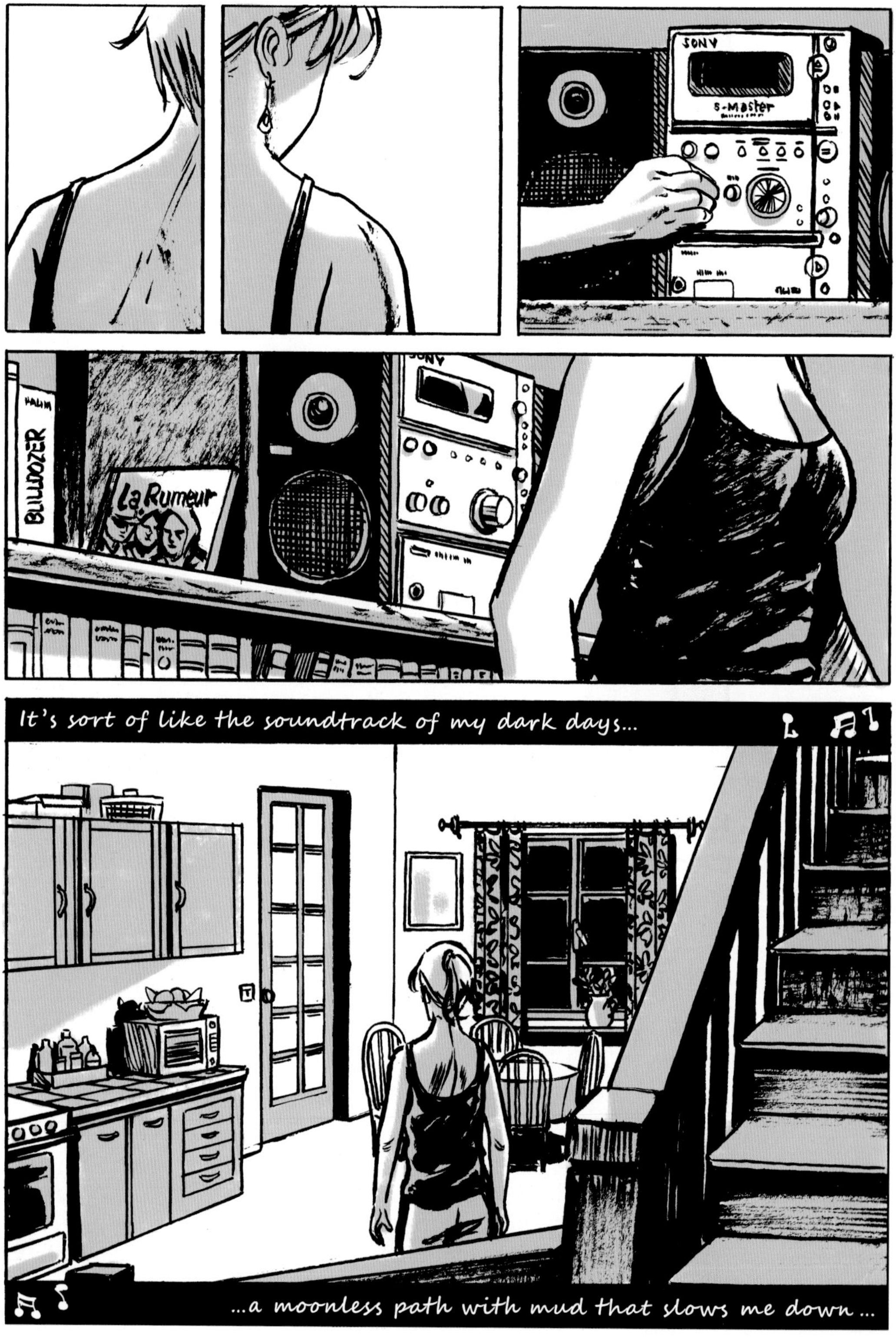
SONY
S-Master
BULLDOZER
La Rumeur
It's sort of like the soundtrack of my dark days...
...a moonless path with mud that slows me down...

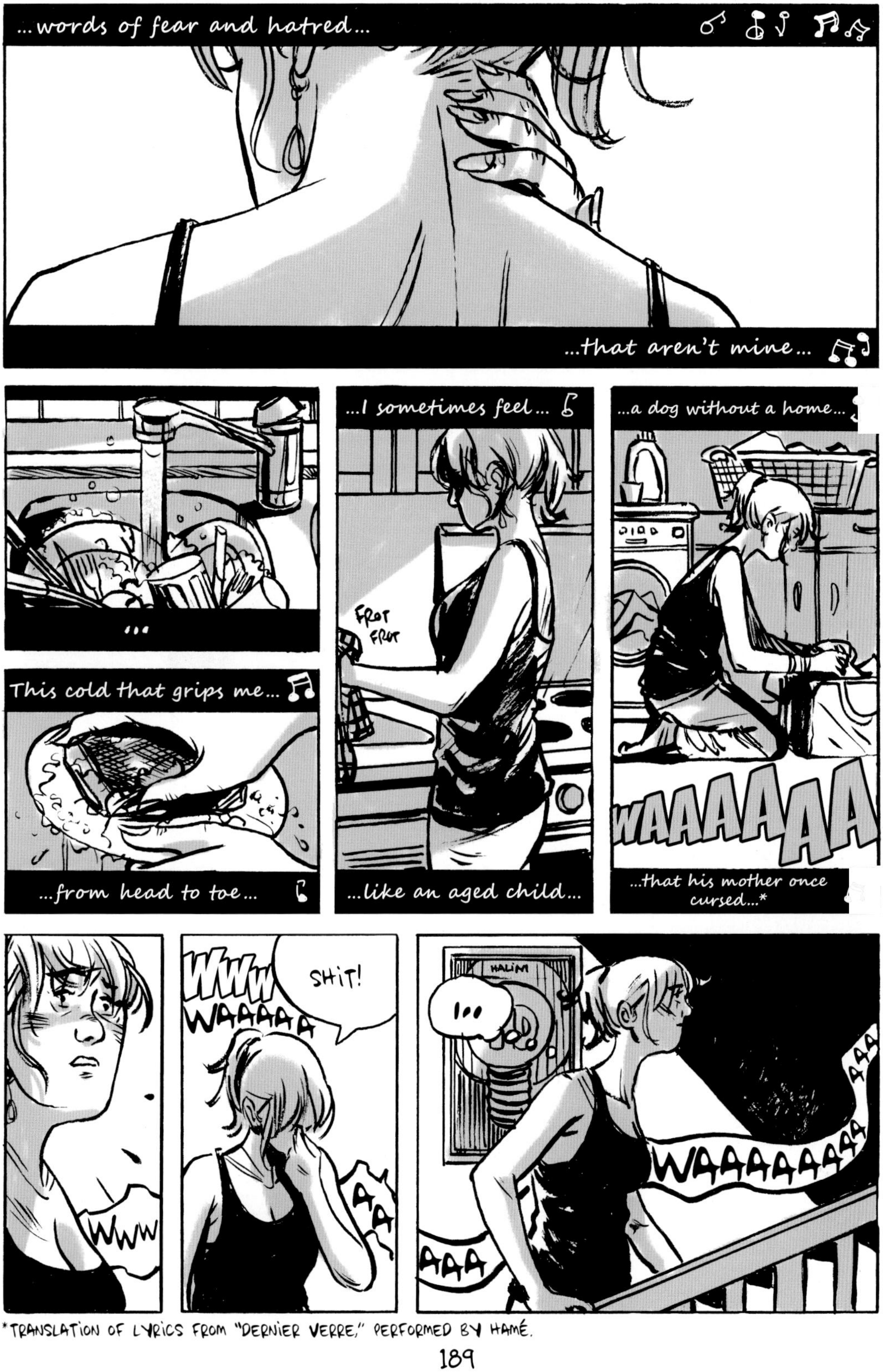
...words of fear and hatred...
...that aren't mine...
...
...I sometimes feel...
...a dog without a home...
FROT FROT
This cold that grips me...
WAAAAAAA
...from head to toe...
...like an aged child...
...that his mother once cursed...*
WWW
WWW WAAAAA
SHIT!
AAA
!!!
HALIM
AAA
WAAAAAAAA
AAA

*TRANSLATION OF LYRICS FROM "DERNIER VERRE," PERFORMED BY HAMÉ.

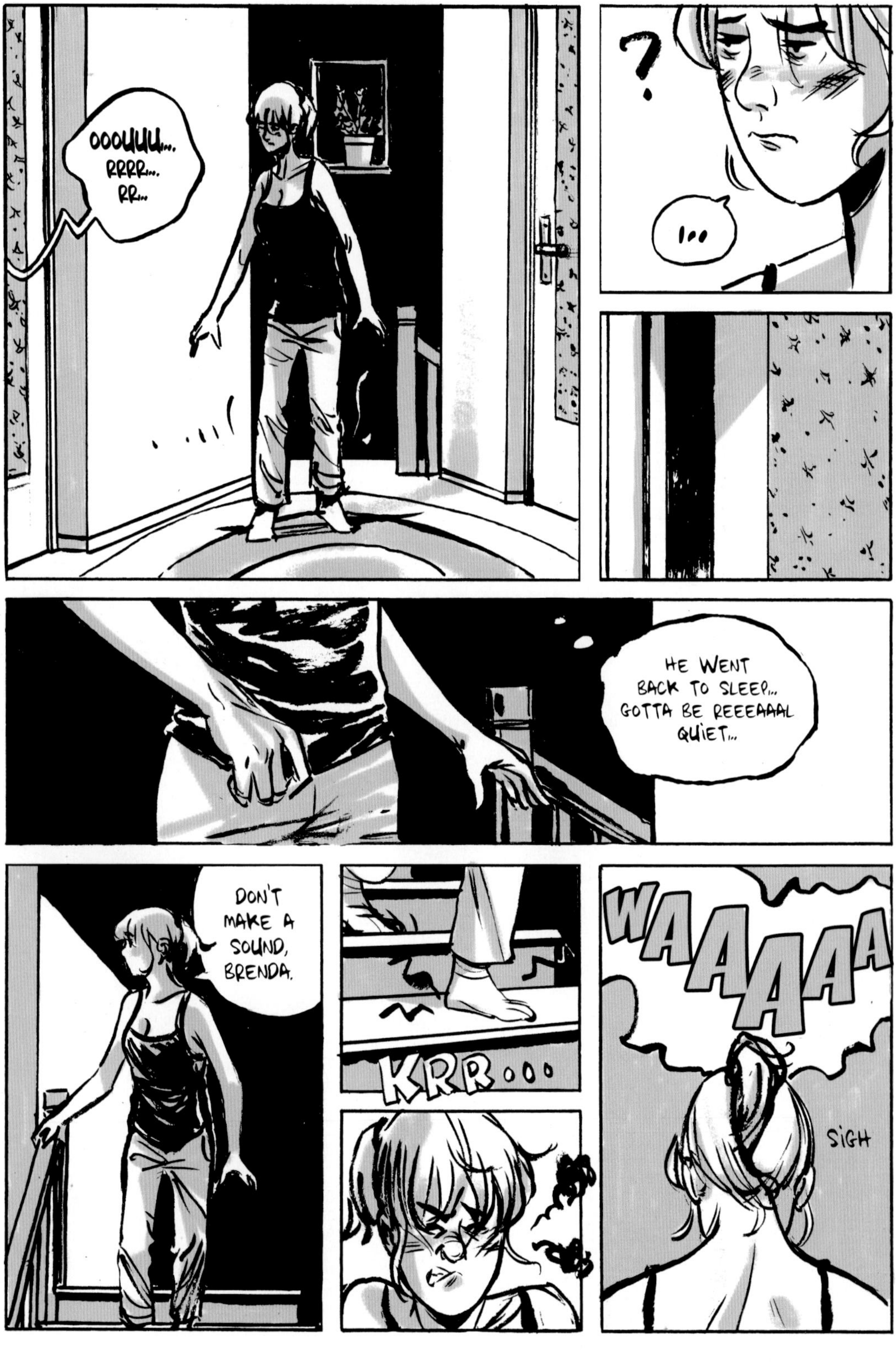
OOOUUU...
RRRR...
RR...
?
...
HE WENT BACK TO SLEEP... GOTTA BE REEEAAAL QUIET...
DON'T MAKE A SOUND, BRENDA.
KRR...
WAAAAAA
SIGH

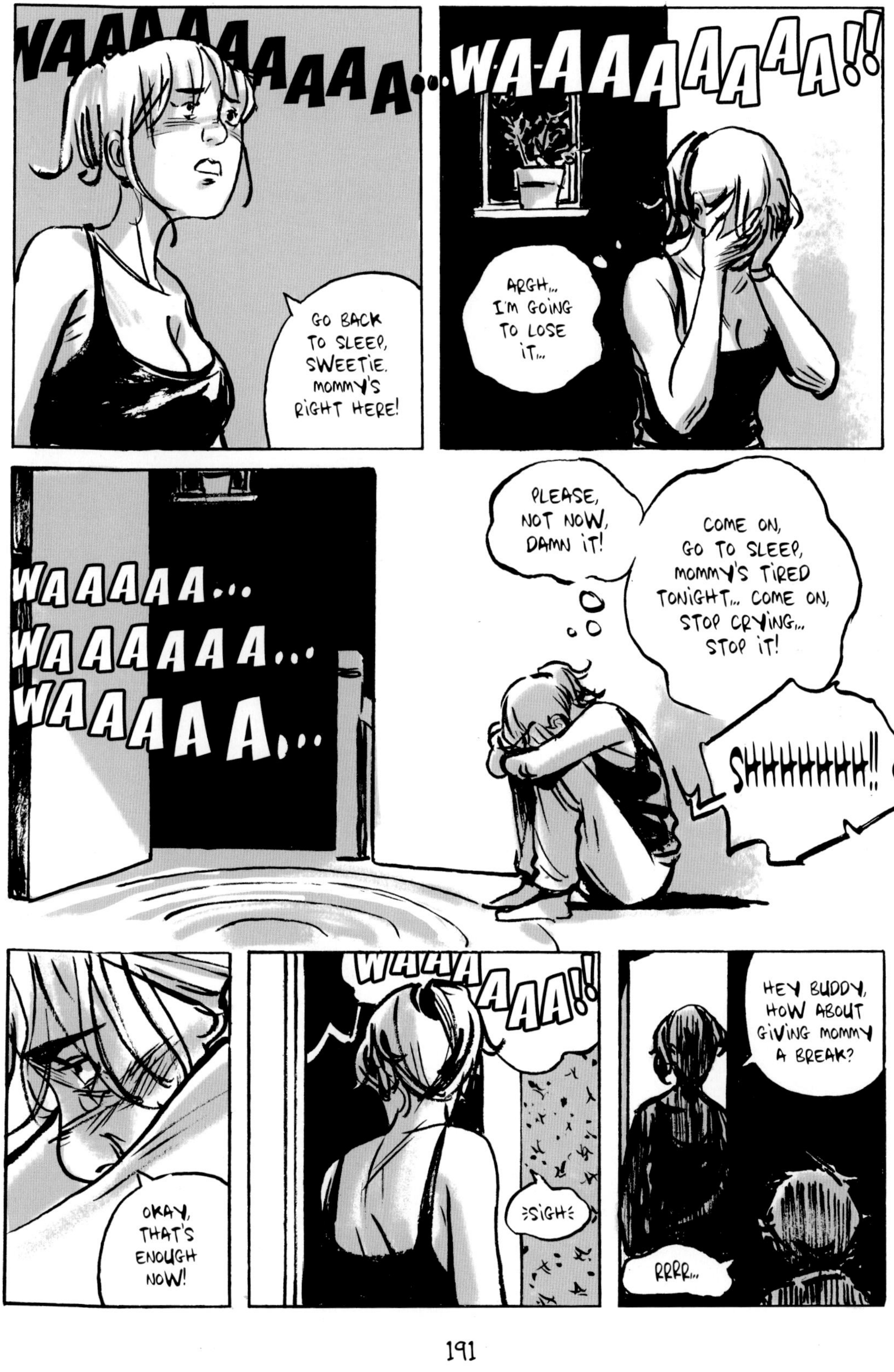
WAAAAAAAAAA...WAAAAAAAAAA!!
GO BACK TO SLEEP, SWEETIE. MOMMY'S RIGHT HERE!
ARGH... I'M GOING TO LOSE IT...
WAAAAA...
WAAAAAAA...
WAAAAAA...
PLEASE, NOT NOW, DAMN IT!
COME ON, GO TO SLEEP, MOMMY'S TIRED TONIGHT... COME ON, STOP CRYING... STOP IT!
SHHHHHHH!!
OKAY, THAT'S ENOUGH NOW!
WAAAAAAA!!
SIGH
HEY BUDDY, HOW ABOUT GIVING MOMMY A BREAK?
RRRR...

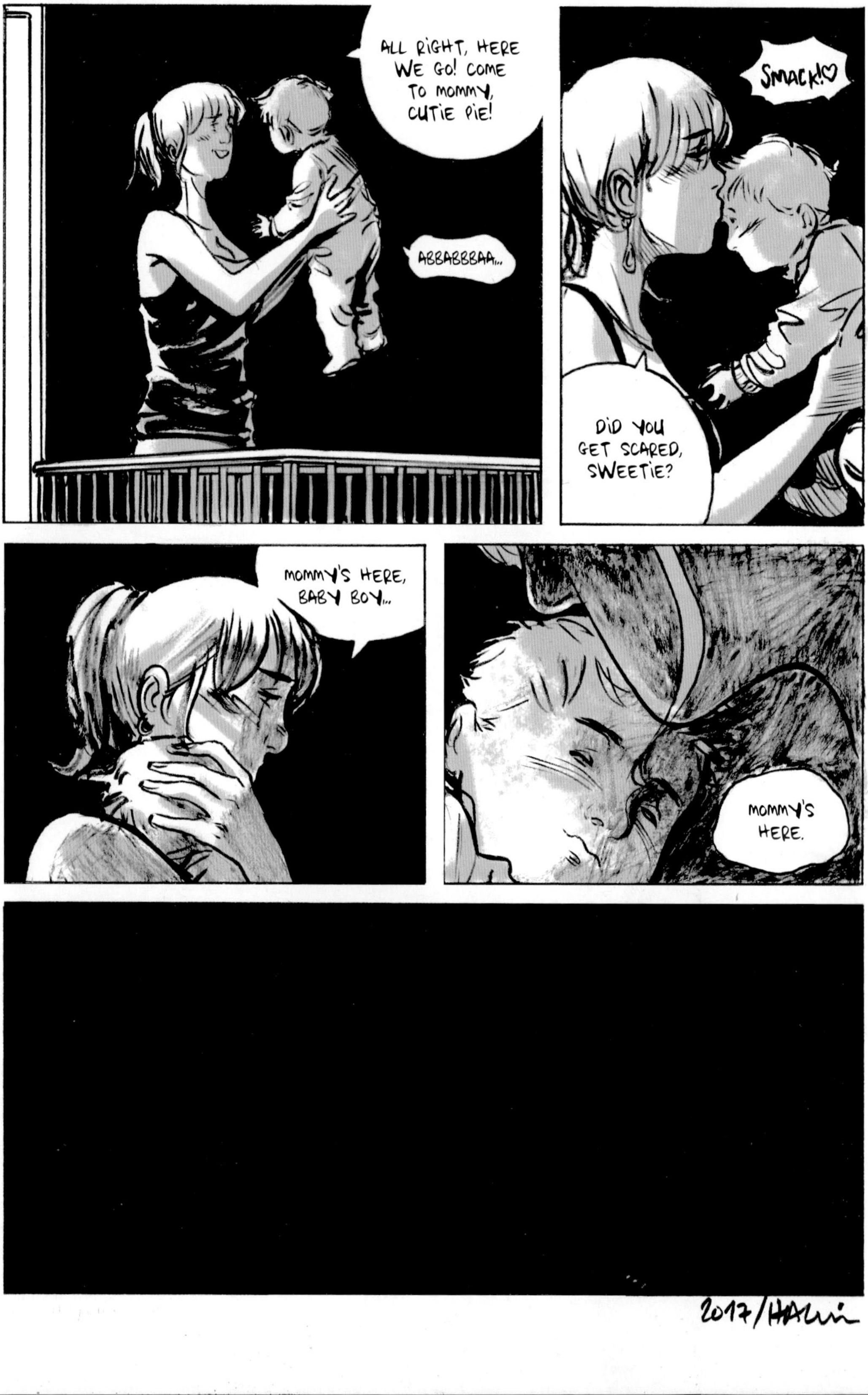
ALL RIGHT, HERE WE GO! COME TO MOMMY, CUTIE PIE!
ABBABBBAA...
SMACK!♡
DID YOU GET SCARED, SWEETIE?
MOMMY'S HERE, BABY BOY...
MOMMY'S HERE.